LINDA A. WALTON is professor of history and international studies and director of the Institute for Asian Studies at Portland State University.

Academies and Society in Southern Sung China

Academies and Society in Southern Sung China

Linda Walton

University of Hawai'i Press
Honolulu

Printed in the United States of America
99 00 01 02 03 04 5 4 3 2 1

Library of Congress Cataloging-in-Publication Data

Walton, Linda A.
Academies and society in southern Sung China /
Linda A. Walton.
p. cm.
Includes bibliographical references and index.
ISBN 0-8248-1962-4 (alk. paper)
1. Education—China—History. 2. Learned institutions and societies—China—History. 3. China—Civilization 960–1644. 4. China—History—Sung dynasty, 960–1279. I. Title.
LA1131.8.W336 1999
370'.951—dc21 98–42955
CIP

University of Hawai'i Press books are printed on acid-free paper and meet the guidelines for permanence and durability of the Council on Library Resourses.

Designed by Deborah Hodgdon
Printed by Maple-Vail Book Manufacturing Group

For my parents

James O. and Elizabeth G. Walton

and

In memory of

Robert M. Hartwell (1932–1996)

Marianne C. Hartwell (1941–1997)

Contents

Acknowledgments

The subject of this book was suggested by my late mentor, Robert M. Hartwell, as a dissertation topic that would allow me to combine interests in both social and intellectual history. When it became clear—to me at least—that a study of Sung academies was too large in scope for a graduate student to tackle, I settled on a more limited local study for the dissertation and postponed study of the broader topic of academies until later. As "later" became nearly ten years later, I was able to benefit from the pioneering work on Sung education and the examination system by John Chaffee and Thomas Lee, as well as from studies by Hartwell, Peter Bol, Hoyt Tillman, Robert Hymes, and Patricia Ebrey. Like many others, this book took far longer to complete than anticipated, and its author incurred many debts in the process.

The research for this book effectively began in 1987–1988 when I was the recipient of a Language and Research Fellowship, jointly sponsored by the Inter-University Program for Chinese Language Studies in Taipei, the Committee on Scientific and Scholarly Cooperation with the U. S., Academia Sinica, and the Henry Luce Foundation. A grant from the ACLS Joint Committe on Chinese Studies subsidized additional study at the Inter-University Program, where Director James Dew provided hospitality and support. During that year, my understanding of Sung texts was greatly improved by the efforts of my teacher, Liu Chi-lun. My stay in Taipei was also enhanced by the presence of other colleagues in Chinese studies: Brian McKnight, Constance Meaney, John Shepherd, David Schak, Hill Gates, Huang Chuh-chieh, Lau Nap-yin, Stephen Durrant, Chiu-mi Lai, and Joseph Allen.

I am grateful to librarians at the National Central Library in Taipei, the Institute for Research in Humanistic Studies in Kyoto, The

Tōyō Bunko in Tokyo, the Beijing Municipal Library, the Beijing University Library, the manuscripts division of the Fujian Normal University Library, and the University of Washington East Asia Library. A Travel to Collections Grant from the National Endowment for the Humanities made possible a research trip to the East Asiatic Library at the University of California at Berkeley in 1989, where Donald Shively provided assistance. Stints as resident director of study abroad programs sponsored by the Oregon University System in 1991 (Fuzhou) and 1994 (Beijing) allowed me the opportunity to do some research in mainland libraries. Two summer stipends from the Oregon Council for the Humanities and two Faculty Development Grants from Portland State University provided support for research that contributed substantially to this book. I appreciate financial support for the production of this book provided by the Department of History, the Friends of History, and the Vice Provost for International Affairs at Portland State University.

Parts of this book in different form have appeared previously: "Southern Sung Academies as Sacred Places," in Patricia B. Ebrey and Peter N. Gregory, eds., *Religion and Society in T'ang and Sung China* (University of Hawai'i Press, 1993); "Scholars, Schools, and *Shuyuan* in Sung-Yuan China," in W. Theodore de Bary and John W. Chaffee, eds., *Neo-Confucian Education: The Formative Stage* (University of California Press, 1989).

I wish to thank my colleague, David A. Johnson, for his unfailing encouragement and support as both mentor and friend. Candice Goucher, good friend and co-conspirator in more than one undertaking, by her creativity and generosity of spirit taught me much about humanistic scholarship and teaching. Sharon Carstens prodded me to refine and sharpen arguments. Frederick M. Nunn, as department head and administrator mentor, provided a model for how to sustain research projects in the midst of administration and teaching. My editor, Sharon F. Yamamoto, carried out her duties with a high degree of professionalism and courteous efficiency. Comments by one of the anonymous referees for the University of Hawai'i Press contributed substantially to improving the manuscript, though any errors remain, of course, my responsibility.

INTRODUCTION

In 1259, Ma Kuang-tsu, prefect of Chien-k'ang (modern Nanking), assembled his colleagues to attend the opening convocation lecture in Spring Wind Hall at Illumined Way Academy, where the audience was said to number in the hundreds.[1] Chou Ying-ho, a protégé of Ma Kuang-tsu and headmaster of the academy, delivered the lecture.[2] Chou Ying-ho drew the topic for his talk from the opening passage of the Confucian *Analects* ("To learn with a constant perseverance and application"), exhorting his audience to take Confucius and the sages of antiquity as their guides in learning.[3] He also quoted the eleventh-century philosopher Ch'eng Hao, whose shrine was the foundation of the academy and whose writings were printed there in the same year (1259) for distribution to students. Chou Ying-ho donated his salary to subsidize the costs of printing the entire corpus of Ch'eng Hao's works, which filled 167 woodblocks and were stored along with other classical texts in the academy library.[4]

Like the official government school and other public buildings, Illumined Way Academy was built on a central north-south axis, was surrounded by a wall, and was entered through a main gate at the south side. Along with the library and lecture hall, other main buildings on the academy campus included the Hall of Repose, which housed images of Confucius and his disciples and was used for the performance of school rites,[5] and the Hall of Reverence, a place for eating and tea drinking. There were six student dormitories, residences for administrators and teachers, and other facilities, including a kitchen, storehouse, and bathhouse. The academy was supported by government allocations of land, grain, and cash, which provided student stipends and staff salaries.[6]

The regulations for the administration of Illumined Way were adapted from the late twelfth-century rules for White Deer Grotto Academy, as were the school rites held on the first and fifteenth of each lunar month in spring and autumn.[7] In addition to stipulating

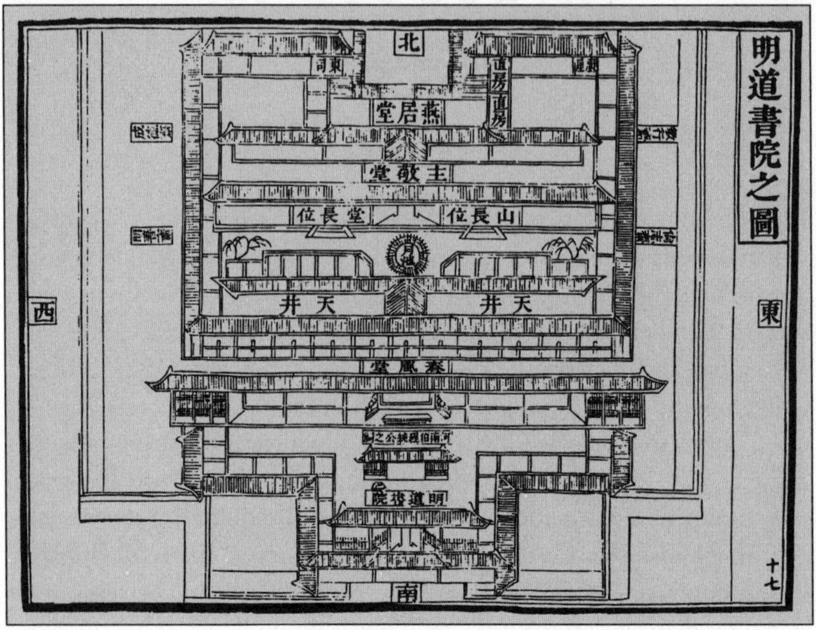

DIAGRAM OF ILLUMINED WAY ACADEMY, CA. 1250S

The main gate is shown at the bottom (south). Directly inside is the shrine to Ch'eng Hao, followed by Spring Wind Hall. Behind that is the entrance to a garden with a pond, leading to the offices of the headmaster on the right (east) and the dean on the left (west). North of this is the Hall of Reverence and, finally, the Hall of Repose. Four student dormitories are located outside this inner structure, two on the west and two on the east.

Source: Chou Ying-ho, comp., *Ching-ting Chien-k'ang chih*, Diagrams, 17.

when and how school rites should be performed, the regulations at Illumined Way were concerned with the formal qualifications for student admission and with establishing standards for both academic work and behavior:

> Every ten days the headmaster entered the hall and gathered the students to receive lecture tallies. Lectures were repeated according to the regulations. There were thirty-eight lectures on the classics, and sixteen on the histories. They were all recorded on the lecture register. Each month there were three examinations: the first ten-day period [examination] was ques-

> tions on the classics; the middle one was questions on histories; the final one was preparation for the examinations. Those who excelled were recorded in the dormitory record of moral achievement. The Rector was in charge of keeping records of whether or not students improved their moral achievement. When going out or coming in, the regular students always had to wear a long gown. There was a register for requests for leave. Those who went out without registering were punished. As soon as they were received by the academy, the scholars and colleagues were not allowed to go out or request visits. Those who transgressed were criticized and punished. Those involved in litigations were given up to one day off. Those requesting over three months' leave were recorded as lacking by the Dean and would not be allowed to participate. If without reason they did not visit the shrine, attend lectures, or prepare their lessons, up to three demerits were recorded in the register. If students went out in disregard of the rules, they would not be allowed to participate again.[8]

This brief glimpse of academy life in thirteenth-century China, captured through its rules, has counterparts in the medieval European university and the Islamic *madrasa* (college of law). European university regulations illustrate common concerns with maintaining order in the academic community. According to the *Early Statutes of the Sorbonne* (before 1274): "[C]oncerning those who are newly received or about to be admitted it is ordained that unless they have made progress in sermons, disputations, and lectures as aforesaid within seven years from the time of their admission, they shall be . . . deprived [of the benefits of the house]."[9] The *Statutes of the Faculty of Canon Law* at the University of Paris (1340) strictly regulated the appearance and behavior of students as well as academic etiquette:

> [T]hey shall wear proper and decent garb, especially the outer garments. Members of religious orders for their outer garments shall have frock or cowl or other habit befitting their order. Also the same, of whatever state or condition they may be, shall not wear pointed or openwork shoes, red hose or sandals, nor knotted hoods, or other clothing or colors of cloth prohibited by law. Also, they shall not impede the doctors or

> other lecturers, or bedells or other officials of the said faculty in the exercise of their scholastic duties by whistling, stamping, and disturbances of any sort.
>
> Also, at disputations, reviews, lectures on solemn decretals, set harangues and feasts of doctors they shall be required to defer to those of older grade and greater importance in seating themselves, so that henceforth the students in such cases shall leave the first and second rows of benches vacant for persons of such grades and others above mentioned, just as is the custom in the faculty of theology.[10]

Although canon law was only one of the key faculties of the medieval European university, the study of religious law was the foundation of the *madrasa*.[11] The *madrasa*, which first appeared in the eastern regions of the Islamic world in the tenth century and spread to Spain by the fourteenth, was an important institution of Islamic civilization.[12] One of the most renowned *madrasas* was the Nizamiyya of Baghdad, founded in 1065, but prominent *madrasas* also appeared in other major cities of the Islamic world (Alexandria, Damascus, and Konya) by the twelfth century. *Madrasas* were funded by endowments (*waqf*), which were given by donors to gain religious benefits.[13] The professors were doctors of Islamic law whose students received instruction in legal studies, which might then be followed by a course of study in the philosophical sciences. In the *madrasa* classroom, seating was arranged according to the accomplishments of individual students: those more advanced were given seats close to the professor, demonstrating their mastery of the subject and consequently their relatively greater intimacy with the professor. Class began and ended with a prayer, in addition to the five daily prayers required of Muslims.[14]

Broad parallels may be drawn between the medieval European university, the Islamic *madrasa*, and the academy in Sung (960–1279) China. In all three settings, students and teachers lived in a community joined by the common pursuit of learning and regulated by standards of behavior based on particular cultural and social norms and rooted in differing ideologies (Christianity, Islam, Confucianism). The transmission and interpretation of Confucian textual tradition was the educational mission of the academy (*shu-yuan*), corresponding to the

Qur'anic legal tradition in the *madrasa* and Christian theology in the medieval European university. All made use of pedagogical techniques that combined memorization and recitation of texts along with disputation. Despite obvious ideological, cultural, and even institutional differences, a remarkable degree of consistency can be seen in the ordering of academic life in these schools.

In addition to suggesting comparison with educational institutions in medieval Europe and the Islamic world, the sketch of Illumined Way Academy highlights aspects of academies in thirteenth-century China that frame the argument of this book. The foundation of Illumined Way was the shrine to Ch'eng Hao (1032–1085), one of the patriarchs of True Way Learning (*tao-hsueh*) as it evolved in the Southern Sung (1127–1279). What was the relationship between the rise of True Way Learning and the academy movement in Southern Sung China? What was the role of shrines at academies? Illumined Way shared architecture, support, and function in common with the prefectural school. What distinguished academies from prefectural schools and what was their significance as educational institutions? Academies were administered by men with scholarly and official credentials who often held the post of headmaster concurrently with another appointment, as did Chou Ying-ho. Academies also provided opportunities for scholars to lecture, discuss, study, or otherwise associate with scholarly colleagues. What was the social and political meaning of academies and what role did they play in shaping the cultural and social identity of the literati elite (*shih*)?

Although precedents can be found in earlier periods, academies originated in the Sung, an era marked by profound changes in the economy, technology, thought, and the social and political order.[15] Institutional innovations of the time included an empire-wide network of state schools, part of a broad constellation of educational institutions that flourished in the Sung.[16] Distinct from the official school system, academies rose in the early Northern Sung (960–1126), declined, and then reappeared in the Southern Sung (1127–1279), when they proliferated widely throughout the empire. The conventional narrative account of Southern Sung academies rests on the assumption that academies were established in opposition to government schools, were "private" rather than "official," and represented a form of resistance to the pedagogical imperatives of education aimed at succeeding in the examination system.[17] This view depicts Northern Sung academies as supplemental schools, which declined with the growth of state education, but sees the revival of academies in Southern Sung as a reaction against official schools and the examination-oriented education they represented.

The impressive growth in numbers of academies during the late twelfth and thirteenth centuries has also been related to the use of academies by leading True Way scholars, particularly Chu Hsi (1130–1200), to promote their doctrines.[18] Southern Sung proponents of True Way Learning claimed that their predecessors in the late T'ang (618–907) and Northern Sung had retrieved the Way, lost since the demise of the philosopher Mencius more than a millennium earlier. Part of a broader renaissance of Confucian learning that began in the late T'ang, True Way advocates believed they alone held claim to an exclusive understanding of the Way and had a mission to transmit and propagate it. As Hoyt Tillman has argued, despite often sharp differences among them, True Way scholars formed a fellowship through both social relations and intellectual discourse that fostered a sense of community and common purpose.[19] Academies served as intellectual centers for the True Way fellowship and were consequently closely associated with the official elevation of True Way Learning from proscribed heterodoxy in 1195 to state orthodoxy by imperial proclamation in 1241.

As contested claims to truth were resolved by state authority through pronouncements of approval or disapproval, the resolution of philosophical disputes became politicized. In the charged political atmosphere of the court, the professional stakes were high: official careers often rose and fell with frequently shifting definitions of orthodoxy. From this perspective, the proliferation of academies in Southern Sung can be seen as a response to ongoing political and ideological struggles at court that produced victims who sought refuge in academies, which provided a sense of community and reinforced elite identity through association with colleagues and the common pursuit of scholarly activities.

This study explains the Southern Sung academy movement not

only as a product of intellectual controversies and a response to political factionalism, but also as part of broader changes taking place in Sung society. The Southern Sung academy movement was produced by a conjunction of several historical trends: a political, economic, and cultural shift from north to south that had been ongoing at least since the T'ang and that was decisively completed with the fall of the north to the Jurchen Chin; a social transformation of the *shih* elite from the hereditary aristocratic pattern of T'ang and pre-T'ang to the examination elite of later imperial China; and finally, the relative weakness of state institutions at the local level that encouraged initiatives taken by *shih* in their local communities, such as the founding of academies.[20] The Southern Sung academy movement was intimately related to the politics of local communities and to economic and technological changes (printing, for example) that accompanied the commercial revolution of the Sung, as well as to the vicissitudes of the True Way movement, political factionalism, and both the threat and reality of war with border states. Academies were also crucial to the redefinition of the social and cultural identity of the *shih* (or *shih ta-fu*), the theme of this book.[21]

In order to explain how ideas expressed in academy lectures made sense of the world and engaged their audience, one needs to locate them in their contemporary social and political context as well as in an intellectual tradition inherited from the past. From this perspective, True Way Learning is treated here as the ideological articulation of a new *shih* identity, rather than as a philosophical system.[22] Ideas are never disembodied, although they sometimes take the form of philosophical abstractions that at least appear quite far removed from concrete social realities. Interpreting True Way Learning as the ideology of the *shih* takes as a point of departure the notion that ideas are inscribed with meaning through social practice: in the concrete material existence of people's lives.[23] What people do and how they explain what they do, both internally to themselves either consciously or unconsciously, and externally in formal ways such as writing or lectures, constitutes ideology.

Like any complex body of thought, True Way Learning encompassed a broad range of ideas that could be used to sustain widely differing points of view. Aspects of True Way Learning resonated with the lives of *shih* in the late twelfth and thirteenth centuries and contributed to the definition of a new *shih* identity. With the rise of True Way Learning as a particular adaptation of new Confucian ideas, a significantly altered view of the ideal *shih* emerged, one that built on earlier ideas of scholarship and service, but adjusted the balance between them in a substantially new way. Embedded in the primary discourse on the transmission of the Way in True Way Learning was a secondary discourse on the *shih* and how the *shih* should act. This particular view of the *shih* developed when it did in response to the political and social circumstances of the Southern Sung, but it also helped to craft a new *shih* identity. Ideological construction is rooted in social, political, and economic conditions, but it does not only reflect them; it also shapes them.[24]

Although many conflicting personalities and ideas contributed to the formation of True Way Learning in the late twelfth century, and consequently differing conceptions of the *shih*, by the thirteenth century these competing strands were increasingly homogenized and woven into one Way that was associated primarily with the philosopher Chu Hsi and institutionalized in academies. This process can be treated as strictly intellectual, a product of the engagement of thinkers operating in a highly abstract world of metaphysical and cosmological concepts. But True Way thinkers also wrote about matters of politics and society, offering their views of how government should be practiced and how society should be ordered. While acknowledging the homogenization of the Way as in part a product of intellectual engagement, this study approaches the process as essentially one of ideological construction, shaped by social forces as well as intellectual ones. This process can be traced to the cult of Chu Hsi that took root in thirteenth-century Fu-chien academies and was spread by his disciples and their students throughout the empire by the late Southern Sung. True Way Learning moved from being a challenge to prevailing dogma, to being a dogma itself, although the full realization of this lay in the future, after its adoption by the Mongols and its continued evolution in the Ming (1368–1644) and Ch'ing (1644–1910).

In addressing the question of why True Way Learning "succeeded," we need to ask why certain ideas appealed, why others did not, and, ultimately, why some were accepted or sanctioned while others were rejected. The authority of the state played a key role but was not the sole determinant of what ideas were sanctioned. State approval or prohibition could exert weighty influence on the process of ideological construction, but it did not operate in isolation, nor was this a one-way process. Rather, there was a dynamic relationship between state authority, represented by decrees that alternately supported or discredited ideas, and social forces, represented by the intellectual and political elite: those who took *chin-shih* degrees, became officials, and were the cultural guardians of Confucian tradition.

Southern Sung academies were founded by alliances of officials and local elites. Even academies most closely associated with True Way thinkers were not distinct from others: nearly every single academy for which there are records was established through the cooperative efforts of local elites and circuit, prefectural, or county officials. Academies provide one of the strongest kinds of evidence in support of the localist argument developed by Robert Hartwell, Robert Hymes, and others. With the retreat of the central government from exercising authority at the local level, documented in recent scholarship on Sung politics and society, academies were one of the institutions that occupied the "middle space" between what was "private" (*ssu*) and what was "official" (*kuan*).[25] Thus the use of the term "private academies" for *shu-yuan* is clearly inaccurate. As soon as a scholar's retreat or study became an academy, it ceased being "private."

Academies were nodes of negotiation between the state and local elites, public (although unquestionably an elite "public") spaces to which officials gave their approval and support but which were dominated by local elites. In promoting the establishment of academies, like community granaries or the community compact, local elites were carving out public space, using voluntary, local efforts to replace state institutions such as schools, the ever-normal granary, or the *pao-chia* system.[26] When family schools were established as academies open to "scholars from the four quarters," they were providing a community service that promoted the family's status locally but also replaced (or supplemented) government schools. The transformation of a lineage school into an academy, or simply the founding of an academy by a lineage, was a move from private (*chia*, the corporate household) to public (the elite community).

When academy lecturers cited the *Four Books* on the duty of the *shih* to engage in self-cultivation and not be concerned about "profit and salary," they were exhorting their audience to seek learning for its own sake, "learning for the self." This stood in sharp contrast to the realities of striving for political office through success in the examination system, but must have offered solace to those who recognized that both degrees and office were increasingly difficult to come by, and that government posts were fraught with political uncertainty and even danger. At the same time, the audience for these lectures—local elites—were increasingly concentrating on their own communities, seeking financial security through land and other investments, building networks of affinal ties, contributing to public works and social welfare projects, supporting religious establishments such as Buddhist temples, and founding academies.[27] Seeking the Way was dependent on reading, on teachers, on the cultivation of human nature, but also on an environment in which to practice: the academy.

Learning, Examinations, and Schools

"Learning" was central to the social and cultural identity of the *shih*, an elite whose status was at least formally dependent on office-holding and scholarly achievement, although these were in turn dependent on family background.[28] There were additional criteria that affected status, such as land-holding and other forms of wealth, but both of these formal qualifications—office-holding and scholarship—were associated with success in the examination system, defined as attainment of a *chin-shih* degree.[29] The examination system was closely tied to educational institutions developed by the Sung state, which administered both the examinations and schools to facilitate the recruitment, training, and selection of government officials. Just as differing assessments of the role of the examination system in conferring status are central to modern debates on changes in Sung society,[30] so, too, did contrasting conceptions of education animate Sung debates on the proper content and goals of learning, and the role of schools and the examination system in this process.

Comprehension of the multiple meanings of education, across cultures and across time, is essential to grasp the issues debated and the principles at stake in the Sung discourse on learning, particularly that of the True Way schoolmen. Learning (*hsueh*) for Confucius encompassed both study and teaching, acquiring knowledge, reflecting on it, and transmitting it.[31] The purpose of learning was the transmission of human culture (*wen*),[32] a task Confucius claimed in deference to the creative work of the sages, who produced the culture that later men merely transmitted. The concept of teaching (*chiao*) was thus paired with learning, and being a teacher in part meant acting as a moral example to transmit understanding of human culture. Both oral and written forms of cultural knowledge were important, along with the performative aspect of learning through the act of teaching and the conduct of ritual: learning was experiential as well as cognitive. The moral component of education was addressed to elites as well as to commoners, since members of the elite were expected to be moral exemplars to the common people and to promote the rituals (*li*) of appropriate social behavior as a means of acquiring, internalizing, and expressing prescribed ethical values.

Thus education in the Confucian tradition encompassed "Learning for one's own sake, rather than for others" (*Analects*, 14.25), the role of teachers as moral exemplars and as transmitters of the traditions of antiquity and the performance of rites to ensure the proper ordering of society. Embedded in early Confucian and Mencian notions of education was a tension between the goal of "learning for one's self" and learning for service to the state. To be sure, these goals were not mutually exclusive, and their relative importance was dependent on historical circumstances, but there was a dynamic tension between them that can be seen in the historical and literary figure of the eremite as well as the upright minister who served his ruler. This tension continued from classical through imperial times, informing changing perceptions of the proper role of the *shih* in the Sung.

During the T'ang, Buddhism also began to lay claim to education in two distinct ways. First, Buddhism offered a different goal for learning: realizing one's true Buddha nature, not one's humanity. Second, Buddhist monasteries provided a setting for learning both Buddhist and Confucian texts, and in the absence of much formal schooling for aspirants to the examinations, many students received training in Buddhist monasteries.[33] Partly in response to the pervasive influence of Buddhism at many levels of society and culture, Confucian thinkers in the T'ang and Sung contributed to important changes in the conception of education. Literary skill was held in high esteem and valued as a means to apprehend the Way, the ultimate object of learning.[34] The T'ang scholar Han Yü (768–824), for example, was noted not only for his influential essay, "The Origins of the Way," but as a master of the "ancient prose" (*ku-wen*) style.

Of far greater consequence for changing conceptions of education during the T'ang was the examination system, which institutionalized a particular definition of education as training for officials and evaluated literary skill along with knowledge of the classics and histories. The examination system laid the groundwork for education to be regarded more as training for bureaucratic office than "learning" in the sense of subjective awareness of one's humanity (*jen*) through the transmission of human culture, a latter-day reflection of the contrast between the ideals of the loyal minister and the eremite. Tension between these two aspects of education informed vigorous debates on the content of the examinations and inspired criticism of the examination system itself as an institution that diverted men from the proper goals of Confucian learning.

Despite rhetorical allusions made by many Sung writers to a hierarchical network of schools in antiquity that extended from ruler's court to rural village, before the Sung most schooling took place within the home and family, through private tutors, or in religious establishments, such as Buddhist monasteries. During the late T'ang and Five Dynasties (907–959) era, in addition to Buddhist monastic schools, individual scholars prepared students for the examinations at their private studies or retreats, and some wealthy families supported schools for their kin.[35] In the early Northern Sung, before the creation of a state system of local schools, academies—many of which originated as private studies, retreats, or even family schools in the late T'ang and Five Dynasties—played an important role in educating men for service in public office.[36] With the educational reforms of the Ch'ing-li era (1041–1048), prefectural and county schools usurped the educational function of academies as training institutions for government officials, and academies were more or less abandoned for the remainder of the Northern Sung.

In Southern Sung, education aimed exclusively at preparation for passing the examinations drew sharp criticism from some scholars, who complained that such utilitarian motivation destroyed the real purpose of learning. Criticism of the examination system—and, by association, of official schools that fostered exclusive concentration on examination success—began to grow in the late twelfth century. One expression of this can be seen in comments made by Chu Hsi:

> Scholars [*shih-jen*] must first make a distinction between the two [separate] things, the examinations and learning, as to which to value as more weighty. If learning occupies seventy percent of the will, and the examinations, thirty percent, then it is all right. But, if the examinations are seventy percent, and learning is thirty percent, then one will surely be defeated [by being focused on external reasons for learning, rather than the self]; how much more if the will is entirely set on the examinations![37]

Although prefectural and county schools continued to exist throughout the Southern Sung, former academies were restored and new ones were founded in increasing numbers. According to one count, although there were nearly six hundred government schools by the end of the Southern Sung, there were also well over four hundred academies.[38] Beginning in the middle to late twelfth century, commemorative inscriptions for the founding or restoration of academies frequently made the point that government schools were nothing but examination mills, grinding out profit-minded pedants who could pass the examinations but were not truly learned in the sense of knowing humanity or realizing the Way. Such criticism must be seen in light of increasing competition in the examination system, which, by the middle to late Southern Sung, made the chances of success exceedingly slim.[39]

Expanded educational opportunities, through greater access to schools and wider availability of books due to advances in printing and paper production, led to an increase in the numbers of educated people in both cities and the countryside. Advances in printing technology not only made the dissemination of knowledge easier and cheaper, thereby aiding aspiring examination candidates, it also created anxiety among the *shih* about competition within the elite and concern about maintaining the distinction between *shih* and commoners. Expanded educational opportunities did not translate into increased rates of success, at least as measured by the attainment of *chin-shih* degrees and appointment to office. Although ever larger numbers of people participated in the examinations, the rates of success dropped dramatically in the face of declining numbers of degrees awarded and official posts available.[40] Viewed from this perspective, criticism of the examinations was a kind of self-justification process, arguing that a system that practically guaranteed failure was itself faulty.

Although candidates surely recognized that success defined by degrees and offices was increasingly elusive, the cultural ideal of education associated with preparation for the examinations remained a powerful force, and membership in the *shih* elite continued to be identified with participation in "examination culture."[41] The founding and support of academies as local educational institutions in Southern Sung thus could be seen as an activity used to define membership in the elite, since academies provided a *shih*-controlled alternative to prefectural or county schools where they could attend lectures, carry out ritual veneration of the sages and local scholars, and in other ways identify themselves as part of the educated cultural elite.[42] Even though individuals had very little chance to qualify as *chin-shih* through the examination system, they were highly motivated to acquire the education that would enable them to participate in it, and potential students far exceeded the capacity of government schools to serve them. This led many Southern Sung men to restore old academy sites and to found new ones, thereby participating in the examination culture associated with status as *shih*.

Confucian Academies and Buddhist Monasteries

Although the discussion of academies so far has treated them solely in the context of educational institutions, perhaps the closest institutional counterpart of the academy was provided by the Buddhist monastery. Comparison between academies and Buddhist monasteries yields parallels at nearly every level. Physically, academies were constructed much like Buddhist monasteries.[43] They centered on a shrine hall for ritual observances, like the Buddha hall in the monastery. Academy scholars lectured from a platform in a central lecture hall similar to that used by Buddhist abbots in the dharma hall. There were dormitories for students, just as for monks, plus the other necessary buildings for communal living: dining rooms, kitchens, bathhouses, and so on. Like the rules for community life in Buddhist monasteries, regulations for living and studying at academies were promoted by Chu Hsi and others.[44]

Printing technology, which originated in Buddhist monasteries for the purpose of proselytization, was similarly important at Confucian academies. In addition to lecturing and rituals, one of the three principal activities commonly associated with academies was the collection of books. Like Buddhist monasteries' printing of scriptures, many large academies sponsored the printing of works by men venerated at academy shrines, such as the writings of Ch'eng Hao printed at Illumined Way. The storage of woodblocks in academy libraries aided in the preservation of such works.

By providing expanded opportunities for teachers to develop a personal following of students and disciples, Southern Sung academies emphasized the teacher-student relationship in a way that paralleled the Ch'an Buddhist doctrine of master-disciple transmission of the dharma. Influenced by the mode of presentation used by Ch'an masters as well as a more general cultural trend toward the use of the colloquial and spoken forms in written texts, a new genre of Confucian teaching text, the *yü-lu*, or "sayings," evolved.[45] The *yü-lu* recorded the oral teachings of Confucian masters as Ch'an *yü-lu* were records of Ch'an masters' sayings. The emphasis on living masters, rather than sacred texts, associated with the use of the *yü-lu* as a teaching device greatly elevated the role of the Confucian teacher, and the enhanced importance of a setting in which the teacher was venerated much like a Ch'an master.

These parallels go beyond superficial similarities. It has long been recognized that Buddhist precedents provided the model and inspiration for new institutions in the Sung by which Confucians sought to appropriate social welfare activities previously associated with Buddhist monasteries, such as the "charitable estate."[46] Considering the Buddhist model for such institutions, parallels between monasteries and academies in structure and practice, and the role of monastic education in the T'ang and Five Dynasties, there is good reason to see a Confucian counterpart to monastic institutions in Sung academies. This is not to say that academy founders consciously (or even unconsciously) adopted Buddhist monastic structures and practices, but simply to stress that these worlds were not rigidly separated.[47] Highly educated abbots and monks moved easily in the world of the Confucian scholar-official, both at court and among their counterparts in areas where large temples and monasteries were located. Confucians wrote funerary inscriptions for Buddhist monks who had been their friends. Institutional boundaries, no less than personal ones, were fluid and permeable, not rigidly drawn. There need not be specific statements by historical actors showing their awareness of influence; it should be sufficient to point out compelling parallels that suggest the vitality and dynamism of interaction among different traditions in a complex social and cultural setting.[48]

Competing Claims and the Anxieties of an Age

Interaction between Confucian scholars and Buddhist clergy also produced tensions that were reflected in relations between institutions associated with each tradition. Both academies and monasteries were supported by land endowments, and there is evidence that academies occasionally appropriated land or buildings that belonged to monasteries or temples. Such cases are not always clearly usurpations, since textual references sometimes indicate that a "ruined" hall or other remains of a temple was occupied by an academy. Still, it is clear that there was an element of competition between the Buddhist community and supporters of academies for both material and human resources as well as territorial claims. Sacred sites were "contested spaces," places known to different traditions as spiritually powerful (*ling*) and appropriated by Confucian academy founders. Mount Lu, the site of White Deer Grotto Academy, was only one of many such places, occupied for centuries by both Buddhist and Taoist establishments. The flagship institution of the Southern Sung academy movement, White Deer Grotto was established in the tenth century at an old Buddhist site on Mount Lu.

By Southern Sung, rather than appropriating Buddhist or Taoist sites, academy founders were more likely to associate the site of an academy with the patriarchs of True Way Learning and to locate the spiritual power of the landscape in the sediment of a Confucian past, the residue of historical figures who marked the landscape with their lives as teachers. Shrines were erected at their former residences or studies, and these often became the foundation of academies. The commemoration of the past in shrines was also part of the construction of an alternative historical memory, as some of the individuals venerated were victims of political purges and others were representative figures in the True Way movement. Religious trends of the time also inspired the erection of such shrines. It was not by chance that intensive shrine-building activity dedicated to True Way thinkers, their students, and local officials who supported academies took place simultaneously with the proliferation of shrines to popular deities.[49]

The flourishing of popular Buddhist associations, such as the Buddha recitation (*nien-fo*) societies in the Southern Sung, should also be seen as contributing to the motives for building academies.[50] These organizations helped to create the perception of need for a Confucian—and distinctly elite—counterpart, the academy, which contributed both to the construction of a new social and cultural identity for the *shih* and to the "transformation through education" (*chiao-hua*) of local society. When the authors of academy inscriptions wrote of *chiao-hua* as a motive for academies or noted the ratio between Confucian institutions and Buddhist or Taoist ones (to the detriment of Confucian ones), they were calling for the cultural conversion of people. This is a familiar motif: an area known for the litigious, unruly nature of its population is brought to order by the actions of a worthy prefect or magistrate, who supports schools and academies. The local official is praised for the attention he gives to local concerns, particularly to the priorities of government to provide education. Officials known for suppressing bandits at times were responsible for the founding or restoration of academies, suggesting the multiple meanings of the institution and the relationship of academies to local politics.

Instability and disruption were produced by official careers, which moved men from their native areas, sometimes to distant regions. Staying only a relatively short time in each post, *shih* often found themselves away from home, without an assigned office but unable (or unwilling) to return home. Academies provided a residence, an occupation (studying, lecturing), and association with men of the same social and cultural background. At academies the younger generation, too, might find productive ways to spend their time, rather than in profligate activities that drained away family resources. When Yuan Ts'ai, the twelfth-century author of a guide to family life, described opportunities for the employment of sons and brothers in the absence of hereditary stipends or real estate, becoming a scholar headed the list.[51] If young men failed to take the *chin-shih* degree and hold office, they were encouraged to become teachers, and academies expanded the opportunities for teachers beyond private families and government schools.

Like the spread of shrines to popular deities, the religious cults that accompanied them, and the growth of popular lay congregational associations such as the Buddha recitation societies, academies were an institutional response to many anxieties of the age, including political turmoil, both domestic court politics and foreign invasion. Academies were also a particular kind of public space for men: distinct from the "inner quarters" of the domestic domain inhabited by elite women and yet separate also from the official world, a masculine space dominated by the authority of the state.[52] Since the rise of footbinding during the Sung has been explained in part as an expression of male anxiety about physical weakness in contrast to the strength of northern nomadic warriors,[53] we might see academies as a refuge for men, a place where they congregated away from the pressures of both domestic and official life.[54] Academies were microcommunities, models of a (male) elite society, from which women were excluded and where men resided together for periods of time and lived according to regulations that governed matters of daily life as well as formal learning.

Sources and Summary of this Study

The numerous commemorative inscriptions on the founding or restoration of academies have not previously been used to provide more precise and detailed information on the setting, origins, and history of academies. Although useful for all periods, such sources are particularly valuable for the Sung, an era with few surviving local histories, but for which there exist numerous collected works of individual authors, as well as epigraphical collections that contain academy inscriptions. Like other kinds of historical documentation, however, inscriptions have certain limitations and lacunae. They were written to "commemorate" and hence preserve in recorded memory the men who founded academies or who were venerated at academy shrines. Authors usually wrote inscriptions at the request of friends or colleagues related to or associated with the men to be commemorated. Inscriptions thus were hagiographic in part, but they were also commonly used as a forum to express criticism of the examination system, schools, or other institutions and government policies. Only infrequently do academy inscriptions reveal much about what went on at academies, what was "taught" there, and so on. Used in conjunction with other sources, however, such as gazetteers, commemorative inscriptions provide a deeper and richer perspective on Southern Sung academies than it has hitherto been possible to achieve with more limited sources.

Part I of this study will focus on "geographies," considering in chapter I the "intellectual geography" of the Southern Sung academy movement: the relationship between the four major True Way thinkers active in the latter twelfth century—Chang Shih, Lü Tsu-ch'ien, Chu Hsi, and Lu Chiu-yuan—and academies in Hu-nan, Fu-chien, Chiang-hsi, and Liang-che. The main portion of the chapter deals with the activities of Chu Hsi and his disciples in Fu-chien and the spread of the academy movement there. I argue that after his death, Chu Hsi's followers developed a cult to him in academies that became the basis for his widespread veneration throughout the Southern Sung empire in the mid- to latter thirteenth century. Chapter 2 documents the spread of the Chu Hsi cult in various geographic regions through the activities of the second generation of his disciples, beginning with Wei Liao-weng. At the same time, the diversity of the academy movement can be seen in academies established in the thirteenth century to venerate a variety of other figures and in academies that were supplemental schools, complements to existing prefectural and county schools. The chapter includes case studies of two well-documented Southern Sung academies. Records of Illumined Way Academy provide unique details on the finances, administration, and ritual activities of one major thirteenth-century example. The other case study, White Egret Islet Academy, is documented almost entirely in a series of inscriptions written over the course of the thirteenth century.

Chapter 3 considers the significance of place in the Southern Sung academy movement from two perspectives: the impact of economic conditions on the geographic distribution of academies and the implications of shifting views of landscape traceable in commemorative inscriptions. More than rhetorical flourishes, the attention paid to landscape by writers of commemorative inscriptions for Southern Sung academies expressed what can be called "geohistorical" memory. These authors inscribed the landscape with new Confucian meaning, recounting the appropriation of Buddhist and Taoist sacred sites and the creation of a new pilgrimage network based on Confucian sacred sites.

Part 2 deals with the social and cultural contexts of the movement in the Southern Sung. Chapter 4 traces the transformation of family schools into academies, showing that these lineage-based institutions also were part of the academy movement. Although people associated with True Way Learning wrote about these institutions and may have taught at them, most family academies originated through the efforts of individuals who sought to provide education for their lineage and often extended this to the local elite community. Expanding on chapter 4's discussion of family schools and academies, chapter 5 takes up the relationship between academies and local elite communities in Southern Sung, showing how academies furthered social integration by fostering networks among scholars from various regions. Like sites of religious pilgrimage, academies were usually associated with a shrine or shrines at which visiting scholars participated in ceremonial veneration of sages and worthies. Academies also provided lodging, occupation, and a sense of community identity for scholars displaced by warfare. Cultural legitimacy, in turn, was promoted by efforts to extend support to refugee scholars. The actions of officials in establishing or aiding academies in areas under their jurisdiction were often identified with the idea of *chiao-hua*, "transformation through education." *Chiao-hua* can be seen as both a political strategy aimed at the consolidation of control over local society through an alliance between officials and local elites and as a cultural strategy to deflect support from Buddhist institutions. Finally, chapter 6 documents the "learning of the *shih*" as portrayed through lectures given at academies in the thirteenth century, showing how ideas derived principally from the *Great Learning* and the *Doctrine of the Mean* were used to redefine the social and cultural roles of the *shih* in the waning years of the Southern Sung. In conclusion, I will argue that the cultural and social redefinition of *shih* identity was as significant in the proliferation of academies in Southern Sung as political and intellectual factors associated with the True Way movement, and that these dimensions of the Southern Sung academy movement were all interrelated.

One

Geographies

Intellectual, Economic, and Sacred

1

From Northern to Southern Sung

Academies and the True Way Movement

When the Southern Sung scholar Lü Tsu-ch'ien (1137–1181) looked back on the great academies of Northern Sung in his inscription for White Deer Grotto Academy, he summed up their development in the following way:

> At the beginning of the dynasty when people had just cast off the tribulations of warfare during the Five Dynasties period, scholars were still isolated. As things grew more settled, culture began to flourish. At first classicists [*ju*] made use of mountain retreats where they taught. The great teachers [gathered] as many as several thousand [students]. Sung-yang, Marchmount Hill, Sui-yang, and the "Grotto" [White Deer]

> were the most famous. They were known throughout the empire as the "four academies." The founders and their successors all honored the classicist profession. These [academies] were apportioned official books, allotted official salaries, and bestowed name plaques.[1]

Although founded at former scholarly retreats, studies, or other kinds of private schools, as Lü Tsu-chi'en noted, Northern Sung academies were distinguished from these earlier sites by state recognition and support through bequests of books, name plaques, and land endowments. Lü Tsu-chien's inscription was written to commemorate Chu Hsi's restoration of White Deer Grotto, which began in the late T'ang as a private scholarly retreat at an old Buddhist site.[2] The origins of this academy can be traced to the Chen-yuan era (785–804), when the T'ang scholar and statesman Li Po (773–831) and his brother lived as recluses at Mount Lu. Their retreat became the site of a school (Mount Lu State School [*kuo-hsueh*]) during the Southern T'ang. After the founding of the Sung, in 977 this school received an official bequest of books and state recognition through the formal bestowal of its name, White Deer Grotto Academy.[3]

Unlike other Northern Sung academies, Marchmount Hill originated not as a scholar's retreat, but as a government school. It was founded in 976 by the prefect of T'an in a hilly area surrounding the modern city of Ch'ang-sha, just one year before White Deer Grotto received a bequest of books and recognition by the Sung government.[4] According to one source, it too was established on the former site of a Buddhist temple.[5] Local people assisted the prefect in building the academy, which included a five-bay (*chien*) lecture hall along with fifty-two bays of dormitories. The academy subsequently declined, but was restored in 996 by the prefect, who added images of Confucius and his disciples. A set of classics was requested from the Directorate of Education, and there were reported to be more than sixty students at the time.[6] In an inscription written in 1000 recording the early history of Marchmount Hill, the scholar and official Wang Yü-ch'eng (954–1001) argued that schools should be the first priority of government officials, supporting his argument with examples from the Han:

> Since the Three Ages [of antiquity], the two [Western and Eastern] Han conformed to principle [*li*] and successively related traditions of good officials to inform later generations. The *Miscellaneous Records of the Eastern Capital* first related [the tradition of] Wen Weng and the *Han Records of the Eastern Chamber* [of the Loyang Southern Palace] first wrote of Wei Sa. [They] observed [Wen Weng's] management of Shu, and [Wei Sa's] teaching in Kuei-yang. Both led by making schools their priority. The barbarians submitted and transformed themselves. Thus do we know that schools are the basis of government![7]

The idea of government traditionally included education, symbolized in the term *cheng-chiao*.[8] The close ties between academies and the state in Northern Sung is revealed in the administration of Marchmount Hill. In 1012 a scholar was appointed headmaster at the academy.[9] Although he was summoned to a post in the Directorate of Education (*kuo-tzu chien*), he later resigned that position and returned to be professor at Marchmount Hill, which was formally granted its name plaque in 1015.[10] Despite its official status, however, Marchmount Hill and other academies were no longer regarded as essential once prefectural and county schools were established by the central government. Marchmount Hill, which flourished for nearly a century, was clearly in decline by around 1065, when the local prefectural school was founded.[11]

As it developed during the early Northern Sung, the typical academy included a central ceremonial hall, usually called the "Hall of Great Completion" (*ta-ch'eng tien*); in front of it was a lecture hall, called the "Hall of Clarifying Human Relations" (*ming-lun t'ang*); and wings of dormitories were placed symmetrically along corridors to the left and right. There was often a library and a sacrificial hall for the worship of Confucius and his disciples, as well as a kitchen, granary, and bathhouse, and pavilions, ponds, and gardens. A wall surrounded the academy, with one or more gates.[12] Land endowments, which might be contiguous with the academy grounds or lie elsewhere nearby, were allotted for support. There were wide variations of scale. The administration of the academy was supervised by a headmaster, usually called *shan-chang*.[13] Numerous other titles and positions might be used, however, depending on the particular circumstances of the individual academy.[14]

The well-known Northern Sung academies were geographically widespread, if not numerous. To the south of Marchmount Hill lay Stone Drum Academy, which began during the early ninth century as a private study at the site of a Taoist temple in Heng-yang County.[15] In 1035 it received land for its support along with the official name of Stone Drum Academy. Sui-yang Academy, to the southeast of the Northern Sung capital, Kaifeng, was the site of the scholar Ch'i T'ung-wen's study in the tenth century.[16] In 1009, after a local man contributed money to build a school at the site of Ch'i T'ung-wen's residence, he was made assistant preceptor at the school. Ch'i T'ung-wen's grandson, a local official, was appointed to manage the academy.[17] In 1035, the same year Stone Drum received its official name, it was granted the name of Ying-t'ien Prefectural Academy.[18] As a prefectural school, it was provided with a substantial endowment of land (ten *ch'ing*, or about 140 acres) for its support.[19] Sung-yang Academy, near the old eastern capital of Loyang, was located at the southern peak of Mount T'ai-shih, and its foundations also date to the pre-Sung era.[20] It was named T'ai-shih Academy in 995 and given a printed set of the Nine Classics and commentaries.[21] Like Stone Drum and Ying-t'ien, it was formally granted a name plaque as Sung-yang Academy by the Sung government only in 1035.[22] Mount Mao Academy in Jun Prefecture (Che-tung) was built during the reign of Jen-tsung (1023–1063) at a famous Taoist site dating to the Six Dynasties.[23] In the early Northern Sung an eremite scholar lived there and taught students. In 1024 the local prefect requested recognition of the academy, and it was granted three *ch'ing* (forty-two acres) of land for support.[24]

Certain aspects common to academies in Northern and Southern Sung are illustrated in the brief histories of the "great" Northern Sung academies: the appropriation of a scholar's residence or study as the site; state recognition through the grant of a name plaque; and an official endowment of land or bequest of books. In some cases, kin of the founding scholar were appointed to administer the academy. Most academies were located at sites originally identified with either Buddhism or Taoism—that is, places of particular spiritual power and appeal. Most were founded by eremite scholars seeking refuge from the chaotic political conditions of the Five Dynasties period, and these men naturally selected places that had been associated with other eremitic traditions, either Taoist or Buddhist ones. The histories of these well-known Northern Sung academies also suggest a uniform chronology: origins in the tenth century (or earlier); formal founding in the late tenth or early eleventh century; and demise in the mid-eleventh century.

Although not included among the category of the four (or six) great Northern Sung academies, Mount T'ai Academy has been described by a modern scholar as "one of the most famous private academies of the time," representing the return to a new appreciation of the classics.[25] Located at the most sacred of the Five Marchmounts, Mount T'ai Academy in the Shan-tung peninsula was the teaching place of Sun Fu (992–1057), one of the leaders in the Confucian revival of the early Northern Sung. Along with Hu Yuan (993–1059) and Shih Chieh (1005–1045), Sun Fu was known as one of the "Three Teachers" of the Northern Sung.[26] The first three chapters of the *Case Studies of Sung and Yuan Scholars* treat Hu Yuan, Sun Fu, and Ch'i T'ung-wen (the scholar associated with Sui-yang [Ying-t'ien Prefectural] Academy), thus beginning the intellectual history of the Sung with these three teachers.[27] Although he does not have his own chapter, Shih Chieh is listed among the disciples of both Hu Yuan and Sun Fu. Shih Chieh's inscription on Mount T'ai Academy, written in 1040, described Sun Fu's teachings as taking up the tradition that began with Mencius and continued through Han Yü.[28] After failing to get a *chin-shih* degree, Sun Fu returned to Mount T'ai, where he studied the *Spring and Autumn Annals* and taught students. He was eventually appointed to an office in the Directorate of Education. Sun Fu's appointment as an educational official at court illustrates the absorption of private teachers by the state in the new school system created just on the heels of Shih Chieh's inscription with the reforms of the Ch'ing-li era (1041–1048).

There are scattered references to other Northern Sung academies, but the numbers do not suggest a widespread movement, even considering the scanty sources. Beginning in 1044–1045, the imperial government encouraged and supported the expansion of prefectural and county schools.[29] Local officials allocated land to establish and support these schools, much as they had endowed earlier academies such as White Deer Grotto.[30] Their educational functions now superseded by prefectural and county schools, and in competition with these schools for land endowments, academies declined. As Chu Hsi later remarked:

> I consider that [when] the teaching of the former era's local schools had not yet been restored, scholars were in distress and lacked the means to study. They frequently selected good sites and established studies as places to gather, lecture, and study. Those in government sometimes designated them [as schools]: like this mountain [Stone Drum], Marchmount Hill, and White Deer Grotto. [This was so] until the Ch'ing-li and Hsi-ning (1068–1077) [eras] when school officials blanketed the empire and the huts of the former day's eremite scholars were without use.[31]

A primary reason for the flourishing of government schools in the late Northern Sung was the linking of schools and examinations that peaked during the administration of chief councillor Ts'ai Ching (1046–1126). In 1101 Ts'ai Ching extended the Three Halls System (*san-she fa*), begun during the reforms of Wang An-shih (1021–1086), to all local government schools.[32] This system instituted a hierarchy of levels, or "halls" (outer, inner, upper), through which students had to progress prior to attaining degrees. Although the Three Halls System was abandoned in local schools after 1121, linkage between schools and examinations fostered by the system continued to be controversial in Southern Sung, eliciting censure from critics such as Ch'en Fu-liang (1137–1203):

> When the Three Halls System was first applied in the Hsi-ning era (1068–1077), all those who desired to become *chin-shih* were forced to go through the schools. Local selection [*hsiang-chü*] increasingly emphasized school officials' recommendations based on family certificates [*chia-chuang*] attest-

> ing to the qualifications [of candidates], and teachers were unable to recommend people on their own. Because of this, literary "technique" [*shu*] determined success, and profit and salary were all that mattered. Teachers and scholars all turned toward academies.[33]

According to Ch'en Fu-liang, these conditions were exacerbated when the Three Halls System was reinstituted under Ts'ai Ching during the Ch'ung-ning era (1102–1107).[34] Ch'en Fu-liang stressed the social factors involved: he objected to the standardization represented by the Three Halls System because it meant that teacher-student ties and personal evaluations were reduced in importance, and dependence on school officials' acceptance of family certification increased. Criticizing the emphasis on achieving success in the examinations—"profit and salary were all that mattered"—Ch'en Fu-liang, like many others, expressed dismay at the strategies employed by his contemporaries to accomplish this goal. Finally, he attributed the academy movement in the twelfth century to the deleterious effects of the Three Halls System, arguing that teachers and scholars rejected government schools in favor of establishing academies where they would not be subject to the institutional legacy of the Three Halls System.

While Ch'en Fu-liang argued that the academy movement grew out of frustration with the effects of the Three Halls System, some modern scholars have found its motivation in the suppression of the ideas of the Northern Sung thinker Ch'eng I and his followers.[35] This point was also made by contemporary observers such as Lü Tsu-ch'ien. In his inscription on White Deer Grotto, Lü Tsu-ch'ien traced the link between Northern Sung thinkers and the Southern Sung academy movement.[36] He decried the rise of Wang An-shih to power and the suppression of Ch'eng I's thought, suggesting that the revival of academies came about because of these difficulties.[37] By the end of the twelfth century the suppression of Ch'eng I's thought had been extended to his transmitter and interpreter, Chu Hsi, who was officially proscribed by government decree along with a number of his followers, associates, and others in the False Learning (*wei-hsueh*) prohibition of 1195.[38] The members of this group identified themselves by the rubric *tao-hsueh* (True Way Learning). The revival and expansion of academies in the Southern Sung has been explained as a product of political factors associated with the True Way movement,[39] and the transformation of True Way Learning from proscribed heterodoxy to official orthodoxy in the mid-thirteenth century has also frequently been attributed to its close association with the academy movement of Southern Sung.[40]

The Southern Sung academy movement began in the late twelfth century with the restoration of Northern Sung academies such as Marchmount Hill, Stone Drum, and White Deer Grotto.[41] Although Marchmount Hill was the first of the major Northern Sung academies to be restored in the Southern Sung, Chu Hsi's restoration of White Deer Grotto in 1179 was the acknowledged model for the widespread founding and restoration of academies that followed. While White Deer Grotto was perhaps not the innovative institution some commentators have claimed, it has nonetheless been regarded as the prototype of the Southern Sung movement.[42] It gained its reputation as the model academy of the Southern Sung through its association with Chu Hsi, who later became the central figure in the True Way movement, but who was only one of many thinkers associated with True Way Learning in the late twelfth century.

The Intellectual Geography of Southern Sung China[43]

The intellectual history of Southern Sung China has conventionally been organized according to schools of thought, defined by particular thinkers and often by geographic regions.[44] This practice is rooted in the tendency of traditional scholars to trace the filiation of ideas from teacher to student in a manner that parallels the derivation of biological ancestry, including emphasis on geographic origins or native place. Without being constrained by this approach to the history of thought, it is fruitful to ground our understanding of academies in relation to intellectual developments in the Southern Sung by viewing major True Way thinkers and their followers in the geographic settings where they were most active and influential. According to Hoyt Tillman, during the first half of the twelfth century two distinct approaches developed within the True Way fellowship.[45] One was centered in Fu-chien, where Ch'eng I's disciples, Yang Shih (1053–1135) and Lo Ts'ung-yen (1072–1135), were active. Lo Ts'ung-yen was the teacher of Li T'ung (1093–1163), who in turn taught Chu Hsi. The other center was located in Hu-nan at Marchmount Hill, where Hu An-kuo (1074–1138), his son Hu Hung (1105–1161), and their most illustrious disciple, Chang Shih (1133–1180), were active.[46] The Hu-nan school can be regarded as a subdivision of the Ch'eng-Chu school, considering Chang Shih's scholarly ties to Chu Hsi and also the Fu-chien origins of Hu An-kuo and Hu Hung, highlighting regional ties to Chu Hsi.[47] In its focus on practical learning, the Hu-nan school can also be seen as linked to the historical school in Che-tung identified with Lü Tsu-ch'ien and the utilitarian philosophy particularly of Ch'en Liang (1145–1194).[48]

In the mid-1160s Chang Shih was an established teacher with his own disciples in Hu-nan, a frontier area distant from concentrations of population and prosperity in the southeast. Chang Shih's teaching at Marchmount Hill focused on the texts of the *Great Learning* and the *Mencius*, emphasizing the relationship between the cultivation of self and the order of state and society.[49] His concern with moral education and practical action, as opposed to metaphysical speculation, was reflected in the educational focus of the academy. When Marchmount Hill was restored in 1165 by the prefect of T'an, it was the first of the four major Northern Sung academies to be revived, and Chang Shih wrote a commemorative inscription for it the following year.[50] After describing its early history, he related its destruction at the fall of the Northern Sung and rebuilding in 1165, drawing a distinction between his goals for academy learning and education tied to the promise of examination success and office: "How could we allow students to gather here, boasting only of examination success and [the potential of] lucrative careers? How could we allow them to study only literary texts? Instead we desire to complete human talents in order to transmit this Way and to save the people."[51] Chang Shih stressed the completion of "human talents," rather than pedantic literary exercises designed to win success in the examinations, as the rationale for education.[52] Completing human talents meant cultivating *jen*, "human-heartedness" or "benevolence." Discussing the transmission of the tradition from Confucius (and Mencius), Chang Shih said: "What exactly is this tradition? It is human-heartedness, [which is just] the human heart. It is what regulates human nature, determines fate, orders the empire, and controls the myriad elements."[53] Chang Shih's criticism of the examinations, in his inscription on Marchmount Hill and elsewhere, fit well with Chu Hsi's own views, and when Chu came to visit Chang at the academy in 1167, they engaged in a fruitful exchange of ideas.[54] By the latter half of the twelfth century the two strands of the Hu-nan and Fu-chien schools were connected through Chu Hsi.

In his inscription on the renovation of Marchmount Hill in 1188, Ch'en Fu-liang drew upon the development of academies in the early Northern Sung to suggest continuity with the academy scholars of that era, such as Ch'i T'ung-wen, Hu Yuan, Sun Fu, and Shih Chieh.[55] The *Case Studies of Sung and Yuan Scholars* regards Ch'en Fu-liang as the major figure in the Hu-nan school after the death of Chang Shih, although he was from Jui-an County in Wen, and has traditionally been associated with the Yung-chia school of institutional and historical studies.[56] A tradition of political loyalty and hostility to the Chin (and later the Mongols) at the academy was a legacy of Chang Shih and his teachers, Hu An-kuo and Hu Hung, both of whom were irredentist patriots and unrepentant critics of submission to the "barbarians." According to Ch'en Fu-liang's inscription, there was a shrine to Chu-ko Liang (a scholar-general of the Three Kingdoms period) at the academy already in 1188, suggesting a military dimension to academy life and curriculum.[57] This would have been of particular interest to Ch'en Fu-liang, the author of the first military history of China.[58] Like Chang Shih and his predecessors in Hu-nan, Ch'en Fu-liang had a practical and pragmatic bent, oriented toward concrete institutional problems rooted in historical analysis.[59] In this light, it could be said that he saw the academy as an institution that could serve both to express and to propagate those values, but the institution itself never became a focus for him as it did for Chu Hsi and his followers.

Although the restoration of Marchmount Hill took the lead in the revival of academies in the Southern Sung, in later times the fame of White Deer Grotto, restored by Chu Hsi, overtook that of Marchmount Hill.[60] In 1178 Chu Hsi became prefect of Nan-k'ang in Chiang-hsi, where White Deer Grotto was located. While on an excursion to Mount Lu in 1179, Chu Hsi had occasion to observe the ruins of the academy and determined it should be restored.[61] Under Chu Hsi's direction and with the support of other local officials, the restoration of the academy was completed in early 1180.[62] Chu Hsi had the old buildings repaired and new ones constructed, and acquired books and a land endowment. He reorganized the academy based on his own teachings and designed regulations for it, consisting of admonitions to follow Confucian notions of proper conduct in the five key human relationships and vague exhortations to study and self-cultivation supported by quotes from the classics.[63] In spring 1181 Chu Hsi requested imperial recognition for the academy through the bestowal of a name plaque and a set of the Nine Classics.[64] In the same year Chu Hsi's intellectual rival, Lu Chiu-yuan, was invited to lecture there.[65] According to the brief record of his lecture, Lu Chiu-yuan focused on Confucius' distinction between "profit" and "what is just," and thus between the "gentleman" and the "petty man": "Those who study cannot but fix their wills on this distinction. The examination system has been used to select scholars for a long time. Famous classicists and great officials have all been produced through it. Today, those who would be *shih* cannot avoid it."[66] Having acknowledged this, Lu Chiu-yuan went on to criticize the inevitable concern with profit and salary that motivated those who studied for the examinations.

Stone Drum Academy in Heng Prefecture, near Marchmount Hill in T'an, was restored in 1185.[67] The following year a ceremonial room for images of Confucius and his disciples was added. Several thousand volumes of books were obtained from the Directorate of Education, and public land and money were allotted by local government authorities to provide material support.[68] Like Marchmount Hill, Stone Drum was restored and supported by government officials. Yet when Chu Hsi wrote an inscription in 1187 to commemorate its restoration and expansion, he related Stone Drum's early history and then justified the restoration by criticizing the standards of government schools:

> Today's commandery and county school officials certify erudites and students without investigating the quality of their virtuous behaviour and moral skill. What they [students] receive, moreover, is entirely the writings of prevalent vulgarity. The process of advancing [through the exams] in order to hold [office] causes men to focus on profit rather than on doing what is right. Scholars are motivated by their own self-interest.[69]

Echoing Chang Shih's criticism of the examinations, Chu Hsi decried the failure to examine students' moral qualities and called what they learned "prevalent vulgarity." Similar to Lu Chiu-yuan's comments in his lecture at White Deer Grotto, Chu Hsi argued that preoccupation with success in the examinations and appointment to office blinded men to what is right and allowed them to see only profit and so to act selfishly.[70]

Finally, in 1194, when he served as prefect of T'an, Chu Hsi also contributed to the continuing restoration of Marchmount Hill.[71] He established the first regulations for the academy based on rules he had created for White Deer Grotto. At that time, according to Chu Hsi, there was a daily allotment of rice and cash for students that was modeled on the regulations of the prefectural school.[72] At the end of the twelfth century, Marchmount Hill was said to have one thousand students, one hundred bays of buildings, and fifty *ch'ing* (about seven hundred acres) of land for its support.[73]

Unlike both Chang Shih and Chu Hsi, Lu Chiu-yuan was unenthusiastic at best about the academy enterprise, even though his followers actively promoted the establishment of an academy devoted to his teachings.[74] He taught students at Elephant Mountain Retreat in Kuei-hsi County (Hsin, Chiang-tung), which he built in 1188.[75] Lu Chiu-yuan described the surroundings in detail to a friend he wished to invite for a visit.[76] But he seemed to regard the retreat simply as a place for students and friends to come and study or converse with him, rather than as a formal institution.[77] Like many other retreats and academies, this one stood on a site with deep Buddhist associations, although Lu Chiu-yuan renamed it "Elephant Mountain" to accord with his impression of the peak as shaped like an elephant.[78]

In contrast to Lu Chiu-yuan, Lü Tsu-ch'ien did take an active role in promoting his own academy. After his mother's death in 1166, Lü Tsu-ch'ien taught at a retreat near his mother's tomb on Mount Ming-chao in Chin-hua. He later built Beautiful Pools Academy within the city of Chin-hua, where he taught as many as three hundred students at one time.[79] Lü Tsu-ch'ien, in fact, had drawn up rules for academy life in 1167, well before Chu Hsi wrote his.[80] Lü Tsu-ch'ien's academy rules were more specific than Chu Hsi's, both in matters of ethical conduct and in practical matters such as note-taking and discussion. In 1170, after students had gathered at Beautiful Pools, Lü Tsu-ch'ien appended seven regulations, the most important dealing with family morality and the behavior of the *shih*.[81] Lü Tsu-ch'ien's rules also focused on the collegial aspect of learning at the academy. The name, Beautiful Pools, seems to reflect this emphasis, as it is an allusion to the commentary on the *tui* hexagram in the *Changes*, interpreted as the mutual encouragement of learning among friends.[82] In his rules, Lü Tsu-ch'ien demonstrated concern with creating a community of learning for *shih*, although at the same time he required that students reside with their families and pay strict attention to family obligations, as suggested by the rules he added in 1170. Although Lü Tsu-ch'ien's involvement in the academy movement as a whole appears to have been modest (perhaps because he died at an early age), in the latter part of the twelfth century his Beautiful Pools Academy rivaled White Deer Grotto and Marchmount Hill.[83] Chu Hsi was able to persuade him to write the commemorative inscription for Chu's restoration of White Deer Grotto in 1179, and there Lü Tsu-ch'ien described the purpose of academies in the following interrelated way: competition with Buddhism and Taoism, the improvement of the educational system, and the promotion of Confucianism.[84]

While Chu Hsi's fame in the Southern Sung academy movement rests on his revival of White Deer Grotto in Chiang-hsi, he was most active in founding academies in his adoptive home, Fu-chien. His ancestral home was Wu-yuan County (Hui, Chiang-tung), but he was born, educated, and spent much of his career both in and out of office in Fu-chien. His father, Chu Sung (1097–1143; 1118 *chin-shih*), was appointed to his first office as sheriff of Cheng-ho County (Chien

Prefecture).[85] During his appointment, Chu Sung's father died, and because the family was too poor to return the body to their ancestral home for burial, he was buried there in the Wu-i Mountains of northwestern Fu-chien.[86] Chu Sung is said to have established two academies in the area around this time, one at the site of his father's grave at Star Creek.[87] He was subsequently appointed sheriff of Yu-ch'i County, and after dismissal from this post served as a tutor in the home of the Cheng of Yu-ch'i.[88] Chu Hsi was born here, and after his father's death he was cared for and taught by local friends of his father: Hu Hsien (1086–1162), Liu Tzu-yü (1097–1146), his younger brother Liu Tzu-hui (1101–1147), and Liu Mien-chih (1091–1149), all of Ch'ung-an County.[89] Chu Hsi later married Liu Mien-chih's daughter (ca. 1133–1176).[90]

Both Chu Hsi's teacher, Li T'ung, and his closest disciple, Huang Kan (1152–1221), were also natives of Fu-chien, and much of Chu Hsi's philosophical writing was done during periods of retirement in northwestern Fu-chien. Despite his frequent refusals to accept official appointments, however, Chu Hsi did hold office in Fu-chien, and even in retirement there was hardly a reclusive scholar: not only did he refine the concept of the community granary and other institutions designed to promote social welfare and harmony, but even before his work at White Deer Grotto commenced, he contributed substantially to the academy movement in Fu-chien.[91]

According to the Yuan scholar Yü Chi (1272–1348), the largest number of academies established by Chu Hsi was in Chien Prefecture in the Wu-i Mountains of northwestern Fu-chien.[92] As early as the Ch'ien-tao period (1165–1173), Chu Hsi built Harmony Culture Academy in Chien-yang County as a place to store books and carry out Confucian sacrifices.[93] In 1170 he built Cold Spring Retreat at the side of his mother's grave in Ch'ung-an County. Some students attended,[94] but it was never transformed into a formal academy as the other two retreats, Wu-i and Bamboo Grove, eventually were.[95] Wu-i Retreat, named for the Wu-i Mountains, was built by Chu Hsi in 1183, and his students went there to hear him lecture.[96] He built Bamboo Grove Retreat in Chien-yang County in 1192 in memory of his father at a place Chu Sung had liked.[97] Shortly thereafter it was renamed

Ts'ang-chou, and many students went there to study during Chu Hsi's lifetime. Formal school rites were held there, as described by Chu Hsi,[98] involving a complicated ceremony venerating Confucius and his disciples, with great attention to details of apparel, ritual implements, proper forms, and procedure. In contrast to the more elaborate school rites held usually on the first and fifteenth of the month, the daily ritual at Ts'ang-chou was much simpler:

> The master arose early every day, and all the students at the academy put on their robes and went to the front of the Reflecting Hall [*ying-t'ang*] where they struck the wooden gong and waited for the master to come out. When they had opened the gate, the master ascended the hall, where the students lined up in order and offered incense, bowed and went out. One of the students went to the altar of the Earth God to offer incense. Next they went to the pavilion and bowed to the image of the Former Sage [Confucius]. Then they took seats in the academy and received the morning salutations, drank soup, and sat for a little while, or they could ask questions and then leave. At the beginning of the lunar month, they presented wine and fruits in the Reflecting Hall; at the end of the month, they presented tea. If there were seasonal things, they presented fresh ones and afterward ate them.[99]

Although the Wu-i landscape had its particular attractions, Chu Hsi did not limit his academy-building activity in Fu-chien to that area alone. In the hinterland of coastal Fu Prefecture, on the border between Fu and Chien, lay Ku-t'ien County, the site of six academies. Nearly all were directly associated with Chu Hsi.[100] Half of them claimed name plaques in Chu's calligraphy, although they were not necessarily established by him.[101] Chu Hsi and Huang Kan lectured at Conch Peak, and Chu's disciple, Yü Ou, a native of Ku-t'ien, founded Indigo Field Academy, where Lü Tsu-ch'ien and Huang Kan both lectured.[102] The reason for this cluster of academies in Ku-t'ien is suggested by evidence that Chu Hsi traveled with Huang Kan to Ku-t'ien during the 1195 False Learning prohibition (the attack on Chu Hsi and his followers by court officials who demoted, dismissed, or barred them from appointment to office). According to an inscription recently unearthed from the remains of Indigo Field, Chu Hsi spent time in Ku-t'ien during the peak of the prohibition in 1197. The inscription states that, after this, "all the elite families' *chin-shih* and their disciples built academies to lodge (*yu-chü*)."[103] It indicates, not surprisingly, that the origins of a large-scale academy movement began at the time of the prohibition, when scholars connected with Chu Hsi were purged from office.

The statement in this inscription also suggests a social explanation for the proliferation of academies: they were established by elite families with members who had attained *chin-shih* status or were anxious to gain a position in this social category. Indirectly we might understand from the phrase "built academies to lodge" that such academies provided a place for either aspiring scholars or those who had achieved scholarly recognition but no official post. This also presents a somewhat different perspective on the contention by Chang Shih, cited above, that teachers and scholars turned to academies because they were dissatisfied with government schools' emphasis on the examinations. Academies were built to provide places, and perhaps occupation, for "*chin-shih* and their disciples." Viewed in the context of increased competition for a limited number of *chin-shih* degrees and official posts, the statement further implies that academies were established to secure a kind of institutional legitimacy for the growing numbers of literati (see part 2).[104]

As Hoyt Tillman has pointed out, longevity played a role in determining the lasting influence of Chu Hsi over Chang Shih, Lü Tsu-ch'ien, and Lu Chiu-yuan, since Chu Hsi survived until 1200.[105] Lü Tsu-ch'ien and Chang Shih died in the beginning of the 1180s, and only Lu Chiu-yuan lived into the 1190s. But longevity is hardly the whole story. Chu Hsi, Chang Shih, Lü Tsu-ch'ien, and Lu Chiu-yuan—the four major thinkers of the late twelfth century—were all associated to some degree with academies, but it was Chu Hsi and his followers who were clearly most active in promoting academies as institutions critical to their mission to retrieve the Way. Chu Hsi's activities in Fu-chien before 1195 already had established the foundations for an academy movement there, both through his own direct efforts in building academies and through those of his students. The flowering of the movement, however, would come only after his death in 1200, with the growth of a cult around his charismatic intellectual leadership.

Academies and the Spread of the Chu Hsi Cult in Thirteenth-Century Fu-chien

Following Chu Hsi's death, many of his disciples and their students founded academies in Fu-chien to venerate him, contributing to the creation of a Chu Hsi cult; this can be seen as part of a broader movement of shrine-building activity associated with the "cult of worthies" that developed in Southern Sung.[106] As Ellen Neskar has shown, although shrines to Chou Tun-i (1017–1073) and the Ch'eng brothers became widespread as part of the "transmission of the Way" ideology during the twelfth century, Chu Hsi did not become part of this pantheon until the thirteenth century.

In 1225 Liu K'o-chuang (1187–1269) built a shrine to Chu Hsi at the site of K'ao-t'ing Study (*shu-t'ang*) in Chien-yang County, a place where Chu Hsi had lived; in 1244 it was officially named K'ao-t'ing Academy.[107] Administration of the academy and responsibility for rites dedicated to Chu Hsi and his father were linked in the appointment of their descendants as headmasters.[108] At the end of the Sung, Chu Hsi's third-generation descendant, Chu I, was made headmaster at K'ao-t'ing Academy.[109] When he committed suicide at the fall of the Sung, students at the academy asked to have Chu Hsi's fourth-generation descendant, Chu Ch'un, take the position.[110] Chu Hsi's descendants also played a key role in transforming Wu-i Retreat into an academy. After Chu Hsi's death Wu-i Retreat was expanded by his son, Chu Tsai (fl. 1225), and later by his grandson, Chu Chien.[111] In 1244 rules were adopted, and in 1262 the position of headmaster was established, along with formal recognition of Wu-i Academy by the court.[112]

Chu Hsi's birthplace in Yu-ch'i County was made into a shrine to both him and his father in 1237 by the magistrate, Li Hsiu, whose father had been a student of Huang Kan.[113] Beside the shrine were two buildings where local scholars were invited to come and read Chu

Hsi's works.[114] The educational function of this academy was expanded in 1245 with the addition of a lecture hall. The academy was restored by the local magistrate Huang Yen-sun (1256 *chin-shih*) in 1269, and four dormitories and a sacrificial hall to Confucius were added.[115] At the time of this renovation, commentaries by Chu Hsi on Chou Tun-i's concept of the Great Ultimate, Chang Tsai's "Western Inscription," and other key works were collected into a book titled *A Compilation of Explanations and Investigations* (*Chi chieh hsin*).[116] Using these materials, question-and-answer pedagogy was employed at the academy.[117] By 1275, when it was formally awarded the name Southern Stream Academy by the court, it had been actively functioning for a generation.[118]

Places where Chu Hsi or his father—sometimes both—had held office also became sites of academies dedicated to him. In addition to Southern Stream, Chu Hsi and his father were commemorated at Stone Well Academy, established in 1211 by the prefect Tsou Ying-lung (1172–1244; 1196 *chin-shih*) and a local official at Stone Well Market in Ch'üan-chou.[119] Chu Sung had held office there and returned during the early Shao-hsing period (1131–1161) to discuss learning with local scholars. When Chu Hsi held office in 1157 in nearby T'ung-an County, he went to Stone Well Market and continued his father's association with local scholars there.[120] When Stone Well was established, Chu Hsi's son, Chu Tsai, who had earlier expanded Wu-i Retreat, was serving in office in T'ung-an and was ordered to manage it.[121] The ancestral cult aspect of the growth of academies dedicated to Chu Hsi (or to both him and his father) lay not only in the transformation of his birthplace and sites where he had visited or held office into academies, but also in the continued appointment of Chu Hsi's descendants to posts at these academies.

When Chu Hsi was prefect of Chang, he reportedly had wanted a lecturing place there, but had not been able to build one.[122] Wei Chi (1187 *chin-shih*) was prefect of Chang and built Dragon River Academy there in 1225 to fulfill Chu Hsi's wishes, adopting the rules of White Deer Grotto.[123] Wei Chi previously had been professor (*chiao-shou*) at Nan-k'ang and was probably inspired by his experience there.[124] In 1246 the prefect Fang Lai (1205 *chin-shih*) added a lecture hall and placed an image of Chu Hsi in the academy to be venerated.[125] Ch'en Ch'un (1159–1223), a major disciple and interpreter of Chu Hsi from Lung-ch'i County in Chang, came annually to lead the ceremonies, and Huang Kan was later venerated there as well.[126]

Huang Kan founded Surrounding Peak Academy, which was granted its name by the court in 1244, in Chien-yang County.[127] The county's Hut Peak Academy, which received a name plaque from Li-tsung in 1255, began as a retreat in the Ch'ien-tao era (1165–1173).[128] It was associated with Ts'ai Ch'en (1167–1230), who also built South Mountain Academy at the third bend of Nine Bends Stream in the Wu-i Mountains,[129] and who was the son of Ts'ai Yüan-ting (1135–1198), one of Chu Hsi's major disciples.[130] Ts'ai Yüan-ting and another of Chu Hsi's disciples taught at what later became Chien-an Academy, established in 1238 in the metropolitan county of Chien Prefecture by the prefect, Wang Yeh (1220 *chin-shih*).[131] A shrine was made at Chien-an for rites to both Chu Hsi and Chen Te-hsiu (Wang Yeh had been Chen's student).[132] In 1263 Hsü Chi, another student of Chen Te-hsiu, was appointed Chien-ning prefectural school professor, and concurrently headmaster of Chien-an Academy.[133] Chen Te-hsiu, from P'u-ch'eng in Fu-chien, was jointly venerated with Chu Hsi because Wang Yeh founded the academy and because of his local origins and association with Chu Hsi. At some time later, probably in the early Yuan, Chu Hsi's fourth-generation descendant, Chu Pin, was appointed headmaster at the academy "to take up [the rites at] the shrine."[134] At K'ao-t'ing, Southern Stream, and Chien-an Academies, descendants of Chu Hsi were appointed to posts, suggesting a strong element of the ancestral cult associated with these academies.

The Wu-i Mountains were also the site of an academy established at the former Chien-yang County residence of Liu Yueh (1144–1216; 1172 *chin-shih*).[135] Liu Yueh had built Cloud Manor Study (*shu-fang*) when he stayed at his home in Chien-yang during the False Learning prohibition.[136] When he was later appointed vice chancellor of the Directorate of Education (*kuo-tzu ssu-yeh*), he requested that the ban on False Learning be abolished and that Chu Hsi's rules from White Deer Grotto be used for the Imperial University.[137] He also undertook the printing of Chu Hsi's commentaries on the *Four Books*, having argued with chief councillor Shih Mi-yüan (1164–1233) that Chu Hsi's works were "in sympathy with the heart of the empire's scholars and gentlemen."[138] Liu Yueh was eventually appointed chancellor of the Directorate of Education (*kuo-tzu chi-chiu*), and Cloud Manor Academy was granted a name plaque in 1210. Only a decade after Chu Hsi's death and shortly after the rescinding of the False Learning prohibition, an academy was established by a powerful Chu supporter from the area where his academy-building activity had been concentrated.[139]

Although Ch'en Mi (1171–1230), a native of P'u-t'ien County along the southern coast of Fu-chien, did not hold high office in the capital as Liu Yueh had, he did build three academies during his tenure as prefect of Yen-p'ing (Nan-chien): Yen-p'ing and Southern Way Academies in his home county and Turtle Mountain Academy in Chiang-lo County.[140] Ch'en Mi was a follower of Chu Hsi's learning through his disciple, Huang Kan; he also had been prefect of Nan-k'ang, where he was involved with White Deer Grotto.[141] When he became prefect of Nan-chien and established Yen-p'ing Academy in 1209, he set it up according to the rules for White Deer Grotto.[142] After Ch'en Mi built Southern Way,[143] he invited an eremite scholar and student of Chu Hsi, Lin Hsueh-meng, from Yung-fu County (Fu) to be head (*t'ang-chang*).[144] Chao Fu (1195–1252; 1235 *chin-shih*), from Yu-hsi County in Nan-chien, whose intellectual lineage can also be traced to Chu Hsi, came to teach at the academy as well.[145] The name of the academy symbolizes the transmission of the Way to the south, and Ch'en Mi's third academy, Turtle Mountain, in Chiang-lo County, was named for Yang Shih, a native of Chiang-lo who was credited with transmitting the thought of the Ch'eng brothers to the south.[146] Turtle Mountain was Yang Shih's honorific name and referred to his residence, which became a sacrificial temple dedicated to him at the very beginning of the Southern Sung.[147] It was then transformed into an academy in the early part of the thirteenth century during the administration of Ch'en Mi.[148] Ch'en Mi himself was venerated at East Lake Academy in P'u-t'ien.[149]

Thus students of Chu Hsi's disciples, such as Ch'en Mi, used their official positions to further the academy movement in thirteenth century Fu-chien. Ch'en Mi was particularly likely to have been involved with the academy movement more than once because of his experience at Chu Hsi's premier academy, White Deer Grotto. He shared with other officials who were academy founders scholarly ties either to a major disciple of Chu Hsi, such as Huang Kan, or to lesser-known followers. The fact that Ch'en Mi himself was venerated at another academy in his native county and that the founder was also headmaster at another academy in P'u-t'ien suggests further that there were networks linking academies through founders, teachers, and headmasters as well as through individuals commemorated at them. The Fu-chien native Yang Shih, like Chu Hsi, was venerated at a number of academies; even a relatively lesser-known figure such as Ch'en Mi might also be honored by the establishment of an academy.

Founded in the last decade of Southern Sung rule, Spring Mountain Academy represents the full development of the Chu Hsi cult in Fu-chien and illustrates its wide scope and adaptability, as particular individuals associated with the academy or the region, in addition to Chu Hsi and others in the True Way pantheon, were venerated there. Spring Mountain was founded in 1266 by Chao Hsi-ch'a, prefect of Ch'üan-chou and an imperial clansman.[150] Chao Hsi-ch'a was the son of Chao Shih-hsia (1190 *chin-shih*), a prominent disciple of Chu Hsi and, like Chu, also a former prefect of Nan-k'ang.[151] Chao Hsi-ch'a was admonished by local scholars for not having done something to recognize his father's position as a disciple of Chu Hsi;[152] in response, he founded Spring Mountain to venerate Chu Hsi, Chu's disciples (primarily those from Fu-chien), and his own father. Although Liu K'o-chuang states that Spring Mountain was built at a site east of the city wall at the ruins of an abandoned temple, another source claims that the "temple was changed to an academy to worship Master Chu."[153]

Based on Liu K'o-chuang's description, Spring Mountain must have been quite a large academy. In front was a Hall of Repose (*yen-chu t'ang*) dedicated to Confucius, his three main disciples, and Mencius. On the hall walls were portraits of Chou Tun-i (1017–1073), the Ch'eng brothers, Shao Yung (1011–1077), and Chang Tsai. The hall's arrangement followed the system of Ts'ang-chou, the retreat of Chu

Hsi's in the Wu-i Mountains that became K'ao-t'ing Academy. [154] "Former worthies" were venerated along corridors (*wu*) behind the hall. On the west side were portraits of Lü Ta-lin (1046–1092), Yang Shih, Hou Chung-liang (a follower of Ch'eng I and Chou Tun-i and teacher of Hu An-kuo), Hu An-kuo, Hu Hsien (1086–1162), Liu Mien-chih, and Lo Ts'ung-yen. On the east side were portraits of Hsieh Liang-tso (1050–1135), Yu Tso (1053–1127), Yin Ch'un (1171–1142), Chu Sung (Chu Hsi's father), Hu Yin (1098–1156), Liu Tz'u-yin (1101–1147), Li T'ung, Chang Shih, and Lü Tsu-ch'ien. Behind the hall was a shrine dedicated to Chu Hsi, Huang Kan, Chao Shih-hsia, Chen Te-hsiu, and Ch'en Mi. The lecture hall stood to the south, with the north side of it used for honoring the teachers. Four dormitories were lined up along the sides. Opening school rites were held once the buildings were completed, and a name plaque was requested from the court.

What was the significance of the men selected for veneration at at the academy? The group included the usual members of the Confucian and True Way pantheon, such as Confucius and his disciples, Mencius, and Chou Tun-i, Shao Yung, Chang Tsai, and the Ch'eng brothers of the Northern Sung. It also included Ssu-ma Kuang, noted more as a historian and statesman than a philosopher, although he had also been venerated by Chu Hsi at Ts'ang-chou Retreat; and Lü Ta-lin, a student of the Ch'eng brothers and younger brother of Lü Ta-chün, who authored the famous Lan-t'ien Lü-*shih hsiang-yueh*, or "community compact," which was adapted and promoted by Chu Hsi.[155] Lü Ta-lin, Hsieh Liang-tso, Yu Tso, and Yang Shih were known as the Four Masters of the Ch'eng school. Hu Yin, Hu An-kuo, Hu Hsien, Liu Tzu-hui, and Liu Mien-chih were all natives of Ch'ung-an, where Chu Hsi settled after his father died, and were all students of Yang Shih and the Ch'eng brothers.

All the Hu were related, and Hu An-kuo was one of the key figures in the Hu-nan school associated with Chang Shih and Marchmount Hill. The inclusion of Hu An-kuo here reinforced the connection between Hu-nan and Fu-chien established by Chu Hsi through his contact with Chang Shih and his visit to Marchmount Hill, and Chang Shih himself was also venerated here along with the other major True Way figure of the late twelfth century, Lü Tsu-ch'ien. The only one of the four key True Way thinkers active in the latter twelfth century not represented here is Lu Chiu-yuan, who did stand somewhat apart from the others in his thinking. After the death of Chu Hsi's father, both Liu Tzu-hui and Liu Mien-chih took care of Chu Hsi as their own son.[156] Lo Ts'ung-yen was a native of Nan-chien and also a student of Ch'eng I. Those venerated in the inner sanctum, Chu Hsi's sacrificial temple, included his major disciple, Huang Kan, Chao Shih-hsia, Chen Te-hsiu, and Ch'en Mi, the former prefect of Nan-chien responsible for the establishment of three academies there. One aspect in particular stands out here: the emphasis on individuals who were students or followers of Northern Sung philosophers and who were also natives of Fu-chien, especially of Ch'ung-an, where Chu Hsi was most active. This suggests that it was important to establish a link between the region and the transmission of learning from the Northern Sung. The most obvious link was provided by Yang Shih, but it is significant that lesser figures in the True Way pantheon, such as Hu Yin, were also included, presumably because of identity with their native area.[157]

In his inscription on Spring Mountain, Liu K'o-chuang, who had erected a shrine to Chu Hsi in 1225 at the site of K'ao-t'ing Retreat (subsequently K'ao-t'ing Academy), suggested the extent to which Chu Hsi's influence had come to dominate the academy movement in Fu-chien and elsewhere by the latter Southern Sung:

> Throughout the empire, the writings of Chu Hsi are read and his Way is honored. In the locality [*hsiang*] where he was born, the districts [*li*] where he resided, and the areas [*pang*] where he held office, together with the elders of the Hsi-ning (1154–1173) and Ch'un-hsi (1174–1189) eras, they discussed so vigorously that "the hair clasps fell out and the cart umbrella broke off." In the places where they lectured on his doctrines and refined them, they frequently erected statues and collected books. Scholars of mature learning assembled and taught in these places. In Hui, Chien, Nan-k'ang, Ching-T'an, T'an-Heng, whether called retreats [*ching-she*] or academies [*shu-yuan*], they all hang out name plaques. Whether administered together with the prefectural literary schools or separately established by teachers and their disciples, the rules are like White Deer.[158]

There are several points to note here. First, Liu K'o-chuang attributed the spread of Chu Hsi's doctrines to Chu himself, in part as his personal charisma stimulated intellectual activity wherever he went. The result initially was the collecting of books and erecting of images—building libraries and shrines where scholars gathered. Second, Liu K'o-chuang recognized both academies and retreats as places that were formally proclaimed by the display of name plaques, often granted by the court.[159]

Academies previously established in Fu-chien by Chu Hsi's followers or otherwise associated with Chu Hsi received name plaques from the court: Huang Kan's Surrounding Peak Academy in 1244, Ts'ai Ch'en's two Hut Peak Academies in 1242 and 1255, and Chu Hsi's Wu-i Academy sometime during Li-tsung's reign (1225–1264).[160] The places listed by Liu K'o-chuang in his inscription on Spring Mountain as centers of Chu Hsi's learning in academies were in fact all places directly associated with Chu Hsi: his home prefecture (Hui); Chien in Fu-chien, where he was most active; Nan-k'ang, the site of White Deer Grotto; and T'an and Heng in Hu-nan, the site of Marchmount Hill and Stone Drum, both of which Chu Hsi visited and wrote about. As Liu K'o-chuang also stated in his inscription, "[I]n the locality where he was born, the districts where he resided, and the places he held office" Chu Hsi was remembered and venerated at academies.

By the reign of Li-tsung, the Chu Hsi cult was well established in Fu-chien through the efforts of Chu Hsi's followers and their students, many of whom held local offices that enabled them to support the building of shrines and academies. To what extent was the academy movement in Fu-chien primarily a product of Chu Hsi and his followers? Both here and outside Fu-chien the academy movement encompassed a wide variety of academies, some dedicated to Chu Hsi or other True Way thinkers, but some also closely related to prefectural schools. Despite rhetorical opposition by intellectual leaders such as Chu Hsi and Chang Shih to government schools and their ties to the examination system, along with criticism of the kind of learning fostered by these schools, many Southern Sung academies in fact were supplemental to local schools, a point suggested by Liu K'o-chuang's assertion that some academies were jointly administered with prefectural schools. Chien-ning's Purple Iris Academy, for example, founded in 1211, was essentially an addition to the prefectural school.[161]

Like the famous teachers associated with Northern Sung academies, such as Ch'i T'ung-wen and Sun Fu, the Southern Sung scholars Chang Shih, Lü Tsu-ch'ien, Chu Hsi, and Lu Chiu-yuan all taught at academies, and all but Lu Chiu-yuan actually participated in the establishment of their own academies, where they taught their followers. Unlike their Northern Sung predecessors, however, these four Southern Sung thinkers were lecturing at academies against the backdrop of major changes: the great political reordering that accompanied the loss of the north, the transformations and disruptions brought about by economic change, and increasing competition in and criticism of the examination system, which was tied to state schools. Southern Sung academies were closely linked to the True Way movement, particularly through the veneration of True Way thinkers at academy shrines. But they were also places that served a number of different purposes, including the education of *shih* who aspired to take the examinations and hold office. In the next chapter I will undertake a broad survey of academies beyond Fu-chien, showing both the diversity of the academy movement and how it was related to True Way Learning.

2

Shrines, Schools, and *Shih*

The Thirteenth-Century Academy Movement

Although intellectual geography continued to play a role in the thirteenth-century academy movement through the legacy of prominent teachers such as Chang Shih in Hu-nan and Chu Hsi in Fu-chien, academies also shared a common institutional character that transcended region. Academies were both regional institutions and sites for the construction of supraregional identity based as much on social class affinities as regional ones. While authors of commemorative inscriptions often referred to local geographical characteristics and wrote of the veneration of local scholars, emphasizing residence or native place, academies were also sites where *shih* from many places congregated and where they developed a bond of common social and cultural identity. Rituals venerating Confucian worthies and local scholars reinforced a sense of community among the *shih*. Lectures and libraries at academies provided the educational resources that enabled *shih* to prepare for the examinations and to participate in the cultural life of the scholar, whether or not they took a degree. Both the ritual and educational aspects of academy life were critical to the construction of a new *shih* identity in the thirteenth century. The development of an empire-wide academy movement was also closely related to the expansion of True Way Learning, as its patriarchs—initially Chou Tun-i and the Ch'eng brothers, and later Chu Hsi—were venerated at academy shrines, not only at places associated with them but gradually as members of an imperial pantheon that linked local figures to a wider intellectual, cultural, and even historical context.[1] The dynamic interplay between locality and the emerging True Way pantheon was reflected in regionally shifting combinations of True Way patriarchs and local scholars venerated at academy shrines.

This chapter surveys the thirteenth-century academy movement first by tracing the expansion of True Way Learning through the activities of followers of Chu Hsi and other True Way thinkers who founded, taught at, or wrote inscriptions for academies throughout the Southern Sung empire (apart from Fu-chien). I will show that, although academies dedicated to a wide range of thinkers—including followers of Lu Chiu-yuan as well as Chu Hsi—were part of the thirteenth-century academy movement, the differences among them were not highlighted by inscription writers (who were often their disciples); rather, the diversity of True Way was submerged in the desire to homogenize the Way as one in contrast to Buddhism and Taoism. The complex relationship between True Way Learning and academies in the thirteenth century is the unifying theme of this chapter, which concerns the expansion of the True Way movement through academies, its initial diversity and eventual homogenization as one Way, and the dual aspect of academies as both shrines and schools.

The Politics of True Way Learning and the Academy Movement

Beginning with the rescinding in 1202 of the False Learning prohibition directed against followers of Chu Hsi, some academies were founded by local officials as shrines venerating individuals persecuted under previous regimes: these foundings occurred most recently during the regime of Han T'o-chou (1152–1207; in power 1195–1224), but reached back to the regimes of Ch'in Kuei (1090–1155; in power 1139–1155), who silenced the opposition to peace with the Jurchen agreed to by Kao-tsung in 1141, and even to Ts'ai Ching (in power 1102–1125), whose repression of officials was associated with the conservative Yüan-yu (1085–1093) faction, which had opposed the reforms of Wang An-shih and his successors.[2] The reputations of men who had been demoted or dismissed during these repressions were rehabilitated through the erection of shrines commemorating them, and these shrines sometimes became the center of academies. West Brook Academy, for example, was established in 1235 on the foundation of a shrine erected during the Shao-hsing era (1131–1162) to the "Three Liu": Liu Huan (1000–1080; 1030 *chin-shih*), his son, Liu Shu (1032–1078), and Liu Shu's son, Liu Hsi-chung (d. ca. 1120).[3] Liu Huan was dismissed from office for criticizing his superiors and retired to Mount Lu. Liu Shu was a historian who worked with Ssu-ma Kuang and later lost his official post because he offended Wang An-shih. Liu Hsi-chung also was a historian and, although initially recommended by Ts'ai Ching, eventually offended him and consequently lost his official position.

Shrines to political figures were part of a broader shrine-building movement that included True Way patriarchs and their disciples, and both kinds of shrines often became the center of academies.[4] After Chu Hsi's death, while some followers led the building of academies to promote his learning in Fu-chien, others spread beyond Fu-chien to establish academies in nearly every region of the Southern Sung empire. The activities of these men dovetailed with policies pursued by Li-tsung (r. 1225–1264) as the court promoted the orthodoxy of the True Way movement and granted official recognition to some academies by bestowing name plaques. By the 1220s the imperial government appeared eager to engage the loyalties of scholars associated with the True Way movement and academies in part because of increased military pressures to the north as the Mongols began their assault on the Chin. Once the Mongols had destroyed the Chin state, they took steps to legitimize their position as rulers by restoring the Confucian temple in 1234 in their capital and laying claim to rights as inheritors of the Mandate of Heaven. This event intensified the need for the Sung state to validate its authority in terms of Confucian legitimacy, a need addressed by the elevation of Chu Hsi's synthesis of Northern Sung thinkers to the status of official orthodoxy during the middle of Li-tsung's reign (1241). The shift from heterodoxy—symbolized in the 1195 proscription of True Way Learning—to orthodoxy has been explained as a product of both political and intellectual factors, and has frequently been attributed to the close association of True Way Learning with the academy movement in the Southern Sung.[5]

During the reign of Li-tsung there was a surge in imperial bequests of books and in the awarding of name plaques in imperial calligraphy to academies. Such acts constituted formal recognition of academies by the imperial government in response to requests from officials. Like the imperial practice of bestowing name plaques on Buddhist monasteries, the granting of a name by the court did not confer special privileges, benefits, or duties on an academy, although the imperial appointment of headmasters at officially recognized academies began in the 1260s.[6] The process for requesting and receiving names was relatively random, dependent on the favor of a powerful official making the request or the political connections of the founder, as well as, perhaps, imperial whim. While the name-granting provided official recognition, it was not a determining factor in either the viability or the importance of an academy, nor was it deemed of sufficient significance to the state to merit notice in annals of the court or in other imperial records. The list of academies awarded names must therefore be reconstructed from accounts in local histories and commemorative inscriptions, which give uneven regional coverage. Because of its limitations, such a list is not a reliable guide to the composition of the thirteenth-century academy movement, although it can serve as a catalogue of its diversity.

Some academies granted names by the court originated as shrines to True Way patriarchs,[7] such as the Lien-hsi Academy dedicated to Chou Tun-i in his birthplace (Tao, Hu-nan).[8] By the thirteenth century, shrines to Chu Hsi could be found at academies beyond Fu-chien, such as White Deer Grotto, where a shrine to him was erected after his death.[9] Like the academies erected in his birthplace and at sites where he held office, lectured, or visited in Fu-chien, Purple Light Academy (built in 1245) was founded by the prefect to "enshrine" (*tz'u*) Chu Hsi in his official native place, Hui (Chiang-tung), and awarded a name by the court.[10] Also dedicated to Chu Hsi was Lin-ju Academy in Fu (Chiang-hsi), founded in 1249 by Feng Ch'u-chi with a shrine to his teacher, because Chu Hsi had been appointed to the same post Feng held (intendant of the Evernormal Granary, Tea, and Salt for Chiang-hsi).[11] Apart from Purple Light and Lin-ju and numerous similar academies in Fu-chien, Chu Hsi was venerated elsewhere along with other True Way patriarchs at places where there was no special connection with the site, suggesting the movement's spread was no longer confined to concrete associations with place or even personality (students or disciples). For example, at Heaven Gate Academy in Tang-t'u County (T'ai-p'ing, Chiang-tung), founded in 1246 by prefect Ch'en K'ai (d. 1268) and granted a name by the court in 1249, there was a shrine hall to the "seven worthies": Chou Tun-i, the Ch'eng brothers, Chang Tsai, Chu Hsi, Chang Shih, and Lü Tsu-ch'ien.[12] A similar shrine to Chou Tun-i, Chang Tsai, the Ch'eng brothers, and Chu Hsi was built at Seal Ridge Academy (also called Seal Light) in Yuan Prefecture's Fen-i County (Chiang-hsi) during the mid-thirteenth century.[13] (Although it should be noted that the shrine was added many decades after the academy itself was founded during the Ch'un-hsi era [1174–1189].)

Other academies awarded names by the court were founded at shrines to local "former worthies," including men who were known as either scholars or officials. For example, East Yung Academy in Ming (Che-tung) was dedicated by chief councillor Cheng Ch'ing-chih (1176–1251; 1217 *chin-shih*) to his teacher, Lou Fang (1193 *chin-shih*), around 1230.[14] Still other academies granted imperial recognition were essentially counterparts to prefectural schools and not associated with a particular thinker or school of thought, such as East Lake Academy in Nan-ch'ang (Chiang-hsi), which was officially named in 1210.[15] Although shrines were not absent from academies like East Lake, their role was ancillary to the identity of the academy. Among the more than twenty-five academies granted names by Li-tsung were some that were barely more than glorified studies of little-known scholars,[16] at least so far as can be judged from extant records, while others, such as Illumined Way (see below), were major regional scholarly institutions. At the same time, some academies not formally recognized by the court were relatively large and important, such as Su-chou's Tiger Hill Academy, established in 1235 to honor the Northern Sung scholar Yin Ch'un (see chapter 5).[17]

Wei Liao-weng and Academies: From Ssu-ch'uan to Su-chou

Unlike Tiger Hill, Su-chou's Crane Mountain Academy was awarded a name during Li-tsung's reign. Founded after the death of Wei Liao-weng (1178–1237), the academy was named for his honorific, Master Crane Mountain.[18] Wei Liao-weng was one of Chu Hsi's followers active in the early part of the thirteenth century whose influence can be seen in academies that spanned a wide geographical range. Like many others of his day, Wei Liao-weng's official career followed a circuitous path, and his political peregrinations created opportunities for him to teach at places that became academies named for him.[19] Between 1205 and 1222 Wei Liao-weng held only local offices in Ssu-ch'uan, having left the capital in disgrace after offending Han T'o-chou. The earliest of several Crane Mountain Academies was established in his native place, Ch'iung Prefecture (Ssu-ch'uan), when he retired in 1210 to White Crane Mountain in mourning for his father, and students went there to study with him.[20] One scholar who went was Wang Ta-fa, who later founded Level Mountain Academy in his home county of Hsiu-ning (Hui, Chiang-tung) after his return.[21] According to the account of Crane Mountain Academy written by Wei Liao-weng, local scholars had no place for study, so when the academy was completed it was used to house the autumn examinations. But there were no books, and Wei Liao-weng criticized the prevalent atmosphere of empty discussion in which scholars tried to outdo each other in fine rhetoric, arguing that this was nothing more than "making notes in literary phrases."[23] When a library was built and one hundred thousand volumes of woodblocks were added, the academy then provided the means for students to undertake serious study beyond empty literary rhetoric.[24] If Wei Liao-weng's claim about the library is even roughly accurate, Crane Mountain must have had a substantial impact on local educational resources, notwithstanding the tendency to inflate numbers like these. In this case, the promotion of True Way Learning, assumed because of Wei Liao-weng's affiliation with Chu Hsi, may have taken second place to the expansion of education in the area.

Wei Liao-weng was finally drawn back into active political life with an appointment from the chief councillor, Shih Mi-yuan, in 1222. But his criticism of the political machinations behind the accession of Li-tsung finally forced Wei Liao-weng out, and he was demoted to a post in remote Ching Prefecture (Hu-pei), where he established another academy in 1227.[25] According to Wei Liao-weng's biography in the dynastic history, "scholars from Hu-nan, Chiang-hsi, and Liang-che did not consider a thousand *li* a great distance to shoulder their books and follow [him]."[26] In 1231 Wei Liao-weng was appointed to a sinecure administering a Taoist temple in the Wu-i Mountains; the following year, he took a similar post at Chiang Prefecture in Yangtze Valley. Both appointments put him in close proximity to sites associated with Chu Hsi: the former at a place where Chu Hsi had also held a sinecure, the latter near Mount Lu and White Deer Grotto. Although Wei Liao-weng was known to have been interested in reconciling the views of Chu Hsi and Lu Chiu-yuan, he was heavily influenced by Chu Hsi's followers, especially Fu Kuang, who was a student of both Lü Tsu-ch'ien and Chu Hsi.[27] Wei Liao-weng was a key figure in the spread of Chu Hsi's ideas to Ssu-ch'uan, and the academies associated with him helped to promote Chu Hsi's thought there in the first quarter of the thirteenth century. The various Crane Mountain Academies venerated this disciple and transmitter of Chu Hsi, although there is no record of a formal shrine to him at any of these places.

Yuan Fu and Academies: Chu Hsi, Lu Chiu-yuan, and Lü Tsu-ch'ien

In contrast to his contemporary, Wei Liao-weng, a student of Chu Hsi who established academies as a private scholar to promote Chu's thought, Yuan Fu's intellectual lineage can be traced to Lu Chiu-yuan, yet he supported the founding or restoration of academies dedicated to not only Lu, but also to Chu Hsi and Lü Tsu-ch'ien while in office as judicial intendant of Chiang-tung. Yuan Fu, who took a first-place *chin-shih* in 1214, was a student of both his father, Yuan Hsieh, and Yang Chien, two of the Four Masters of Ming Prefecture, the foremost disciples and transmitters of Lu Chiu-yuan's thought.[28] In 1232 Yuan Fu oversaw the completion of Elephant Mountain Academy, built at the site of Lu Chiu-yuan's Elephant Mountain Retreat in Kuei-hsi County (Hsin, Chiang-tung).[29] Although the new academy was dedicated to Lu Chiu-yuan, the rules of White Deer Grotto were used to administer it, and in his lectures on the *Doctrine of the Mean*, Yuan Fu argued that the ideas of Chu Hsi and Lu Chiu-yuan were "in harmony" and that both expressed the unity of the Way.[30] In his annunciatory prayer for the school sacrifices at Elephant Mountain, Yuan Fu explained how Lu Chiu-yuan had distinguished Buddhists from Confucians, not how his thought may have differed from Chu Hsi or others: "Buddhists act for the self, while we Confucians act for the public [good]. Buddhists leave the world, while we Confucians order the world."[31]

"Ordering the world" apparently included appropriating Buddhist property, as Elephant Mountain used an abandoned temple's dharma hall (*fa-t'ang*) to house "students from far and near who collected like clouds" when Yang Chien's major disciple, Ch'ien Shih, was made headmaster there.[32] Feng Hsing-tsung (1176–1237), from Tz'u-hsi County (Yang Chien's home), was also a student of Yang Chien's whom Yuan Fu later invited to become headmaster at Elephant Mountain.[33] In the winter of 1231 Yuan Fu had the collected works of Lu Chiu-yuan printed at Elephant Mountain, along with his (Yuan's) father's *Chia-shu shu-ch'ao* (Documents on the family school).[34] When the academy was completed in the spring of 1232, school rites were held. In formal attire, students and teachers lined up according to rank to pay homage at the shrine of the "Three Gentlemen" (Lu Chiu-yuan, Yang Chien, and Yuan Hsieh), acting as though they were in the presence of their deceased teachers.[35] In the fall of that year, it was granted a name by the court.[36]

During the five years he was judicial intendant of Chiang-tung,

Yuan Fu also restored White Deer Grotto.[37] He appointed as headmasters T'ang Chin, who had taken a *chin-shih* in the same year as himself (1214), and Chang Hsia (1161–1237; 1208 *chin-shih*), with whom he had held office in Ch'ih.[38] According to Yuan Fu, both were followers of Chu Hsi's learning, and therefore appropriate appointees for this post, although T'ang Chin, in fact, was said to have turned toward Lu Chiu-yuan's thought.[39] Yuan Fu also explained that it was these personal ties with both men that led him to appoint them. This sheds light on how officials interacted with their colleagues in the appointment of academy administrators, and suggests one of the most important dimensions of academies: providing employment for men seeking official posts. Personal relations were a key element in the formula for success: "school" ties (taking degrees in the same year or being students of the same teacher), bonds created by holding office either in the same local area or at court, and both native place and affinal ties.[40] Just as regional and philosophical connections linked Yuan Fu to headmasters Ch'ien Shih and Feng Hsing-tsung at Elephant Mountain, so, too, did school and office-holding ties link T'ang Chin and Chang Hsia to Yuan at White Deer Grotto.

In a commemorative inscription on the restoration of White Deer Grotto, Yuan Fu traced a line of intellectual and political development back to the mid-eleventh century with the reform era of Wang An-shih, arguing that the Ch'eng brothers provided the illuminating leadership to restore the Way, in contrast to Wang and his associates, whom he characterized as "utilitarians."[41] He brought his argument up through the Chia-ting period (1208–1224), suggesting that the "classicists" of this era continued the line of the Ch'eng brothers as had Chang Shih, Chu Hsi, and Lu Chiu-yuan before them. Not long after this (1238), Yuan Fu was asked to write an inscription for Bamboo Pavilion at Lü Tsu-ch'ien's former academy, Beautiful Pools.[42] In the 1208–1224 era Lü Tsu-ch'ien's disciples had erected a shrine to him after Beautiful Pools had fallen into disrepair.[43] In 1237 the academy was restored, with substantial support from local officials, and in 1240 it was officially granted the name Beautiful Pools.[44] Wang Po (1197–1274) was later appointed to manage the academy, and his mentor, Ho Chi (1188–1268), was named headmaster in 1263.[45] Ho Chi and Wang Po were the first two of the Four Masters of Chin-hua (Wu,

Che-tung), followers of the True Way in that region. When Ho Chi was appointed headmaster at Beautiful Pools, he was said to have "received the true tradition of *li-hsueh*."[46] Both Ho Chi and Wang Po were followers of Chu Hsi through his disciple, Huang Kan, although Wang Po was also influenced by Lü Tsu-ch'ien through his own father, who was one of Lü's disciples.[47] Thus, although on the surface one might see the dominance of Chu Hsi's thought through the individuals active at Lü Tsu-ch'ien's academy, in fact there was a good deal of diversity in the influences evident at Beautiful Pools just as there was at White Deer Grotto.

Yuan Fu appeared anxious to downplay differences among Chu Hsi, Lu Chiu-yuan, and Lü Tsu-ch'ien and instead emphasize commonalities, and men associated with White Deer Grotto, Elephant Mountain, and Beautiful Pools likewise displayed diverse sources of intellectual influence. By tracing, as he did in his essay on White Deer Grotto, developments beginning with the domination of the reform party in Northern Sung through the False Learning prohibition and finally its rescinding, Yuan Fu reduced any sense of conflict among these thinkers and represented them instead as all inheritors of one Way, in contrast not only to Buddhism and Taoism, but also to "utilitarian" political leaders such as Wang An-shih.

Just as the unity of the True Way movement was stressed by Yuan Fu in writings on academies associated with Lu Chiu-yuan, Chu Hsi, and Lü Tsu-ch'ien, the perpetuation of the late twelfth-century True Way fellowship was reflected in the diversity of the academy movement in the mid-thirteenth century. Unity for Yuan Fu did not privilege Chu Hsi, particularly considering Yuan's own family background and ties to the home of Lu Chiu-yuan's major disciples, nor did diversity necessarily threaten the viability of the True Way movement. In fact, diversity was more likely to be a source of vitality, encouraging the promotion of True Way Learning as a broad movement of moral regeneration. Unity and diversity can be understood in this sense as two sides of the same coin: both suggest the plurality of the True Way movement in the mid-thirteenth century and the inclusion of a broad spectrum of figures among those venerated at academies. While Wei Liao-weng transmitted his teacher Chu Hsi's thought through private teaching at academies in Ssu-ch'uan during the early thirteenth century, students of Chang Shih, Lü Tsu-ch'ien, and others in the late twelfth-century True Way fellowship used their official positions to promote the veneration of their teachers at academies founded in areas under their jurisdiction. Like Yuan Fu, these officials propagated True Way Learning not as an exclusive enterprise but as a movement of moral education; unlike Yuan, whose administrative duties placed him at Elephant Mountain, White Deer Grotto, and Beautiful Pools, mid-thirteenth century officials whose administrative assignments took them to more distant regions of the empire carried the diversity of the True Way fellowship to new frontiers.

The Regional Expansion of the Academy Movement: The Southern Tier

By the mid-thirteenth century, academies associated with the True Way movement were founded along the southern frontier (southern Hu-nan, Kuang-tung, and Kuang-hsi) and granted official recognition by the court. One of the earliest and most important of these was Hsiang River Academy, built in 1247 along the banks of the Hsiang River in Ch'ü-chiang County (Shao, Kuang-tung).[48] Like Yuan Fu, who held the office of judicial intendant when he oversaw the restoration of Elephant Mountain and White Deer Grotto, Yang Ta-i (1220 *chin-shih*) was judicial intendant for Kuang-tung when he established Hsiang River Academy.[49] The history of the academy illustrates a common pattern of shrine-building—in this case, a shrine to True Way patriarchs—associated with a local school, followed by the moving of the shrine to a new site and the founding of an academy. In 1165 a shrine to Chou Tun-i and the Ch'eng brothers had been built to the east of the prefectural school's lecture hall.[50] This shrine was renewed in 1183 by Professor Liao Te-ming (1169 *chin-shih*), a prominent disciple of Chu Hsi, and Chu wrote a commemorative inscription for it.[51] Although the account in the dynastic history biography of Yang Ta-i says that he moved this shrine and founded Hsiang River Academy to venerate the T'ang prime minister Chang Chiu-ling (673–740), an inscription by Yang made no reference to Chang, but emphasizes rather the link with Chou Tun-i, including discussion of his philosophical contributions.[52] Ch'ü-chiang County was both Chang Chiuling's home and a place where Chou Tun-i had held office. Conflating the two figures—a T'ang statesman and a True Way patriarch—Hsiang River Academy brought together links to place with both political and philosophical leadership stretching across several hundred years.

Images of Chou Tun-i, the Ch'eng brothers, Chu Hsi, and Chang Shih were venerated in the academy shrine, where school rites were performed.[53] Judicial intendant Wu Sui (1200–1264; 1229 *chin-shih*) requested and received a name from the court in 1254.[54] When the academy was rebuilt in 1265 and the first headmaster was appointed "to take up the sacrifices to Chou Tun-i," Ou-yang Shou-tao (b. 1209; 1241 *chin-shih*) wrote a commemorative inscription, noting that the rebuilding of the academy took place under the leadership of Yang Ta-i's nephew, Yang Ch'ung-kung (fl. ca. 1250s).[55] Previously, as prefect of Tao (Chou Tun-i's native place), Yang Ch'ung-kung had requested a name for Lien-hsi Academy when it was renewed in 1262.[56] Ou-yang Shou-tao stressed the family connection through Yang Ta-i in Shao and through his nephew in both Tao and Shao, alluding to similarities with the disciples of Confucius and Mencius continuing their teachers' efforts: "Tao is like Lu, and Shao is like Chi."[57] Founded initially by the local prefect, supported by another official who had been involved elsewhere with academies, and recognized by the court, Hsiang River Academy in many ways typified thirteenth-century academies. At the same time, according to one modern scholar, this academy was the earliest and most complete in Kuang-tung.[58] He attributes this to the fact that Ch'ü-chiang was a major transportation route from Chiang-hsi southward, its proximity bringing influence from the academy movement's stronghold there (see chapter 3).[59]

Later, while serving as judicial intendant for Kuang-hsi, Yang Ta-i also took part in the 1262 founding of Hsuan-ch'eng Academy in Ching-chiang Prefecture (modern Kuei-lin), which commemorated the visits of both Chang Shih and Lü Tsu-ch'ien to this area.[60] Yang Ta-i's support of this academy may have been related to his own background: his native place was T'an in Hu-nan, the home of the Hu-nan school centered at Marchmount Hill, and he was a student of Hu Hung, Chang Shih's teacher. Li-tsung granted a name, transforming the shrine to Chang Shih and Lü Tsu-ch'ien into an academy and recognizing it as an outpost of Han culture in the far southwest; there were monthly examinations and annual support for a period of fifteen years, until it was destroyed by the Mongols. Both Hsiang River Academy and Hsuan-ch'eng provided educational resources to areas that lay in the frontier zone of Han civilization, were officially recognized by the court and supported by government officials, and venerated patriarchs of the True Way pantheon.

Elsewhere along the southern tier, academies that shared similar structural features and were also recognized by the court were not closely identified with True Way figures, although Chu Hsi's disciples were in evidence. We have seen that Wei Liao-weng's involvement with the academy movement stretched from his home in Ssu-ch'uan to Su-chou. Wei Liao-weng's friend Lin Chieh was prefect of Ch'üan (southern Hu-nan) in the 1208–1224 era and built a hall at the ruins of the study of Northern Sung literary figure Liu K'ai (947-1000) along the Hsiang River in Ch'üan prefecture to store books and to provide a place where local scholars could come for lectures.[61] Wei Liao-weng composed an inscription for a newly built hall at Clear Hsiang (River) Academy when the academy was expanded under the administration of prefect Chao Pi-yuan (1214 *chin-shih*), a descendant of the chief councillor Chao Ju-yü (1140–1196).[62] Although the initial request was rejected, the academy was officially recognized by the court in 1227, the same year Wei Liao-weng founded Crane Mountain Academy in exile in Hu-pei. Wei Liao-weng likened Clear Hsiang to the four academies of the Northern Sung (Sui-yang, Mount Sung, Marchmount Hill, and White Deer Grotto); and in his inscription, Ch'eng Pi (1163–1242) argued that Clear Hsiang should be accorded the same recognition as East Lake and Lien-hsi Academies, both of which had previously been granted names.[63]

Ch'eng Pi praised the ancient prose (*ku-wen*) movement of the Northern Sung, recounting that Chang Ching (971–1019) had established a study to commemorate Liu K'ai's literary skill—which he compared to that of Han Yü—at the site that later became Clear Hsiang Academy.[64] What is striking about this is the veneration of literary figures of the Northern Sung ancient prose movement and the absence of any clear references to True Way ideas or thinkers.[65]

Perhaps this is a matter of timing: since True Way Learning had yet to be pronounced orthodox by the court, academy founders were careful to validate their enterprise in relatively safe terms, such as the veneration of acknowledged literary models. Alternatively, it is possible to see this as simply a manifestation of the diversity of the academy movement in at least the first half of the thirteenth century, when academies might be associated with the veneration of literary figures, historians, or even politicians, as well as philosophers.

Like other academies in southern Hu-nan, Kuang-tung, and Kuang-hsi, Han-shan Academy was also an educational resource and cultural outpost along the southern frontier, although it was not officially recognized by the court. Named for the T'ang scholar Han Yü, Han-shan Academy was built on the foundations of a shrine to him in Ch'ao Prefecture at the eastern end of Kuang-tung, where he had been exiled to the post of prefect.[66] Although he held office in Ch'ao for less than a year, the legacy of his administration was widely known and included the famous expulsion of crocodiles along with the establishment of a school.[67] The depth of local people's feelings was shown in the naming of geographical sites after him, such as Han River and Han Mountain (Han-shan), where a shrine was erected to venerate him.[68]

Jao Tsung-i has argued that the appointment of officials from Ssu-ch'uan and Fu-chien, places where Han Yü's influence was greatest, to posts in Ch'ao helps to explain the high regard for Han Yü there.[69] According to a poem by Ch'en Yao-tso (963–1044; 989 *chin-shih*) from Ssu-ch'uan, Han Yü's educational legacy made Ch'ao the "coastal Tsou and Lu."[70] Another famous Ssu-ch'uan native and exile in Ch'ao, the Northern Sung poet Su Shih, wrote an inscription on the shrine to Han Yü in which he claimed that Confucian learning in Ch'ao began with Han Yü.[71] In the late eleventh century (Yuan-yu era [1086–1094]), the shrine was moved to a location south of the prefectural city wall; and in 1243 during the tenure of prefect Cheng Liang-ch'en (1217 *chin-shih*), Ch'eng-nan *shu-chuang*, a school named for its location "south of the city wall," was built at the shrine.[72] An inscription written in 1269 by Lin Hsi-i (1210–1273; 1235 *chin-shih*) details the structure of what he called Han-shan Academy at the time it was restored by the assistant prefect of Ch'ao, Lin Shih-chih.[73] The academy had twenty students divided among four dormitories and was supported by land allocated by Cheng Liang-ch'en and purchased by Ch'en Kuei (d. 1272), intendant of the Evernormal Granary for Kuang-tung.[74]

Following Jao Tsung-i's argument, although the influence of officials from Ssu-ch'uan was strongest in the Northern Sung, by the Southern Sung those from Fu-chien were most influential.[75] For example, Cheng Liang-ch'en was from Fu-chien's Fu Prefecture, as was Lin Hsi-i;[76] Lin Shih-chih, Lin Hsi-i's former student and friend, was from Fu-ch'ing in Fu-chien's Fu Prefecture.[77] Ch'en Kuei was from Fu-chien's P'u-t'ien County, had previously held office as prefect of Chang in Fu-chien, and was the son of Ch'en Mi, founder of three academies in Fu-chien (see chapter 1).[78] Liao Te-ming, founder of Hsiang River Academy, was from northwestern Fu-chien's Shun-ch'ang County (Nan-chien), and he held office in Hsing-hua's P'u-t'ien County along the coast. He had also held the post of prefectural school professor in Shao, where he renewed the school shrine to Chou Tun-i and the Ch'eng brothers prior to founding the academy there.[79] Teacher-student, official, and regional ties were blended here to produce powerful connections, a network that linked Ch'ao to Fu-chien, which lay in close proximity, unlike Ssu-ch'uan.

Lin Hsi-i's inscription records the words of the prefect to students gathered at the shrine to Han Yü, linking his role in local education with that of Han and T'ang figures who were famous for their support of schools in Ssu-ch'uan and Fu-chien:

> The tradition of learning among the scholars of Ch'ao began with Wen-kung [Han Yü]. It is like Wen Weng in Shu [Ssu-ch'uan] and Ch'ang Kun in Min [Fu-chien]. Their countrymen offer up incense [to them]. Up to the present [even though] it has been several hundred years, [Han Yü's] teaching has not been forgotten. Since [the beginning of] our dynasty, the local figures who have gone up to [the Imperial University] to study, to hold high office, and to take degrees have been many. In the homes the sound of chanting and recitation, and official lineages lined up in the neighborhoods are all the bequest of [Han Yü]. Former men built this place, and thus transmitted his teachings. Would it not be our shame if we did not restore it? . . .
>
> For scholars there is nothing more difficult than learn-

> ing. In learning there is nothing more difficult than [being a] teacher. The teacher of our men of Ch'ao was [Han Yü]. . . . Daily viewing his image, how can we not know what to respect and admire?[80]

An image of Han Yü was placed at the center of the shrine building, with an image of Chao Te, a local scholar appointed by Han Yü to teach at the school, on the left; images of Chou Tun-i and Liao Te-ming were placed on the right.[81] Thus the cult to Han Yü was integrated by the late thirteenth century with disciples of Chu Hsi (Liao Te-ming) and with the True Way pantheon (Chou Tun-i). Enshrining local or regional figures at Han-shan Academy (Chao Te and Liao Te-ming) along with Chou Tun-i and Han Yü symbolized an ideological connection with the restoration of the Way in the eleventh century and its continuation both temporally into the thirteenth century and spatially into the malarial southern regions of exile.[82]

From Clear Hsiang in southern Hu-nan to Hsiang River, Hsuan-ch'eng, and Han-shan in Kuang-tung, academies established along the southern tier from the mid- to late thirteenth century either were recognized by the court or, in the case of Han-shan, were founded with the support of local officials who identified the sites of these academies with late T'ang and early Northern Sung cultural icons, epitomized by Han Yü and Chou Tun-i. Both shrines and schools, the purpose of these academies was to bring education to relatively remote areas, associating that mission with the ancient prose movement (Han Yü and Liu K'ai), as well as with the True Way fellowship through veneration of both True Way patriarchs (Chou Tun-i, the Ch'eng brothers, Chang Shih, Lü Tsu-ch'ien, and Chu Hsi) and local figures at academy shrines.

Returning to Roots: Chu Hsi and Lu Chiu-yuan in Che-tung

"Pillowed in the great sea, Ssu-ming [Ming prefecture] is the easternmost commandery of the empire; in the eastern part [of Ming] lies Ch'ang-kuo county in the midst of the sea; and in the eastern part [of

Ch'ang-kuo] in the midst of the sea lies Mount Tai."[83] So begins an inscription on Mount Tai Academy written in 1275 by Huang Chen (1213–1280; 1256 *chin-shih*), one of Chu Hsi's noted thirteenth-century followers whose native place was Ming's Tz'u-hsi County, also the home of Lu Chiu-yuan's major disciple, Yang Chien.[84] Mount Tai's remote location in the Chou-shan archipelago off the coast of Ming made it a kind of maritime frontier, somewhat comparable to the inland frontiers of the south and southwest. In 1271 a scholar named Wei Chü, a follower of Yang Chien and Yuan Hsieh, and others requested the establishment of a place for "impoverished scholars" at the ruins of a distillery on Mount Tai.[85] Prefect Liu Fu complied with the request and contributed the old distillery foundation as well as additional financial aid.[86] Another local scholar, also a follower of Yang Chien and Yuan Hsieh, was made teacher at the academy.[87]

In their inscriptions on Mount Tai Academy, both Chao Yü-ho,[88] a later prefect, and Huang Chen stressed its importance in providing educational resources on the maritime edge of the empire. Chao Yü-ho's inscription, written in 1273 to commemorate the academy's founding, linked the economic and social development of the area to the need for education: "Since the establishment of the county in the Hsi-ning era [1068–1078], our place has been a solitary sea islet. During the Ch'un-hsi era (1174–1190), imperial favor made it a market town [*chen*], and the sea turtle's [the island's] mountains and streams were transformed. All the local elders shouldered their book satchels and went to the gates of Yang Chien and Yuan Hsieh."[89] Citing the essays by Chu Hsi on Stone Drum, Lü Tsu-ch'ien on White Deer Grotto, and Chang Shih on Marchmount Hill, Chao Yü-ho distinguished Chu Hsi and the academy from Taoist eremitism and linked local founders of the academy to famous predecessors:

> Yuan-hui [Chu Hsi] was a classicist [*ju*]. When he used learning to manage his locality and to perfect his disciples, it was not like the hermits and eremites who seclude themselves in the mountains and valleys, clothing themselves in air and [living on] fungus in order to imitate the prevalent customs of the Taoists. . . .
>
> If [the academy founders] emulate the followers of Con-

> fucius and Mencius, if [they] are able to imitate the rules of Stone Drum, White Deer, Marchmount Hill, and Wu-i, even if they cannot be like Confucius and Mencius, [the] Ch'eng [brothers], and Chou [Tun-i], can they not be compared with Chu [Hsi], Chang [Shih], Lü [Tsu-ch'ien], and Han [Yü]? Even if they cannot be like Chu, Chang, Lü, and Han, can they not be compared with Hsu, Wei, and Hsu [local scholars who founded the academy]? . . . Honoring the former sages in the present day is the purpose of establishing academies.[90]

Although Chao Yü-ho has emphasized here the enshrinement of former sages (and teachers) at the academy, elsewhere in the inscription he also underscored the importance of study. Chao Yü-ho commended the dedication of scholars who pursued learning even "by reflected light from the snow [in winter] and bagging fireflies [for light in summer]," and in uncomfortable circumstances, "having no stove in winter and no fan in summer."[91]

While Chao Yü-ho's essay made the connection between Ch'ang-kuo's economic development and the establishment of Mount Tai Academy, Huang Chen noted the lack of local schools in the area as justification for the academy:

> Even though scholars desire to shoulder their book satchels and go to local schools, they cannot. How are they then to have a place for collegial learning? In ancient times, 500 households made a *tang* and each *tang* had a local school [*hsiang*]. Today Mount Tai has perhaps 3,000 households and yet, contrary to [the custom in] antiquity, it is not even as good as one *tang* [it has not even one local school]. [Because of this] in 1271 Wei Chü and others petitioned Prefect Liu Fu to obtain the abandoned distillery foundation to build Mount Tai Academy in order to sacrifice to former sages and to study their teachings.[92]

From Huang Chen's perspective, the goals of learning and the ritual veneration of sages and teachers were dual aspects of education intertwined in the academy movement, each dependent on the other. As a follower of Chu Hsi, Huang Chen also stressed not just the activity of study, but its content, describing the orthodox nature of learning at Mount Tai Academy despite its remote setting:

> The many scholars of Mount Tai are on the incline of a dangerous place, and yet their learning is orthodox. . . . Now what is this orthodox learning? . . . Master Yang's egotism and Master Mo's universal love were not orthodox. Mencius explained it and returned to the orthodox. Lao-tzu's pure seclusion and the Buddhists' individual extinction were not orthodox. Master Han [Yü] explained it and returned to the orthodox. Those who discuss emptiness transgress the heights, and those who strive for profit [utilitarians] transgress the depths. This is not orthodox. Master Chou [Tun-i] and [the] Ch'eng [brothers] explained it and returned to the orthodox. For every heterodox doctrine that rose up, there was always an orthodox doctrine to save posterity. . . . Mount Tai's lecturing on Wen-kung's [Chu Hsi's] learning is orthodox indeed![93]

Unlike Chao Yü-ho, who highlighted Chu Hsi but also included his contemporaries Chang Shih and Lü Tsu-ch'ien, Huang Chen identified Mount Tai's intellectual orientation with Chu Hsi alone. Even though its founding was associated with Yang Chien and his followers, Huang Chen projected Chu Hsi's thought as dominant and ignored any reference to Yang Chien or the ideas of Lu Chiu-yuan.

Founded at the same time as Mount Tai, Compassion Lake Academy in Ming's Tz'u-hsi County was dedicated to Yang Chien; his residence at Compassion Lake was made a shrine to him around the time of his death.[94] A prefectural official moved the shrine to an islet in the middle of the lake during the Chia-hsi period (1237–1240), and when Liu Fu established Compassion Lake Academy in 1271, he located it on the shores of the lake beside a Buddhist temple.[95] Liu Fu had been master of the hall in the Imperial University where Yang Chien had studied, and there Liu Fu had become acquainted with his ideas. When he became prefect of Ming, he memorialized to the court to honor Yang Chien by establishing an academy, although there is no record of the granting of a name by the court. In 1272 Liu Fu allocated "officially confiscated land" (*mo-kuan-chih t'ien*) in Ting-hai County to support it.

Wen Chi-weng (1253 *chin-shih*), a student of Yang Chien, wrote an inscription in 1273 to commemorate the founding of Compassion Lake Academy.[96] Criticizing contemporary standards of learning, he elaborated on the doctrine of "mind" associated with Yang Chien as Lu Chiu-yuan's disciple and defended his teacher's ideas against charges of Ch'an influence:[97]

> The learning of Yang Chien is "mind" [*hsin-hsueh*]. . . . The *Changes* explains "mind"; the *History Classic* transmits "mind"; the *Rites* orders "mind"; the *Music* [Classic] regulates "mind"; the *Odes* give sound to "mind"; the *Spring and Autumn* [Annals] censure [the iniquities of] "mind." . . . How can there be learning apart from "mind"? . . . The *shih ta-fu* as youths study empty confusion and deception. They do not know what kind of thing "mind" is. They spew blood and breath, vying for a meritorious name. They determine their fate by grasping at riches and wealth, destroying their pure spirit [*ching-shen*] and thereby losing their original spiritual nature [*hsu-ling*]. . . .
>
> The volumes stored in the mountains number in the thousands, the scrolls stored on the shelves number in the tens of thousands. Hands ceaselessly unroll them, and mouths endlessly repeat them, taking this to be learning. In other words, they only fish for the sound of praise to achieve profit and salary. They lubricate the lips, decorate the documents, and nothing more. The learning that goes in the ears and comes out the mouth they regard as true; instead they consider the doctrine of "mind" to be false, even to the point of faulting the Master's [Yang Chien's] learning as "Ch'an learning."[98]

Wen Chi-weng's harsh criticism of contemporary learning allowed him to ridicule accusations against Yang Chien, and his views apparently had official support. Ch'en I-chung (1262 *chin-shih*), who became chief councillor in 1275, and Ming prefect Ch'en Ts'un (1247–1252 *chin-shih*) both put their names to the inscription, indicating official recognition and support for Compassion Lake Academy, although it was not granted a name by the court.[99] Despite his ardent defense of Yang Chien, however, Wen Chi-weng also used a phrase, *hsu-ling*, drawn from Chu Hsi's commentary on the *Great Learning*, thereby revealing the influence of Chu Hsi's writings on his own vocabulary and thought and suggesting the convergence of schools of thought at the end of the Southern Sung.[100]

The founding of both Mount Tai and Compassion Lake Academies in the 1270s illustrates several key aspects of the late Southern Sung academy movement and its relationship to the True Way school. Mount Tai was established as a school, at the request of local scholars who saw the need for added educational resources in the rural maritime fringes of the flourishing southeast coast. Compassion Lake exemplified academies that originated as shrines. Although Huang Chen vociferously declared the learning of Chu Hsi as the orthodoxy taught at Mount Tai, in fact the founders of the academy (and its official sponsor, Liu Fu) were closely tied to Yang Chien and his local colleague Yuan Hsieh, both followers of Lu Chiu-yuan. Similarly, although Wen Chi-weng vehemently defended his teacher, Yang Chien, Wen's own writings reveal his intellectual debt to Chu Hsi. At the close of the Southern Sung, the two academies reflect both the weaving of the major threads of True Way Learning into a single fabric, even in the heartland of Lu Chiu-yuan's disciples, and the dual nature of academies as shrines and schools.

A Transmission Shrine Academy: Illumined Way

Like many other academies founded at shrines to patriarchs of the True Way movement, Illumined Way Academy in Chien-k'ang (modern Nanking) began as a shrine to Ch'eng Hao built around 1175 at the prefectural school.[101] In 1214 the shrine was separated from the school and buildings were added. Commissioner Chen Te-hsiu's (1178–1235) 1215 inscription commemorating this event related Ch'eng Hao's service in the area as registrar of Shang-yuan County to the carrying out of the cosmological concept of Heavenly Principle (*t'ien-li*).[102] Chen Te-hsiu allocated support to the shrine (which at that time appeared to be much like an academy), including Spring Wind Hall, which housed images and had a second story that was probably used as a library, and two "schools" (*shu*) at the sides.[103] When the academy was completed, scholars and students carried out the opening school rites. No date is given for the beginning of these activities, although elsewhere 1241 is given as the founding date of the academy, the year True Way Learning was declared orthodoxy.[104] The school later fell into disuse, and it became a hostel for soldiers.[105] In 1249 the library was struck by lightning and destroyed in the ensuing fire.[106] Wu Yuan (1190–1257; 1214 *chin-shih*), a native of Chien-k'ang, subsequently rebuilt and enlarged the academy, following the rules of White Deer Grotto for its regulations.[107]

Although Illumined Way was clearly supported by local government officials, formal imperial recognition of the academy came only with the granting of a name by Li-tsung in 1256.[108] Prefect Wang Yeh (1220 *chin-shih*), a follower of Chen Te-hsiu, had written in 1253 to request the name plaque, couching his request in terms of the preservation of "this culture" (*ssu-wen*).[109] As a student of Chen Te-hsiu, Wang Yeh made use of his position as prefect to continue his teacher's support of the shrine to Ch'eng Hao by transforming it into Illumined Way. In 1258 the prefect Ma Kuang-tsu wrote a colophon to Chen Te-hsiu's shrine inscription in which he referred to Chen Te-hsiu's equation of the "heart/mind of the Way" (*tao-hsin*) with Heavenly Principle as what should be taught.[110] Ma Kuang-tsu also wrote a preface for the printing of Ch'eng Hao's writings at the academy in 1259 in which he stated that "ascending the hall of Master Ch'eng, then one must read the writings of Master Ch'eng; only then is one able to clarify his Way, keep it in one's heart, and carry it out in one's being."[111] As Han Yü claimed that the Way began from Mencius, so Ma Kuang-tsu claimed that after Mencius, the Way resumed only with Ch'eng Hao.[112] The creation of an orthodoxy of academy learning can be seen in the evolution of Illumined Way as an official institution sanctioned by the imperial government in the mid-thirteenth century.

Both Illumined Way and the prefectural school lay on the east side of the prefectural city and shared similar architecture. Although different names were used for various buildings in each complex, there were roughly parallel functions for each of the principal components of both institutions. For example, the prefectural school's "Hall of Great Completion" (*ta ch'eng-tien*) was used for the performance of rites, like the "Hall of Repose" at Illumined Way.[113] Lectures were held at the prefectural school's "Hall of Illumined Virtue" (*ming-te t'ang*), as they were at Spring Wind Hall at the academy. In addition to the structural similarities, since Illumined Way was administered and supported by officials, some of the same individuals were involved with both institutions. For example, Yu Chiu-yen, who commemorated the shrine to Ch'eng Hao in 1196, also wrote an inscription for the library at the prefectural school.[114] In 1263 Yao Hsi-te, area military commander-in-chief, renovated Illumined Way and renewed buildings at the prefectural school.[115]

A charitable estate (*i-chuang*), modeled on that of the Ming prefectural school charitable estate, was established in 1251 to support the school under the administration of Wu Yuan, who also supported Illumined Way.[116] The account of the prefectural school charitable estate justifies the need for support by saying that "the *shih-tzu* of Chien-k'ang who are poor and in want are many, and those who meet with misfortune are many."[117] A half million strings of cash were used to buy nearly 7,280 *mou* of lakeland to set up the charitable estate; this land produced an annual income of over 4,300 piculs (*tan*) of polished rice and unhulled rice.[118] Half of this income went to the support of the school, and half went to fulfill requests for aid from school administrators, students, and needy scholars (*shih-tzu*), including "itinerant *shih-tzu* who are not registered as native residents" (*t'u-chu pu-chi yu-hsueh chih jen*).[119] Those who petitioned for aid received eight piculs of unhulled rice and seven piculs of polished rice; these amounts were calculated in cash value at thirty-six strings for each picul of polished rice and twenty-five strings for each picul of unhulled rice.[120] As the local history states, "[T]herefore, itinerant scholars from elsewhere who attend the school here, or those who sojourn in this prefecture without being registered here can be subsidized, if they encounter misfortunes."[121] This amounts to a modest social welfare system for itinerant or indigent *shih*, who would undoubtedly be encouraged to attend the school with the promise of support.

Although Illumined Way had no charitable estate, like the prefectural school it was supported by government allocations of land, grain, and cash (see the appendix). A total of nearly 5,000 *mou* of tenant land in five counties was allotted to support the academy, along with 1,270 piculs of polished rice, 3,662 catties (*chin*) of unhulled rice, a modest amount of other crops (beans and wheat), and a small amount of tax monies (110 strings).[122] In addition, rental property income in a very modest amount—less than one hundred strings—was allotted. Although comparison is complex, since there are somewhat different sources as well as amounts of funding, the level of support for both the prefectural school and Illumined Way appears to have been roughly similar. The prefectural government allocated to Illumined Way a monthly amount of five thousand strings of cash to support scholars, along with firewood. Salaries for school administrators and teachers, along with student stipends, were paid in cash, grain, and fuel allotments. In addition to the precise amounts listed for both income and expenditures, like the regulations for the prefectural school charitable estate, the finances of Illumined Way were overseen through regular meetings, to prevent abuse and to maintain fiscal control and solvency.[123]

In terms of both support and activities, Illumined Way was a major local institution, with extensive funding, precise rules for its fiscal and institutional operations, and a hierarchy of administrative officials. The position of headmaster at Illumined Way dates to the 1240s. From the time of the founding of the academy until 1260, headmasters were concurrent appointees selected from among the ancillary officials of the prefectural government.[124] In 1259 the headmaster requested that the office of educational intendant be established, following the example of East Lake Academy, and Wen Chi-weng was appointed to the post.[125] The practice of appointing headmasters concurrent with another central government position is exemplified by Wu Chien (1244 *chin-shih*), who is listed as holding the post of headmaster while serving as pacification commissioner of Chiang-tung in 1252.[126] After 1260, headmasters were appointed by the Ministry of Personnel;[127] this was part of court policy by the end of Li-tsung's reign.[128] According to an inscription written for the headmaster pavilion at White Egret Islet Academy by Ou-yang Shou-tao in 1263, Li-tsung's policy included conferring authority on headmasters to oversee prefectural school professors.[129] A decade later, Huang Chen similarly wrote an inscription for the headmaster pavilion at Lin-ju Academy in Fu, Chiang-hsi, where he was prefect.[130] Both praised Li-tsung's granting of name plaques to academies and appointment of headmasters, which was seen as further evidence of imperial support for academies and recognition of their importance in conjunction with prefectural and county schools.

In addition to formal school rites performed on the first and fifteenth of each lunar month in spring and autumn, rites were also carried out on a daily basis by the appointed heir of Ch'eng Hao at the central shrine to him.[131] The court had previously named Ch'eng Yen-sun, a fifth-generation descendant of Ch'eng Hao from Ch'ih Prefecture, to oversee the shrine.[132] After his death, a member of the Ch'ih branch of the Ch'eng line was recruited in 1262 to fulfill the obligations of Ch'eng Hao's descendants at Illumined Way.[133] A ten-year-old boy was named heir to the deceased Ch'eng Yen-sun to perform ancestral rites at the shrine. The boy was officially renamed Yung-hsueh, literally "elementary learning," to reflect his new position in carrying on the lineal descent line at the shrine to Ch'eng Hao. Yung-hsueh studied with his uncle, who lectured and gave him examinations every ten days. Thus, according to the account in the local history, "'this culture's' teachings were completed, and the sacrifices to the former worthies were not abandoned."[134] Support for these descendants and their supervision of ancestral rites was provided by the prefecture and Illumined Way.

Continuity with the original foundation of the academy, the shrine to Ch'eng Hao built around 1175, was reflected in the care taken to maintain the involvement of a descendant of Ch'eng Hao at the academy nearly a half century later. Illumined Way continued the ancestral link to Ch'eng Hao by providing for his descendants to maintain sacrifices to him at the academy shrine. At the same time, the acceptance and promotion of ideas associated with the lineal transmission of True Way were represented in the dedication of Illumined Way to the patriarch, Ch'eng Hao. The granting of a name by the court in 1256 affirmed imperial support for the institution as a symbol of ideological orthodoxy. Chu Hsi reportedly wrote an inscription on the shrine to Ch'eng Hao early in its history, and although neither Chu nor his followers were notably involved with Illumined Way, it was clearly a True Way transmission shrine academy as well as a local educational institution. Other academies given names by the court, however, were not identified with shrines to True Way patriarchs or shrines of any kind. These academies were essentially counterparts or supplements to prefectural schools and stressed teaching and learning for the examinations as well as for the purpose of self-cultivation.

"To Supplement the Inadequacies of Schools"

Like government schools, academies were places of lecturing and studying, and in this regard, despite criticism that state schools taught to the examinations and not for "true learning," academies also provided training in classical and historical texts that would equally serve the needs of students preparing to take the examinations. Some thirteenth-century academies were established for this very purpose. Awarded a name by the court in 1210, East Lake Academy in Nan-ch'ang County (Hung) was built to "house itinerant scholars" and "supplement the inadequacies of [government] schools."[135] Established at the request of the assistant prefect, the argument was made in support of it that there was no place to invite famous scholars to lecture.[136] Founded at the same time as East Lake, although not granted a name by the court, Purple Iris Academy in Chien-ning (Fu-chien) was commemorated in an inscription by Lou Yueh (1137–1213; 1163 *chin-shih*).[137] He described both the economic and academic prosperity of the region, including a prefectural school with three hundred students divided up among twelve dormitories. According to Lou Yueh, however, this was inadequate for local needs, and even though the prefectural school was expanded, it was still insufficient to meet the demand. Consequently, Purple Iris was established next to the school, with support of three thousand strings of cash, including a donation from the prefect's own salary.[138] Lou Yueh recounted the history of the prefectural school and refuted criticism that the academy duplicated the prefectural school and was therefore extravagant.[139]

Dragon Islet and White Egret Islet Academies at Chi (Chiang-hsi), like East Lake and Purple Iris, were essentially supplements to the prefectural school. At the beginning of the thirteenth century and near the end of his political career, Chou Pi-ta (1126–1204; 1151 *chin-shih*) from Lu-ling (Chi) commemorated the establishment of Dragon Islet at the confluence of the Chang and Kung Rivers, where they joined to make the Kan River in Chi's T'ai-ho county in 1202.[140] After describing the landscape and historical background of the place, Chou Pi-ta related the earlier history of the academy site as a hostel and a drinking place. When the academy was built to replace the hostel, it had twenty rooms and was modeled on Marchmount Hill, Stone Drum, and White Deer Grotto.[141] The *Spring and Autumn Annals* were used as the basis for examinations, and there were ten students as well as a headmaster. Echoing Lou Yueh's justification for Purple Iris, Chou Pi-ta argued that Dragon Islet was a necessary addition to the prefectural school:

> Someone asked: "The county already has a school. Is it not too much [to add an academy]?" I answered: "Examining into the records, there are 100 Buddhist places and fifteen Taoist places; and that doesn't include the places that have been abandoned for which only a placard with a name survives. In Ou-yang Hsiu's "Essay on Fundamentals," he said that in the era of the Three Dynasties, if people did not work in the fields, then they worked at rites and music [were either farmers or scholars]. If they were not at home, then they were in the schools. This was the means by which kingly government was made clear and the teachings of the sages were carried out. Although there was Buddha and Lao-tzu, there was no means for them to enter. Today the former schools have all been turned into Buddhist and Taoist temples. How can you not question that situation and yet question this [adding another school by establishing the academy]?[142]

Chou Pi-ta also wrote an inscription for Le-shan Academy in Jui (Yun) Prefecture's Kao-an County, founded in 1203 by the prefect Wang Yen (1201–1204 *chin-shih*) and devoted to the education of the imperial clan.[143] Wang Yen was the sixth-generation descendant of one of the most influential chief councillors of the Northern Sung, Wang Tan (957–1017; 980 *chin-shih*).[144] According to Chou Pi-ta, Wang Yen was inspired to found the academy because of his desire to support the cultivation of talent among the imperial clan in recognition of his ancestor's close relationship with the emperor.[145] Chou Pi-ta recounted the educational history of the early Sung, emphasizing schooling associated with the imperial family and concluding with the imperial clan school (*tsung-hsueh*) established in Hang-chou at the founding of the Southern Sung. The academy was located at the side of the prefectural school; its structure was similar to other academies of the day, centered around a lecture hall with east and west wings that each had three dormitories.[146] There was a quota of twenty students, and one thousand *mou* was allocated for support, which was said to be sufficient for its needs. Lecturers were chosen to give instruction in the classics and history, and opening rites were held.[147] Like Dragon Islet, Le-shan functioned as a supplement to the prefectural school, and was related by its commentator, Chou Pi-ta, to imperial needs for education in the early thirteenth century. Chou Pi-ta was one of the most respected chief councillors of the Southern Sung, but he had been accused of being part of the False Learning prohibition and demoted by Han T'o-chou, probably because he had recommended both Chu Hsi and Lü Tsu-ch'ien.[148] Chou Pi-ta's interest in Dragon Islet and Le-shan was that of a senior statesman supporting education for state objectives through writing commemorative inscriptions on them. There is no hint in either inscription of True Way Learning, despite the inclusion of Chou Pi-ta in the proscription on True Way. He barely lived to see the lifting of the proscription.

A successor to Chou Pi-ta's Dragon Islet, White Egret Islet Academy was founded in 1241 by Chiang Wan-li (1198–1274), like Chou Pi-ta a chief councillor of the Southern Sung, although a generation later.[149] Both Chiang Wan-li and Ou-yang Shou-tao (b. 1209; 1241 *chin-shih*), who assisted in the founding of White Egret Islet, were from Lu-ling, as was Chou Pi-ta.[150] As mentioned above, Ou-yang Shou-tao later wrote an extensive inscription on the headmaster pavilion there, beginning with the imperial proclamation in 1263 to make academy headmaster a concurrent appointment with prefectural school professor.[151] He named Huang Chia (1256 *chin-shih*) as the current holder of the position.[152] He also stated that White Egret Islet had the capacity to serve several hundred students at the time he took up office there as a lecturer. He described the problems in finding sufficient housing for the students, and finally the granting of land from the prefectural government to rebuild the academy, and particularly a residence for the headmaster.[153] This must have been in the mid-1260s, some two decades after the official founding of White Egret Islet.

In his essay Ou-yang Shou-tao discussed at some length the capital and local schools of antiquity in relation to eremitism in more recent times, suggesting that academies such as White Egret Islet drew recluse scholars out of mountain fastnesses, and implying that concentrating schools in central areas only forced scholars to "avoid the world," because they had no schools (or academies) in areas where they lived.[154] He pointed out that before the Northern Sung proclamation to establish schools in prefectures and counties throughout the country, recluse scholars lectured to students on their own and were often granted books and other signs of imperial favor.[155] He cited as an example Hu Yuan, who relinquished his official appointment in order to become headmaster at Marchmount Hill. He contrasted that time, when headmasters were not officially appointed, with contemporary conditions in which academies flourished and had imperial support and recognition, extending to the appointment of officials to supervise them.[156] Finally, Ou-yang Shou-tao made the point that, unlike antiquity and even later times, his own day saw the joining of government schools with the teaching of scholarly recluses in the academies.[157] He claimed that school professors (*chiao-shou*) and academy headmasters were essentially the same, citing Han Yü on teachers and using Confucius' relationship with his disciples as supporting evidence. He described Chiang Wan-li's interaction with students at White Egret Islet as intimate and warm, allowing them to forget that he was a personage of high official status. Ou-yang Shou-tao argued for a close, personal teacher-student relationship, which he likened to that idealized between father and son and between elder and younger brothers.[158] At the same time, Ou-yang Shou-tao was explicit in his characterization of the academy as parallel with government schools, suggesting that the distinction of academies was to provide a place for "scholarly recluses" who could be drawn out of their remote settings into more central places where they could congregate with other scholars and serve society rather than remaining isolated in rural retreats.

Still later, near the end of the Southern Sung, Hsieh Fang-te (1226–1289; 1256 *chin-shih*) composed a colophon to Chou Pi-ta's inscription on Dragon Islet Academy.[159] He repeated a passage from the original inscription and appended his own comments to it, justifying the need for an academy in addition to the prefectural school. Hsieh Fang-te described White Egret Islet Academy as located on Dragon Islet, and noted that forty-eight years after the death of Chou Pi-ta (1252), an academy was there still.[160] He also pointed out that the academy and the prefectural school looked out on the same water, and thus the academy simply supported what the school was supposed to do. Hsieh Fang-te agreed with the idea that the academy headmaster should take responsibility for local education, a notion put forward by Ou-yang Shou-tao as well. Not only in cultural backwaters, such as southern Hu-nan or Kuang-tung and Kuang-hsi, but even in areas that would not be considered remote, such as northern Chiang-hsi, a major academy, White Egret Islet—with a long history that stretched throughout the thirteenth century—was promoted and justified as a necessary supplement to the prefectural school. Finally, Liu Ch'en-weng (1232-1297; 1262 *chin-shih*), like Chou Pi-ta, Chiang Wan-li, and Ou-yang Shou-tao also from Lu-ling, wrote an inscription on the shrine hall for Chiang Wan-li at what he called Egret Islet Academy.[161] Because he jointly founded the academy with Chiang Wan-li, Ou-yang Shou-tao also was venerated at the shrine, which was built by the headmaster in 1279.[162]

The history of Dragon Islet/White Egret Islet Academy in Lu-ling can be traced through several inscriptions from its origins in the beginning of the thirteenth century into the Yuan. From its first appearance as Dragon Islet, it served as a supplement to the prefectural school. By the late thirteenth century, Chiang Wan-li and Ou-yang Shou-tao were venerated at the academy shrine, reflecting a widespread movement of shrine-building that included not only members of the True Way pantheon, but also local scholars and officials.[163] These men were venerated here because of their association with the academy; unlike academies founded at shrines to True Way thinkers, literary figures, or officials, this academy originated as a supplementary school, and its founder and his successor were venerated to honor their contributions to this enterprise. Here, the shrine was not central to the role of the academy, but rather was a product of the passage of time, as the founders of White Egret Islet were venerated at the end of the Southern Sung.

In no perceptible way were noted proponents of True Way Learning associated with these academies, nor were they established in opposition to government schools.[164] Academies such as Dragon Islet/White Egret Islet were products of local men working in cooperation with local officials, expressions of local elite identity. Chou Pi-ta was a local man who had achieved high political office and returned home at the end of his career to commemorate Dragon Islet as an institution that represented educational ideals of antiquity and also served local needs in the present. Chiang Wan-li, who held office at Dragon Islet, collaborated with the local scholar Ou-yang Shou-tao to continue Chou Pi-ta's enterprise. Finally, although the author of one record of this academy, Hsieh Fang-te, was from Hsin in Chiang-tung, Chou Pi-ta, Chiang Wan-li, Ou-yang Shou-tao, and Liu Ch'en-weng were all from Lu-ling—local men commemorating a local institution. In this regard they differed both from Chang Shih, Chu Hsi, Lü Tsu-ch'ien, and other True Way thinkers who wrote about academies in the late twelfth century from a perspective critical of government education, and from chroniclers of the great Northern Sung academies who saw the founders of these institutions as Confucian scholars motivated by a desire to teach students in an era before the state school system was in place. Rather, the several extant accounts of Dragon Islet/White Egret Islet all stress the complementary and supplementary relationship between the academy and the prefectural school.

But considering some academies as supplementary to government schools still to some degree begs the question of why officials chose to allot resources to the support of academies rather than to the expansion of government schools. I believe the answer to this lies at least partly in the idea of control. Although they were far from being private institutions, academies were places where—in contrast to government schools—*shih* could assert some degree of intellectual, political, and social autonomy. By supporting academies, prefectural and county officials were supporting the interests of local elites and thus promoting local social harmony and order. Local elites, in turn, by supporting academies, were also contributing to the creation of jobs for themselves, quasi-official positions that were eventually appropriated by the central government as the position of academy headmaster was made concurrent with prefectural school professor by the 1260s. In some measure, academies were social welfare institutions, providing occupation and support for local *shih*, some of whom were probably newly arrived residents or itinerant scholars. From the perspective of local government, academies provided a means to employ such men and to prevent their becoming a problem for the maintenance of social order (see chapter 5).[165]

The Unity of the Way and the Academy Movement

Founded in the 1240s and dedicated to Chu Hsi, Purple Light Academy was rebuilt in the winter of 1276 at the old foundation of the prefectural school and the ruins of a Taoist temple. Fang Hui's (1227–1307; 1262 *chin-shih*) commemorative inscription associated the original site with Chu Hsi, referring to one of his sobriquets, Master Tzu-yang (Purple Light), from the mountain nearby.[166] Fang Hui described the previous location of the academy outside the south gate of the city wall, amid mountains and streams, with "vermilion placard and golden script," and the conventional layout of wings of dormitories to the east and west of a central lecture hall, along with a library and other pavilions.[167] He closed the inscription with a comparison of She County, the site of the rebuilt academy, with Confucius' state of Lu, emphasizing that Chu Hsi was the heir of Confucius and Mencius. Like Purple Light, Lin-ju Academy was founded in the 1240s and dedicated to Chu Hsi, but it was granted a name plaque only in 1271, and the first headmaster was appointed in 1273, simultaneously with the founding of Mount Tai and Compassion Lake in Ming.[168] Written the same year, Huang Chen's inscription on the headmaster hall at Lin-ju begins with a discussion of the transmission of the Way from antiquity through his teacher, Chu Hsi, and then concludes with the statement, "Our emperor Li-tsung elevated [the learning of Chu Hsi] and carried out sacrifices [to Chu Hsi] in order to proclaim his learning as the learning of the empire. The *shih ta-fu* therefore establish academies in order to chant and practice this doctrine."[169]

Like his contemporary Huang Chen, the erudite encyclopedist Wang Ying-lin (1223–1296; 1241 *chin-shih*) was also a native of Ming's Tz'u-hsi County. While living at home in seclusion after the fall of the Southern Sung, Wang Ying-lin recorded the restoration of Compassion Lake Academy in 1292.[170] He presented Yang Chien as an orthodox thinker, linking Yang's teacher, Lu Chiu-yuan, to Chu Hsi: "The learning of the Master [Yang Chien] is the learning of Wen-an [Lu Chiu-yuan]. When Wen-an lectured on the *Analects* at White Deer . . . [t]hose who listened were excited and their hearts were moved. . . . Chu Wen-kung [Hsi] also declared that what Master Lu said concentrated on 'revering moral nature.'"[171] Tutored by his father, a student of Lü Tsu-ch'ien and Lu Chiu-yuan through their disciples, Wang Ying-lin was exposed to a diverse array of intellectual influences, including his teacher Wang Yeh, a student of Chen Te-hsiu.[172] Wang Ying-lin's interests were eclectic, not exclusive, and were reflected in his weaving together the thought of Chu Hsi and Lu Chiu-yuan at Compassion Lake.

In the early Yuan, Jen Shih-lin (1253–1309) composed an inscription for an academy in Ming's Feng-hua County that was dedicated to Chu Hsi.[173] It recounts the academy's Southern Sung origins:

> Formerly, when Wen-kung [Chu Hsi] was intendant of the Evernormal Granary for Che-tung, he frequently traveled to T'ai and Wen prefectures by boat across Dragon Ford. The elders led all the students to request that he give lectures in the school. In around 1260, Yao Hsi-te established the sea boundary [*hai-kun*] and [with] Hsieh Ch'ang-yuan, a prefectural official, planned [the academy]. Former *chin-shih* Li Hsiao, Shu Mi, and T'ung Yao requested to establish an academy to the east of the ford where students could gather and study. . . . The sign read "Dragon Ford Academy." It was subsequently moved to the east of the Confucian temple-school [*miao-hsueh*]. In 1281 the name was changed to Wen-kung Academy [to honor Chu Hsi].[174]

Jen Shih-lin's Northern Sung ancestors were from Ssu-ch'uan, as were both Yao Hsi-te and Hsieh Ch'ang-yuan, providing a link that may have facilitated Yao's and Hsieh's cooperation in the establishment of this academy and perhaps encouraged Jen's commemoration of it.[175] Yao Hsi-te was active in the renovation of Illumined Way in 1263, and he became minister of war in 1264. His official action cited in the above quote was probably related to his military responsibilities, as coastal defenses were mounted in the face of the growing Mongol threat. Hsieh Ch'ang-yuan had been a student of Chu Hsi's disciple, Wei Liao-weng, in Ssu-ch'uan, where he took first place in the Ssu-ch'uan examinations. Interestingly, Shu Mi (1244 *chin-shih*) was the grandson of Shu Lin, one of the Four Masters of Ming, disciples of Lu Chiu-yuan.[176] It is not inconceivable that, looking back from the perspective of the early Yuan, Jen Shih-lin may have constructed a link with Chu Hsi to add legitimacy, since it is likely that the original purpose of Dragon Ford was primarily to serve the needs of local scholars, including descendants of followers of Lu Chiu-yuan, and thus may have been a supplementary school. Most telling, however, is the name change after the fall of the Sung that made the identification of the academy with Chu Hsi unmistakable. Thus in Ming Prefecture, the home of the major disciples of Lu Chiu-yuan, by the early Yuan either Lu Chiu-yuan and Chu Hsi were woven together, as in Wang Ying-lin's inscription on the restoration of Compassion Lake, or Chu Hsi was the dominant figure, as the evidence from Dragon Ford suggests:

> The [school] system of the former kings of antiquity is truly distant, indeed! The T'ang proclaimed that schools should be established throughout the empire's prefectures and counties. After that, the fame of the four academies was widely known. With the gradual flourishing of schools in the Sung Ch'ing-li (1041–1048) and Hsi-ning (1068–1077) eras, the huts of retired scholars consequently were abandoned until Hui-kuo Chu Wen-kung began to restore the ancient sacrifices to Confucius at White Deer Grotto, like the rites of K'ai-yuan (713–741). He subsequently established Bamboo Grove Retreat, elevating Tseng-tzu and Tzu-ssu to the Confucian temple to match Confucius and following sacrifices to the

> seven masters: Chou [Tun-i], Ch'eng [I and Hao], Chang Tsai, Shao Yung, Ssu-ma [Kuang] and Li Yen-p'ing.[177] Thereupon, those who established academies at the lecturing places of the Classicists were numerous. When Wen-kung died, then among all the places where he resided or held office there were none that did not [regard him as] teacher and honor him, thereby seeking to explicate his learning. For this reason, academies increasingly flourished.[178]

Echoing Liu K'o-chuang's assertion in his 1268 inscription on Ch'üan-chou's Spring Mountain Academy—"Throughout the empire, the writings of Chu Hsi are read and his Way is honored"—Jen Shih-lin has made a similar claim from his perspective in the early Yuan. In Jen's view, the key reason behind the spread of academies is veneration of Chu Hsi and his doctrines, not learning in opposition to the examinations, nor even necessarily to promote success in the examinations. For Chinese literati under Mongol rule, the promise of the examinations was much less attractive and even less realistic than in the late Southern Sung; but they could retain their scholarly association with colleagues at academies.

Conclusion

Official recognition of academies through the granting of names by the court during the last two reigns of the Southern Sung was an attempt by the state to shore up its support by recognizing the claims of the True Way school, understood as an umbrella that covered a multiplicity of thinkers, not just those directly affiliated with Chu Hsi. The homogenization of the Way reflected during the 1230s in Yuan Fu's support of academies associated with Lu Chiu-yuan, Lü Tsu-ch'ien, and Chu Hsi, and expressed in his comments on them as all proponents of one Way, culminated by the 1270s in the encompassing of diverse thinkers under the cult of Chu Hsi carried out at academies throughout the Southern Sung empire, including those most closely associated with the transmission of Lu Chiu-yuan's thought in the thirteenth century. Yuan Fu's descendant, Yuan Chueh (1266–1327), wrote in an inscription on an academy in 1307 that "the regions of Wu [Liang-che], Shu [Ssu-ch'uan], Min [Fu-chien], and Yueh [Kuang-tung] all revere only Chu Hsi as teacher."[179] A generation later than Liu K'o-chuang, Yuan Chueh could expand the geographical perimeters laid out by Liu, who drew the boundaries of the academy movement associated with Chu Hsi in Hui (Chiang-tung), Chien (Fu-chien), Nan-k'ang (Chiang-hsi), and north central Hu-nan. Yuan Chueh's list extended to the distant regions of Ssu-ch'uan and Kuang-tung.

Just as academies granted names by the court cut a broad geographical swath throughout the Southern Sung empire, the diversity of the academy movement in the thirteenth century is reflected in the range of these institutions from transmission shrines such as Illumined Way to supplementary schools such as White Egret Islet. By the thirteenth century, as Chu Hsi's followers expanded the academy movement to all regions of the Southern Sung empire, their activities dovetailed with the growing need for *shih* to confirm their social and cultural identity as an elite defined by their pursuit of education. Thus while some academies flourished as places where members of the True Way fellowship congregated, studied, and taught, and where True Way patriarchs were enshrined, others were educational institutions supplementing prefectural schools. Chu Hsi's followers popularized the institution, but the academy movement had a momentum that was propelled by the needs of *shih* as well as the promotion of True Way Learning. These two developments overlapped and reinforced each other, producing both the dynamism and the diversity of the academy movement in the thirteenth century.

During the half century encompassed by the reigns of Li-tsung and Tu-tsung, academies were established throughout the Southern Sung empire. Stretching from Fu-chien in the southeast, where the roots of the movement were planted, to Chiang-hsi, Chiang-tung, and Hu-nan, to Ssu-ch'uan in the far west and Kuang-tung and Kuang-hsi in the south, academies were both shrines and schools. Chu Hsi's association with the academy movement, particularly through the activities of his disciples and their students at academies throughout the Southern Sung empire, gave his doctrines a critical advantage. Although White Deer Grotto was not the innovative institution many have claimed,[180] and although a broad range of thinkers associated with the True Way movement were involved with academies, by the last decade of the Southern Sung Chu Hsi was the focus of both teaching and ritual veneration at academies.[181] The promotion of academies by Chu Hsi and his students in Fu-chien, where it could be said the academy movement really began to grow before Chu Hsi's death in 1200, was also influential in the spread of academies beyond Fu-chien through his disciples and their followers. After 1200, Fu-chien academies continued their growth through the Chu Hsi cult, as "sacred" places identified with Chu Hsi became the sites of academies. Beyond Fu-chien, networks of Chu Hsi's followers carried the model, and the charisma of their teacher, to all regions of the Southern Sung empire.

3

The Academy Movement

Economic and Sacred Geography

Academies were concentrated in the very regions of the Southern Sung empire known to be the most economically advanced, populous, and prosperous, and for which we have the best records: Chiang-hsi, Chiang-tung, Fu-chien, Che-tung, and Che-hsi. Hu-nan, Ssu-ch'uan, and Kuang-tung also have relatively high concentrations of academies.[1] Regional variations and patterns in the academy movement at times were due to the influence of particular individuals, such as Chang Shih in central Hu-nan or Chu Hsi in northwestern Fu-chien, each of whom gathered large numbers of followers and inspired the building of academies. In addition to "intellectual geography," discussed in chapter 1, other geographical conditions need to be considered in evaluating the regional distribution of academies. Although not as closely related to urban development as academies became in the Ming and Ch'ing,[2] Southern Sung academies were by no means isolated scholarly refuges. The ideal of late T'ang retreats where scholarly recluses taught their students persisted in the origins of early Northern Sung academies. But the data for Southern Sung suggest very clearly that, although shrines at scholars' studies may have been

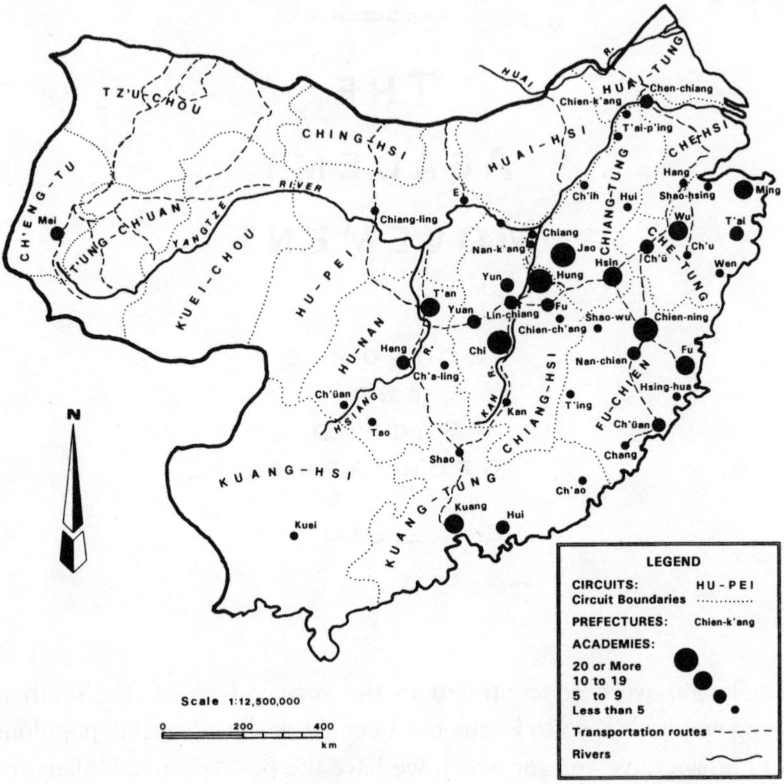

SOUTHERN SUNG CHINA

located in rural settings, as these shrines were transformed into academies with the support of government officials, they were frequently moved into or close to urban centers, walled city enclaves that served as county or prefectural seats of government. In his inscription on White Egret Islet Academy in the 1260s, Ou-yang Shou-tao distinguished academies from prefectural schools by arguing that academies provided places for scholarly recluses to be drawn out of their rural retreats into more central locations where they could associate with other scholars and serve the needs of more students (see chapter 2).[3] Li-yang Academy began as a shrine to Fan Chung-yen at the site of a Taoist temple where he had studied as a youth.[4] After the shrine was destroyed (probably at the fall of the Northern Sung), his residence was restored beside the Taoist temple around 1195, and when it became an academy in 1226 it was moved near the city wall.[5] Lü Tsu-ch'ien's Beautiful Pools Academy was located within the Chin-hua city wall. As Yuan Fu noted: "Although it is close to the market, it is not noisy. It is like fleeing the world, but not being an eremite."[6] The names of many academies bear witness to a nostalgia for the rural landscape, as academies named for mountains, gardens, streams, and other aspects of the natural environment continued to reflect the ideal of reclusion and retreat, even as they were moved to more urban settings. Although the phrase "beautiful pools" comes from the *Changes* commentary on the *tui* hexagram, referring to the collaboration of friends in study and moral self-cultivation, the name "Beautiful Pools" also directly alluded to two lakes in front of Lü Tsu-ch'ien's original retreat to the west of the city.[7]

Looking at the broader context of location, we can identify clusters of academies along major transportation arteries, suggesting that accessibility was important in the selection of their sites. When Yuan Fu decided to build Elephant Mountain Academy, because the original site of Lu Chiu-yuan's retreat was "in the mountains and not close to a thoroughfare," he assigned one of Lu's followers to find a similar place that would be more accessible.[8] Ming, the site of ten academies, was the terminus of the canal between the Southern Sung capital, Hang-chou, and the seaport of Ming-chou (modern Ningpo), which served as the transshipment center for ocean-going trade to domestic markets.[9] Hung, with twenty-four academies, lay in close proximity to P'o-yang Lake and at the point where a tributary of the Yangtze divides into the Kan and Hsin Rivers. Hung was also the intersection of two major highways: a north-south road from Chiang on the Yangtze that continued to its terminus in Kuang-chou, and an east-west road that could be followed east and north to Che-tung and Che-hsi or south to Fu-chien. Chi, with twenty-one academies, lay in the Kan River basin along the major north-south highway from P'o-yang Lake to Kuang-chou. Hsin in Chiang-tung, with thirteen academies, lay at the crossroads of the Hsin River and the intersection of two highways, one leading into Chiang-hsi and one into Fu-chien, thus placing it at a major transportation node. Tai Piao-yuan's (1244–1310) inscription on an academy founded there at the end of the Southern Sung explicitly mentioned the location: "Kuang-hsin [Academy] lies at the crossroads of Chiang, Min, and the two Che [Chiang-tung and Chiang-hsi, Fu-chien, Che-tung and Che-hsi]. . . . The site . . . is a most flourishing central place."[10] Chien in Fu-chien, with twenty-two academies, lay at the crossroads of two major highways: one leading from Hsin to Fu along the Fu-chien coast, and one leading from Ch'ü farther east along the Hsin River to the southern Fu-chien ports of Ch'üan and Chang. Lou Yueh, in his inscription on Purple Iris Academy in Chien-ning, began with the statement that "Chien-ning is the major thoroughfare between Min (Fu-chien) and Che (Che-tung and Che-hsi)."[11] T'an in Hu-nan, with sixteen academies, lay along the Hsiang River at the convergence of two major north-south highways; farther down the Hsiang River, Heng, with eight academies, lay along that highway as it turned in the direction of Kuang-chou, to separate from the southwesterly flowing Hsiang. Hsiang River Academy in Shao (Kuang-tung) was located at a key transportation site in Ch'ü-chiang, which offered access to Chiang-hsi.

Academies also tended to be clustered around commercial and industrial centers.[12] Jao, with twenty-three academies, lay along the shores of P'o-yang Lake, a rich agricultural area, and also the site of a mint. Both Fu (eleven) and Lin-chiang (five) in Chiang-hsi were sites of mints. Hsin (thirteen) in Chiang-tung produced swords and weapons. Both T'an (sixteen) and Heng (eight) in Hu-nan were shipbuilding centers; and Heng was the site of a mint, while T'an was a textile center. Hui (eight) in Kuang-tung was the site of a mint. Ming (ten) was both a textile and shipbuilding center. The founding of Mount Tai Academy in Ch'ang-kuo County, Ming, was associated with the economic development of an area that became a market town in the twelfth century and began to establish schools to serve local scholars, culminating in the late thirteenth century with Mount Tai. Chien in Fu-chien had twenty-two academies, including Chien-an County with eight and Chien-yang with seven, and was a commercial center with a mint and ceramics and printing industries. Finally, Mei in Ssu-ch'uan was a printing center.

The fact that virtually all of the prefectures with relatively high concentrations of academies were also located on important transportation routes and/or were centers of vital economic or technological activity suggests that we should look not only at intellectual factors as explanations for the growth of academies in certain places associated with famous teachers, but also at conditions of economic geography that led to the concentration of academies in such propserous and easily accessible places. In addition to intellectual and economic geography, we need to consider elements of cultural geography. What did place mean to the people who founded academies? How did changing perceptions of landscape express ideological transformations? How was "contested space" appropriated through power conflicts between groups seeking either to retain or gain control of the landscape?

Sacred Geography and Northern Sung Academies

The commercial revolution of the Sung altered the physical landscape through the impact of industrial developments such as mining, the enhancement of transportation routes, and the creation and expansion of urban environments.[13] Just as the commercial revolution had an impact on the physical landscape, the intellectual transformation of the late T'ang and Sung eras reshaped the "iconography of landscape."[14] Since the idea of nature itself is a cultural construction, even in the absence of the physical imprints of human habitation, the natural landscape has cultural meaning that can be deciphered. Any landscape contains a variety of ideological representations, so that a description of its appearance must also logically be "thickened" (in Geertzian terms) into an interpretation of its meaning.[15] The built environment adds layers of meaning to conceptions of the natural landscape, reshaping and reconstructing the landscape according to shifting material and ideological conditions. Like temples, shrines, gardens, walled towns, and rural villages, academies were part of a built environment that people imposed on the natural landscape. If we regard culture as a text to be read and interpreted,[16] then both the natural landscape and the built environment are part of that text and, as with any other text, can also be read at multiple levels of meaning. In China there was a powerful and coherent intellectual system constructed to guide people in their creation of a built environment,[17] commonly described as "geomancy" (*feng-shui*, literally, wind and water).[18] The belief that human dwellings and graves needed to fit into their natural surroundings in such a way as to maximize positive chthonic energies and defuse noxious ones was central to geomancy.[19] Although scholars wrote about the theory of geomancy, its practice often cut across social barriers, as scholars sought the advice of geomancers (who were not necessarily members of the educated elite) for the siting of graves as well as dwellings.[20]

Great interest in the physical landscape was demonstrated in countless administrative geographies and topographical works, such as the two Sung compendia, *Fang-yü sheng-lan* and *Yü-ti chi-sheng*.[21] By the Sung, travel diaries (*yu-chi*) such as Southern Sung poet Lu Yu's Record of a *Journey to Shu* (*Ju-Shu chi*) were common, as scholars recorded their observations from travels to new posts or for pleasure.[22] Poems were written for academies as they were for temples, shrines, and other sites encountered on a journey.[23] Travel in the form of pilgrimages to sacred sites such as mountains or temples was embedded in complex cultural patterns created by the interweaving of popular religious practices, institutionalized religion, historical tradition, and elite literary memory.[24]

Students of religion have made use of the term "sacred geography" to describe the perception of landscape as endowed with religious meaning.[25] There was an obvious sacred geography in such works as the *Shan-hai ching* and in the concept of the "Five Marchmounts," the sacred mountains of predynastic China that continued to wield great power in later centuries, foremost among which was Mount T'ai in Shan-tung.[26] By the Southern Sung, five sacred Buddhist mountains, modeled on those of India, were assigned a position of prominence by the state: three were in the Southern Sung capital of Hang-chou, the remaining two in adjoining Ming Prefecture.[27] Of greater importance, however, to both clerical and lay believers, were the "four famous mountains" (*ssu-ta ming-shan*), dwellings of the bodhisattvas Manjusri (Wu-t'ai in Shan-hsi), Samantabhadra (O-mei in Ssu-ch'uan), Avalokitesvara (P'u-t'o in Che-tung), and Ksitigharba

(Chiu-hua in An-hwei).[28] Taoism, too, had its Five Peaks, envisioned as part of the larger scheme of cavern-heavens (*tung-t'ien*) and "blessed lands" (*fu-ti*) under these sacred peaks.[29] Confucianism has not usually been related to sacred geography, although the viability of the imperial state and the sanctity of the throne were closely connected to the performance of the *feng* and *shan* sacrifices on Mount T'ai, described by Ssu-ma Ch'ien in the *Shih chi*.[30] Few emperors dared to perform these rites, since they were an expression of the moral perfection of imperial rule, but the symbolism of the mountain linking the emperor's ritual place with cosmic order nonetheless remained powerful.

Beyond these central sites were other mountain peaks and ranges, hills, and caverns that acquired spiritual meaning through association with the quality of *ling*, frequently defined as "numinosity." In the context of both elite and popular religious traditions in China, sites that were *ling* were considered to be manifestations of the power of a deity.[31] Typically, a temple or shrine on a mountain peak housed an image of the deity, and paying homage to this image was the goal of pilgrimages to the peak. The importance of mountains as sites of religious activity is reflected in the use of the term "mountain gate" (*shan-men*) to designate the entrance to ordinary temples.[32] Similarly, *shan-lin* (mountain and forest) is the term commonly used to refer both to the dwellings of recluses and to Buddhist monasteries.

The works of countless poets and painters who transcended the confines of association with any one particular tradition (Buddhism, Confucianism, Taoism) bear witness to the power of landscape in the aesthetic and intellectual consciousness of the cultural elite.[33] For example, the Northern Sung poet Su Shih's writings—on landscape paintings, temple inscriptions, eulogies—display a profound sense of the interconnectedness of human life and the natural world.[34] Scholars and officials of the state expressed such ideas in their writings; and academies, like temples, monasteries, and shrines, inspired rumination on the power of landscape and its relationship to the built environment of the human social world. In 969 Hsu K'ai (901–974), a Southern T'ang literary scholar, composed a commemorative inscription on the Ch'en Family Academy (*shu-t'ang*) in the southern foothills of Chiang-hsi's famed Mount Lu in which he drew a distinction between the functions of natural landscape and the human intellect, while at the same time stressing the complementary nature of the relationship between them: "For correlating similarities and differences and distinguishing true from false, the land is not equal to men. For nourishing *ch'i* and moral substance [*chih*] and for steeping the spiritual essence [*ling*] of mind, men are not the equal of the land. Scholars consider this and thereby determine [where] to take up residence."[35] The idea that landscape played a role in the cultivation of human moral and spiritual character was not a new one: for example, it was associated with the late T'ang practice of scholars studying in secluded mountain temples.[36]

How is the interesting commentary by Hsu K'ai on the relationship between the landscape and the human mind to be understood as a product of earlier trends of scholars retreating to mountain landscapes as well as in the context of evolving Confucian ideas? Hsu K'ai's comments were an exception for his time, at least in writings on academies by prominent scholars. His better-known elder brother, Hsu Hsuan (917–992), wrote an inscription on Floriate Forest Academy in Hung Prefecture to the south of Mount Lu in the Kan River basin, founded by the lineage of Hu Chung-yao.[37] Hsu Hsuan described the planting of pine and bamboo and the making of a pond to create a pleasant environment for the students.[38] Despite its name, however, and the description of the physical surroundings, the natural setting of landscape was not critical. Unlike his brother, Hsu Hsuan made no statement about the landscape and its relationship to human activity at the academy,[39] nor did the Northern Sung literary scholar, Yang I (974–1020), mention the landscape in his inscription on Thunder Lake Academy, founded by the lineage of Hung Wen-fu at Chien-ch'ang (Nan-k'ang commandery).[40]

Inscriptions on the four "great" academies of the Northern Sung similarly focus on the importance of education to the state and the models of schools in antiquity, not the landscape where these academies were built. Wang Yü-ch'eng's inscription commemorating the restoration of Marchmount Hill Academy in 1000 made no mention of landscape, referring only to the link between education and government and the necessity of training in the classics to prepare officials for service to the state (see chapter 1). The early Northern Sung scholar Shih Chieh's inscription on Mount T'ai Academy in 1040 placed his teacher, Sun Fu, directly in the line of transmission of the Way from Han Yü.[41] The lineage begins with Mencius, goes to Yang Hsiung in the Han, then Wang T'ung in the Sui, and finally to Han Yü in the T'ang.[42] Shih Chieh pointed out that these men transmitted their learning to disciples, who then repeated and transmitted it in texts. He equated his master, Sun Fu, with the line of transmitters beginning with Mencius and suggested that the process of disciples transmitting their teacher's learning through writing continued with his teacher. After listing the written works of Mencius and the others, he stated: "The Master [Sun Fu] considered the *Changes* as the ultimate [expression of] the heart of Confucius. The ultimate of Confucius' practice lies in the *Spring and Autumn Annals*. These two great Classics are the ultimate writings of the Sages. They are the great way to order the world!"[43] There is no indication anywhere in Shih Chieh's inscription that the location of the academy in the most sacred of Confucian state sites, Mount T'ai, had any bearing on the transmission of the Way, other than that it is in an untroubled place where students can come and learn. The Way is understood to be embedded in the texts of a succession of masters, transmitted through their disciples and in their writings. There is no significance attached to the landscape, despite its sanctity as a site of imperial ritual. Shih Chieh's concern, and that of others who wrote on Northern Sung academies discussed here, was with the revival of the Confucian Way and the logic of its transmission through generations from teacher to disciple, as elucidated by Shih.

Like Shih Chieh's inscription on Mount T'ai Academy, there is little or no obvious concern with the landscape itself in most documentation on Northern Sung academies on any of the mountains, so why were they located in those mountain landscapes? Many academies began in the late T'ang-Five Dynasties era as scholarly retreats in the mountains where it was possible to avoid or escape military and political disorder. The location of these academies in secluded mountain settings also drew on a tradition of Confucian eremitism traceable to Han retreats called *ching-she*, a term appropriated by Buddhists as a translation for the Sanskrit *vihara* and later revived by T'ang scholars for their studies. With the founding of Sung, the new rulers sought the support of scholars and conferred official recognition on the most important of existing retreats, and family schools such as that of the Ch'en at Mount Lu, as academies. These institutions were initially useful as schools to educate officials for the new government, and so received books and name plaques from the state.

The revival of the Confucian Way lay at the heart of Northern Sung efforts to build Confucian schools and academies in mountain landscapes that were part of an existing sacred geography. Like mountain imagery employed at Buddhist temples and used for the retreats of recluses, the term for headmaster at an academy (*shan-chang*) similarly incorporated mountain imagery. The use of such imagery and the mountain settings of prominent Northern Sung academies such as White Deer Grotto, Marchmount Hill, and Stone Drum should not obscure their evolving roles as official institutions. At the same time, the Confucian and state orientation of these academies did not mean that their founders were oblivious to the spiritual power (*ling*) of sacred sites long appreciated by Buddhists and Taoists. Stone Drum originated as a private study established at the site of a Taoist temple during the T'ang Yuan-ho era (806–821),[44] and Marchmount Hill was said to have been founded on the former site of a Buddhist temple.[45] The construction of academies in such places can be seen as a means to lay claim to a landscape that had been inhabited, shaped, and given meaning by the spiritual "Other." The physical presence of academies then began the interpretive reshaping of the landscape according to a Confucian vision. This process is vividly portrayed in the interaction of Buddhist and Confucian communities and attempts to appropriate contested spaces at Mount Lu during the Sung.

SUNG ACADEMIES AND THE APPROPRIATION OF SACRED SPACE

Mount Lu was a visually arresting mountain landscape studded with Buddhist and Taoist sacred places. Although not a sacred mountain like Mount T'ai or Mount Heng, Mount Lu was famous as a Buddhist site because of its early association with Hui-yuan and his legendary

Pure Land Society there, and it was also a place that attracted people because of its fantastic landscape. By the Sung, White Deer Grotto on Mount Lu was as important as the Buddhist site of Hui-yuan's Eastern Grove Temple. In Chu Hsi's writings about White Deer Grotto, he praised the landscape of Mount Lu as the "best in the southeast,"[46] but elsewhere he decried the flourishing of Buddhist and Taoist places on the mountain: "The Taoist and Buddhist residences on Mount Lu number one hundred and ten. Of those that were dilapidated and run down, there are none that have not been restored. But as for the Confucian dwellings, there is only one, the remains of the former dynasty's famous worthies."[47] Chu Hsi was building his case for the restoration of White Deer Grotto, but he was also echoing a familiar refrain about the relatively plentiful Taoist and Buddhist sites on Mount Lu in comparison to Confucian ones. This was apparently the case throughout the Sung, at least until Chu Hsi's revival of White Deer.

According to the *Lu-shan chih*, during the Sung seventy-four Buddhists, twelve Taoists, and about seventy-six lay people resided on Mount Lu.[48] The largest number of Buddhists were followers of the Ch'an sect, and many of the literati who came to Mount Lu during the Northern Sung were deeply involved with Ch'an priests.[49] In 1079 Hui-yuan's Eastern Grove Temple was elevated to a Ch'an temple, and the Nan-ch'ang prefect, Wang Shao, requested the appointment of an abbot, who thus became the first-generation Ch'an patriarch of Eastern Grove Temple.[50] Ch'ang-tsung Chao-chueh, of the Shih lineage of Yu-hsi County (Nan-chien, Fu-chien) and the thirteenth "dharma heir" of Nan-yueh, the founder of Lin-ch'i Ch'an, was named abbot in 1088.[51] Chang Shang-ying (1043–1121; 1065 *chin-shih*), later chief councillor near the end of the Northern Sung, went to Mount Lu when he encountered political problems at court and there developed a deep relationship with the new abbot.[52] As head of Mount Lu's Eastern Grove Temple, Ch'ang-tsung Chao-chueh led the Yellow Dragon sect of Lin-ch'i Ch'an that flourished at many temples on the mountain, which together formed the Mount Lu Buddhist "society"(*chieh-she*).[53] The Cloud Gate sect of Lin-ch'i Ch'an likewise flourished on Mount Lu, with famous priests and official eremites who supported it. In fact, the growth of Ch'an in general during the

Sung was due in large part to official patronage and support, such as that reflected in the close relationships between officials and priests on Mount Lu.

Just as Chang Shang-ying's political misfortunes led him to withdraw to Mount Lu, so did the experiences of Liu Huan (1000–1080) and Ch'en Kuan (1057–1122) draw them to the mountain.[54] Each, in different generations, was dismissed from office for frank criticisms of their superiors.[55] Ou-yang Hsiu (1007–1072) wrote a prose poem (*fu*), "Mount Lu is High," to honor Liu Huan, and Huang T'ing-chien (1045–1105) also composed a poem that described him at Mount Lu.[56] Together with Ch'en Shun-yü (d. 1074), the author of *Lu-shan chi*, Liu Huan would mount an ox and ride back and forth into the mountain; the Northern Sung landscape painter Li Kung-lin (1049–1106) painted this scene and together Liu Huan and Ch'en Shun-yü composed poems on it.[57] Liu Huan held in particularly high regard the priest Pao-feng chieh-mao of West Brook Mountain, and attended him there.[58] Ch'en Kuan fled from chief councillor Ts'ai Ching's wrath to Mount Lu, and there he became acquainted with a disciple of another prominent Yellow Dragon Ch'an priest, Pao-feng K'e-wen.[59]

Through the Northern Sung there were two distinct, although interrelated, trends on Mount Lu of concern here. One was the interaction between Ch'an priests and Confucian literati, which reflected continuity from earlier times when T'ang and Five Dynasties scholars and poets sought spiritual sustenance and refuge there. The other trend was that of academies founded at Mount Lu to provide education for the examinations. We can see this trend as early as the Five Dynasties with the establishment of the Ch'en Family Academy in the foothills of Mount Lu during the Southern T'ang. Similarly, the beginnings of White Deer Grotto (as it was renamed in 977 and restored by Chu Hsi more than two centuries later) lay in the Mount Lu State School, also established during the Southern T'ang. By the early Northern Sung there were schools on the mountain that were part of state efforts to recruit and train officials for government service. Sites of earlier retreats, such as White Deer Grotto, were appropriated by the state, while local family schools, such as that of the Ch'en, were encouraged by official recognition. Meanwhile, Buddhist institutions continued to expand, as seen in the growth of Ch'an sects on the mountain, although these, too, were drawn into the state sphere by becoming part of the *shih-fang* system of abbot selection, as in the case of Eastern Grove Temple.[60]

Although there was no direct or obvious connection between the growth of a monastic establishment on Mount Lu in the Sung and the development of White Deer Grotto, the latter may be seen as part of a Confucian effort to appropriate the mountain's powers and redefine them in order to stake out a space for Confucian literati among the profusion of Buddhist sites. To this end, Chu Hsi (and others before him) drew on the pattern of reclusion characteristic of the late T'ang and Five Dynasties that led Li Po and his brother to build a retreat on the mountain. There is no overt suggestion of competition over territory on the mountain between Buddhist and Confucian groups during the Northern Sung, but by the Southern Sung this had changed, with explicit expression by Chu Hsi, among others, of concern over the proliferation of Buddhist (and even Taoist) sites and the lack of Confucian ones.

In earlier times Mount Lu had been a hotbed of local cults, as well as a place where struggles were played out between such cults and both Taoists and Buddhists.[61] Just as Mount Lu was associated at first with Hui-yuan and the Pure Land sect, and later with Ch'an sects during the Sung, Mount Mao in Che-hsi near the Yangtze River can be seen in many ways as the quintessential Taoist mountain. It was the uncontested site of the Shang-ch'ing school of Taoism, dating from the Six Dynasties and the T'ang.[62] Before the reign of the Sung emperor Jen-tsung (1023–1044), a local scholar resided at Mount Mao and built an academy there.[63] In 1024 the local prefect requested official recognition of the academy, and Jen-tsung bequeathed three *ch'ing* (about forty-two acres) of land. For a decade the academy was self-sufficient, relying on the estate at Mount Mao. After the death of the founder, the academy was taken over by a Taoist temple, and a pattern of struggle over the site was repeated throughout the remainder of the Sung (see below). Although Mount Mao Academy never achieved—at least in the documentary sources that remain—the status of White Deer Grotto, it is significant that the academy nonetheless was cited among the four (or six) "great" academies of the Northern Sung.[64] This may be because it was viewed as a kind of conquest over an area that had been so thoroughly identified with Taoism, as Mount Lu had been associated with Buddhism. The case of Mount Mao vividly illustrates the Confucian invasion of a landscape previously occupied by institutions primarily identified with a competing set of ideas—in this case, Taoism. Confucians attempted to reshape the landscape according to their own vision, while appropriating its power.

Academies added meaning to the built landscape that often challenged existing constructions, such as Buddhist and Taoist temples and shrines to local deities, or incorporated earlier sites. Yang Ta-i observed in his inscription on Hsiang River Academy that numerous shrines, pavilions, and halls to popular or local deities, other non-True Way men, and Buddhist or Taoist deities stood in comparison to the lack of shrines to True Way figures, such as the shrine to Chou Tun-i he used as the foundation of Hsiang River.[65] In his inscription on East Lake Academy, Yuan Hsieh recounted the selection of a location in a scenic place where various pavilions and shrines were taken over to build a hall to house traveling scholars invited to lecture.[66] In the mid-thirteenth century the original site of Chang Shih's study, located behind the abbot's quarters of Heavenly Blessings Temple in Chien-k'ang, was made into a shrine to Chang, which became Nan-hsuan Academy during the last decade of the Southern Sung.[67] Lu Chiu-yuan resided in the former abbot's quarters of an abandoned Buddhist temple at Elephant Mountain;[68] and the temple's dharma hall was used to house the many students who "collected like clouds" at Elephant Mountain Academy in the early 1230s.[69] The former site of a T'ang Buddhist temple and of the Northern Sung scholar Yang I's retreat, Embracing Jade Academy was established during the Southern Sung after Chu Hsi, Lu Chiu-yuan, and Wang Ying-ch'en all lectured here.[70] Spring Mountain Academy (see chapter 1) was built in 1266 to venerate Chu Hsi and a host of others at the ruins of Heavenly Repose Temple, formerly the site of a T'ang Taoist shrine, Purple Pole Palace.[71]

Although academies frequently were simply fused onto earlier abandoned sites, as in the above examples, other cases suggest that some sites were contested spaces, where the interests of academy supporters competed with those of Buddhist and Taoist institutions and their communities. One model of interaction between Buddhist/Taoist and Confucian traditions is that of tension and conflict, as academy inscriptions suggest the dynamics of contested space, particularly the absorption of Buddhist land or buildings by academy founders, or the reverse, in which academy property was appropriated by monasteries or temples. Struggles over property took place when academies were built in close proximity to temples, or when temple land was allocated to support academies. Compassion Lake Academy was established next to the T'ien-t'ai sect's P'u-chi Temple;[72] land disputes with priests from the temple spilled over into the Yuan.[73] Tiger Hill Academy in Su-chou, located to the west of Cloud Cliff Temple, was founded at the site of a shrine to the scholar Yin Ch'un (1071–1142).[74] Tiger Hill was built in 1235 by a regional official on the model of the four great Northern Sung academies "in order to reform the people of Wu, who were seduced by Buddhism."[75] At the fall of the Southern Sung, Tiger Hill was taken over by Buddhist priests, likely from neighboring Cloud Cliff Temple.[76] Lien-hsi Academy in Jun, dedicated to Chou Tun-i, was located outside Crane Forest Gate at Golden Crane Mountain; at the beginning of the Yuan, priests from Crane Forest Temple occupied the academy's land.[77] Huai-hai Academy, founded in the mid-thirteenth century for refugee scholars, was overrun by Buddhist monks from Sweet Dew Temple in the early Yuan (1290).[78] In the 1250s, neighboring Buddhist priests took over part of Angling Terrace Academy to build a dharma hall.[79] Only after litigation and orders from the prefect was half of the land eventually returned to the academy and the dharma hall moved to a new site.[80] East Yung Academy, established by the Southern Sung chief councillor Cheng Ch'ing-chih to honor his teacher, Lou Fang, was reportedly built "at the side of a Buddhist temple."[81] During the disruption attending the fall of the Southern Sung, the temple's priests must have usurped the academy's property, since it is recorded that in 1281 the Buddhist priests were removed.[82]

The usurpation of property was also carried out to the advantage of academies, usually through efforts of local officials. Five hundred *mou* (about seventy acres) of Divine Mystery Temple land was allocated to the support of students at T'ai-fu Academy in the 1250s.[83] Abandoned land was taken from Lotus Spring Temple to support

Locust Tree Hall Academy.[84] In the mid-1220s, Ch'üan-chou's Stone Well Academy was enriched by abandoned temple land.[85] When Cinnabar Sun Academy was established and a name plaque from the court granted in 1264, two *ch'ing* (about twenty-eight acres) of "officially confiscated" land (*mo kuan-chih t'ien*) from a Buddhist temple were allocated by the prefectural government to support the academy.[86] But Wu Ch'eng's inscription states that "after this, the Buddhists took it back, and the academy lacked the means to support scholars."[87]

There was also competition over Taoist sites. After Mount Mao Academy was absorbed by a Taoist temple in the Northern Sung, it was not restored until the mid-1230s, when Liu Tsai (1166–1239) rebuilt it.[88] It was later abandoned and then rebuilt again about a decade later by the prefect Wang Yeh, who confronted the Taoists there and had their lands and property confiscated.[89] The county magistrate, Sun Tzu-hsiu (1212–1266; 1232 *chin-shih*), expanded the academy and used the confiscated land for the support of scholars.[90] Other Taoist sites not as well known as Mount Mao were also places of conflict. Clear Orthodoxy Academy, dedicated to Wang Ying-ch'en (1118–1176) and his son—who were known to have strong Taoist leanings but were also associated with Chu Hsi and the True Way movement—was established at a site in Ch'ü Prefecture (Che-tung) that in the early Southern Sung had been a shrine to them and was later turned into a Taoist temple.[91] When the academy was founded near the end of the Southern Sung, the Taoists were displaced, and legal disputes over land continued into the early Yuan.[92] Contested spaces clearly were more than sites of spiritual efficacy: they were also sites of competition over land.

Although tension and conflict were expressed in competition over land, academies closely resembled Buddhist monasteries in their architecture and physical layout. Thus we might see convergence as an alternative model for relations between Buddhism and Confucianism.[93] Much of the information gleaned from regulations at Illumined Way Academy (see introduction), as well as from the description of its buildings and their functions, suggests parallels with the community life of Buddhist monastic institutions, regulated by codes such as the *Ch'an-yuan ch'ing-kuei* of 1103.[94] Even terminology used at Illumined Way and other academies mirrored Buddhist monastic institutions in a variety of ways. *K'ai-shan* was the term used for the founding abbot of a public (or Ch'an) monastery[95] and certainly bears some relationship to the term *k'ai-t'ang*, used for the opening convocation at Illumined Way, signaling the installation of a new headmaster. Similarly, the term *shang-t'ang*, to "ascend the hall," used to describe rites performed by the abbot of a public monastery in which he ascended a high seat in the center of the dharma hall and lectured, is echoed in the use of the term *teng-t'ang* to describe ascending the shrine hall to Master Ch'eng (Hao) at Illumined Way.[96] The parallel becomes even more compelling through the description of Spring Wind Hall, the lecture hall at Illumined Way corresponding to the dharma hall at a Buddhist monastery: a lecture seat in the center, surrounded by places for listeners on all four sides, was on a platform elevated on four pillars with a hanging bamboo curtain.[97] The new headmaster ascended this platform to deliver the opening lecture, just as the abbot of a monastery "ascended the hall" to deliver a sermon and inaugurate his term in office.

Like the patriarchs halls at Ch'an monasteries, which were used for enshrining portraits of former abbots with portraits of lineage patriarchs, shrine halls at academies enshrined patriarchs of True Way along with local scholars and other figures associated with the academy (but not headmasters).[98] Although at Illumined Way Ch'eng Hao was the singular figure venerated in the shrine hall, at other academies combinations of True Way patriarchs and local scholars and officials were venerated in shrine halls. For example, at Spring Mountain Academy in Fu-chien's Ch'üan-chou, in addition to the individuals venerated by placement of their images along two corridors behind the lecture hall, the central shrine to Chu Hsi, to whom the academy was dedicated, included the founder's father and a local official known for his support of academies in the region, along with Chu Hsi's major disciple, Huang Kan, and Chen Te-hsiu, also from Fu-chien and a prominent True Way scholar.[99] The veneration of True Way patriarchs and local scholars and officials at academy shrines closely resembled the patriarchs halls at Buddhist monasteries and adds further evidence of the institutional affinities of monasteries and academies.

Culture—and landscape as a representation of culture—is not only a text that can be read; it is also a domain in which power is negotiated, and where meanings are not just imposed, but contested.[100] A landscape may have several different systems of symbolic representation existing within it simultaneously, and sometimes antagonistically.[101] Both conflict and convergence characterized the relations between academies and their Buddhist (and sometimes Taoist) counterparts as academy supporters sought to appropriate sacred landscape and transform it.

THE SACRED LANDSCAPE OF SOUTHERN SUNG ACADEMIES

Unlike the limited sources we have for Northern Sung academies, many Southern Sung academy inscriptions pay a good deal of attention to the landscapes in which academies were built. Chu Hsi, active in the restoration of Marchmount Hill as well as White Deer Grotto and author of an inscription to commemorate the rebuilding of Stone Drum, was deeply moved by the mountain landscapes where these academies were built. Chu Hsi began his inscription on Stone Drum with a statement on the physical environment: "Heng-chou's Stone Drum Mountain, based on the confluence of the Cheng and Hsiang Rivers, is surrounded by flowing rivers; and it is the most excellent place in the commandery."[102] In his inscription on Marchmount Hill, Chang Shih said that Chu Hsi "loved the beauty of its mountains and rivers."[103] When Chu Hsi visited Chang Shih there, in addition to their philosophical discussions, they climbed the peak together as part of their shared experience.[104] The observation of nature aided comprehension of the cosmic principles by which the human and natural worlds were ordered. In Chu Hsi's inscription on the restoration of Chou Tun-i's retreat (Lien-hsi Academy) on Mount Lu, he wrote in an almost mystical fashion, describing a cosmological order as it related to ethical concepts:

> Now, heaven is above and earth is below; but the two *ch'i* and Five Phases intermingle, alternate, rise up and descend, go back and forth in its midst. In creation and transformation, issuing forth and nourishing things, dispersing and collecting, there is not a single thing that does not have a fundamental principle

> [*li*]; and the greatest among these is the essence [*hsing*] of humanity [*jen*], propriety [*i*], rites [*li*], and wisdom [*chih*].[105]

For Chu Hsi, knowledge of nature that yielded understanding of universal principle (*li*) was a means to pursue individual moral self-cultivation in order to achieve Confucian sagehood, the ostensible goal of those who founded or studied at academies. Accordingly, great importance was attached to the physical environment of academy sites, where the pursuit of sagehood was to be conducted, since the process of moral self-cultivation was dependent both on the historical "sediment" of those who had gone before, preserved in the ecology of a particular locale, and on acquiring knowledge and understanding of nature in order to comprehend universal principle.

Chu Hsi spent many of his days in retirement from office in the Wu-i Mountains of northwestern Fu-chien, where the beauty of the landscape inspired him to build several retreats, two of which later became formal academies (see chapter 1).[106] In his inscription on Wu-i Academy (originally Wu-i Retreat), established in 1183, Chu Hsi wrote much about the landscape:[107]

> The Wu-i stream flows east through nine bends, and the fifth one is the deepest. Thus, from north to south, the mountains here are the loftiest. The stones make a peak, rising above the ground a thousand feet.[108] On the top there is a small level place where a plot of earth produces a grove of trees. . . . The outer water comes from the northwest of the mountain, twisting four times, passing south and doubling back, winding around the mountains, flowing to the northeast. The four twists produce streams that flow out from them. On the two sides rise cinnabar and kingfisher blue-green cliffs. The grove stands up encircling and crowding together. Deities [*shen*] carved it out and spirits [*kuei*] shaped it: one cannot give a name to its form. Those who travel up and down by boat are amazed and dazzled. In a little while they suddenly encounter a level ridge and a long mound. Blue-green wisteria bushes and trees spread elegantly, and sticky bean vines provide covering shade. It causes men's hearts and eyes to be open and at ease, profoundly deep. When you can't go any higher, there is the location of the retreat.[109]

The Wu-i Mountains are full of fairy lore; even now the boatmen who guide the bamboo rafts down the Nine Bends Stream for tourists tell many fantastic stories about the spirits embedded in the landscape. Clearly Chu Hsi was deeply influenced by this atmosphere; perhaps he was drawn to the place because of it. In the above passage, although he goes on to describe the locations and purposes of various buildings, he is moved by the landscape and dedicates most of the piece to a description of it. The setting of Wu-i Retreat was also vividly described by Han Yuan-chi (1118–1187):

> Mount Wu-i is directly north in Min-Yueh. Its mountains are strong and heroic, deep and great. . . . Min's many mountains all come after it. The greatest of its peaks is like a hat worn on the top of a giant's head. Along the steep pathways and narrow crevices you can look but you can't climb. The legendary immortals who fled from the Ch'in [crawled] caterpillar-like along here; brooks flow out below it and there are sharp-angled and steep-sided cliffs; thus big rocks stand up like trees and groups of rocks make strange shapes. . . . Those who come by boat on the stream call it the "Nine Bends," viewing to the left and right [from the boat as the stream winds sharply back and forth nine times].[110]

But this late twelfth century chronicler of Wu-i Retreat took care to distinguish the activities of Chu Hsi and his followers from those of Taoist eccentrics and eremites:

> When I held office in Chien-an, my friend Chu Hsi lived there at Wu-fu in the Wu-i Mountains. . . . He and his students used to tuck their books under their arms and go out to chant old poems and drink wine. . . . [But] Chu Hsi was a classicist [*ju*] . . . unlike those who sequester themselves in the mountains and valleys, clothing themselves in air and eating fungus in order to imitate the prevalent customs of the Taoists.[111]

In appropriating sacred space, Southern Sung academy founders went beyond simply using Buddhist and Taoist sites or appreciating beautiful landscapes: they crafted their own vision of the power of the landscape. Many academies neither intruded on Buddhist or Taoist sacred space nor were located in spectacular mountain settings; rather, they were founded at the residences, studies, or retreats of scholars, many of whom were associated with True Way Learning. In contrast to Northern Sung writers such as Shih Chieh, who saw the Way embedded in transmitted texts, Southern Sung authors of academy inscriptions identified the landscape as the repository of the Way, the concrete physical embodiment of the legacy of human teachers. Shrines that venerated these teachers at academies, and the academies themselves, contributed to the construction of a Confucian sacred landscape. Rites performed at academy shrines commemorated men who were cultural symbols and transmitted values associated with these symbols to new generations. The consecration of sacred space took place with the opening school rites performed upon completion of an academy's construction or restoration and often commemorated in an inscription that infused these sites with meaning by linking scholars in both time and geographical place.

Academy sites were sometimes characterized by inscription writers as *ling*. In his description of the setting of Locust Tree Hall Academy Yeh Meng-te wrote: "Brush Peak towers at the front; Embroidery Valley surrounds it at the back. Kingfisher Blue Cloud Immortal Mountain encircles it to the left and right. The land is *ling* and excellence is put forth, as if it were established by Heaven itself. . . . Contemplating the teacher tablets of the two masters . . . today we make known this . . . numinous place where sojourners can lecture and take their ease."[112] Yeh Meng-te also associated the concept of *ling* with the teachings of the two masters, Lu Chiu-yuan and his brother, whose family school was the origin of Locust Tree Hall.[113] The site for Li-yang Academy, dedicated to Fan Chung-yen, was "divined" (*pu*), and the landscape where it was built was described as manifesting *ling*: a mountain in front, peaks surrounding it, and water flowing at the sides to the east and west.[114] Water was a crucial component of geomantic beliefs, and as central to sacred landscape as mountains. The metaphor of flowing water was often used for the Way. Ho Meng-kuei (1265 *chin-shih*), writing on Hundred *Chang* Creek Academy, quoted a passage from Mencius on water and then opined: "The Way is like water. It goes back and forth in Heaven and Earth without ceasing even for a moment. . . . Therefore, those who observe the Way can do no better than to observe water."[115]

Authors of commemorative inscriptions for academies frequently suggested that there was an organic relationship between the natural beauty of mountains and rivers, where "vital forces" (*ch'i*) collected, and the production of eminent scholars. The idea that *ch'i* accumulated in the mountains and rivers of beautiful landscapes and produced talented men appears with significant frequency in Southern Sung academy inscriptions. The idea reflects a mentality in which the natural and human worlds are closely interrelated in history, both in geological time and in human historical time. In his inscription on Dragon Islet Academy at the beginning of the thirteenth century, Chou Pi-ta described the physical beauty of the island setting in the Kan River, with a lofty peak called "Heavenly Pillar."[116] Following this, he related the immediate background of the academy founding:

> At first, to the east of the county seat, they built a hall to serve the needs of guests passing through. Not long after, it became a hostel, and then a drinking place. . . . [The magistrate] . . . sighed, saying, "The ethers of heaven and earth collect in the mountains and rivers. The excellence of the mountains and rivers thus produces men. How much more [when] the elders passed on the tradition of the islet excelling in the county and producing first place *chin-shih!*"

Chou Pi-ta concluded with the statement that "not only through the examinations does one obtain the help of the mountains and rivers,"[118] suggesting that although an ecohistorical process provided the basis for the production of eminent men, a human-controlled process, either the examination system or educational institutions, like the academy, was necessary to cultivate the talents native to a particular area.

Just as Chou Pi-ta stressed the importance of what men did to transmit learning— "elders passing on the tradition"—Chen Te-hsiu made a similar point in commemorating the family school of the Huang in Chi's Yung-feng County (see chapter 4):

> [It was where] the Five Mountains coiled like a dragon. A brook crossed in front, clear as a mirror. The front looked out toward Spirit Peak and Embracing Jade, both excellent peaks and heavenly manifestations. The Master [Huang] said: "This is appropriate as a place for scholars to retreat, reform themselves, and complete their strength." . . . The talents produced here all were excellent. . . . It is not only the spirit of the mountains and rivers that here move and issue forth [talents]. It is also the result of education.[119]

Chen Te-hsiu echoed the idea expressed by Chou Pi-ta that both the geohistorical process that creates *ch'i*-endowed landscapes and the education provided by the academy are complementary elements in the production of human talents.

Caves or grottoes, as well as mountains, were also places associated with spiritual power, particularly in the Taoist tradition. Just as mountains were viewed as protuberances of chthonic power, so caves were seen as places where humans were able to gain direct access to that power. Even so pragmatic and utilitarian a thinker as Yeh Shih (1150–1223) could wax eloquent on the subject, as he recounted the founding of Stone Cavern Academy:[120]

> Stone Cavern is [at] a famous mountain [that belongs to] the Kuo lineage. At first, the cavern was deep and lacked any way through; it was only a place for woodcutters. Kuo began to think about clearing it out; before this was accomplished, the obstructions and cliffs were such that no one knew how to do it and they wanted to stop. Kuo, pressing forward, saw a crack; and in the distance he heard the sound of water coming out of the innermost recesses. He said, "Ah! This is it." So, after many steps of obstructions, he could climb up the levels and enter behind [the cavern]; the earth opened and the valley was light. Suddenly it was as if it were a [completely] different place. On the level ground of the highest part, the stones soared high and crouched low; and the hard bamboos and lean trees clothed it above. The water flew in rushing torrents and flowed violently; and the red plantain and green rushes covered it below. . . .
>
> Kuo was deeply pleased by the beauty of the mountains

> and water. For a thousand years it was hidden, like the Chao jade or the Sui pearl, uncut jade on the outside [the precious part], enclosed in the center. One day it was suddenly displayed. How is this different from Wu-ling and T'ien-t'ai, manifested in the present and hidden in the past?[121]

Yeh Shih goes on to recount the building of the academy at this site by Kuo in order to provide a place for his descendants and others to study, allocating his family resources to the support of the public good. Although Yeh Shih makes it clear that such a place is not essential for study, the inscription itself suggests that the place in fact did have special powers. The rich and vivid description of the location dominates the inscription. It is more than beauty of the landscape, however, that makes it an attractive and appealing place for the academy. The implication is that there is a connection between the hidden treasure of the landscape through the cavern, and the special quality this confers on the place, as an analogy is made to Wu-ling in Chiang-hsi and T'ien-t'ai in Che-tung "manifested in the present but hidden in the past."

The importance attributed to landscape by Southern Sung writers of commemorative inscriptions on academies was more than rhetorical convention: it expressed a shift in focus among literati that was both intellectual and social. The intellectual shift from literary to ethical concerns in the Northern Sung, documented by Bol, can be extended in Southern Sung to an integration of the ethical with the cosmological.[122] The cosmological concerns of Southern Sung True Way thinkers were reflected in an enhanced interest in the environment of academies because the landscape was seen as the physical embodiment of *tao-t'ung*, the historical transmission of the Way, reflected in individual thinkers connected in space as well as time. A particular academy locale was often identified as having produced a series of thinkers who, in succession, left an imprint on the place through their influence on others who then built shrines to them and thereby transformed the landscape.

Southern Stream Academy in Yu-hsi County (Nan-chien, Fu-chien) was located at Chu Hsi's birthplace. A Southern Sung inscription for this academy identifies the "Three Masters"—Yang Shih, Lo Ts'ung-yen, and Li T'ung—as natives of the area and links their origins to the ecohistorical background:

> The luxuriance of the mountains and rivers of Yen-p'ing [Nan-chien] specially produced Kuei-shan Yang [Shih], Yu-chang Lo [Ts'ung-yen] and Yen-p'ing Li [T'ung] within several decades. The brilliant splendor of the mountains and rivers collected to make Chu Hsi, who died thirty-eight years ago. Thus, there was extreme flourishing of the currents and ethers [*feng-ch'i*], but a shrine had not yet been established. . . . After it was established, even common laborers knew that his father [Wei-chai] had held office here and that Chu Hsi was born here.[123]

The birth of Chu Hsi in this place is associated with the verdant beauty and richness of the mountains and rivers, where *ch'i* collected to produce human talents. His birth there is connected historically to Yang Shih, who transmitted the Way of the Ch'eng brothers to his native south, and also to Lo Ts'ung-yen, who continued this tradition, and to Li T'ung, who then transmitted it to Chu Hsi in his teachings. The passage of time and the production of scholars were directly linked to the topography of the locale. This notion built on an obsession with the historical transmission of the Way through individuals who were seen as connected over time through identification with specific landscapes. Particular landscapes were made sacred by their association with such individuals, who were often venerated at shrines that became the foundation of academies.[124] This development converged with—and was partially an expression of—a social historical shift that may be described as a growing emphasis on locality and regional identity, reflected in part in the attention paid by authors of commemorative inscriptions to the physical settings of academies and to local figures venerated at academy shrines.[125]

By the late Southern Sung and early Yuan, ideas about the transmission of the Way through men over time embodied in a particular landscape appear to be a common assumption. Hsiung Ho (1253–1312), writing on the restoration of Wu-i Academy at the end of the Southern Sung, begins with the physical landscape:

> Of the thirty-six famous mountain places within the cosmos, there is none as flourishing as Wu-i. After Confucius and Mencius, for over 1500 years the Way had no one the equal of Chu Hsi to honor. The grass-green mountains and the blue waters [are] just as the vermilion letters and the green [literary] "patterns" [*wen*]. The diagrams and books here explicate and clarify the Way, which truly began at this mountain. The Four Books opened the tradition of Chu and Ssu [Confucius and Mencius]. [Chu Hsi's *Tzu-chih t'ung chien*] *kang-mu* received the brush of the *Spring and Autumn Annals*. Today who does not read these books? How can students in the halls of one acre in the empty mountains not grasp it? For several years the rain poured and the wind thundered. One morning the land closed and Heaven opened . . . [then Chu Hsi came here and established the academy].[126]

A direct association is made here by Hsiung Ho between the physical landscape and culture in ascribing similarity to mountains and waters and texts. Unlike his early Northern Sung predecessors, Hsiung Ho saw the "literary patterns" embedded in the landscape, not in the writings of a Han Yü or Liu K'ai, nor in the transmitted texts of antiquity.[127] His depiction of the physical transformation of the landscape—"the land closed and Heaven opened"—preparatory to Chu Hsi's establishment of an academy there echoes the almost mystical experience described above by Yeh Shih.

Wu Ch'eng's (1249–1333) inscription on the Yuan restoration of Marchmount Hill emphasized the special power of that mountain manifested in the activities of key philosophers:

> For the length of a thousand and several hundred years the spirit [*ling*] of Heng's Marchmount has collected extraordinary men. There was Master Chou [Tun-i] who was born at Hu-kuang's Tao-chou. . . . After more than 100 years, there was Kuang-Han Chang [Shih], whose home was in T'an. When Master Chang was not yet ill, Master Chu [Hsi] came from Fu-chien to T'an. He stayed there for two months. They discussed together and opened up the secrets of the distant past. They went to Marchmount Hill, climbed up to the top of the peak together and afterward [Chu Hsi] departed. Following this, Marchmount Hill became an academy. . . . It was

> not the former Marchmount Hill. It is because of men that the place is important.[128]

Wu Ch'eng suggested that the sacred aura of the mountain attracted men, but that the collective presence of these men over time endowed the mountain with special importance.

Sacred Geography: The Landscape of Historical Memory

Academies can be considered a kind of mnemonic architecture that constructed a landscape of historical memory through the veneration of teachers and scholars at academy shrines.[129] In their discussion of pilgrimage in China, Susan Naquin and Yü Chün-fang have pointed out that places where philosophers such as Chu Hsi traveled in the course of teaching and lecturing became sites that drew literati visitors, "who came in remembrance and so recharged the sites with new attractive power."[130] Naquin and Yü mention White Deer Grotto as one such site.[131] Pushing this point further, it can be argued that the Southern Sung academy movement created a network of sites that became destinations for literati "pilgrims," who visited these sites, complete with shrines, to venerate scholars and patriarchs of the True Way, and to participate in the communal life of the academy. Southern Sung academies were clustered along important transportation routes (see above), suggesting the framework of a pilgrimage network. Some people stayed at academies for relatively lengthy periods of time; but clearly many also came and stayed only briefly, as little as three days if one takes the rules for stipends provided at some academies as a guide.[132] The location of academies, coupled with provisions for traveling scholars, and the background of some academies as hostels, provide substantial evidence of a pilgrimage network.[133]

The sites of pilgrimage were academies themselves or the shrines within, which were often dedicated to a local scholar or, increasingly in the Southern Sung, a local scholar in combination with a figure (or figures) in the True Way pantheon. Academy shrines erected to venerate such men, often at the sites of their former studies or residences, consecrated these places in the True Way sense of linking people of the time to their scholarly antecedents. As shrine-building expanded in the Southern Sung, both independently and with the academy movement, the landscape in which academies and their shrines were built took on new and greater meaning. True Way thinkers, who often wrote commemorative inscriptions, constructed in the thirteenth century a sacred geography that endowed the landscape with a particular cosmological and historical meaning. In some cases, sites associated with historical figures from as early as the Han, or more recently the T'ang and even Northern Sung, were appropriated by Southern Sung founders of academies.[134] Nostalgia for the past inspired the erection of shrines and academies dedicated to such historical figures.

Angling Terrace Academy originated as a shrine to a Han eremite, Yen Kuang (37 BCE–43 CE), at a site associated with him in T'ung-lu County (Yen, Che-tung).[135] An intimate associate of Han emperor Kuang-wu (r. 25–57), Yen Kuang rejected office and retired to T'ung-lu County. During the Northern Sung, Fan Chung-yen held office as county magistrate and erected a shrine at the site of Yen Kuang's fishing place in the Fu-ch'un Mountains.[136] Following Fan Chung-yen's death, local people remembered him and made offerings for him to the right of the shrine.[137] In an inscription on this site in 1180, Lü Tsu-ch'ien recorded the construction of the shrine by Fan Chung-yen, who also incorporated an image of a T'ang eremite poet, which was placed to the left of Yen Kuang's shrine.[138] Lü Tsu-ch'ien described buildings there that were much like the academy, which Lu Yu's son, Lu Tzu-i, founded at the shrine in 1228 when he was prefect of Yen.[139] By its completion in 1251, it was clearly well supplied and functioning as a school; the following year the prefectural school professor began to serve concurrently as the academy headmaster.[140]

The history of Angling Terrace provides a context for understanding how academies incorporated earlier associations with a site and used them to impose a particular meaning on the landscape. In the case of Angling Terrace, layers of meaning were represented by Yen Kuang, Fan Chung-yen, and Lü Tsu-ch'ien. The temporal and spatial were brought together in the series of shrines that became the foundation of the academy, as Yen Kuang, Fan Chung-yen, and Lü

Tsu-ch'ien were linked through time in the physical space of the shrine, and later, the academy. Confucian historical memory was represented in the layers of meaning that accrued to this site through the commemoration of Yen Kuang and Fan Chung-yen by Lü Tsu-ch'ien, and with the erection of the academy by Lu Tzu-i as an institution of "transformation through education" (*chiao-hua*).[141] Although some of its property was absorbed by a neighboring temple within ten years after its completion, an account in the local history suggests that spiritual power returned to the site when the prefect ordered the Buddhists to return the land where they had built a dharma hall:

> In 1261 the new prefect observed the demise [of the academy] and the absorption of the Guest Star Pavilion by Buddhist priests. He ordered them to separate what was formerly the dharma hall and divine a new foundation for it to the east of the dharma hall. With this, the mountain grasses and trees were restored to the "pure spirit" [*ching-shen*].[142]

A similar process of layering over a long span of time can be seen in the background of the early Yuan Mount T'ao Tall Bamboo Academy.[143] An inscription on the academy describes a fascinating train of events in which a dream about a landscape painting became the inspiration for the establishment of an academy at the burial site of Lu Yu's grandfather, Lu Tien (1042–1102), where the landscape apparently corresponded to that portrayed in the painting:

> In the year 1285 I was a guest together with my compatriot Ch'en Yung-pin at the home of the gentleman [Wang Ying-sun].[144] Around midnight, Yung-pin pulled at my bedding. I woke with a start and asked him why [he woke me]. He said: "I dreamed I accompanied Wang to Wu-lin [Hang-chou] to visit Chou Mi, who was peacefully residing there. In the middle of his residence there hung a painting, and we observed the landscape [in the painting]. It was splendid and unique, unlike other places. A mountain rose up from the land directly into the clouds. At the bottom was a poem in small official script, altogether sixty-five characters, entitled 'Lu Wu-kuan,' praising his [Lu Yu's] literature. . . ."
>
> I said, "How strange! What meaning can this have?" We

> cast the *Changes* and the results were auspicious for the culture of the dynasty. Yung-pin could not sleep for happiness. The next day he told Wang, who also thought it strange, and he ordered it to be written down. Four years later [1289] [a member of] the Lu lineage returned to Wang's by way of Mount T'ao. The peaks emerged like [the tips of brushes in] a brush holder from the Cloud Gate Mountains, and the foothills were thick with tens of thousands of bamboo. Six years later [1295], the academy was completed. Wang took his guests on a walk to view the scenery. Wang looked at Yung-pin and said: "Don't you remember the dream you had before?" Yung-pin suddenly apprehended it. I was also at his side and saw [the similarity of the landscape] at the same time. With joy I said: "Ah! How can this be the [result of] human effort? Heaven rains water [down] and [earth's] *ch'i* [pushes] upward. . . ."
>
> Since antiquity the beauty of the mountains and rivers were the Heaven-made repository for bequeathing its men. When T'ao Hung-ching [452–536] lived here . . . it was illustrious in Taoists. After several hundred years had passed, during the Sung Hsi-ning era [1068–1078], Lu [Tien] retired here and collected books. Today his grave is under the branch peak. Two hundred years later it began to belong to Wang. This land is not of itself superior; it is excellent because of men. Men are able to make the land excellent, to make it excellent with the Way.[145]

Great importance is attached to the physical landscape and its historical associations with T'ao Hung-ching and other Taoists, as well as with Lu Yu's family.

Wang Ying-sun and Chou Mi (1232–1298) were part of a circle of eremite literati who retired after the fall of the Southern Sung and lived in fairly close proximity to the former capital.[146] The emphasis above on the auspicious signs for the "culture of the dynasty" is characteristic of Wang Ying-sun's and Chou Mi's optimistic longing for the revival of the Sung. Lu Yu's own bitterness over the loss of the north to the Chin is echoed in the sentiments of these men after the establishment of Mongol rule in the south. The presence of successive human figures over time endowed the landscape with spiritual power that was both symbolized and generated by the mountain itself. The inscription goes on to discuss the political difficulties of Wang Ying-sun, who had offended the prime minister when first appointed to office, and was out of favor for ten years, leading to his life as a eremite scholar.[147] Similarly, during the Northern Sung Lu Tien earned Wang An-shih's disfavor and so retired to Mount T'ao to collect books and study.[148] The two experiences of Lu Tien and Wang Ying-sun resonated in the place they shared through the integration of historical time and place at Mount T'ao; and their lives as recluses echoed the early association of the place with the Taoist master, T'ao Hung-ching. Heaven bestowed its favor through the collection of *ch'i*, which produced eminent men and which was physically manifested in the beauty of the mountain landscape. A complex of past historical figures were brought together in this academy site, where the power of the mountain was represented in multiple layers and traditions.

The relationship between the land and human culture stressed here echoes the ideas expressed by Hsu K'ai in his inscription on the Ch'en Family Academy, cited earlier. But in the more than three centuries that had passed, the relationship between landscape and human culture became much more than an abstract notion, as articulated by Hsu K'ai. It had become identified with specific individuals, linked over time through the landscape. Humans endowed the landscape with power, and the landscape, in turn and over time, endowed people with the accumulated power of their human predecessors. The quality of *ling*—numinosity or spirit energy—ascribed to certain landscapes is seen as the historical bequest of humans in the past, such as Chu Hsi's predecessors in Nan-chien: Yang Shih, Lo Ts'ung-yen, and Chu's teacher, Li T'ung. Such an idea is not at all alien in the context of a tradition that places strong emphasis on an individual's and family's "native place." Just as family lineage is rooted in a specific place through the residence of biological ancestors, so scholarly lineage can also be rooted in a landscape identified as the residence of intellectual ancestors.

The evolution of the relationship between landscape and human culture, traced here through academies, was not an isolated intellectual phenomenon. It must be seen against the background of broad social and political changes occurring in the course of the transition from Northern to Southern Sung that placed new emphasis on local ties and underscored the importance of regional identities. In contrast to Northern Sung, where academies did not appear to be significantly tied to their locales and which represented central state interests, in Southern Sung expressions of local identity can be seen both in attention paid to landscape and in emphasis on the relationship between that landscape and local figures. Many of these local figures, however, were also embedded in a far broader context as local representatives of True Way, much in the same way that academies, by Southern Sung, provided a mnemonic architecture that transcended region and linked local identity to a new ideology that was both historical and cosmological.

If "all cultural landscape represents an architecture of one or more ideologies,"[149] then Confucians could be said to have attempted, with considerable success, to reshape the cultural landscape in a form consistent with their own ideology. They did this by constructing academies that in many ways replicated Buddhist monasteries and by placing them in physical settings that mirrored belief in the natural beauty of a landscape as an ecohistorical endowment that, over time, produced men of outstanding scholarly ability and moral quality. The appropriation of earlier Buddhist and Taoist sites by academies was one element in the construction of Confucian sacred space. The creation of a sacred geography reflected in the academy movement was also related to the construction of a new identity for Southern Sung *shih*. The ideal of self-cultivation, which provided cultural and ideological sanction to the activities of *shih* who congregated at academies, was dependent on a redefinition of space. The sacred space represented by Southern Sung academies enabled and supported the ideal of self-cultivation, focused on the exemplary lives of scholars and worthies of the past in a landscape of historical memory. We might think of academies in this way as imposing a kind of Confucian "cognitive grid" or template on the landscape,[150] constructing an ideology by giving meaning to the experiences of people who assembled at academies, took part in rituals at academy shrines, read books, listened to lectures, and discussed ideas with colleagues.

Two

Academies in the Society and Culture of the Southern Sung *Shih*

4

Kin and Community

From Family School to Academy

As active as Chu Hsi and his followers were in promoting academies, they had no monopoly on the institution. While Chu Hsi may have seen the academy as a community institution that provided proper learning for the *shih*, in contrast to examination-oriented government schools, some Southern Sung lineages used family property and resources to found academies where their sons could be educated in preparation for taking the examinations. Academies dedicated exclusively to the education of family members were essentially private family schools known otherwise by terms such as *chia-shu*. Frequently, however, those attending family academies included affinal kin, and often the local *shih* community, sometimes extending even to *shih* who traveled from a distance to attend. Family academies open to the larger community of *shih* were one of a range of institutions in the "middle space" between the individual *chia*, or household unit, and the state, or "official" (*kuan*), level.[1] Like lineage charitable estates that provided support for members of a common descent group,

Southern Sung family academies educated descendants of particular lineages; and, like community charitable estates that provided economic support for local *shih*, academies founded by individual lineages often served the educational needs of the larger community of *shih*, not just those of one lineage.[2] Building an academy open to the *shih* community was one way for a lineage to enhance its standing and authenticate its claim to membership in the local elite: it was a form of investment in cultural and social capital, exchanging property for status.

Delving more deeply into the motives behind the founding of family academies, we might ask why families—or at least certain individuals in these families—chose to donate resources to support a family school rather than, for example, to transmit property to heirs. Patricia Ebrey has written about the growth during the Sung of practices, such as the building of ancestral halls and the endowment of estates or schools, that both strengthened group consciousness and positively contributed to the physical perpetuation of the descent group.[3] Academies founded by lineages in the Southern Sung to educate their sons and thereby maintain or elevate status could also be used to enhance the cohesion of the kin group by commemorating ancestors. The twin themes of education for sons and ancestral veneration were often united in these academies. Founding an academy to honor an ancestor not only commemorated that individual but also publicized the commitment to education, and the academic ambition, of his descendants. It was a means of enhancing group identity that invited official approbation, since educational enterprise conformed well with Confucian state norms. Similarly, academies as an expression of kinship group solidarity that simultaneously provided education for office-holding avoided potential official censure of overly zealous kinship group activity that might be seen as threatening to state authority.[4]

This chapter will focus on the development during the twelfth and thirteenth centuries of family schools that were called academies, tracing the concurrent evolution of these institutions as counterparts to academies associated with True Way thinkers and to those that were similar to prefectural schools. Family academies, like their counterparts, proliferated in the twelfth and thirteenth centuries, but they also had a history that substantially predated the Southern Sung academy movement. A brief survey of this background will highlight the changed circumstances of Southern Sung family academies and their significance in the Southern Sung academy movement.

FAMILY, SCHOOL, AND STATE

Before the rise of the great Northern Sung academies, and even before the founding of the Sung, there were notable cases of lineages who established schools for their kin that were called academies (*shu-t'ang or shu-yuan*). The Ch'en Family Academy (*Ch'en-shih shu-t'ang*), in the southern ranges of Mount Lu, was founded in the early tenth century by the powerful Ch'en, who claimed pre-T'ang noble descent and were recognized both by the last ruler of the Southern T'ang (Li Yü, r. 961–975) and by early Sung emperors.[5] The tenth-century scholar Hsu K'ai's inscription for the Ch'en Family Academy, cited in chapter 3, commemorated the founding of that academy in 939 following an imperial proclamation honoring the Ch'en for the longevity of their large joint residence. The number of people who shared a joint residence as members of the Ch'en lineage ranged from seven hundred in the early tenth century, at the time of the academy's founding, to one thousand in mid-century.[6] The size of the school was commensurate with the size of the family, with extensive buildings, including a library with several thousand volumes, and twenty *ch'ing* (about 280 acres) of land for support.[7] One source states that the Ch'en Family Academy was open to students "from the four quarters," clearly implying that it was not just a family school. The sequence of events here—an imperial proclamation recognizing the lineage's common residence, the founding of an academy, and the writing of a commemorative inscription—follow a logic grounded in the exigencies of state formation, in which the Sung founders co-opted powerful elite lineages who had served rulers of former dynastic houses.[8]

There are records of at least two other schools like the Ch'en Family Academy that served a similar purpose for the state by providing education for government service in the early Northern Sung and whose histories follow a roughly similar chronology. Floriate Forest

Academy in Hung Prefecture to the south of Mount Lu in the Kan River basin was the family school of Hu Chung-yao, who founded it in the late tenth century.[9] The Hu lineage, like that of the Ch'en, was said to have maintained a common residence for several generations and reportedly included several hundred members. For the school built at Floriate Forest Mountain, Hu Chung-yao collected many volumes of books, set up a kitchen and granary, and invited "scholars from the four quarters" to come and study.[10] Later the family was conferred an imperial banner by T'ai-tsung, probably in recognition of their contributions to local culture and also to engage their loyalties to the new regime, as Hu Chung-yao had held a minor office under the Southern T'ang.[11] In the 990s, Hu Chung-yao was given a local educational post following local philanthropic activities, and finally a position in the imperial Directorate of Education.[12]

The relationship created between the family of Hu Chung-yao and the early Sung state was one in which a leader of local society was wooed by imperial recognition of his family and by his appointment to office. The early Sung state recognized previous status associated not only with the fallen Southern T'ang regime, but also with local wealth and power reflected in the establishment of a school, charitable activities, and other community contributions. The local family then continued to exercise leadership and to assume a degree of responsibility for education. During the late tenth century the lineage of Hung Wen-fu at Chien-ch'ang along the Kan River, midway between the sites of the Ch'en Family Academy to the north and Floriate Forest Academy to the south, built a library (*shu-she*) and invited scholars, calling this the Thunder Lake Academy.[13] Like the Ch'en and the Hu, who were praised for their harmonious joint residence over generations, the Hung were similarly honored by T'ai-tsung, receiving an imperial banner along with scrolls in imperial calligraphy for their school library.[14]

The dynamics of interaction between well-established elite lineages and the early Sung state are suggested by the relations between the Ch'en, Hu, and Hung and the Sung founders during the transitional period of the consolidation of Sung rule. The Ch'en Family Academy and academies founded by the other lineages in the late tenth century are examples of private efforts encouraged by the Sung (or even pre-Sung) state because lineage-based schools—particularly when open to others outside the lineage as well—could provide important resources for the state by training potential officials. The Ch'en, Hu, and Hung were responding appropriately to the exigencies of the time by providing educational facilities not only for members of their own lineages, but also to "scholars from the four quarters." They were rewarded for their efforts with imperial recognition of their adherence to Confucian family ideals by being awarded imperial banners, and they received more substantive rewards for support of the state's educational needs through the granting of money and office. In the cases of the Hu and Hung, coming somewhat later in the tenth century after the founding of the Sung, the sequence of events led to official appointments, and even the taking of a *chin-shih* degree by Hung Wen-fu's eldest son.[15] Lineages such as these were absorbed into the power structure of the new Sung state, shifting their loyalties to the newly established imperial government of Chao K'uang-yin (Sung T'ai-tsu, r. 960–976) and his brother (Sung T'ai-tsung, r. 977–997).

Northern Sung family academies can be seen from the perspective of the interests of these lineages as the result of private efforts to bolster the educational underpinnings of the new political order so as to enhance their own opportunities and display their support of the new regime, with whose interests their own were now aligned. Although documentation exists for only a few examples of family academies, like those cited above, likely there were others, perhaps many, on a much smaller scale. For example, there are records of two Teng brothers who each established academies in Hung Prefecture (Chiang-hsi) during the late tenth century.[16] Teng Yen, who was reputed to be learned in the *Changes*, was appointed to a local educational post (*tien-chiao*) in the late 970s, and Luxuriant Creek Academy was set up for him to teach local people.[17] Since it was supported by allocations from the county and prefecture, it was not, strictly speaking, a family school. However, given evidence supplied by the brief notice in the local history of Teng Yen's brother, Teng Wu, establishing Fragrant Creek Academy in the same county, the Teng likely were local magnates of some status who were being brought into state service much like the Ch'en, Hu, and Hung. Later in the Northern Sung, Bamboo Flute Academy was founded in the 1017–1021 period in Hsiang-yin County (T'an, Hu-nan) by the scion of a local Teng lineage known for its support of education to serve both kin and traveling scholars.[18] Since much education prior to the Sung took place with private scholars sponsored by wealthy families, the expansion of tutoring into a school for kin was probably not all that uncommon if resources were sufficient.

Both family schools, such as those of the Ch'en, Hu, and Hung and academies that grew out of scholarly retreats, such as White Deer Grotto, either disappeared or were absorbed by the initiatives of the state in promoting local education during the second half of the eleventh century. Along with the demise of the great Northern Sung academies, the apparent absence of large lineage schools in the later Northern Sung can also be attributed to the growing role of the state in education. Since both the administration and the curricula of official schools were tied to the examination system, families sent their sons there in the hope that their attendance would lead to success in attaining the *chin-shih* degree and in appointment to office. Although family academies may have continued to exist in the late Northern Sung,[19] they were relatively peripheral to the interests of rising elite lineages whose fortunes were tied to success in the examination system, achieved through participation in local government schools.

Southern Sung Family Academies

In the twelfth century, although on a smaller scale than the schools of the Ch'en, Hu, and Hung in the early Northern Sung, family schools—established through the contributions of prosperous members of some lineages—resurfaced in response to frustration with state schools and perhaps the inadequacy of these schools to serve increasing numbers of potential students from *shih* families or those who aspired to *shih* status. Although the founding of such schools was couched in terms of Confucian educational ideals, in fact, immediate pragmatic concerns were undoubtedly foremost among the motives for their establishment. Families wanted to use their resources to provide schooling for their kin, affines, and even other people in their common social circle who might be prospective affinal kin or might in other ways support the interests of these families.[20] By the late twelfth and early thirteenth centuries schools founded initially to serve members of a lineage were likely to become academies and serve the needs of a wider group of *shih* families resident in a community. A classic example of this can be seen in the origins of Illumined Good Academy.[21] In 1182, when he was intendant of the Evernormal Granary, Tea, and Salt for Che-tung, Chu Hsi visited the family school (*chia-shu*) of Yeh Chen.[22] Chu Hsi discussed the *Analects* and the *Mencius* with him, was impressed, and encouraged Yeh Chen in his teaching. In the last decade of the Southern Sung, the family school became Illumined Good Academy. Although the transformation took nearly a century, the process was replicated in numerous cases. A more unusual, but still illustrative, example from the late twelfth century can be seen in Clarified Classics Academy. When General Yueh Fei (1103–1141) met with disgrace, he was feted by a military man named Yin Yen-te in Ch'a-ling County (Heng, Hu-nan), where Yueh Fei had gone with his army. To reward Yin Yen-te, Yueh Fei was said to have requested that the court depute students from the Directorate of Education to teach the sons of the Yin family. In the late 1170s Clarified Classics Academy was founded, and although later it was turned into a "Long Life" Taoist temple, the sons of the Yin family continued to be educated in it.[23] Mount T'ai Academy, also in Ch'a-ling, was founded by a man named Yin I in the Chia-ting era (1208–1224).[24] Both academies likely were linked through generations of the Yin family.

The transformation of family schools into academies in Southern Sung can be seen as one dimension of the concentration of *shih* on their local elite community. From this perspective, Southern Sung family academies are distinct from those of families such as the Ch'en in the early Northern Sung and before.[25] The Ch'en, Hu, and Hung negotiated with the state for status and power in the new regime, and the state, in turn, manipulated their interests to serve its own. In contrast, in the Southern Sung, families who established schools that became academies did so largely in terms of local concerns: lineage interests in educating sons or venerating ancestors, and community interests in supporting both themselves and others like them who were part of the *shih* elite.

Records of two academies in Jao Prefecture (Chiang-tung) founded during the latter twelfth century suggest the circumstances surrounding the founding of such family schools that became academies. East Mountain Academy in Yü-kan County was the family school of the chief councillor, Chao Ju-yü (1140–1196).[26] It was established by his younger cousin, Chao Ju-ti, who invited Chu Hsi to lecture there.[27] Chao Ju-yü's eldest son was also Chu Hsi's student, and Chao's elder and younger brothers taught the Chao sons at the academy. New Field Academy was founded during the Shao-hsing era (1131–1162) by Li Ch'un-nien (d. 1159; 1118 *chin-shih*) in his native place, Fu-liang County, and was restored during the Chia-ting era (1208–1224) by Li Ta-yu (1159–1224; 1196 *chin-shih*).[28] Li Ta-yu was from Tung-yang County (Wu, Che-tung) and was a follower of Lü Tsu-ch'ien.[29] He and his younger brother, Li Ta-t'ung (1223 *chin-shih*), both held official appointments.[30] Li Ch'un-nien, the founder, had served as prefect of Wu, and some contact may have been established with the family of Li Ta-yu and Li Ta-t'ung during that time; but Li Ch'un-nien died the year Li Ta-yu was born (1159), so any contact would have been with Li K'an, Ta-yu's and Ta-tung's father. We can speculate further that Li Ch'un-nien and the Li of Tung-yang may have been related. In fact, this is strongly suggested by two things: Li Ta-yu restored the academy established by Li Ch'un-nien, and he invited a man named Li Te-hsun to teach the descendants (*tsu tzu-ti*) of the Li.[31] It is likely that Li Ch'un-nien in Jao and Li Ta-yu in Wu represented two branches of a common Li descent group, and that this relationship led to the restoration by Li Ta-yu.[32]

Although the above two examples might seem to suggest that either a family associated with a prominent official or one that had recently produced *chin-shih* were most likely to have both the resources and the influence to found an academy, in fact, the founding of an academy was one strategy that could be employed by a family desirous of enhancing its local status by laying claim to some degree of scholarly commitment, if not achievement. Li Ta-yu's native place, Wu Prefecture's Tung-yang County, was the site of a unique cluster of academies established through the efforts of two local families in the mid- to late twelfth century. In the circumstances surrounding the use of a family's resources to found academies, we can observe a model conjunction of wealth and accompanying local scholarly and social status, including marriage ties, in the absence of degree-taking and significant office-holding. One line, in particular, seems to have exercised a remarkable degree of influence locally through its wealth and philanthropic activities, with no visible signs of either achievements or aspirations to status beyond the local community.

Five academies were established in Tung-yang by two prominent local families, the Kuo and Wu. The academy for which the most detailed account exists is Stone Cavern, founded by Kuo Ch'in-chih in 1148.[33] A half century later, in response to a request from Kuo Ch'in-chih's son, Kuo Chin, the Southern Sung scholar Yeh Shih composed a commemorative inscription in which he described the founding of the academy following the clearing of land and the discovery of a previously hidden place where the landscape provided an appropriate setting for study (see chapter 3).[34] Kuo Ch'in-chih's decision to build an academy there was based on his desire, as Yeh Shih recounted it, to make use of this natural bequest for educational purposes rather than transmit it to his heirs as family property:

> [Kuo] sighed and said: "I was a poor student. That this site was suddenly produced from my property is not a bequest for my private use. How can I therefore use it for my private pleasure [only]? In the future I want to enable my descendants to work hard and study here . . . and this will help to raise the academic accomplishments of the locality." Thus he planned an academy, where famous scholars supervised learning. He donated his family's books to it and allocated land to support it.[35]

Kuo Ch'in-chih determined that the academy site should not be privately held by the Kuo family, and after his death it was apparently maintained by his heirs as a community school.[36] Yeh Shih emphasized the altruism of Kuo Ch'in-chih's actions in establishing the academy, which clearly did not serve simply the sons of the Kuo lineage but the *shih* community as a whole: "Ah! Master Kuo is distant indeed! He replaced traveling [for study] with a school, and did not squander his resources for private interests. Because he was concerned with the [good of the] community [*chung-ho*], he did not use his landed wealth to enrich his own family."[37] Yeh Shih went on to say that learning does not depend on having a good place to study—even "firefly lanterns and snowy rooms" are adequate—since what is important is having the will to learn and devoting oneself completely to accomplishing it.[38] Like many of his contemporaries, he took the opportunity to criticize those who set their sights on the superficial achievements of the examinations, but who did not really have the true will to learn. Lacking the right intention at the beginning, these students will have not the means to complete the learning process.[39]

Kuo Ch'in-chih studied with Chang Chiu-ch'eng (1092–1159; 1132 first-place *chin-shih*), a disciple of Yang Shih who was both a classical scholar and a student of Buddhism. Chang Chiu-ch'eng has been described as a transmitter of the intellectual legacy of Ch'eng Hao and a close associate of the Ch'an priest Ta-hui Tsung-kao (1089–1173).[40] Kuo Ch'in-chih's sons, Kuo Chin and Kuo Hao, studied with Chu Hsi and Lü Tsu-ch'ien.[41] Kuo Ch'in-chih's cousin, Kuo Liang-ch'en, who established West Garden Academy using Stone Cavern as a model, invited Lü Tsu-ch'ien to teach, and Liang-ch'en's sons, Kuo Ch'eng (1150–1179) and Kuo Chiang (1153–1217), studied with Lü there.[42] According to Yeh Shih, who composed a funerary inscription for Kuo Liang-ch'en, both sons were born with weak constitutions, so their father provided for their education at home by hiring teachers and recruiting young men from the area to come and study together with them.[43] Kuo Ch'eng occasionally went away to study with a teacher and then returned to teach at his family's school. South Lake Academy was established by Kuo Ch'in-chih's and Kuo Liang-ch'en's nephew, Kuo P'u, but little more is known about either P'u or the academy he founded.[44]

In his funerary inscription for Kuo Liang-ch'en, Yeh Shih described the periodic rise and fall of followers of the thought of Chou Tun-i, Chang Shih, and the Ch'eng brothers. In discussing the attacks on these thinkers in 1169–1170, Yeh Shih suggested a link between the political situation and the activities of local elites in supporting academies: "Lecturers fled to Min [Fu-chien] and Che [Liang-che], hid in Chiang [Chiang-hsi] and Hu [Hu-nan]; and scholars contended in the mountains and valleys. They abandoned their homes and neighborhoods, renting houses and begging food, and all listened to them."[45] In this respect, the founding of family academies can be related to the True Way movement in the twelfth century. Scholars who were dismissed from office or otherwise persecuted provided a rich source of teachers to staff such schools. At the same time, family academies were places for these scholars to find occupation. It is worth recalling here the comment on Fu-chien's Indigo Field Academy cited in chapter 1 that at the time of the False Learning prohibition "all the elite families' *chin-shih* built academies to lodge (*yü-chü*)." Clearly, this phenomenon extended beyond Fu-chien and through the end of the twelfth century. Families with the means to do so took advantage of the opportunity to hire displaced scholars to teach at family academies.

The *Case Studies of Sung and Yuan Scholars* notes that Stone Cavern Academy was where Chu Hsi stayed the longest during the False Learning prohibition.[46] Others who went to Stone Cavern besides Chu Hsi included Ch'en Fu-liang, Ch'en Liang, Lu Yu, and Wei Liao-weng, along with T'ang Chung-yu (1136–1188; 1151 *chin-shih*), Hsu Ch'iao (1160–1237; 1187 *chin-shih*), and Tu Yü, all of whom were natives of Wu.[47] This roster of individuals represents the very broadest spectrum of late twelfth-century intellectuals, including those who found themselves on opposite sides politically. For example, T'ang Chung-yu was impeached by Chu Hsi for alleged official improprieties while he was prefect of T'ai in 1182–1183 (when Chu was intendant of the Evernormal Granary, Tea, and Salt for Che-tung); but T'ang Chung-yu and Lü Tsu-ch'ien were the only two men from Chin-hua during the Sung to be awarded the coveted Erudite Literatus (*po-hsueh hung-tz'u*) degree, and thus had claims to high scholarly status.[48] Although famous scholars from outside the area came to Stone Cavern, given the location of the Kuo family's academies in Lü Tsu-ch'ien's native area and the evidence that Lü taught many members of the Kuo family, his influence and that of his students was perhaps greatest. According to one source, the Kuo invited followers of Lü Tsu-ch'ien and Hsueh Shu-ssu (d. 1211), a scholar who was dismissed from office by Han T'o-chou, to teach at their academies.[49] As a youth, Hsu Ch'iao, who was invited to teach at Stone Cavern, studied with a disciple of Lü Tsu-ch'ien's, and later became a student of Chu Hsi, who praised him.[50] Tu Yü and his five brothers came under the intellectual influence of Lü Tsu-ch'ien through their father, who studied with Lü.[51] Lu Yu and Ch'en Liang, both of whom came to the academy, praised the literary skill of Tu Yü.[52]

Despite the ardent efforts of several members of the Kuo family in promoting education, there is no indication that any of the Kuo took degrees, although Kuo Ch'in-chih's son, Kuo Hao, held a minor local office.[53] Still, it is clear that the family's local status could be parlayed into wider prominence even outside Tung-yang. Ch'en Liang, who had some association with Stone Cavern, wrote of the great wealth built up by Kuo Liang-ch'en's father.[54] Yeh Shih's funerary inscription for Kuo Liang-ch'en provides some details on the Kuo line's prominence, beginning with Liang-ch'en's great-grandfather:[55] "From his great-grandfather on, they were wealthy in their locality; and from Liang-ch'en and his brothers on, they were all scholars. Because they were not appointed to office [in other places], they were still able to divide the property and not to decline. Thus the Kuo surname's rise began with Liang-ch'en."[56] Interestingly, Yeh Shih attributes the prosperity of the Kuo to their *not* being appointed to office, since it meant that division of the family property did not necessarily split up family resources, as it would have done had individual office holders moved away. Office-holding in other areas should not in theory have contributed to the dispersal of family property, since office-holders could be expected to return to their native areas when they had completed a term of office, for mourning or retirement. In fact, however, by the Southern Sung many elite families were changing residence through office-holding.[57] Yeh Shih suggests that the Kuo were able to consolidate their property because they concentrated their interests locally and did not divide them. From this perspective, Kuo Ch'in-chih's establishment of Stone Cavern is a good example of the contribution the Kuo were able to make to the local community because their interests were focused there and not on office-holding elsewhere.

The status of the Kuo in Tung-yang is highlighted further in Yeh Shih's funerary inscription for Kuo Liang-ch'en's brother, Kuo Liang-hsien (1137–1190), who was known for helping those in need:[58] "In the eastern part of Che, among the several great families, the Kuo are first. They do not have noble titles or positions, nor does their wealth exceed others; yet they are considered a great family. Why is that?"[59]

Yeh Shih went on to describe in conventional fashion the violent customs of the area, including the litigious nature of the inhabitants and their tendency to solve disputes by force, and juxtaposed the harmony and learning of the Kuo household with the vulgar customs that surrounded them. Their social and economic strategies were perhaps even more important in guaranteeing them a position of local eminence:

> They married their women to famous men and provided them with dowries. They treated with familial love even those not of the same surname [affinal kin]. They responded to those in need. . . . When traveling scholars passed by their home, they fulfilled their needs. . . . Even though their sons-in-laws and guests were numerous, they did not treat them indifferently. . . . It is fitting that, even though they are not wealthy and do not hold office, they are one of the most prominent families in Che-tung, and it is because of this [their treatment of others detailed above].[60]

Two things may be noted from this presentation of the Kuo line. First, despite Yeh Shih's disclaimer, they must have been relatively wealthy, enough that they could afford a modest degree of philanthropy. In fact, we know this from what Yeh Shih wrote in Kuo Liang-ch'en's funerary inscription about his father, grandfather, and great-grandfather. There are also other suggestions of the role played by the Kuo as local philanthropists: in 1179 Kuo Ch'in-chih donated books to the library of the county school, which was built at that time.[61] Second, locally recognized wealth preceded scholarly achievements, and wealth and scholarship without the addition of either degree-taking or office-holding still enabled the Kuo to arrange good marriages for their daughters.[62]

Through the writing of his commemorative inscription for Stone Cavern in 1198, as well as funerary inscriptions for various members of the Kuo family, Yeh Shih was able to promote the idea of local elite responsibility for education. Yeh Shih himself was brought up in an environment in Wen Prefecture where family schools provided education for local people. In the epitaph for his teacher, Liu Tzu-i, an eremite scholar who studied Buddhism and helped people in times of famine, Yeh Shih mentioned the private local school where he learned from Liu.[63] In an epitaph for one of his contemporaries, Lin Cheng-chung, Yeh Shih noted the existence of another family school in Wen.[64] Thus from the perspective of personal experience, as well as pragmatic social policy, Yeh Shih argued for the value of family responsibility for education, exemplified in Stone Cavern.

The other prominent family from Tung-yang associated with academy building in the area are the Wu, who built Peaceful Fields Academy.[65] Although it is not clear from the sources, it may have evolved from a "charitable school" (*i-shu*) built by Wu Wen-ping in 1174.[66] The school was for both agnatic and affinal descendants (*tsung-yin tzu-ti*), and there is evidence that others studied there as well.[67] Wu Wen-ping's eldest son, Wu K'uei (1145–1217), carried out other philanthropic activities in the local community, so the academy likely was part of these activities.[68] Yeh Shih's funerary inscription for Wu K'uei states that since the time of both his great-grandfather and grandfather the Wu were prominent in Tung-yang, and Yeh compares their wealth and status to that of the Kuo.[69] Wu K'uei invited local scholars T'ang Chung-yu (who also taught at Stone Cavern) and Hsu Chi (an eremite scholar from Lan-hsi County in Wu who gained a reputation only after his association with Peaceful Fields) to teach at the academy, where they were said to have attracted more than one hundred students.[70] Fu Yin, a disciple of T'ang Chung-yu and an affinal relative of Wu K'uei, was also invited to teach at Peaceful Fields.[71] In addition to inviting Fu Yin, Wu K'uei helped his household financially.[72]

Clearly the Wu, like the Kuo, had financial resources that enabled them to act as philanthropists locally and to provide education for their kin, both agnatic and affinal, as well as the local community, in order to gain scholarly status for themselves and their native area.[73] Writing in the late twelfth century, roughly contemporaneous with the charitable school attributed to Wu Wen-ping, the Southern Sung author Yuan Ts'ai argued that charitable schools (and hence lineage academies) were a better investment for the descent group than charitable estates.[74] He implied that family resources were better spent on education than on maintaining joint property, which was subject to potential dispersal by unscrupulous descendants. Education, on the other hand, would enhance prospects for the lineage to rise in status even if it did not result in *chin-shih* degrees, and resources spent on a school, teachers, books, and so on, would not be so easily subject to misappropriation. The support of scholarly activities through establishing an academy, as exemplified by both the Kuo and the Wu in Tung-yang, was sufficient for them to lay claim to local academic credentials.

As appeared to be the case with Peaceful Fields, an academy could simply be founded as a family school, with the term *shu-yuan* being adopted and used for it rather than a more common alternative, such as *shu* or *chia-shu*.[75] In some cases, a family school appears to have been changed into an academy with no evidence of a change in function, although the change might mean that the school was open to the entire elite community, not just descendants of one lineage. Frequently, academies founded initially for the benefit of a descent group were also opened to the *shih* community and not limited to the founder's agnatic or even affinal kin, and in these cases there appears to have been no necessary tension between the interests of that descent group and the community of *shih* as a whole. Rather than seeing the interests of individual *chia* or *tsu* in competition or conflict with each other, both were viewed as part of an expanding series of concentric circles that comprised the elite community.

An example of such a school is Teak Spring Academy in Kuei-ch'i County (Hsin, Chiang-tung) founded by the local Kao family in the late twelfth century, but open to the *shih* community.[76] The Kao traced their descent to a T'ang official, Kao K'uan-jen, who held the post of surveillance commissioner in Fu-chien.[77] In his inscription for this academy, Wang Ying-ch'en (1118–1176) claimed that each generation following Kao K'uan-jen produced men who were outstanding for their literary skills.[78] Kao K'o-yang, a seventh-generation descendant of Kao K'uan-jen, built the academy at the side of his residence, where he taught members of his own descent group and others from the community.[79] After Kao K'o-yang took a degree, he was appointed to office as instructor (*hsueh-lu*) in the Directorate of Education and left his home, suggesting one pattern of academy participation: individuals taught at an academy until they took a degree or, after taking a degree, until they were appointed to office. Given the frequent gaps between posts in the course of an official career, as well as the many who waited to take the examinations and get a degree, academy teaching would have been a reasonably attractive temporary occupation. Wang Ying-ch'en compared the Kao academy to the community schools (*lü-shu*) of antiquity and stated that students could go from the academy to prefectural schools, and then on to the Imperial University in the capital.[80] Clearly this academy functioned as a supplementary school, but at the same time it resulted from the efforts of a particular descent group claiming distinguished ancestry, and was open also to others in the local *shih* community who were neither agnatic nor affinal kin.

Other family schools that were transformed into academies with a correspondingly wider clientele of *shih* include Apricot Embankment Academy, which was set up at the home in Lo-an County (Fu, Chiang-hsi) of a marriage relative of Tseng Feng (b. 1142; 1169 *chin-shih*), probably in the late twelfth century.[81] The founder's uncle had taught at this family school. In his inscription for the academy, Tseng Feng described the uncle in this way: "[H]is occupation was [that of a] classicist [*ju*]. His character was that of a widely learned and elegant gentleman [*chün-tzu*]. He was recorded at the Ministry of Rites as a "tribute scholar" [*kung-shih*]. After this, he studied as a local scholar [*hsiang-shih*]."[82] Tseng Feng identified this individual first by classifying him as *ju*, and then traced his scholarly career through two separate categories of "tribute scholar" (one who is recommended to the emperor to hold office) and "local scholar" (one who remains at home and studies). He praised what this man did as a teacher at the academy, equating his teaching at Apricot Embankment with service to the state. In the conclusion of the inscription, Tseng Feng stated that, although the academy was formerly an old family school, during his generation it was used by other "scholarly colleagues" in the community as well.[83]

The collection and storage of books, often cited as one of the main purposes of Sung academies, was important not only at major academies but also at smaller, lesser-known ones such as those founded by individual lineages. Kuo Ch'in-chih, for example, moved his family's collection of books to the academy he founded in Wu, and also donated books to the county school. In Hu-nan's T'an Prefecture the Liao family's Dragon Pool Academy, established in 1195, became famous as a library.[84] Although founders Liao Yang-chih and Liao T'ien-ching were too obscure to have been recorded elsewhere, their father, Liao Yen-hsiu, held a local office.[85] The Liao family was not one of great historical repute, but in an inscription written to commemorate Dragon Pool, the Southern Sung poet Yang Wan-li (1127–1206) described them as bibliophiles:

> South of the lake (Hu-nan), the great households who are rich in property are not few. It is [rather] those rich in books who are few. Those who are not wealthy are not [so] because they are not old. Among those few [who are rich in books] and barely have any [property] are the Yu-ch'uan Liao brothers, Chung-kao [Yang-chih] and Wen-po [T'ien-ching]. . . . Whether in Min and Che to the east, or Ch'iung and Shu to the west, there are precious books and there is fine paper, and there are books with large characters. One must empty one's pockets to purchase them, and send workmen to the mountains to cut wood for building an academy to house them.[86]

Yang Wan-li went on to describe the academy the Liao brothers built and their invitation to famous teachers to teach the sons of their family, plus the many scholars who came from far places to study there. This family academy, then, served as an important library and teaching place, according to Yang Wan-li at least.[87] Yang Wan-li suggests that the Liao spent whatever means they had on books, and therefore were to be lauded, as opposed to others who were wealthy in property but did not support learning. To what extent this is rhetoric composed to exhort people to pay attention to learning rather than wealth and property is unclear; it certainly seems related to the notion put forth by both Yuan Ts'ai and Yeh Shih in different contexts that it is better to invest in education than to depend on bequeathing property to descendants.

Yeh Shih's contemporary, Chen Te-hsiu, expressed similar ideas in his inscription for the Huang family's Dragon Mountain Academy, which bore some resemblance to the Kuo family's Stone Cavern Academy.[88] Established nearly three-quarters of a century later (1221) than Stone Cavern, in Yung-feng County (Chi, Chiang-hsi), the motives that led Huang Hsing-chih to found Dragon Mountain were not unlike those that inspired Kuo Ch'in-chih at Stone Cavern:

> Dragon Mountain Academy was established by Yung-feng Huang. He was very learned and known in his locality. He taught his sons and younger brothers. But since it was not in a settled place, his will could not be carried out. Thus he sighed and said: "I fortunately have some narrow land. Rather than selfishly pass it on to my descendants, why not make it into a private school, collect talented ones and educate them, in order to fulfill my will?" Therefore, he looked for land. . . . So it was built . . . and completed in 1221. The master allocated half of his property to support it. In stipends and exams, all imitated the rules of the prefecture and county. Examinations were overseen by local *chin-shih* or officials. The master managed it himself, with daily lectures and monthly examinations. Scholars came and all encouraged each other.[89]

Like Yeh Shih, Chen Te-hsiu emphasized the selflessness of Huang Hsing-chih in deciding to devote the use of his property to education rather than simply passing it on to his heirs. As the inscription makes clear, providing for the education of one's descent group and its affines was considered preferable to bequeathing property directly to individuals. Like estates that provided support for indigent members of a descent group, Stone Cavern and Dragon Mountain, among others, were funded primarily by bequests of land. Possibly Dragon Mountain accommodated others besides agnatic and affinal relatives, although these are the clientele named in the academy's surviving records. Huang Hsing-chih's nephew, Huang Ts'ung-lung, served as head of the academy until he took a degree in 1224 and left—further evidence that academies provided occupation as well as training for aspiring examination candidates and officials.[90] Chen Te-hsiu explicitly makes it clear, too, that Dragon Mountain functioned more or less as an adjunct to government schools, tied to them by similar rules and by administration by local *chin-shih* and officials.

Chen Te-hsiu took the opportunity in this inscription to criticize the scholars of his own day, complaining that "the *shih* know how to glorify themselves, but they do not know how to reform the self; and they know how to seek profit, but they do not know how to seek the Way."[91] Chen Te-hsiu claimed that Huang Hsing-chih longed to improve upon the government schools by encouraging learning that was not tied to the examinations. It is difficult to see this as more than rhetoric, however, since the form of Dragon Mountain, flowery prose aside, was modeled on official schools in its rules and administration. How are we to understand this? It does make sense if viewed in light of increasing competition among candidates for the examinations—competition that made it not only even more important to focus family resources on education but also increasingly unlikely that someone would be successful. Thus on the one hand, the Huang family, like the Kuo and others, invested substantial resources in an academy and modeled it on local government schools; on the other hand, Chen Te-hsiu, like other True Way writers, while praising the efforts of the Huang, took the opportunity to criticize the examinations and exhort people to turn their attention away from "seeking profit" (i.e., success in the examinations, followed by official careers) to "seeking the Way." Such views also provided justification to those who did not succeed in the examinations, so it was possible to have it both ways.

Along the lines suggested by Yuan Ts'ai (see above), some charitable estates included schools. One such school was Inculcating Duty Academy in Chin-t'an County (Jun, Che-hsi), established by Chang Kao to teach the sons of his lineage, probably in the early thirteenth century,[92] using a passage from Mencius to name it: "Let careful attention be paid to education in schools, inculcating [*shen*] in it especially the filial and fraternal duties [*i*]."[93] The Chang surname was said not only to be illustrious locally, but also to have a venerable heritage that included high ministers of the state.[94] The school was part of a charitable estate, modeled on that of the Fan lineage, set up at the former residence of Chang Kao's grandfather, Chang Kang (1083–1166), who entered the Imperial University, took a *chin-shih* degree in 1115, and has a biography in the dynastic history.[95] In his inscription commemorating this charitable estate, Liu Tsai first recalled the circumstances of the famous Fan estate, stressing responsibility to ancestors to ensure that their descendants are not in want:[96]

> Would I prefer my own lake of wine and forest of meat, and take no heed of kin crying out in hunger? Would I prefer to have a lovely home and beautiful clothes, and take no heed of kin having no clothes? Would I prefer piling up things to bequeath like clouds to unknown descendants, and pay no heed to the immediate emergencies of [kin]? Would I rather give a lot to the ridiculous Taoists and Buddhists, whom I don't believe in, and pay no heed to to the dispersal of [kin] flesh and bones [because of not having adequate funds for burials]?[97]

Although the Chang estate and academy were dedicated to members of their lineage and Liu Tsai's inscription emphasizes duty to kin in this regard, Liu's own career included at least one highly visible instance of community philanthropy that was carried out in the same area. During a famine in 1224 in Chin-t'an County, Liu Tsai started a soup kitchen that was said eventually, after donations from others, to have fed fifteen thousand people each day.[98] Liu Tsai was a contemporary and colleague of Yeh Shih, Chen Te-hsiu, and Wei Liao-weng, all of whom wrote inscriptions for academies and were prominent officials whose ideas about social policy were influential. Both Chen Te-hsiu and Wei Liao-weng were more actively involved with the academy movement in the early thirteenth century, but as we have seen, Yeh Shih was also eager to promote family academies at least as a strategy for providing access to education in local communities.

That thinkers such as Yeh Shih and Chen Te-hsiu could use their composition of an inscription commemorating these academies to grind their own ideological axes should come as no surprise. Their rhetoric emphasized the benevolence of the founder in diverting family resources to educational enterprise, but it should not obscure for us some of the more homely reasons for lineages to found academies. Family academies can be explained as one strategy lineages used to establish local scholarly credentials. Founding an academy did not by any means guarantee success in the examinations, but it surely was a way to provide an opportunity for sons to get ahead. In this sense, family academies were closely tied to official government schools, and in some cases explicitly sought to replicate them. Yet, given the enormous obstacles to success in examination competition, preparation for the examinations cannot be regarded as the sole, or even necessarily the most important, reason that families allocated property and resources to the support of academies. The scholarly credentials themselves provided sufficient justification for the academies—credentials that were less tangible than a *chin-shih* degree, but important nonetheless. A family that built an academy was proclaiming to the local community and its immediate social world that it was committed to investing in education and therefore it upheld the values of scholarship and learning. This point was strengthened when the academy was open to the *shih* community, who could use it as a community resource serving the common interests of all *shih*. The founding of Tiger Creek Academy in Hsin-chien County (Hung, Chiang-hsi) illustrates an interesting twist on the relationship between family schools, *chin-shih* degrees, and academies. A T'ang prefect of Hung moved his family to Hsin-chien and began a family school.[99] In the 1208–1224 era two of his descendants "took *chin-shih* degrees and therefore changed it [the family school] to Tiger Creek Academy," thus suggesting that success in degree-taking provided the reason for changing a family school into an academy and assuming community responsibility for education.[100]

A tradition of family learning sometimes inspired the building of an academy, even without any clear connection to degree-taking. In his inscription on Wooden Slip Creek Academy of the Wu family in Yen Prefecture (Che-hsi), the Southern Sung writer Ch'eng Pi described the family tradition of learning, specializing in the *Odes* and *Documents*.[101] Wu Ying-yu (fl. ca. 1214) continued family tradition by building an academy so extensive it must have rivaled prefectural schools.[102] Wooden Slip Creek included a lecture hall, a study, dormitories, a library, and a shrine with images of Confucius and his disciples in it.[103] Although Wu Ying-yu's grandfather was said to have followed a Taoist path and become an immortal, his father, Wu Shun-shen, had a "talent for learning," which he instilled in Ying-yu.[104] According to Ch'eng Pi, the Wu were affinal kin of the Hung of K'ang-lü, who established Thunder Lake Academy in the early Northern Sung. In concluding his inscription, Ch'eng Pi used a riparian metaphor to make the point that the ancients nurtured scholars at home, providing a pool of prospective officials for employment by the ruler: "This is flowing from the spring to the stream."[105] Using a horticultural metaphor, Ch'eng Pi argued that after holding office, one should return home to study and teach: "the leaf returning to the seed."[106] Finally, Ch'eng Pi noted that the inscription he wrote for Wooden Slip Creek was for Master Wu (Ying-yu) to put on his deceased father's funerary tablet.[107] This is an interesting and important piece of information, suggesting the close tie between maintaining the family line and building an academy. In the case of Wooden Slip Creek, Wu Ying-yu continued a family tradition of learning by building an academy. By requesting that Ch'eng Pi,[108] who must have had some kind of tie to the Wu, write a commemorative inscription, Wu Ying-yu was also venerating his father.

Similarly, Hundred *Chang* Creek Academy was established by Ch'en Tou-lung for his father, Ch'en T'ien-tse (fl. ca. 1255), in Jui-an County (Wen, Che-tung), at the site where T'ien-tse had lectured.[109] Ch'en Tou-lung, who had returned home to care for his aged father and mourn his death, was appointed headmaster at Honoring Chu Hsi Academy in Wen.[110] Later, Ch'en Tou-lung was appointed to office elsewhere, and when he came home again he established Hundred *Chang* Creek Academy at the place where his father had lectured and was now interred.[111]

As can be seen in the above two examples, academies were sometimes built as family schools in connection with venerating a deceased father. In Southern Sung, honoring ancestors was at times cited as a reason for the founding of academies, much as reference was made in the record for Tiger Creek Academy to the T'ang ancestor who began the tradition of the family school. Cassia Cliff Academy in Kao-an County (Yun, Chiang-hsi) was erected at the old site of a school founded by Hsin Nan-yu, who held the post of director of education (*kuo-tzu chi-chiu*) during the T'ang.[112] His descendant, Hsin Yuan-lung (1195–1200 *chin-shih*), wrote an inscription in 1211 describing his visit to the site, where local people still sacrificed to his ancestor, and his decision to rebuild it as a shrine to Hsin Nan-yu.[113] In addition to the shrine, buildings for lecturing and residence were erected, along with other facilities. Both Chou Pi-ta and Wei Liao-weng wrote name plaques for it, and classes were held regularly.[114]

Shrines to both ancestors and famous scholars at some academies combined elements of worthies' or transmission shrines with ancestral veneration. At the death of Chung Ju-yü (fl. late twelfth century), a disciple of Chang Shih, Chung Ju-yü's son, Chung Chen (a student of Chu Hsi), built a lecture hall (*chiang-she*) in Hsiang-t'an County (T'an, Hu-nan) with an allotment of five hundred *mou* (about seven acres) for support to offer sacrifices to both Chang Shih and his father.[115] Chung Ju-yü took a *chin-shih* degree but did not hold office until his later years, when he was appointed to a minor post. In his declining years he returned home and was made headmaster at South Marchmount Academy and superintendent of South Marchmount Temple (*miao*).[116] The son used his father's honorific name, "Chu-i," to transform the lecture hall in Hsiang-t'an County into an academy, and he invited Chen Te-hsiu to teach there when Chen held office in T'an Prefecture (ca. 1222–1225).[117] Orchid Jade Academy in An-fu County (Chi, Chiang-hsi) was established (probably in the late thirteenth century) to honor native son Liu Yen (1048–1102; 1079 *chin-shih*).[118] Liu Yen was the first of his family to hold office, and he was followed by descendants who also achieved successful official careers, including one who attained the post of chief councillor.[119] Orchid Jade was called the "Liu family school" by Liu Ch'en-weng, the author of a commemorative inscription for it who may also have been a descendant of Liu Yen.[120]

Both Liu Ch'en-weng and his son, Liu Chiang-sun (b. 1257), composed inscriptions on Double Peak Academy in Shun-ch'ang County (Nan-chien, Fu-chien). Double Peak was established shortly before the fall of the Southern Sung at the request of the intendant, Liao Pang-chieh, to honor his forebears, Liao Kang (1071–1143; 1106 *chin-shih*) and Liao Te- ming.[121] Liao Kang had studied with Yang Shih and Ch'en Kuan (1057–1122), and Liao Te-ming was an important disciple of Chu Hsi, whose "questions in the *yü-lu* are most numerous." Liao Te-ming was also venerated at Han-shan Academy in Kuang-tung (see chapter 2). Both Liao Kang and Liao Te-ming received the posthumous name of "Wen-ching," the same as Yang Shih, Lo Ts'ung-yen, and Li T'ung, all of whom were also from Nan-chien.[123] Liu Ch'en-weng, the author of an inscription for Double Peak, declared that it was "the fate of Heaven and Earth that after such a long time they [Yang Shih, Lo Ts'ung-yen, Li T'ung, and Liao Kang and Liao Te-ming] have come together in this place."[124]

In addition to their scholarly lineage, both Liao were known for their actions as officials. In 1131, Liao Kang left his position as prefect of Hsing-hua to retire to his home in Shun-ch'ang to mourn his father's death. When bandits arose in neighboring areas, and the local officials and clerks fled, the people of Shun-ch'ang turned to Liao Kang for leadership. He sent his eldest son, Liao Ch'ih, to deal with the bandits, and they were dispersed.[125] Liao Kang was then appointed judicial commissioner for that circuit.[126] When Liao Te-ming was judicial intendant of Kuang-tung, he deputed troops to quell bandits who had created fear among the population of Shao Prefecture.[127] Although Liao Kang achieved high national office as minister of public works and Liao Te-ming held office in the Ministry of Personnel, both were remembered and venerated for their actions as regional judicial officials, in Liao Kang's case for actions taken while formally out of office.

When local students at Double Peak requested an inscription from Liu Chiang-sun, they prefaced their request with a statement referring to the importance of the Liao surname in Shun-ch'ang, comparing it to famous surnames of the Ch'u state during the Warring States period.[128] The students traced the prominence of the Liao name in the area over a period of one hundred years to Liao Pang-chieh, the academy founder. In his inscription, Liu Ch'en-weng reached back before the Hsia and Shang to a putative ancestor and claimed that over the intervening millennia the Liao had produced talented and famous men, as well as recluses such as Liao Jung of the Five Dynasties period.[129] Thus the claimed continuity of a surname, and the official prominence of the line in the recent past, were cited as justification for founding an academy dedicated to two generations of the Liao. Double Peak's function was to perpetuate the legacy of the Liao through educating local men so they could achieve success in the examinations and hold office. Although the academy was dedicated to two of the founder's ancestors, apparently it was not limited in its function as a school to his descendants. It served the community while honoring two generations of one line.

Unlike Double Peak, which did not receive imperial recognition (i.e., it was not granted a name plaque), Weng Islet Academy, the family school of the Ying, was granted a name plaque in imperial calligraphy in the Ch'un-yu period (1241–1252). The academy was located at the former residence of Ying Su (1193 *chin-shih*) in Ch'ang-kuo County (Ming, Che-tung)[130] His son, Ying Yu (1223 *chin-shih*), assisting civil councillor of state under Li-tsung, was responsible for the creation of the academy at this site in the Chou-shan archipelago off the coast of Ming, close to Mount Tai Academy (see chapter 2).[131] Members of the Ying family were educated at Weng Islet, but it must also have served as a school for the community, since later accounts attribute the decline of the academy to the growth of a prefectural school.[132] Although Weng Islet began as a family school, there are other indications that it closely resembled academies built around shrines that functioned as schools. A Yuan inscription says that Weng Islet honored Chu Hsi and followed the pattern of White Deer Grotto, and when it was founded it was granted books by the court (probably since its founder was an important official).[133] Commentators also remark on the academy as an outpost of defense against the forces of Buddhism and Taoism, a characteristic more often associated with officially established academies in frontier zones than with family schools.[134]

Elsewhere in Ming Prefecture, Kuang-p'ing Academy in Feng-hua County was the former family school of the Shu, named after the honorific title of Shu Lin (1136–1199), one of the Four Masters of the Ch'un-hsi era (1174–1189), who was known as Master Kuang-p'ing.[135] The school was established in 1275 by Shu Mi (1244 *chin-shih*), Shu Lin's grandson.[136] Shu Mi's grandson, in turn, became headmaster at the academy sometime during the last two decades of the thirteenth century.[137] This academy provides another example of the combination of a family school with an ancestral shrine. Wang Ying-lin's inscription on Kuang-p'ing, written in 1275, emphasized the role of the family in education for the benefit of the state. Implicit in his discussion of the importance of family schools is recognition of the benefits that accrue to families who sponsor and support education for their descendants. Education provides the foundation for a family to produce successive generations of officeholders who, because of their positions, will be able to protect the interests of the family as a whole: "When the master died, his disciples paid respect to him with diligence. They put up an image of him in the school. . . . His sons and grandsons, as well as the 'excellent ones' of the patriline and agnates [*tsung-tsu*] morning and evening carried out the rites. . . . Lecturing and teaching also were diligently carried out."[138]

Wang Ying-lin discussed the educational system of antiquity that was organized along various levels of family, community, and finally, state. He also held up as a model the classicists (*ching-hsueh*) of the Han and T'ang who "grasped their family regulations [*chia-fa*]" and the clans (*shih-tsu*) who paid attention to their genealogies (*tsung-p'u*).[139] They are compared with those who took the examinations, were "seduced by profit and salary," and were not "Heaven's titled nobility."[140] Wang Ying-lin contrasted the policies of the current court (end of Southern Sung) with those of previous eras, arguing that the Sung in its policies toward education was linked with Tsou and Lu, the home states of Mencius and Confucius. He cited examples of stellar figures from the Northern and early Southern Sung: Ch'i T'ung-wen, who founded Sui-yang Academy (see chapter 1); Tseng Kung (1019–1083; 1057 *chin-shih*), a noted scholar and official of the Northern Sung who founded a charitable estate for his family; and Liu Ch'ing-chih (1134–1190; 1157 *chin-shih*), who was known for care of his homeless kin.[141] Chu Hsi's compilation of his own *chia-chuan* (literally, family tradition, or family biography) was similarly cited as a precedent linking the actions of Shu Lin's descendants with earlier attempts to consolidate and maintain family interests through activities that enhanced awareness of family identity and simultaneously promoted the elevation of family status through education and officeholding. Wang Ying-lin concluded with the conventional assertion that the diligence and commitment of Shu Lin's descendants was not simply one family's story and that a state's humanity (*jen*) began with one family (*chia*).[142]

CONCLUSION

Written at the close of the Southern Sung, Wang Ying-lin's inscription on Kuang-p'ing Academy comes full circle from the great lineage schools of the pre-Sung era to late Southern Sung family academies as the root of state education. Linking them to classical ideals, Wang Ying-lin argued for the primacy of family as the basis of the state. But, unlike the family schools of the Ch'en, Hu, and Hung in the late Five Dynasties–early Northern Sung, family academies of the Southern Sung were founded against the backdrop of an extensive system of government schools dating to the eleventh century. Whether linked by kinship ties through the founder or set up primarily to venerate ancestors and secondarily provide education to the *shih* community as well as the lineage, the proliferation of such academies in the late twelfth and thirteenth centuries was the result of increasing competition for status and office. In many of the cases cited in this chapter, an academy founded by a particular family was expanded to include members of the local *shih* community, or a family school was transformed into an academy. A striking example of the latter is seen in the case of Locust Tree Hall Academy in Chin-hsi County (Fu, Chiang-hsi). In 1233 the prefect established an academy at the site of a shrine to Lu Chiu-yuan and his brother, natives of the county, adopting the name of the Lu family school for it.[143] This illustrates perhaps an extreme case of the transformation of a family school into an academy, where a local official relied on associations with the family school of well-known philosophers to sanction the founding of an academy that served the needs of the local elite community.

The transition from family schools to academies in the Sung can be seen as part of a broadening of the sphere of activity of local elites.[144] Members of local elites supported the establishment of academies in cooperation with local officials because the interests of both intersected, as the elite sought to affirm its status and prestige, and officials to confirm the authority of the state. By the mid- to late thirteenth century the central government was increasingly willing to entrust local institutions such as schools to local elites in cooperation with prefectural and county officials, because both financial strain due to military pressures and political instability in the face of constant diplomatic maneuvering with northern enemies made the state increasingly reliant on local elites for maintaining order in their communities.

Academies can be understood as community institutions in two ways. First, they were local institutions that were expressions of community identity. In this sense, academies helped provide educational training for sons to succeed in the examination system and thus elevate the status of the local community. Despite criticism by thinkers such as Chu Hsi of pedantic education aimed only at success in the examinations, clearly many academies functioned as supplements to government-sponsored schools. Following the institution of the Three Halls System as part of the New Laws of Wang An-shih in the Northern Sung, the role of official schools was gradually reduced to a selection place for examination candidates, where they qualified for taking the examinations. Thus official schools came to have less of an educational function and more of a role to play as an arm of the administration of the examination system.[145] Second, academies were community institutions for the *shih* to consolidate their identity as a group separate from commoners. Ritual activities at academies contributed to this distinction, as both True Way figures and local scholars were venerated at academy shrines, validating and reinforcing the importance of scholarly activities. Schools and academies were also places to establish communication between local scholars and officials because they were the site of rites that bonded the elite community.[146] This point helps to explain cooperative efforts between local officials and elites attested to in the sources describing the founding of academies. The usual pattern would be for an official or a member of the local elite to propose establishing an academy, and then for both the local government and the elite community to support it with land endowments from the government or with cash, land, or other kinds of contributions. Contributions to support local schools meant that local *shih* were expanding their concerns and activities from the *chia* to the descent group (*tsung-tsu*), and finally to the community (*hsiang-tang*), thereby reducing the role of the central government in local community education.[147]

The interests of local elites and officials intersected as the power of the central government was reduced in the Southern Sung. In addition, bitter factional strife during the Northern Sung contributed to the uncertainty that clouded official careers in the Southern Sung central government, providing both teachers and students for academies. When we consider the support of local education through the founding of academies dedicated either to a descent group or to a wider circle of the local community, we can interpret such efforts as part of a complex of localized strategies to claim status and exercise power rather than as a way to achieve status and position through the state. Educational opportunities provided by academies would aid students in preparing for the civil service examinations, and the awarding of a *chin-shih* degree to a local candidate would bring state-determined status to that individual, his agnates, and his descendants and affines, as well as his locality. In the Southern Sung, however, this status was more useful to aspiring elites in the local community because of what it represented locally rather than as a means to obtain office in the imperial government. The instability and uncertainty of official careers in the face of constant factional strife, particularly over the issues of war and peace, surely made public life in the central government less attractive and less secure than it once had been. Two major aspects of social change in the Southern Sung influenced and helped to shape the academy movement. Growing emphasis on the patrilineal descent line—described by Robert Hymes as a "lineage orientation"[148]—led to the founding of academies to venerate ancestors and to provide educational support for the members of a particular descent group. And the increasingly local focus of elite activities was expressed in the founding of academies that reflected the local status concerns of a particular descent group and the local nature of their ties and aspirations in common with other members of the local elite community.

5

Social Integration and Cultural Legitimacy

Academies and the Community of *Shih*

By the Southern Sung, the local elite community included not only native resident *shih*, but also frequently others who resided there on either a temporary or relatively permanent basis. There are many examples of *shih* residing more or less permanently, without holding office, in areas other than where they were officially registered.[1] The term *chi-chü* (sojourner) was used already in the late Northern Sung to describe *shih* with official status but no current administrative appointment who continued to reside where they had previously held office.[2] The proliferation of academies in the Southern Sung can be accounted for in part by the general phenomenon of *chi-chü* and the consequent presence of unemployed people of official status in areas where they were not registered as native residents. In many cases individuals invited to lecture at academies, or those who were involved with their founding in some way, were *shih* of former official standing but with no current administrative responsibilities. Academies provided a place for these *shih* to identify themselves as members of the elite, whether they were native to the area or not. For those away from their native places, identification with other *shih* was particularly important, and the sense of community fostered by ritual activities at the academy provided social support for "sojourners" classed as *shih*.

One of the most vivid, if relatively late, examples of the relationship between academies and sojourning (also termed *yu-chü, ch'iao-yü, ch'iao-chü*) concerns Ou-yang Shou-tao and his kinsman, Ou-yang Hsin, in the late thirteenth century.[3] Both were natives of Chi Prefecture (Chiang-hsi), but Ou-yang Hsin and his son sojourned in Liu-yang County (T'an, Hu-nan). When Ou-yang Shou-tao was appointed assistant headmaster at Marchmount Hill Academy, Ou-yang Hsin heard that he was in T'an and paid him a visit:[4]

> At first [Shou-tao] did not recognize him, but after they met face to face they developed a mutual bond. Shou-tao thereupon requested to the Hu-nan vice fiscal commissioner, Wu Tzu-liang, to arrange for Hsin to lecture at Marchmount Hill. Hsin lectured on the chapter from the *Record of Rites* entitled "Heaven Sends the Timely Rain; Mountains and Rivers Give Forth Clouds." Shou-tao rose and said, "If Ch'ang-sha has Chung-chai [Hsin], why have I come here?"[5]

From similar accounts in the Sung dynastic history and the *Case Studies of Sung and Yuan Scholars*, it appears that Ou-yang Shou-tao initially was reluctant to acknowledge Ou-yang Hsin, who was undoubtedly seeking help from his well-placed kinsman. Once Ou-yang Hsin proved himself, however, Ou-yang Shou-tao afforded him recognition and support at the academy. This case provides direct evidence of the role of academies as places where sojourners could establish their identity as part of a scholarly community, and where they could find occupation. References to some academies explicitly state that they were founded to serve itinerant scholars. Recognized by the court in 1210, East Lake Academy in Nan-ch'ang County (Hung, Chiang-hsi) was built by the prefect "to house traveling scholars" (*i-kuan yu-hsueh-*

chih shih).[6] There is also scattered evidence of various levels of support provided at academies for itinerant scholars, who would be expected to stay only for a limited period of time. By the late thirteenth century Marchmount Hill allotted itinerant scholars (*liu-shih*) a daily amount of rice and cash.[7] At West Brook Academy in Jui Prefecture (Chiang-tung) the rules stated that scholars who came to stay temporarily at the academy would be allowed three days of rice; if they wanted to stay on as resident scholars they would be supplied with rice on a more permanent basis.[8] Thus occupation, support, and identity as part of a scholarly community could be provided for sojourners by an academy.

In the course of official careers, many *shih* traveled extensively: first going to prefectural centers and the capital to take the examinations, then moving from post to post as they were transferred every one to two years. As this geographic mobility brought *shih* from different places into contact with each other, academies provided an institutional setting that fostered the growth of intellectual and social networks among *shih* from various regions. Academies not only brought them into personal contact with other thinkers and new students, they also enabled these men to be introduced to a broader range of ideas than would have been possible through texts and written communication. By means of formal lectures and study, as well as less formal contacts, people transmitted new ideas and formed personal bonds, many of which led to further family, ideological, or even political alliances.

Such networks at the academies provided an alternative, horizontal mode for relations among *shih*, in contrast to the hierarchical and pyramidal structures of the state tied to the recruitment process (the examination system) and to ranking and promotion in office.[9] The teacher-student relationship could also be seen as hierarchical, but it was based on personal charisma and ties distinct from those of the examination system and official appointments. The nature of such ties was inherently different from those established by sharing the same office, degree year, rank, or seniority. Relations based on scholarly association promoted by academies belonged to a node-and-network model that differed fundamentally from the vertical and hierarchical pyramid of official recruitment, selection, appointment, and promotion. Unlike the fixed number of degrees and offices in the essentially static pyramid structure, the node-and-network model has an almost infinite potential for expansion and multiplication.

The potential for alliances among the *shih* that were not encompassed by state mechanisms of recruitment and office undoubtedly worried government officials. Not surprisingly, there were voices in the central government that expressed dismay and concern at the mobility and apparent independence of the *shih*. Around the beginning of the thirteenth century, vice minister of war Yü Ch'ou (1163 *chin-shih*) wrote a memorial complaining that local government schools were in decline, school officials were increasingly acting on behalf of local interests, and although schools continued to increase in number, they were quickly abandoned:[10]

> The court has raised up the Imperial University and employed famous teachers there. Scholars from the four quarters come here in great numbers, and it can be said to be flourishing, indeed! I am concerned, however, that in recent years the prefectural and commandery schools continue to grow in number, but then are abandoned and decay. The scholars [*shih-tzu*][11] have become itinerant lecturers in order to support themselves. Morning and evening they thus take leave of their official positions and deviously [engage in] prevalent vulgarities [*liu-su*]. The arrogant ones of the localities pass the gates [of the schools] and don't enter. Educational officials consider themselves to be independent and do not serve [the interests of the central government]. If they do serve, it is only from the perspective of one commandery [rather than the empire]. How can this not be deeply harmful?[12]

In referring to "itinerant lecturers" Yü Ch'ou was talking about the very kinds of activities that academies promoted. Although he did not specifically attack academies, they could certainly be seen as major culprits in luring prospective students away from their proper places in government-administered prefectural and county schools. As seen in chapter 4, where family academies were transformed into local elite community institutions, some academies began usurping the functions of local government schools, to the dismay of officials such as Yü Ch'ou. His memorial expresses concern over the fluidity and laxity of lecturing taking place outside the confines of official institutions, as well as with the notion of itinerant scholars, who were not in their proper places, either at home or holding office elsewhere. That Yü Ch'ou's comments did not reflect his views alone is clear from evidence about government problems with sojourners and regulations developed to control them.[13]

Yü Ch'ou went on to discuss problems of selecting educational officials for local schools, an issue that hearkened back to Wang Anshih's reformist attempts to appoint "teaching officials," which resulted in the institution of a special recruiting examination for teachers.[14] The Office of Educational Intendant (*t'i-chü hsueh-shih ssu*) similarly was an outgrowth of Northern Sung concerns to coordinate education from the center, a task that grew increasingly unwieldy as local schools expanded.[15] Yü Ch'ou's point was that too much control was being exercised by local officials such as prefects, who were seen as too closely identified with local interests, rather than with those of the central government. By the reign of Li-tsung, however, rather than resisting the actions of local officials in founding academies, the imperial government appropriated them, validating academies with imperial recognition through granting official name plaques and, by the 1260s, with the court appointment of headmasters. The strategy was designed to enhance support for a financially and militarily weakened central government among the community of *shih*.

The twin themes of the Southern Sung state's quest for cultural legitimacy in the face of the Jurchen and Mongol threats and the desire of *shih* to confirm their identity as a scholarly elite in conditions of intense competition for degrees and offices were interwoven in the political and social contexts of the thirteenth century. Cultural legitimacy was enhanced through the appropriation of cultural icons by state support for academies dedicated to Northern Sung scholars and early Southern Sung loyalist officials and patriotic poets. Identification with these figures as symbols of cultural continuity helped to sanction the Southern Sung state and thus strengthen the official hierarchical order of society. At the same time, the construction of cross-regional social and intellectual networks through academies contributed to the horizontal integration of Southern Sung society by providing both material and ideological support for the *shih* community. Both at the time of the fall of the Northern Sung and as the Mongols launched their attacks on the borders of the Southern Sung empire beginning in the 1220s, *shih* were displaced from their homes as they fled the Jurchen or later the Mongol armies. Academies provided an important institutional support for scholarly immigrants to establish themselves among the local elites in their new homes. The state's appointment of headmasters was an attempt to gain control over this cultural resource by strengthening its own role in academy administration. In some instances, the needs of refugee scholars were directly addressed by the founding of academies in border regions, a clear demonstration of high-level official strategy to secure support from the *shih* elite. Finally, academies were also closely related to the politics of "transformation through education" (*chiao-hua*), as local officials sought to maintain social and political order through the support of academies as a means to achieve this transformation.

Sojourners and Academy Networks

References to the social category of sojourners—individuals who resided outside their native places without holding office—abound in a variety of sources. The *Chia-ting Ch'ih-ch'eng chih*, a local history of T'ai Prefecture (Che-tung) compiled in 1223, contains a separate category on the *chin-shih* lists for *ch'iao-yu*, defined in the following way: "Those who were not born and raised here but resided here are [known as] *ch'iao-yü*. Their sons and grandsons were born and raised here, and those who took degrees are entered on the *chin-shih* lists."[16] Nearly all twenty-six entries on the *chin-shih* list date their "lodging" (*yu*) in various counties of T'ai Prefecture to either 1126–1127 or to the Shao-hsing era (1131–1162), most to the latter. Different reasons are given for their moving to T'ai: most moved from areas that were either taken over by the Jurchen or endangered by the Jurchen conquest, but some also moved because of paternal office-holding in the area and stayed on. Among those who moved to T'ai, for example, was Lü I-hao (1071–1139), who fled to Lin-hai from Chi-nan in the Shantung peninsula in 1130 and who became chief councillor in the early Southern Sung under Kao-tsung.[17]

Less common, although still not all that unusual, was the case of the Northern Sung scholar Hsieh Liang-tso (1050–1103), one of the Four Masters of the Ch'eng school.[18] Hsieh Liang-tso was from the north but died in exile in Lin-hai before he could be rehabilitated following severe punishment for a frank expression of political opinion.[19] His son, Hsieh K'o-nien, fled with his father to T'ai.[20] Hsieh K'o-chia (d. 1134; 1097 *chin-shih*), who must belong to the same generation and be a close agnatic relative of Hsieh K'o-nien, sojourned in (*yu-chü*) Lin-hai at the beginning of the Shao-hsing era.[21] Both men resided in T'ai, although their native place was formally listed as Shang-ts'ai (Ts'ai, Ching-hsi North), Hsieh Liang-tso's native place.[22] Yeh Shih wrote about Hsieh Liang-tso's descendants in T'ai in an inscription on the shrine to Hsieh Liang-tso erected at the prefectural school.[23] Yeh Shih related that all of Hsieh Liang-tso's sons fled when he was punished, perhaps fearing for their own safety. One son died in Ch'u (Hunan), another in Min (Fu-chien); only Hsieh K'o-nien survived in T'ai. In 1136 he was recommended for an official appointment, but he subsequently died. His son, Hsieh Chieh, and Chieh's three sons, according to Yeh Shih, were without clothing and food and depended on others to support their aged mother. In 1212, in the course of revising the local history, the prefect learned of them and received them formally. He provided them with clothing, money, and rice, bought land for them to live on, and enshrined Hsieh Liang-tso in the school.[24] Other sources say that fifty years later, in 1262, the prefect established Shang-ts'ai Academy to continue the sacrifices to Hsien Liang-tso.[25]

In the final years of the Southern Sung, a complex web of cross-regional ties was represented at Shang-ts'ai Academy.[26] When the academy was founded, court approval was granted for Yang Tung (1229 *chin-shih*), then serving as chief councillor, to become headmaster.[27] Yang Tung was a descendant of the illustrious Mei-chou Yang, members of the Ssu-ch'uan elite diaspora described by Paul Smith.[28] Yang Tung had served earlier as judicial intendant of Fu-chien and prefect of Fu and Hsing-hua, where he established Han River Academy, and he had also been prefect of Wu.[29] Wang Po from Wu, who earlier had managed Beautiful Pools Academy there and was later known as one of the Four Masters of Chin-hua (see chapter 2), became headmaster (*t'ang-chang*) of Shang-ts'ai.[30] While at the academy, Wang Po became the teacher of his successor, Wang Pen, a scholar from T'ien-t'ai County in T'ai.[31] Wang Pi (fl. ca. 1250s) from Wu was another student of Wang Po who studied with him at Shang-ts'ai Academy.[32] One final detail on the academy's personnel concerns Wang Yueh (1220 *chin-shih*) from Hsin-ch'ang in Yueh Prefecture, who was invited by Tu-tsung to become headmaster at Shang-ts'ai in 1271.[33] Wang Yueh hailed from the ancestral home of the Shih lineage, who had an outstanding record of degree success.[34] During the mid-eleventh century, Shih Ya-chih (1042 *chin-shih*) moved to Lin-hai in T'ai and founded Stone Drum Academy there.[35] A descendant of the Shih of Hsin-ch'ang, Shih Yen (1128–1182; 1145 *chin-shih*), traced his family residence in Lin-hai County to his grandfather's generation.[36] Like other immigrants to the area, Shih Yen's grandfather had moved to Lin-hai around the time of the fall of the Northern Sung.

People associated with Shang-ts'ai Academy exhibited cross-regional ties within Che-tung that extended most noticeably southwest to neighboring Wu, but that also stretched north to Yueh. Connections beyond Che-tung extended to neighboring Fu-chien as well as distant Ssu-ch'uan. Yang Tung and Wang Pi both held office in Fu-chien around the same time, and both established academies there.[37] A good example of the cross-regional network that was shaped by the larger historical context of the mid-thirteenth century is Chang Hsu (1236–1302), a refugee from Ssu-ch'uan whose father migrated to the southeast at the time of the Mongol invasions of Ssu-ch'uan in the 1230s.[38] Although a child prodigy who was introduced to Chen Te-hsiu when still quite young, Chang Hsu nevertheless failed the special *chin-shih* examination given to Ssu-ch'uan refugee scholars. After this, his education was aided by Yang Tung, a fellow Ssu-ch'uan native and former headmaster of Shang-ts'ai, who encouraged him to study with Wang Po at the academy.[39] The reconstruction of these connections among individuals active at Shang-ts'ai highlights the importance of bonds among people who were from the same place, had held office in the same area, or were students of the same teachers. The reconstruction also suggests that the academy provided an important setting for the continuous reweaving of the fabric of local elite identity, incorporating new threads represented by individuals from as close as neighboring counties and prefectures or as distant as the Ssu-ch'uan basin. The cumulative nature of teacher-student ties—the layering of scholarly generations—is exemplified by Wang Po and his students, who in turn created their own secondary networks among those they influenced.

The pattern that emerges from the evidence of Shang-ts'ai Academy began with the sojourning in T'ai of descendants of Hsieh Liang-tso, one of the Four Masters of the Ch'eng school, whose home was in the north. His descendants moved south at the fall of the Northern Sung, and future generations continued to reside in T'ai. A decade after the rescinding of the False Learning prohibition in 1202, the prefect recognized their ancestor by declaring sacrifices to him at the prefectural school. Fifty years later, near the end of Li-tsung's reign, which witnessed widespread court support and recognition of academies, Shang-ts'ai was formally established by the prefect to commemorate Hsieh Liang-tso. The establishment was significant in two ways. First, Lin-hai, Hsieh Liang-tso's adoptive home, where he died and where his descendants fled at the fall of the Northern Sung, was recognized, initially through school sacrifices and ultimately through the founding of an academy. The veneration of Hsieh Liang-tso at Shang-ts'ai associated T'ai with the transmission of the learning of the Ch'eng brothers, just as Yang Shih, also one of the Four Masters of the Ch'eng school, was venerated at academies in Fu-chien. This process provided a ritual integration of Northern and Southern Sung, linking T'ai to the True Way orthodoxy that gained widespread acceptance during Li-tsung's reign. Second, the establishment of an academy in the mid-thirteenth century provided support and legitimacy not only to the heirs of Hsieh Liang-tso, but also to other scholarly sojourners in T'ai. In the volatile political and social circumstances of the thirteenth century, academies continued to be a source of occupation and identity for *shih*, in addition to places where "former worthies" such as Hsieh Liang-tso were venerated.

Notable among the first major group of sojourners who moved south at the fall of the Northern Sung was Yin Ch'un (1071–1142).[40] Although he lived a generation later and the political circumstances that forced him to sojourn in the south were different, he, like Hsieh Liang-tso, was a Northern Sung scholar of the Ch'eng school who became the object of veneration at his grave sometime after his death. Tiger Hill Academy in Su-chou was established at a shrine to Yin Ch'un by the prefect Ts'ao Pin (1170–1249; 1202 *chin-shih*) when he served as fiscal intendant of Che-hsi around 1235.[41] Both Hsieh Liang-tso and Yin Ch'un were venerated at academies established in the thirteenth century to commemorate their sojourning in the south after the fall of the Northern Sung.

The Southern Sung poet Hsin Ch'i-chi (1140–1207) belonged to the next generation of sojourners, those who traced their family origins to the north, but who were born after the fall of the Northern Sung. Near the end of the Southern Sung, Kuang-hsin Academy was built at the former residence of Hsin Ch'i-chi, whose forebears, like the early Southern Sung chief councillor Lü I-hao, originally came from Chi-nan in the Shantung peninsula.[42] According to an inscription on the academy by Tai Piao-yuan, the location drew many sojourners:

> Kuang-hsin lies at the crossroads of Chiang, Min, and Liang-che. At another time [fall of Northern Sung], the eminent *shih ta-fu* of the Central Plain moved south and in large numbers sojourned [*ch'iao-chü*] here. The site of Chi-nan Hsin Yu-an's [Ch'i-chi] residence is a most flourishing central place. . . . At that time [when Hsin lived here] literati culture converged in Kuang-hsin, and its fame reached to the four directions. The many followers of Chu Hsi came and Chia-hsuan [Hsin Ch'i-chi] ardently followed them. Thereupon, Goose Lake rose in the east and Elephant Mountain in the west. Scholars hid themselves [here], and our country was regarded as the [ancient] districts of Chu and Ssu. But the dwelling of Chia-hsuan soon became dilapidated, and his family was not able to keep it. In 1271 prefect T'ang Chen of K'uai-chi, because of the litigations of powerful people [*hao-min*], examined the [land] registers, and thus this site became official land. In the next year a *ching-she* was built to house students, and then a Confucian altar [*fu-tzu yen-chü*] and a shrine to former True Way

> Confucians [*tao-hsueh ju hsien tz'u*] were added. After T'ang left, P'o-yang Li Yang-lei came and completed it. The name plaque read: Kuang-hsin Academy. It was the spring of 1274.[43]

Several things should be noted here. First, the location of Hsin as a "crossroads" naturally drew many sojourning literati fleeing the north. A brief notice in the *Case Studies of Sung and Yuan Scholars* lends credence to the view of Hsin as a center of scholarly refuge in the late thirteenth century. A reference to an obscure scholar named Yang Ying-kuei, from I-yang County in Hsin, states that at the end of the Southern Sung "Jao and Hsin were the 'hideouts' (literally, caves) of the *shih ta-fu* of Chiang-tung."[44] This made it a prime location for academies, if we consider providing temporary lodging and employment to displaced literati or officials as one of the major functions of Southern Sung academies. Such evidence helps to explain why both Jao and Hsin—areas not noticeably identified with any prominent intellectual group or individual thinker (apart from Lu Chiu-yuan in Hsin)—show one of the heaviest concentrations of academies in the Southern Sung. Second, a sequence of events took place with regard to the founding of Kuang-hsin that was repeated in similar patterns elsewhere. The residence of a venerated scholar was threatened by "powerful families," a situation that typically occurred close to the end of Southern Sung, when social order broke down and opened up possibilities for the usurpation of land. A local official—often, and in this case, the prefect—stepped in and was able to have the property under dispute turned over to the authorities to become official land. This act was then sanctioned by the erection of a shrine to the scholar, and an academy that was named for the scholar.

Shang-ts'ai, Tiger Hill, and Kuang-hsin Academies all were founded in the period between 1235 and the fall of the Southern Sung in 1275. Local officials established them to commemorate a thinker (Hsieh Liang-tso), an official (Yin Ch'un), and a poet (Hsin Ch'i-chi). Only Hsieh Liang-tso was known primarily as a thinker; both Yin Ch'un and Hsin Ch'i-chi were literati who held office, but who were known best by their reputations as loyalist patriots. All were originally northerners, at least by ancestry if not by birth, and all became the focus of ritual veneration in academies established to commemorate them during the last two reigns of the Southern Sung, as it became increasingly important to consolidate support among local elites. The founding and support of academies by local officials reaffirmed a sense among local elites (including sojourners) of common social identity as *shih* as well as political identity with imperial concerns, particularly as the Mongol threat grew. By the 1220s, tensions with the Mongols led to a second wave of sojourners fleeing military chaos along the northern borders. Unlike those scholarly sojourners who fled south at the fall of the Northern Sung, and who were later commemorated in shrines and academies, and unlike prominent individuals such as Yang Tung and Chang Hsu, who fled with their families from Ssu-ch'uan to the southeast, these men moved in a mass migration from threatened areas to relatively safe ones nearby, taking refuge in academies that had been specially established for them.

Border Academies and Refugee Scholars

In 1234–1236 Mongol attacks on the borders of Southern Sung precipitated an influx of refugees from the Huai region to the southeast. The vice minister of the Court of Imperial Sacrifices, Kung Chi-hsien, led the establishment of Huai-hai Academy in Tan-t'u County (Jun, Che-hsi) for displaced scholars fleeing military disorder in Huai-nan.[45] Kung Chi-hsien was originally from Kao-yao County in Huai-tung but had moved to Jun. Considering his own background, he was probably unusually sympathetic with the plight of scholars from Huai-nan. The senior compiler of the palace library, Chang Yen (1226 *chin-shih*), who cooperated with Kung Chi-hsien in establishing the academy, was from Jun, but his ancestors before his father's generation had migrated from Huai, and thus he, like Kung Chi-hsien, had ties to the region.[46] When Huai-hai Academy was renewed in 1248 and granted a name plaque by Li-tsung, Chia Ssu-tao was military commissioner for Liang-Huai and allotted fifty thousand strings of cash to support the academy.[47] The local history states that "the annual income was rich," although there is no record of a land endowment or other sources of support.[48]

Heaven Gate Academy in Tang-t'u County (T'ai-p'ing, Chiang-tung) was founded in 1246 by the prefect "as a place to train sojourning Huai scholars" (*wei Huai-shih liu-yü-che i-ye-chih suo*).[49] Wu Yuan, who rebuilt and enlarged Illumined Way Academy, requested a name plaque for Heaven Gate in 1249. Later, Ma Kuang-tsu, like Wu Yuan a key figure at Illumined Way, and Chiang Wan-li, a founder of White Egret Islet Academy, contributed to the expansion of Heaven Gate. Although Heaven Gate (like Huai-hai) was established specifically to provide a place for scholars fleeing the Huai region, officials who supported other kinds of academies elsewhere took an active role there. Hsu Li, who assisted the prefect in the renewal of Huai-hai in 1248, later became prefect of Jun and in 1253 established Lien-hsi Academy (named for Chou Tun-i) in Tan-t'u County there "to provide a residence for scholars from everywhere" (*i-chü ssu-fang-chih shih*).[50] These connections highlight not only the unsurprising fact that individuals who founded, restored, or supported one academy were likely to be involved with others throughout the spans of their official careers, but also the diversity of origins and purpose that the academy movement encompassed and the multiple communities that academies served: itinerant and refugee *shih* as well as promoters of True Way Learning. At the same time, the convergence of different aspects of academies can be seen in the erection of a shrine at Heaven Gate to the seven True Way patriarchs: Chou Tun-i, Chang Tsai, the Ch'eng brothers, Chang Shih, Lü Tsu-ch'ien, and Chu Hsi.[51]

In 1242 the pacification commissioner Meng Kung (1195–1246) led efforts to create an academy—Kung-an Academy—to succor refugee scholars from Ch'eng-tu in Ssu-ch'uan, which had been invaded by the Mongols in 1236.[52] It was founded in Kung-an County (Ching, Hu-pei) at a shrine venerating the Northern Sung military hero, K'ou Chun (961–1023).[53] Another academy, Nan-yang, also founded by Meng Kung at the same time as Kung-an to support scholars fleeing from war, was built in neighboring Chiang-ling County at a site where Chu-ko Liang had lived.[54] Kao Ssu-te (1229 *chin-shih*) wrote an inscription commemorating the two academies, both of which were awarded name plaques from Li-tsung:

> Since we have had military difficulties, ninety percent of the men of Hsiang and Shu have been "blood in the tiger's

> mouth." Those who were fortunate enough to avoid this have gathered in Ching and E. Everyone who fled here is poor, but especially the scholars. Therefore, pacification commissioner Meng Kung was sympathetic, and wherever they gathered he built a place for them to study. The one at Kung-an was named "Kung-an Academy." It was the old site of a sacrificial altar to K'ou Chun. The one at Wu-ch'ang [E] was called Nan-yang Academy. Thus it took [Chu-ko Liang's] place as a name. Kung-an housed those from Shu; and Nan-yang, those from Hsiang. They reported it to the court and requested name plaques. It was granted.[55]

The statistics on these academies suggest fairly large institutions with substantial endowments. Kung-an was sixty *ying* (columns or pillars) in size, with over two thousand piculs of tax rice allocated annually, plus profits from mountain marshes and two million cash. It supported 120 men.[56] Nan-yang had more than sixty ying in buildings, and substantially more support: over six thousand piculs of tax rice, profit from fish ponds and mountain marshes, and four million cash. Nan-yang supported only twenty more men than Kung-an, despite the fact that it had an allocation of three times the tax rice and double the cash.[57] Li Tseng-po's inscription on Kung-an, written on the occasion of its renewal in 1251, calls it Kung-an Bamboo Grove Academy, for the bamboo grove that was said to have sprung up magically at the grave of K'ou Chun.[58] As he did later at Huai-hai's renewal, Chia Ssu-tao supported Kung-an Bamboo Grove by allotting money to the granary.[59] The academy apparently doubled in size in less than a decade, if the numbers Li Tseng-po cites are accurate. According to him, the buildings were 123 *ying* (twice the original size), and they included a hall for the performance of school rites, a public lecture hall, gates, verandas, four sacrificial altars, and eight dormitories.[60]

All of these academies—Huai-hai, Heaven Gate, Kung-an Bamboo Grove, and Nan-yang—were founded to support refugee scholars fleeing warfare in the mid-thirteenth century. All were initiated by relatively highly placed officials and received government support, including name plaques from the court. The sites of both Kung-an Bamboo Grove and Nan-yang were associated with military heroes. The rhetoric of the commemorative inscriptions emphasizes the heroism of these figures, especially that of K'ou Chun, whose struggle against the Khitan paralleled the struggle of men of the late Southern Sung against the Mongols. The inscriptions also place the academies in an appropriate classical context by quoting or referring to *Mencius*, the *Analects*, and so on, but it is clear they were primarily places for refugee scholars. We can speculate that officials were motivated to establish them not only out of humanitarian concerns but also because the influx of a group of scholars might well enhance the local cultural climate and shore up the crumbling foundations of imperial legitimacy in the face of Mongol assaults. Certainly substantial resources were allotted to these academies at a time when there must have been financial pressures because of the military emergencies. As Huang K'uan-ch'ung has shown, the Southern Sung court was ambivalent about the loyalties of people fleeing the north, but as the Mongol threat grew in the thirteenth century and the state weakened, the court was forced to try to accommodate refugees and gain their allegiance, rather than attempt to impose restrictions on them.[61] The economic and military value of elite refugees was apparent, but their cultural role as inheritors of the legacy of Chinese tradition was also important.[62]

Academies and the Politics of *Chiao-hua*

In the thirteenth century, as relations with the Mongols deteriorated, the authority of the central government to maintain local order declined and banditry and rebellion increased. The careers of many people associated with academies in various regions were characterized by actions against rebels. The commemoration of such actions may be seen as one aspect of the cultural integration of Southern Sung elite society, since these officials' actions represented the interests of local elites in maintaining order, especially as the power of the central government to maintain local order waned. Hsu Yuan-shu (1194–1245; 1232 *chin-shih*), who was venerated at an academy established by his son in his home county of Shang-jao (Hsin, Chiang-tung), was active in the suppression of rebels when he was prefect of

Nan-chien (Fu-chien) in 1241.[63] Hsu Yuan-shu lectured at Yen-p'ing Academy in Nan-chien, and eventually there was a shrine to him in the prefecture.[64]

While prefect of Jun in the 1240s, Wang Yeh supported Huai-hai and Mount Mao Academies, and later, in 1253, wrote an inscription on Illumined Way. Earlier, when he was prefect of Chien-ning (Fu-chien), he had established Chien-an Academy there. In addition to his active promotion of academies, Wang Yeh's biographers in the dynastic history noted his success in suppressing bandit activity in Fu-chien, suggesting a link with his subsequent military career: "When bandits arose in T'ing and Shao, he was put in charge of Shao-wu County, and later the commandery. The bandits arose in T'ang-shih and he personally managed the troops. Later he was made junior compiler in the Bureau of Military Affairs, concurrently examining editor. When there was a military emergency in Hsiang and Shu, he was deputed to the peace talks."[65]

Wang Yeh's predecessor in supporting the renewal of Mount Mao Academy, Sun Tzu-hsiu, was also noted for quelling rebel groups of various kinds.[66] A brief sketch of some of the highlights of Sun Tzu-hsiu's career as a local official is instructive in gaining a sense of how the support of academies fit into the broad range of actions cited by official biographers. Sun Tzu-hsiu's first appointment was to the post of registrar of Wu County in Su. He surely earned the favor of the prefect, Wang Sui (1202 *chin-shih*), when he destroyed a local cult Wang had been unable to control:[67] "There were strange [*yao*] people who were called the 'Water Spirit Grand Brigade' [*shui-hsien t'ai-pao*]. Wang Sui wanted to control them, but he dared not carry it out. Sun Tzu-hsiu enthusiastically asked to do it. He burned their huts, demolished their images, and drowned them in Lake T'ai. He [sarcastically] said, 'This truly is like the "water spirit"!' The cult was accordingly destroyed."[68] He subsequently became magistrate of Chin-t'an County, where Mount Mao Academy was located and which, coincidentally, was also the home of Wang Sui. Sun Tzu-hsiu's service to Wang Hsiu likely was advantageous to Sun, if not in getting the post, then in carrying out his duties there. Sun Tzu-hsiu's biographers in the dynastic history note that in Chin-t'an he "encouraged schools, transforming [local customs] through education (*chiao-hua*), and carried out the local libation rites (*hsiang yin-chiu li*)."[69] In line with this, he visited the ruins of the former Mount Mao Academy and renewed it "to serve traveling scholars from distant places."[70]

Like Sun Tzu-hsiu and a number of other officials who supported academies, Lu Tzu-i, who was the son of the Southern Sung poet Lu Yu and who established Angling Terrace Academy at a shrine to the Han eremite Yen Kuang in 1228 while prefect of Yen,[71] had prior experience as an official with demon-quelling and the suppression of local religious practices associated with shamanism. During his tenure as magistrate of Li-yang County in Chiang-ning (Chiang-tung), he destroyed a profane cult and set up a school in order to transform local customs.[72] By then, Chu Hsi's disciple, Ch'en Ch'un, had given a famous series of lectures there, and followers of Lu Hsiang-shan were active in the area as well.[73]

In at least one notable case, the suppression of domestic rebellion by a local official led to the establishment of an academy to venerate him. Ch'en Wei (ca. 1180–1261), who built Former Worthies Academy in Kan at the southern end of the Kan River basin at the site of a scholar's study, was also associated with the founding of a far less conventional academy in Fu-chien.[74] As specially appointed pacification commissioner, Ch'en Wei led a successful campaign to suppress bandits in the Fu-chien hinterland in 1229–1230.His success was attributed to his skillful military strategy, commemorated in the establishment of Sleeping Dragon Academy, named for Chu-ko Liang, the famous strategist of the Three Kingdoms period.[75] An image of Chu-ko Liang was placed in the academy, and phrases from his writings were inscribed on the wall. The academy functioned partly as a shrine to Chu-ko Liang and to commemorate the success of Ch'en Wei, and partly as a school for teaching the strategic skills associated with Chu-ko Liang. The erection of an academy to commemorate the actions of an official, and the focus on a historic model of strategic skill, were part of the process of "deifying" a human figure recognized for his administrative or military leadership.

Another layer is added to this story by Chen Te-hsiu's fortuitous recording in 1231 of an account of a "shrine to a living person" (*sheng-*

t'zu)[76] that was erected to venerate Ch'en Wei.[77] After repeating the story of Ch'en Wei's strategic success in eradicating the bandits in Fu-chien, Chen Te-hsiu describes the steps taken by the people of Yen-p'ing to honor Ch'en, and notes the historical precedents drawn upon by them:

> The scholars and people of Yen-p'ing gathered to plan, and said: "The merit [*kung-te*][78] of Ch'en was received by seven [prefectures of] Min, but ours received the most. How could we ignore that extreme benevolence?" Therefore, they divined the old site of the Dragon Ford postal station to the east of the prefectural city to make a "shrine to a living person" for sacrificing to his image. They took the T'ang precedent of Ti Liang-kung [Ti Jen-chieh] to name its hall . . . for the people of Chien loved Ch'en Wei as the people of Wei loved Ti Jen-chieh.[79]

Ti Jen-chieh (630–700) was a model upright and talented T'ang minister who faithfully served his sovereign, Empress Wu, even when her policies were questionable, trying to moderate her mistakes and encourage wiser courses of action.[80] Even though Ch'en Wei was not in as high or difficult a position as Ti Jen-chieh, Chen Te-hsiu presented him as beloved of the local population, and in this way conferred on him some of the aura of greatness surrounding the idealization of the scholar-official embodied in the career of Ti Jen-chieh.[81] When Ch'en Wei heard that a shrine was being erected in his honor, he modestly argued that he had only been doing his duty and thus did not merit such attention, but the people, according to Chen Te-hsiu, persisted. Not only did they draw an image of him to be venerated at the shrine, they also added images of the fiscal intendant for Fu-chien, Shih Mi-chung (d. 1244), a cousin of the chief councillor, Shih Mi-yüan (1164–1233), and the military commissioner for western Huai, Tseng Shih-chung.

What did it mean for an official to be worshipped as an image at a shrine? How did this differ from shrines to local deities? That so orthodox a thinker as Chen Te-hsiu would write as positively as he did about such a practice suggests that it was relatively common and one that elicited no censure from True Way ideologues. But it is the latter part of this inscription that reveals the cosmological interpretation of Ch'en Wei's success and thus sheds some light on the religious and intellectual dimensions of this kind of shrine-building activity:

> Ch'en clearly obtained the great merit of the empire from Heaven. From the time he was small he was extraordinary. . . . His talents and simplicity went beyond others. . . . [When he responded to the crisis] . . . it was the determination [*ming*] of myriad vital spirits [*sheng-ling*]. Thus his sincerity and talent converged. It is appropriate that he was able to manage great affairs. The former classicists said: "What will be wrought by Heaven in the transformation of our world, will be produced by its men." The bandits rose in Min, and Ch'en was born in Min. Heaven truly engaged Ch'en in order to carry out its transformation. His pure loyalty was Heaven's heart manifested in him. . . . Heaven and man's mutual convergence is just like this. It was fitting that he be able to complete the great merit. Alas! How can we attribute this simply to chance?[82]

The point is clear: Heaven only operates through men, and thus men can be worshipped as manifestations of, and agents of, Heaven's will.

Although at times academies were built by officials who had acted to suppress popular cults or other religious practices, destructive banditry or rebellion, such as that quelled by Ch'en Wei, was equally harmful to both elites and common people. Therefore, the actions of an official such as Ch'en Wei were regarded with appreciation by common people as well as the elite, at least according to official sources. More often, however, *chiao-hua* was likely to be directed at the transformation of popular culture. An inscription by Wen T'ien-hsiang (1236–1283) on Peace Lake Academy in Hsing-kuo County of Kan Prefecture in the Kan River basin provides a good example of this: "The Confucian temple in Kan's Hsing-kuo County is at the north gate of the county seat. The people of five of the six cantons [*hsiang*] come there to study and chant. They are 'attired in Confucian elegance.' Two hundred *li* to the east there is I-mien canton . . . [its people are rough and ungovernable]. . . . In 1272 Lin-ch'uan He Shih came to govern. He sympathetically said: 'If these people cannot be transformed, then the Way of Heaven-endowed nature [*hsing*] and fate [*ming*] will fade away.'"[83] The magistrate observed that there was no local school and proceeded to establish Peace Lake. When the building was completed and Confucian rites were held there, "all those who surrounded and watched held their breaths in wonder, and the dark-faced old ones,[84] along with the women and children were all happily transformed."[85] As a sign of its cultural transformation, or "Confucianization," this canton was renamed "*Ju-hsueh*" (Confucian learning)![86]

Hsieh Fang-te's colophon on Chou Pi-ta's inscription on White Egret Islet Academy (see chapter 2) justified the need for additional schools in the form of academies, concluding that: "If you consider that educational transformation (*chiao-hua*) is not complete, how can you say that this is too much?"[87] Liu Ch'en-weng's later inscription on White Egret Islet referred to the undeveloped nature of the area, despite the location of the prefectural center on a major transportation route: "Even though the mountains and valleys are barren and empty, people are crowding in because of the flourishing of this learning."[88] Similarly, late Southern Sung inscriptions on Mount Tai Academy off the coast of Ming Prefecture stress the isolated location of the area and the role of the academy as an outpost of cultural orthodoxy (see chapter 2).

Chiao-hua described a policy carried out by local officials to pacify and culturally integrate inhabitants of not only peripheral zones, such as Ch'ang-kuo in the Chou-shan archipelago, but also central areas, such as Su-chou. In his inscription on Tiger Hill Academy in Su-chou, dedicated to Yin Ch'un, Liu Tsai (1166–1239) ended with the laconic statement that the "[people of] Wu [Su-chou region] are seduced by Buddhism."[89] He praised the official who supported the academy, Emperor Kao-tsung, and finally the transmission of the Way through Yin Ch'un as a means to achieve *chiao-hua*.[90] Liu Tsai stated that Tiger Hill was built in imitation of the system of the "four academies," that land was bought to support it, and that the works of Yin Ch'un and his colleagues were collected in it.[91] He went on to suggest that the academy, with its teaching and collection of books, was a means to combat the spread of Buddhist propaganda.[92] Buddhism was a frequent target of *chiao-hua* promoters, along with other potentially heterodox beliefs among the elite; but *chiao-hua* was also directed at populations conventionally characterized as litigious, licentious, or otherwise disorderly, such as those who lived where Peace Lake was built in Kan's Hsing-kuo County. Academy-building was a major aspect of *chiao-hua* policy, reflected in the actions of numerous local officials who both suppressed rebels or religious heterodoxy and also established academies. Even though these two kinds of activities often were not necessarily carried out in the same region by the same officials, they can be seen as two poles of *chiao-hua*: suppression of rebels and religious heterodoxy was the reactive policy, while building academies was the proactive one. Although at one time such independent actions may have been perceived as inimical to the interests of the central government, as evidenced by Yü Ch'ou's memorial in the early thirteenth century (see beginning of this chapter), by the reign of Li-tsung this was no longer the case. Certainly from the more distant perspective of the dynastic history, officials who built academies as part of a general policy of *chiao-hua* were praised for this, not condemned.

Conclusion

The enshrinment of Hsieh Liang-tso in the T'ai prefectural school, and later the establishment of Shang-ts'ai Academy dedicated to him, transformed this Northern Sung disciple of the Ch'eng brothers into a cultural symbol associated with the transmission of orthodoxy from the northern heartland. Loyalist heroes such as the official Yin Ch'un and the poet Hsin Ch'i-chi were similarly appropriated through the establishment of academies to them. The manipulation of such cultural symbolism was a means to restore legitimacy to the imperial government in the face of persistent military and financial pressures associated with the Mongol threat. By the mid-thirteenth century, as the Mongol threat intensified, academy-building became an enterprise associated with the maintenance of cultural legitimacy. Framed in the context of *chiao-hua*, both local officials and high-ranking statesmen of the central government founded, restored, and supported academies, eager to shore up support among *shih* by offering them educational resources in addition to prefectural and county government schools. From an alternative perspective, that of the *shih*, thirteenth-century academies were sites of both cross-regional and local networks, playing an important role in the integration of *shih* society, not only for increasing numbers of sojourners but also for resident *shih*. Both sojourners and refugee scholars, such as those at Huai-hai, Heaven Gate, Kung-an Bamboo Grove, and Nan-yang Academies, were coopted by officials who, through their support of academies, defused potentially disruptive social forces.[93] Academies founded to aid refugee scholars or to house itinerant ones provided a means to support the cultural legitimacy of the Southern Sung state as well as provide for the social integration of an influx of *shih* from one region to another.

The founding of academies in the thirteenth century was also a means to consolidate local social order, as shown in the example of Peace Lake. An academy also could be used to commemorate the restoration of order through the efforts of an official, as in the well-documented example of Sleeping Dragon in southwestern Fu-chien. The founding and support of academies was an important dimension of the activities of local officials in promoting *chiao-hua*, whether to integrate local elites in officially sanctioned ideology or as a means to temper local customs seen as inimical to state interests in promoting social order. Local officials who were cited in their biographies for the suppression of popular cults were often also noted for their support of academies. Thus the dynamics of elite and popular cultural relations were mediated through the institution of academies. The manipulation of cultural symbols—True Way thinkers, loyalist heroes, and so on—by local officials dovetailed with policies pursued by Li-tsung and Tu-tsung in the last two reigns of the Southern Sung, as they conferred imperial recognition on academies throughout the Southern Sung empire. These academies ranged widely in scale, origin, and function, but they were appropriated in common by the central government to consolidate its cultural legitimacy.

To what extent local officials, by their support of academies, may have served their own individual interests or those of local elites they governed, independent of concerns about imperial cultural legitimacy, is unclear. At the very least, the interests of individual officials and local elites overlapped with those of the central government insofar as support for and recognition of academies was concerned. Both local elites who aspired either to maintain or achieve *shih* status and immigrant *shih* who needed to establish themselves in new surroundings found in academies a means to accomplish this by participating in the rituals of education once focused on success in the examinations, but now broadened to a general emphasis on the cultivation of scholarship distinct from service. Although from the perspective of the state academies were cultural resources to be appropriated and controlled—through the granting of names and the appointment of headmasters—academies were also sites for the social integration of the *shih* community and for the reconstruction of *shih* identity in the conditions of the late Southern Sung.

6

ACADEMIES AND THE LEARNING OF THE *SHIH* CA. 1225–1275

Although few records remain of the content of academy teaching in the thirteenth century, fifteen extant lectures, ten of which were given at Illumined Way Academy, suggest how philosophical concepts were transmitted to academy audiences by both scholars invited to lecture and officials who served as academy administrators. Through interpretations of classical texts that validated the role of the *shih* in Southern Sung society, lectures given at thirteenth-century academies articulated the ideological basis of a new *shih* identity. Lecturers concentrated almost exclusively on discussion of passages from the *Four Books*. A text was selected from one of the *Four Books* as the basis for commentary explicating not only what constituted learning but also how the *shih* should act. *Shih* were exhorted to strive for self-cultivation without the guarantee of material rewards in the form of degrees and office. How did lectures at academies resonate with the lives of *shih* in the thirteenth century? How did ideas expounded by academy lecturers give meaning to the intellectual culture and social world of the *shih*? These discussions often included oblique—at times direct—criticism of the conduct of contemporary political affairs, education, and the examination system. While illuminating anxieties that surfaced in the thirteenth century concerning the role and status of the *shih*, the lectures also demonstrate the application of ideas derived from classical texts to the social and political concerns of the *shih*. Close scrutiny of these lectures, along with background on the people who presented them and the academies at which the lectures were given, provides concrete evidence of these concerns as they were voiced in the formal setting of academy convocations, often at the "opening rites" ceremonies.

True Way Learning: Lectures at Illumined Way Academy, ca. 1225–1275

Ten lectures given at Illumined Way Academy from the 1250s through the 1260s, at the annual "opening of the hall" (*k'ai-t'ang*) ceremony, were presented by individuals who held concurrent posts as headmaster of the academy and one of several regional appointments, such as pacification commissioner of Chiang-tung. These lectures probably had more to do with institutional formalities than with educational content, much like annual convocation speeches at modern academic institutions. Nevertheless, also like their modern equivalents, the lectures do shed some light on contemporary social and educational concerns and suggest how it was believed the *shih* should act as well as how they should view their obligations to society.

The first lecture, which is anonymous and undated, takes its text from the *Great Learning* and the *Doctrine of the Mean*.[1] Beginning with the opening passage from the *Great Learning*, the author immediately turns to discussion of the hexagrams, heaven (*ch'ien*) and earth (*k'un*), from the *Changes*. He relates this both to the proper behavior of the gentleman and to the content of learning:

> Heaven and earth in the *Changes* are the nature [*hsing*] and responsive circumstances [*ch'ing*] of heaven and earth. The image of heaven says: heaven acts with strength. The gentleman by his own strength does not rest and thereby imitates heaven. The image of earth says: earth is strong and "earthly." The gentleman by his broad virtue leads things and thereby regulates the earth. . . . What men study is heaven and earth. . . .
>
> Learning begins with imitating and modeling [oneself after] the forms [*hsiang*] of heaven and earth. It ends with attaining heaven and earth. From this one achieves a position. [Learning] begins with exhaustively investigating the principles of the myriad things, and culminates in the myriad things being cultivated. It begins in the expansion of learning by the investigation of things [*ko-wu chih-chih*], sincere intention [*ch'eng-i*], upright mind [*cheng-hsin*], and self-cultivation [*hsiu-shen*]; and is completed in the household being regulated, the state ordered, and all-under-heaven pacified.[2]

Following the Ch'eng brothers (and Chu Hsi), universal principle is identified with human nature, and the "myriad events" with "circumstances."[3] Both are brought together in "mind," which is derived from heaven, and thus is called "virtuous." After a detailed explication of the opening passage of the *Great Learning*, phrase by phrase, the author takes up more specific contemporary affairs, beginning with the social background of prominent men from the region:

> Many of the famous families from Chin-ling [modern Nanking] established themselves in the south during the Six Dynasties, not to mention our dynasty's great Confucian Ch'eng [Hao], who held office in this area. During the Hsi-ning era [1068–1077], Prime Minister Wang [An-shih] lodged here. The various gentlemen in their travels passed by Wild Pear Garrison's Snowy Cedar Temple in Shang-yuan County [Chien-k'ang]. They also knew how to distinguish between the learning of Master Ch'eng and Master Wang. I am ignorant, but I have heard that Master Ch'eng put first the bequeathed words of the *Great Learning*, exhorting people to express them and carry them out in the policies they adopted, thus penetrating and carrying out the [ways of] the hundred

> kings without change or corruption. The learning of Wang relied on forced clarification and produced new meanings, creating [false] clarity by bringing chaos to the ancient texts in order to update the classics. This corrupted the mind of the *shih* and caused it to decay.[4]

The point here is that Ch'eng Hao transmitted the true meaning of the classic, while Wang An-shih distorted ancient texts by forcing meanings into them. If the *shih* would pay attention to the dictates of the *Great Learning*, then they would understand the false nature of Wang An-shih's learning and the truth of Ch'eng's.[5]

After citing the first passage of the *Doctrine of the Mean*, and relating this to the sages and rulers of antiquity, our anonymous speaker elaborated on several critical terms:

> How is it that what is decreed by heaven [*t'ien-ming*] is called [human] nature [*hsing*]? What is spontaneously so [*tzu-jan er jan*] is heaven. What is ordered [chih] without being ordered, is fate [*ming*]. What one is born with is [human] nature. What is bestowed on men is called fate. What is endowed in men is called [human] nature. Heavenly decree is just human nature; and human nature is just the decree of heaven. Therefore, it is said that human nature is what is decreed by heaven. How is it that following human nature is called the Way? Human nature is just principle; and principle is just humanity, righteousness, rites, and moral knowledge.[6]

The speaker continued in this vein, explicating each phrase in the opening passage to identify principle (*li*) with human nature and with what is decreed by heaven, thus giving the fundamental concept of *li* a genesis that was unassailable in the decree of Heaven, embodied in human nature. He concluded with the statement that "since Mencius, the one who opened and clarified human nature and principle, with efficacy toward men's minds and supplementing the world's teachings, there is just Master Ch'eng and no other."[7]

Wu Chien (1244 *chin-shih*), who served as headmaster at Illumined Way concurrent with his appointment as pacification commissioner of Chiang-tung in 1252, was the author of the next lecture in the extant series.[8] He was a student of the *Spring and Autumn Annals* who five years later was appointed erudite of the Court of Imperial Sacrifices and assistant in the palace library. Wu Chien's lecture for the "opening of the hall" was based on the famous passage from the *Analects* in which Confucius classified the stages of his life from age fifteen to age seventy according to degrees of wisdom attained. Wu Chien said that this was the Sage's method of teaching people what learning is, and he went on to argue that the most important aspect of learning was not to lose the "original mind" (*pen-hsin*). By this, Wu Chien implied that learning took place in a series of stages moved forward by self-reflection, culminating in restoration of the original mind.

A lecture by Hu Ch'ung, who had held the same concurrent posts as Wu Chien in 1251, focused on the *Great Learning*.[9] Like the anonymous lecture discussed above, Hu Ch'ung took as his text the opening passage of the *Great Learning* and in his own words repeated much of the same commentary as the anonymous lecturer. He concluded with these words: "Going to the hall of Ming-tao [Ch'eng Hao], reading his writings, and reciting his words, thus can one reflect on and seek the entire self and entire mind, open its clarity and diagram its renewal, and return to the place of ultimate goodness."[10]

Chu P'i-sun's (1244 *chin-shih*) lecture in 1254 began on a more pragmatic and practical note than his predecessors, with a description taken from the *Rites of Chou* of how local officials taught in antiquity, pointing out that the recruitment system of antiquity put teaching before selection:[11]

> "The great officers in the local schools [*hsiang*] taught the multitudes the 'three things' and [thereby] raised up candidates for office [*pin-hsing*]. First were the six virtues: knowledge, humanity, sageliness, righteousness, loyalty, and harmony. Second were the six conducts: filial piety, friendship, harmony, affinal love, tolerance, and sympathy. Third were the six arts: rites, music, archery, charioteering, calligraphy, and mathematics." The method of selecting and raising up [candidates] in antiquity was in general to teach them first and select them after. This was the means by which human talents flourished. If they were not to teach [but then] select, it would

> be like not plowing and then harvesting; or like not planting but expecting cultivated fields. This is unreasonable.[12]

Explaining the details of the virtues, conduct, and arts, Chu P'i-sun pointed out that although these three categories are varied in their components, they are unified in a single Way.[13] He continued in a historical mode of argumentation:

> Lacking the teaching of the Chou, the Western Han fell because the Confucian techniques [*ju-shu*] were corrupt. Lacking the teaching of the Chou, the Eastern Han fell because scholars with reputations for moral integrity declined. The Chin lacked the teachings of the Chou, and human talents were weakened by "pure discussions [*ch'ing-t'an*]." High T'ang lacked the teachings of the Chou, and human talents were consumed with literary works. . . . Alas! Although the Chou is distant, how can the [basic] teachings of the "three things" exist or disappear according to the times? When the scholar gentleman [*shih chün-tzu*] is at home, he goes to his local school [*hsiang-tang*]; when he travels, he attends [other] schools [*hsiao*]. All are places for training and teaching.[14]

Chu P'i-sun pointedly described the proper behavior of the *shih* in going to his local school when residing at home and in attending other such schools, presumably academies, when away in office. He concluded his lecture by quoting both Ch'eng brothers on the relationship between teaching and selection:

> Master I-ch'uan said: "Men all say that if someone doesn't teach men [but] selects them for office, then can selection for office be sufficient to award them a degree? If for two days out of ten one is trained for occupation, then the remaining days one only studies." [This was what] Master Ming-tao [Ch'eng Hao] called the "great transformation," and what Master I-ch'uan [Ch'eng I] called study. Now, how can it be something other than the "six virtues," "six conducts," and "six arts?" In order to select according to the teaching of the Chou, one must follow the instructions of the two masters, Ming-tao and I-ch'uan; then can one be considered to have the ability of a worthy.

> The holy Son of Heaven has carried out this [ancient method of] "selecting and raising up to be teachers and administrators [*pin-hsing shih-shuai*]." Furthermore, he is able to use the Way to transform the individual schools of thought of the scholars . . . [and enable them to complete their learning according to the dictates of the Chou teachings].[15]

Chu P'i-sun based his description of learning on what was ascribed to the schools of antiquity, stressing teaching first and selection after. The emphasis, then, was on learning the "three things," the categories of learning that incorporated virtues, conduct, and the arts, presumably in that order. This placed the learning of the *shih* in an orthodox classical setting and reaffirmed the importance of teaching and learning in schools as a prerequisite for holding office, even if office-holding was a less and less credible goal.

The following year, Chao Ju-chou, concurrent headmaster and Chien-k'ang prefectural judge in 1255, presented a short convocation lecture on the first chapter of the *Great Learning*, focusing on *ko-wu chih-chih*, "the expansion of knowledge by the investigation of things." Pan Chi, concurrent headmaster and Chiang-tung military commander, delivered the convocation lecture in 1256, taking his text from commentary on hexagram number twenty-four—*fu* (return)—of the Changes.[17] Revived interest in the *Changes* in Sung times is reflected in his lecture, as Pan Chi cited the *T'uan-chuan* ("Commentary on the hexagram statements"), ending with the line: "Does not *fu* make apparent the mind [*hsin*] of heaven-and-earth?" He went on to discuss the concept of this "mind" at some length, relating it to conceptual categories derived from the cosmology of the *Changes*:

> What is this "mind?" Heaven-and-earth by producing things [*wu*] creates mind and thereby gives birth to man. Thus [man] obtains the mind of heaven-and-earth as [his] mind. This being so, then from the Great Ultimate [*t'ai-chi*] first dividing and separating *yin* and *yang*, there were the principles of opening and closing, movement and stillness; revolving without cease, going to the extreme and then returning. [This is] the principle of lacking an end point and also of lacking a pause. Therefore, the former Confucians [*ju*] considered the principle [*tuan*] of movement as the mind of heaven-and-earth.[19]

The gentleman (*chün-tzu*) must nourish *yang* essence (*ch'i*) by regulating himself, and thus he will realize the mind of heaven and earth. Drawing on Mencian notions, Pan Chi continued: "The human mind embodies four principles: empathy, shame, compliance, and a sense of right and wrong. The humanity of these four principles is the origin of the four virtues. It is the same as mind, which is the mind of heaven-and-earth through its production of things."[20] He went on to describe how the gentleman should seek humanity through "return" (the *fu* hexagram), which is interpreted as a return to the Mencian original mind.

Turning to historical themes, Pan Chi said that beginning with the Eastern Han, study of the *Changes* was not transmitted, and so the mind of heaven and earth had not been seen for a thousand years until the time of Ch'eng Hao:[21]

> Ch'eng Hao stayed here in Shang-yuan. For a long time there has been a shrine to him where the gentlemen learn. Annually in *ping-chen* in the eleventh month, on the day *kuei-hsiu*, the sun is at the extreme south. After five days is the first of the twelfth lunar month. *Yang* is hidden, movement is limited, and life begins to return. Because great Confucians of the time who took up the orthodox transmission of the learning of the Way were unjustly judged, Master Yü-chai [Ma Kuang-tsu] placed [images of them] in the upper part of the hall. He ordered me to lecture on the *fu* hexagram in order to observe the mind of heaven-and-earth. . . .
>
> I have heard that *fu* has two meanings. *Fu* is the Way of heaven, and it is also the Way of man. . . . [*F*]*u* is the means by which the movements of the heavens are constant and regular; and *fu* is the means by which the *chün-tzu* strengthens himself without rest. Thus, the Way of heaven has no beginning apart from man.[22]

Pan Chi skillfuly manipulated the *Changes* and its commentarial tradition to develop the notion of "return" as returning to a Mencian original mind, which, in turn and in harmony with the cosmic rhythms described in the *Changes*, placed the learning of the *shih* in a cosmological setting, even as the anonymous author of the first lecture discussed the heaven and earth hexagrams in the *Changes*. Pan Chi also made reference to Ma Kuang-tsu, who erected images in the academy of individuals who had been persecuted politically for their views, thereby commemorating them and preserving their ideas. Pan Chi's reference to this action implied that this, too, was a kind of return, a rehabilitation of reputations.

Chou Ying-ho (1213–1280; 1250 *chin-shih*), who later edited the local history of Chien-k'ang, was concurrent headmaster and pacification commissioner of Chiang-tung in 1259 when he gave the opening lecture, using two passages from the *Analects*.[23] His lecture was unusually long, taking up six double-sided pages in the local history. After citing the opening passage of the *Analects*, Chou Ying-ho discussed the importance of the first chapters, or sections, of writings by the sages. He said that the first task of students must be to grasp this: "[It is essential to] realize [*wu*] what has not been said from what has already been said; to completely realize that the main point of the first section lies in the heading of the first chapter, and that the main point of the head phrase lies in the first character. . . . As 'learning' [*hsueh*] is the first word in the *Analects*, so it should be first for men."[24] Chou Ying-ho went on to define learning as "imitation":

> What is called learning is just imitation [*hsiao*]. To imitate what one ought to imitate is the orthodox [way] of learning. To imitate what one ought not to imitate is the mistaken [way of] learning. To imitate emptiness and extinction in order to be like the "high" is the learning of wrong principles [*tuan*]. To imitate recording what one has heard, words and essays, in order to be like those who boast [of their literary skills] is the learning of contemporary vulgarity. All these are what is imitated and called learning, but this is not what the sages called learning. This [the learning of the sages] lies in clarifying goodness and returning to the beginning.
>
> Everyone is good at the beginning because human nature is derived from heaven. Human nature is principle [*li*], and has nothing that is not good. . . . In order to examine and transform the "psychophysical stuff" [*ch'i-chih*], one must take the sages and worthies as models . . . like Yen-tzu, Yin I, and so on. . . . As Confucius said: "King Wen is my teacher."[25]

Having made the argument for imitating past models of sages and worthies as the essence of education, Chou Ying-he castigated Buddhism by reference to "emptiness and extinction" and denigrated the display of literary skill as "contemporary vulgarity," in contrast to the learning of Confucius. He then reflected on the relationship between knowing and ability:

> To know [*chih*] filial piety and brotherliness, one must be practiced [*hsi*] in the affairs [*shih*] of filial piety and brotherliness. . . . One must study the ancients [for models] of this, [and likewise for obtaining the principles of loyalty and sincerity]. . . . But if you imitate without practicing, this is not learning. And if you practice, but don't persevere, it is insufficient to complete learning. This is why *hsueh erh shih hsi* [to learn with constant perseverance and application] is the first phrase of the *Analects*.[26]

Emphasizing the need to examine one's inner self in the process of learning, Chou Ying-ho carefully distinguished between this goal (*wei-chi*) and that of seeking selfish ends (*wei-wo*).[27] The latter results in self-aggrandizement; the former leads to the recovery of man's original goodness. The petty man and the gentleman are distinguished on the basis of this: for example, to feel indignant (*yun*) at not being known (recognized in an admirable way) by men is selfish (*ssu*), and characteristic of the petty man.[28] Chou Ying-ho also suggested that "those who practice are not as good as those who explain," a seemingly overt self-justification.[29]

Chou Ying-ho defined the "good" (*shan*) as the principles (*li*) of humanity, justice, rites, and moral knowledge.[30] Quoting Ch'eng Hao on humanity: "[It is the] root of public good of all-under-heaven. It is what Heaven has decreed to men, and what makes men. Those who have not lost what it means to be a man, then can be considered sages and worthies."[31] What this means is that those who have maintained their original heaven-decreed nature are considered sages and worthies. Ordinary men have lost this nature and must struggle to restore it. This is why the first chapter of the *Analects* discussed the word *hsueh* and why the second and third discussed the word "humanity," because there is nothing in learning apart from humanity.[32] Developing the concept of humanity further, Chou Ying-ho looked more closely at the second and third chapters of the *Analects*, noting that humanity is said to begin with filial piety and brotherliness: "Humanity is like cultivating grain. Filial piety and brotherliness are the sprouts. Humanity to men and love of things are the various grains produced from the sprouts."[33] Finally, he quoted Ch'eng Hao and Chu Hsi, the former on the importance of reading the *Analects* first, using it as a measure for everything else, the latter on his caution that being too "ornate" (in literary ways?) risked losing the virtue of the original mind.[34] Chou Ying-ho also mentioned the patronage of Ma Kuang-tsu, who supported his official career and invited him to lecture at Illumined Way, following his demotion for criticism of Chia Ssu-tao.[35]

Chang Hsien (1244 *chin-shih*) served concurrently as headmaster and as prefectural professor of Chiang in 1259 until 1261.[36] His lecture text for the opening ceremony in 1259 was the twentieth chapter of the *Doctrine of the Mean*.[37] After explicating section nineteen on the steps to attain sincerity (*ch'eng*), Chang Hsien pointed out that the rules for Chu Hsi's White Deer Grotto Academy set forth the five requirements named here for the order of learning at the academy: extensive study, accurate inquiry, careful reflection, clear discrimination, and earnest practice.[38] Chang Hsien emphasized the importance of truth (*shih*) and sincerity in the practice of these five techniques:

> To question without extending [one's knowledge] is not truth. To inquire without care is not truth. To discriminate without clarity is not truth. To carry out without diligence is not truth. The beginning does not lie in discussing high and subtle theories, but only in daily regular carrying out what must be done. The mutual refining of teachers and colleagues by this means [achieves] the true mind. Lecturing on this [achieves] true learning. Working on this [achieves] true nature.[39]

Like his predecessor, Chou Ying-ho, Chang Hsien was a protégé of Ma Kuang-tsu and was recommended by him to Li-tsung for his filial and harmonious qualities, a recommendation that earned him a special appointment to the History Bureau in 1261. Near the close of his lecture, Chang Hsien mentioned the beneficent influence of Ma Kuang-tsu's administration, and the printing of a work of Chen Te-hsiu on mind, along with the true learning of the *Doctrine of the Mean*. Chang Hsien also stated that he had given the opening lecture in 1256, after repeated requests from Ma Kuang-tsu, and that the current lecture (in 1259) repeated some of that.[40]

Hu Li-pen was appointed in 1260 through the Ministry of Personnel to be concurrent headmaster.[41] He took as his text the first passage in the *Great Learning*, following Chu Hsi's commentary explaining what age level this passage referred to and the content of education in antiquity: "What they were taught in the greater school was self-cultivation, the way of ordering men. It was not just 'sprinkling and sweeping, answering and responding, advancing and retreating; rites, music, archery, charioteering, calligraphy, and mathematics.' Thus, the *Great Learning* begins as it does."[42] Hu Li-pen went on to describe the metaphysical background of this educational goal:

> The heavenly Way circulates and gives rise to the myriad things. The means by which it creates and transforms is just *yin*, *yang*, and the Five Phases. What is called *yin*, *yang*, and the Five Phases always has this principle, and later has its "psychophysical stuff." When it comes to producing things, then by the clustering of this *ch'i* afterward, there is this form [*hsing*]. Therefore, the production of people and things obtains this pattern. And, after this, there is the means to strengthen and order the nature [*hsing*], which is benevolent, just, and [attuned to] rites and moral knowledge [*chih*]. Obtaining this *ch'i*, then there is the means to make the body, which is [composed of] the soul [*hun-p'o*], the five viscera [heart, liver, lungs, stomach, kidney], and the hundred bones [skeleton]. *Ch'i* is just the human mind; and *li* is just the mind of the Way [*tao-hsin*].[43]

Finally, although no date is given, Weng Yung was appointed headmaster temporarily through his post as Shang-yuan County sheriff.[44] He also lectured on the first passage from the *Great Learning*: "'Unobscured virtue' [*ming-te*] is what men receive from Heaven. It is the virtue of complete clarity. Chu Hsi described it as 'the empty spirit unobscured' [*hsu-ling pu-mei*]. This means the mind. 'Empty spirit' means its *ch'i*; 'unobscured' means its *li*. . . . If men are sunk in 'psychophysical stuff,' and weakened by material desires [*wu-yü*], they are not able to clarify it on their own [and so they need the process of learning described to help them]."[45] Weng Yung noted that he was a student of the "former teacher," probably referring to Chu Hsi, since he did study with Ts'ai Yuan, a son of Ts'ai Yuan-ting, one of Chu Hsi's major disciples.

All ten lectures at Illumined Way were given by individuals who held concurrent appointments as headmaster and some regional office. In some cases at least—Chang Hsien and Wu Chien, for example—the lecturers went on to be appointed to higher offices. None of the speakers were known as important thinkers in their own right, either at that time or later.[46] But their very unremarkability makes the ideas they expressed useful as an indication of general attitudes and understanding among the *shih*. All addressed the issue of learning for the *shih*. The most frequently cited text was the *Great Learning*, followed by the *Doctrine of the Mean* and the *Analects*. Apart from these texts, one speaker focused on the *Changes* and one cited the *Rites of Chou* and the *Book of Documents*.

Common to all of the lectures was an emphasis on the need for students to develop moral character, in accord with human nature as endowed by heaven. Using the *Great Learning* and other texts as interpreted by the Ch'eng brothers and Chu Hsi, the lecturers presented metaphysical assumptions that supported their exhortations to students to concentrate on the development of moral character. They then explained how students should accomplish this. Both Wu Chien and Hu Ch'ung argued that the purpose of learning was to restore the original mind or to "return to the place of ultimate goodness." Pan Chi's discussion of the *fu* hexagram emphasized the need for students to return to the original mind, the "mind of heaven-and-earth."

Having established the purpose of learning as the restoration of the original mind, students were exhorted to imitate the model of the sages and worthies. The common goal of students should be self-cultivation, the method of restoring original mind. Self-cultivation was what was taught in the "greater schools" of antiquity, according to Hu

Li-pen—not just the ritual behavior of education and particular skills, such as calligraphy and mathematics. Self-cultivation meant preparing for service, not seeking selfish ends. But self-cultivation for service should not be understood as meaning preparing for the examinations, either: this was viewed as falling prey to the desire for profit, in the material terms of official salary and in less concrete terms as public recognition.

Chou Ying-ho went so far as to define learning as imitation, expanding on this concept to link knowledge and ability through practicing what the study of the ancients taught. Chu P'i-sun used the description of teaching in the local schools of antiquity to support the idea that teaching took precedence over selecting, suggesting that virtues and good conduct were taught before the arts, and that teaching in general took place prior to selecting men for office. For Chang Hsien, following Chu Hsi, practice was the final stage in the order of learning to be followed by academy students, at Illumined Way as well as at White Deer Grotto. These steps must be carried out and practiced with sincere effort, in order to achieve the goal of restoring original mind. This could not be accomplished on one's own. As Chang Hsien pointed out, the support of colleagues and friends was essential, as was the process of lecturing. An academy could thus be seen as providing the necessary setting for the intellectual and social support of colleagues and friends and for inspirational lectures.

The learning of the *shih* presented in these lectures is ethical and cosmological/metaphysical, but it is also placed in both historical and classical textual settings. For example, Chu P'i-sun held up the teaching of the Chou as the pedagogical model of antiquity and cited the *Rites of Chou* as its source. The classical textual settings include the *Four Books*, plus the *Changes*, which also provides grounding for the cosmological context. According to both Chen Te-hsiu and Ma Kuang-tsu, heavenly principle was the proper subject of learning, expressed by Ch'eng Hao and taught in the academy dedicated to him. At the same time that students were urged to practice self-cultivation, they were cautioned that they might not have the opportunity, because of political circumstances, to serve. They nevertheless needed to prepare themselves through learning and to carry out what they learned in seclusion, if necessary.

These ideas were not limited to Chien-k'ang commandery and Illumined Way. They resonated in inscriptions and in the few extant lectures that can be documented for other academies in the mid- to late thirteenth century. Like the authors of lectures at Illumined Way, these other writers were not the foremost intellectual figures of their day; but their articulation of contemporary views on learning opens a window on the framing of a new social and cultural identity for *shih*.

CH'EN WEN-WEI AT DRAGON MOUNTAIN, NAN-HSUAN, AND WHITE DEER GROTTO ACADEMIES

Ch'en Wen-wei (1154–1239; 1208–1224 *chin-shih*), a student of Chu Hsi from Shang-jao County in Hsin (Chiang-tung), lectured at Dragon Mountain, Nan-hsuan, and White Deer Grotto Academies in the 1230s.[47] Dragon Mountain in Yung-feng County (Chi, Chiang-hsi) was the family school of the Huang, established in 1221 by Huang Hsing-chih with an endowment of personal property. In the inscription he wrote at the time of its founding, Chen Te-hsiu commented on the proper goals of learning:

> In ancient times the sages . . . put first moral knowledge [*chih*] by lecturing and investigating principle in order to manifest the knowledge of innate mind [*liang-hsin*]. They followed this with [the realization of] humanity through earnest will and energetic action in order to complete the virtue [*te*] of original mind [*pen-hsin*]. . . . In later times, Confucius and Mencius taught in Chu and Ssu and they also put first knowing and humanity. . . . How can those who have set their will on learning do otherwise than to take the sages and worthies as their teachers? . . . I have often contemplated that in high antiquity they did not have examinations as a means to advance [candidates] and select [them]. Scholars [*shih*] practiced on their own. . . . That time is distant and the teachings have been lost. The *shih* know how to make themselves eminent, but not how to refine themselves. They know how to seek after profit, but not how to seek after the Way. The loss of the innate mind stems entirely from this. . . . If one considers only literature and arts or only

> office and rank, as the schools of the prefectures and counties do, it is inadequate.[48]

Chen Te-hsiu then argued that Master Huang, the founder of the school, encouraged teaching of the Way of the former sages and worthies, who were to be followed as exemplars of moral behavior. This was contrasted with current practices that encouraged consideration only of the embellishments of learning (literature and arts) and its rewards (office and rank).

Echoing these ideas, Ch'en Wen-wei gave a lecture based on the *Great Learning* at Dragon Mountain sometime after its founding in 1221 and before his death in 1239.[49] Like Chen Te-hsiu, Ch'en Wen-wei criticized literary learning for its own sake and, following the doctrine of the *Great Learning*, emphasized self-cultivation [*hsiu-shen*] as the essential basis of the political and social order.[50] Like other writers of his day, he also stressed the deleterious effects of the examination system: "From latter ages, the examinations [*k'o-mu*] have been used to select scholars. What has been emphasized is classical learning and literary skills . . . and these do not clarify the dictates of the sacred classics, nor are they able to refine the sagely Way, serving only literary talents. . . . This causes men to seek profit and salary, and to lose true talents."[51] Ch'en Wen-wei suggested that Huang's action in establishing Dragon Mountain came from an admirable desire to counteract this trend by supporting the academy:

> Master Dragon Mountain allotted his own personal funds to open a school. He bought land to support it. He invited teachers to teach, and welcomed excellent scholars from the four quarters. He considered the completion of human talents to be his own personal responsibility. . . . The gathering of the present day is not only by means of culture to associate with colleagues and rectify desires, [but] to support humanity by means of collegiality. The various gentlemen do not shirk the effort of shouldering umbrellas and book satchels to gather together in a group, just like the worthies [of earlier times]. In following affairs it is like the ancients' studying for themselves. The investigation of things, the extension of knowledge, and self-cultivation [means] setting the will on all-under-heaven,

> not on the self alone. This will shine like a bright beacon in generations to come.[52]

Like Chen Te-hsiu, who contrasted the scholars of antiquity—who "trained themselves"—with contemporary scholars who studied only for attaining office and rank through the examinations, Ch'en Wen-wei held up the image of students at the academy coming to seek learning "like the ancients' studying for themselves." Thus the *shih* should strive to emulate the sages and worthies of ancient times and thereby refine themselves, not for selfish purposes, but to carry out the Way in the world.

In the mid-1230s Nan-hsuan Academy was built by the local prefect at a shrine to Chang Shih in I-ch'un County (Yuan, Chiang-hsi), and Ch'en Wen-wei gave a lecture there on the *Doctrine of the Mean*.[53] A lecture he gave at the Yuan prefectural school (also in I-ch'un County), probably around the same time,[54] focused on the *Great Learning*. Following the *Great Learning*, self-cultivation is understood not as an end in itself, but as a means to bring order to the world, and a careful distinction is made by Ch'en Wen-wei between selfishness and service. He criticized Confucians (*ju*) of his own day: "Confucians seen in the present generation are mean; they reside at ease and take their leisure, lacking even a little concern for all-under-heaven and the state. When they do gather to discuss things it is only to make themselves famous and rich, and their discussions are concerned with nothing beyond the household."[55] Ch'en Wen-wei's comment attacked the localized, family-centered concerns of *shih*, who are seen as self-interested rather than dedicated to public service. It is both an acknowledgment of the local focus of elite interests in the thirteenth century and a hortatory reminder to his audience of the origins of their status. He regarded concern with the economic and social welfare of individual households or even lineages as selfish, since the proper focus of their interest should be humanity as a whole. One might even extend this criticism to the community of elite families, concerned only with their own economic and social welfare rather than service to the state.

Ch'en Wen-wei argued that the essential nature of all men, from the sages and worthies to himself, was the same, and that all could thus carry out self-cultivation in order to know how to act. The means to carry out self-cultivation is "the extension of learning by the investigation of things" as described in the *Great Learning*, and is central to Chu Hsi's thinking. The proper duty of the *shih*, according to Ch'en Wen-wei, is to carry out self-cultivation by discovering the inner capacity of human nature ordained by heaven. The transmission of literary texts cannot be used to accomplish the goal of self-cultivation, although clearly classical texts, such as the *Great Learning*, are essential. Furthermore, once the *shih* have completed self-cultivation, the purpose of which is to enable them to know how to act to achieve what is good and just, they should consider the welfare of the empire as their central concern. Quoting both the *Analects* and *Mencius*, and reflecting the conditions of his time, Ch'en Wen-wei acknowledged, however, that often *shih* must adjust to retirement, and being unable to carry out their principles in the world of office and public duty.[56] Citing Mencius, he said that when *shih* are disappointed in their desire for office, they should nevertheless practice their principles in seclusion; and if the opportunity is presented, they should use their self-cultivation to achieve good in the world.

In his lecture at Nan-hsuan, which was based on the *Doctrine of the Mean*, Ch'en Wen-wei emphasized, as he did in much of his extant writing, the concept of sincerity. To carry out the Way, knowledge, humanity (*jen*), and courage (*yung*) were required; all were said to be common to human beings, who must practice them with sincerity, the thread tying all three virtues together.[57] Quoting the *Doctrine of the Mean*, he distinguished among those who are born knowing the Way, those who know it through study, and those who know it only after painful recognition of their ignorance. Similarly, he distinguished among those who carry it out easily and naturally, those who carry it out to gain advantage, and those who carry it out only with strenuous effort.[58] But the end results, he argued, are nonetheless the same, however they were achieved. Thus, although natural endowments may differ, the sages never rejected men on the grounds of these differences, but rather emphasized heaven-endowed humaneness. Quoting the *Doctrine of the Mean* again, Ch'en Wen-wei noted that the love of learning is close to knowing; practicing what one knows with vigor and energy is close to humanity; and knowing shame is close to having courage.[59] The knowledge of these things makes it possible to carry out self-cultivation, and thereby to know how to order state and society. He concluded by pointing out the similarity of the *Great Learning* and the *Doctrine of the Mean* in emphasizing the essential importance of self-cultivation: "The *Mean* is within the self."[60]

Ch'en Wen-wei also lectured at the most famous academy associated with Chu Hsi, White Deer Grotto. Although the extant lecture is not dated, it was probably given in the 1230s.[61] Ch'en Wen-wei based the lecture on several texts from *Mencius*, beginning with the distinction between righteousness and profit.[62] He developed this idea to present a parallel distinction between human desires and heavenly principle, a distinction, according to Ch'en, clarified by the rules for learning established by his teacher, Chu Hsi, at White Deer Grotto. Ch'en Wen-wei also claimed that officials who came to the academy learned the distinction between righteousness and profit and were able to discuss this as they had not been able to before.[63] Quoting the *Analects*, he contended that the Confucian school is concerned only with humanity, the root of learning; if students study without knowing this and without basing their studies on humanity, then all will be for nothing.[64] Close to the end of his lecture, Ch'en Wen-wei quoted from a chapter in the *Analects* that treats individuals known for service to their rulers or for their conduct in retirement from public duties. Those who lost their honor or lives because they upheld ideals of service are regarded equally with the famous figures of Po I and Shu Ch'i, whose humanity lay in their retreat from public service.[65] Ch'en Wen-wei concluded his lecture with the following comments on Chu Hsi: "Master Wen-kung raised up White Deer Academy on abandoned ruins; he established upright regulations for residence and lecturing. The various gentlemen daily study in it, and refine themselves. Thus, in the future they will be able to develop their virtue and broaden their practice, and thus return to [the capacity to] act as the sages and worthies."[66]

According to Ch'en Wen-wei, justification for the *shih* lay in their self-cultivation, accomplished through the mutual support of like-minded colleagues who followed the prescriptions of the *Four Books*. Their aim should be to emulate the sages and worthies of antiquity and to eschew the literary embellishments of later ages, embodied in one sense in the examination system. The goal of self-cultivation was one way to rationalize the probability of failure, as competition for degrees and office grew increasingly intense in the late Southern Sung. One should note, however, that the lectures exhorting *shih* to adhere to these ideals generally were given by a *chin-shih*, or someone who held an official post.

Wen T'ien-hsiang at West Brook Academy

A sharp contrast to the situation of the *shih* who had no opportunity to serve is offered by the example of Wen T'ien-hsiang (1236–1283; 1256 *chin-shih* number one), the most renowned loyalist martyr of the Southern Sung.[67] Unlike those who did not hold office, Wen T'ien-hsiang served the Southern Sung as an official and military leader and died a heroic death at the hands of Khubilai Khan when he refused to serve the new regime, upholding the highest ideals of loyalty. Early in his career, Wen T'ien-hsiang lectured at West Brook Academy in Jui (Chiang-hsi), where he was prefect in 1263–1264.[68] The lecture was presented at the opening rites ceremony and drew on the *Mencius*, the *Changes*, and the *Doctrine of the Mean*, while commenting on contemporary social and political issues. Beginning with a citation from Mencius interpreted as critical of men who assume the role of teachers, Wen T'ien-hsiang referred to Han Yü's famous essay on teachers to support the position of local scholars involved with schools. Wen T'ien-hsiang identified his own responsibilities as prefect with the duty to carry out *chiao-hua* (transformation through education), even though he recognized that his position as a government administrator relegated him to a limited role compared with that of the teachers and students involved with the prefectural school and the academy. Like his later inscription (1272) on Peace Lake Academy in Kan's Hsing-kuo County (see chapter 5), in his West Brook lecture Wen T'ien-hsiang emphasized the importance of *chiao-hua*, not only as the duty of an administrator, but also as the responsibility of local scholars. He alluded to the emphasis in antiquity on *chiao-hua* as an essential function of government, and the secondary importance attached to "[keeping] records and meetings," suggesting that his own administration aspired to the model of antiquity, unlike the prevailing climate in government.[69]

Wen T'ien-hsiang criticized the *shih* for abandoning their central responsibility to teach the Way. Citing the *Changes* on the gentleman, he argued that the basis for the gentleman's position in society rests on his loyalty (*chung*), honesty (*hsin*), and sincerity, all of which are combined in the concept of virtue (*te*). More interestingly, Wen T'ien-hsiang connected the idea of virtue as "what is 'spoken' in the heart" with the gentleman's occupation (*ye*) as "what is 'spoken' in affairs."[70] He developed this idea further, arguing that one's words (*wen*) and actions (*hsing*) cannot be separated from loyalty and honesty; one would necessarily be the product of the other. Citing the *Analects*, he said, "Let words be sincere and truthful and actions honorable and careful." Emphasizing the link between words and action and the necessary base of sincerity behind them, Wen T'ien-hsiang exhorted the *shih* to strive for sincerity. For Wen T'ien-hsiang, sincerity was the thread binding words and actions, and it was the "ultimate realization of the Way."[71]

Wen T'ien-hsiang's words may be seen as a prescient comment on his own future conduct as a loyalist martyr, but they must also, at the time he spoke them, have carried particular significance for the audience at this academy. West Brook Academy was established to venerate the "Three Liu": Liu Huan; his son, Liu Shu; and Shu's son, Liu Hsi-chung (see chapter 2). All three were demoted or dismissed from office for offending their superiors.[72] When Wen T'ien-hsiang spoke of the sincerity of words and the accord between words and actions, he was implicitly making reference to the troubled political careers of the three Liu, and thereby criticizing indirectly the actions of many of his contemporaries.[73]

CH'ENG JO-YUNG: AN ACADEMY CAREER

While Wen T'ien-hsiang's lecture at West Brook and inscription on Peace Lake Academy may have been incidental to his own political and military career, the career of Ch'eng Jo-yung (1268 *chin-shih*), a

Chu Hsi follower who studied with Jao Lu, intersected with several major academies of the late Southern Sung.[74] He was headmaster at An-ting and Lin-ju Academies during the 1240s before he took his *chin-shih* degree, and headmaster at Wu-i Academy in the 1270s.[75] He also gave a lecture at Peck Peak Academy in Yü-kan County (Chiang-tung), probably sometime in the 1270s, although the date is unclear.[76] Continuing a theme observed in lectures at Illumined Way, Ch'eng Jo-yung began his lecture with a lengthy quote from Yang Shih:

> In ancient times, scholars took the sages as their teachers. . . . All those who studied took the sages as their model. . . . Today's scholars . . . must study the Way of the sages and worthies. If they only emphasize erudite knowledge of antiquity and penetrating the present as culture [*wen*], and do not practice loyalty, faith, and honesty, they will not be upright scholars. Since ancient times there have been many men who heard the Way but were not able to carry it out [because of the circumstances of the times]. For example, in the declining days of the Eastern Han, eremites and scholars who had a reputation for moral integrity were many. When they did hold office, they relied on the Way of the sages and worthies. . . . Those who went against the Way were those who had not heard it. Today's scholars claim that their "faction" follows the ancients [but in fact they do not]. . . . Learning, but not reaching the Way, is like not learning.[77]

Following this quote from Yang Shih, Ch'eng Jo-yung described the Way as formed from the principles of *yin* and *yang*, the Five Phases, and the myriad things (*wu*) and events (*shih*). The learning of scholars is the same as that of the sages and worthies; however, sages need not strive to "get it," whereas worthies must put forth effort to do so. Students simply follow the lead of the sages and worthies: "In studying the Way known by the sages and worthies, there is nothing apart from 'sitting in reverence' [*chü-ching*] in order to establish its fundamentals and investigating principle [*ch'iung-li*] in order to extend knowledge; and self-cultivation in order to seek its reality."[78] Following his teacher, Ch'eng Jo-yung also ranked those who studied according to their aims:

> Chu Hsi was a master who came last but benefited from the labors of his predecessors, from Kuei-shan [Yang Shih], Yü-chang [Lo Ts'ung-yen], and Yen-p'ing [Li T'ung]. His teaching is so clear and complete and is suitable for extension of education in the world and for later generations. I have studied the latter part of the collection of his *Literary Works*, and derived some diagrams of the four levels from my understanding of his "Letters in Reply to Liu Ch'i-chang." The highest level of study is to aim to become a sage or worthy. The second level is for an understanding of humanity and righteousness. The third level is for the study of literary works and the last is for candidature at the civil examinations.[79]

Ch'eng Jo-yung made clear the hierarchy of learning, placing literary study and preparation for the examinations pointedly below aspiring to the self-cultivation of sages and worthies and the understanding and practice of humanity and righteousness. Finally, Ch'eng Jo-yung described the content of the learning of the *shih*, drawing on the link in the *Great Learning* between self-cultivation and service:

> The learning of the sages and worthies is the beginning of what it means to be a *shih*. In the end it is what it means to be a sage. In the beginning it is the means to self-cultivation. In the end it is the means to pacify the world. It is knowing that the Way is the natural principle of heaven-and-earth. And it is also knowing that this learning is the matter of fundamental distinctions among men. . . . That whereby *shih* hear the Way is what is called the learning of the sages and worthies. Yang Shih said: "To study and not hear the Way is like not studying." I also say, "To establish an academy but not to lecture on clarifying this Way is just the same as not having an academy." . . . When talking of mind, there is nothing as important as sincerity. Sincerity is the basis of the Five Regularities and the Hundred Actions. In speaking of principle, there is nothing as important as centrality [*chung*]. Centrality is the standard rule of responding to affairs and connecting with things. . . . Simply put, mind is nothing other than principle, and principle is nothing other than mind.[80]

Echoing themes discussed in lectures at Illumined Way in the 1250s and 1260s, Ch'eng Jo-yung emphasized the need for self-cultivation with the aim of service— "pacifying the world"—but he also implicitly recognized the unlikelihood of utlizing the fruits of self-cultivation in office by stressing the importance of the learning itself and imitation of the sages, whether serving in office or not.

Fang Feng-ch'en at Stone Gorge Academy

Like the lecture of Ch'eng Jo-yung at Peck Peak Academy, a lecture by Fang Feng-ch'en (1221–1291; 1251 *chin-shih* number one) at Stone Gorge Academy in Ch'un-an County (Yen, Che-hsi), is extant in the *Case Studies of Sung and Yuan Thinkers*.[81] Stone Gorge was one of two academies granted name plaques by Tu-tsung (hence gaining imperial recognition) near the end of the Southern Sung (1271).[82] A critic of chief councillors Cheng Ch'ing-chih and Chia Ssu-tao, Fang Feng-ch'en requested to return home to Ch'un-an because of illness. Even when appointed minister of rites and personnel, he preferred to stay at home and lecture. In his Stone Gorge lecture, Fang Feng-ch'en focused on the concept of humanity, identifying it with *hsin* (the Mencian original mind) and using a horticultural metaphor to explain it:

> Among the former classicists who discussed humanity, the most excellent and famous one was Hsieh Liang-tso. He pointed out that the seeds of grasses and trees are planted and then produce [living things]. . . . Wherein lies the "seed" of men? [It is] called mind. Wherein lies the "seed" of heaven and earth? [It is] called men. . . . [Since mind cannot exist on its own], men receive the material force [*ch'i*] of heaven and earth, which becomes form [*hsing*]; [they] obtain the principle of heaven and earth, which becomes human nature [*hsing*]. . . . The various principles of the Way are all produced from the opening up and dispersal of the human mind. Like the sprouting of grasses and trees, it cannot be stopped. . . . Shang-ts'ai [Hsieh Liang-tso] said: "What is alive is humane; what is dead is not humane. If human minds are not humane, then the mind of heaven and earth is also dead." Mencius said that

> humanity is just the human mind. . . . [One should] exhaustively reflect and examine the self to serve the life of the original mind. If it is not like this, then it is just dead ashes, rotten wood, hard stone, and that's all.[83]

An inscription on Stone Gorge Academy written by Fang I-k'uei (fl. ca. 1265), a descendant of Fang Feng-ch'en, states that it was built to promote "Ch'eng-Chu learning."[84] Both Fang Feng-ch'en and his younger brother, Fang Feng-chen (1262 *chin-shih*), lectured at the academy.[85] Fang Hui (1227–1307; 1262 *chin-shih*), prefect of Yen and author of a prose poem (*fu*) on Stone Gorge, stated that the Fang of She (Hui; his own lineage) and the Fang of Mu (Yen; the lineage of Feng-ch'en and Feng-chen in Ch'un-an County) were descended from a common ancestor in the Latter Han.[86] Whatever the truth of this claim, it is clear that kinship bonds were an important aspect of the academy, and it is likely that the Fang in the two neighboring prefectures of Hui and Mu were, in fact, related. All three Fang brothers—Feng-ch'en, Feng-chen, and Feng-chia—were eremites after the fall of the Sung, although Stone Gorge was already a center of study and teaching established by Fang Feng-ch'en in the waning years of the Southern Sung.[87]

CONCLUSION

In lectures at Illumined Way and other academies delivered from the 1230s through the 1270s, *shih* were cautioned not to study for selfish ends—defined as seeking success in the examinations and appointment to office—but to cultivate the self in order to realize "original mind," inherent in people as heaven-endowed human nature. *Shih* were exhorted to prepare themselves to serve, understood in the broad sense of serving humanity and the ends of helping to bring about or restore heavenly principle in ordering the empire. The rationale and justification for the social status of the *shih* and their cultural role lay in self-cultivation, achieved with the support of their peers and colleagues who gathered at academies. They were urged to model themselves on the sages of antiquity, rather than to strive for worldly success in the terms of their own times: examination degrees and office-holding.

Ch'en Wen-wei in particular, perhaps in part because he lectured at the Huang family's Dragon Mountain Academy, where the message was especially apt, criticized the serving of narrow family interests as opposed to the use of private resources to support education for the broader community of *shih*. Wen T'ien-hsiang, in his capacity as prefect where West Brook Academy was built, also stressed the role of officials in supporting such efforts. Both Ch'en Wen-wei and Wen T'ien-hsiang, although their lectures came a generation apart, emphasized the concept of sincerity—for Wen especially, the link between words and actions. Since West Brook was established to venerate men who had paid a high professional price for refusing to compromise their ideas to political exigencies, Wen T'ien-hsiang's emphasis on sincerity in words and actions may be seen as a comment on the three generations of the Liu as models for local *shih* to emulate. It was not office-holding in itself that mattered, but standing by the principles one learned from the classics and the words and conduct of the sages. Ch'eng Jo-yung put it even more directly, explicitly stating the definition of what it meant to be a *shih*: the learning of the sages and worthies, not examination success or office-holding.

At the end of the Southern Sung, in the 1270s, Fang Feng-ch'en represents a final evolution in the complex of ideas about the social, cultural, and political role of the *shih*: eremitism. Like Hsiung Ho (1253–1315; 1274 *chin-shih*) and Hsieh Fang-te, who retired to Turtle Peak and Vast Spring Academies, respectively, in Fu-chien at the end of the Southern Sung,[88] Fang Feng-ch'en's retreat into eremitism became one way for *shih* to meet honorably the circumstances of their times. The groundwork, however, had been laid already in the early years of Li-tsung's reign, when *shih* were encouraged to engage in self-cultivation but not to expect to hold office. The ideas expressed in lectures at Illumined Way and other academies from the 1230s through the 1270s articulated a view of the role of the *shih* in response to the social conditions of the first half of the thirteenth century that ironically resonated with the collapsing political order at the fall of the Southern Sung and provided justification for some for the retreat into eremitism.

Conclusion

Benjamin Schwartz noted long ago the tension between the demands of personal self-cultivation and public service that was central to Confucianism.[1] After the examination system was introduced in the T'ang, education was tied to the process of recruitment and selection for government office, thus privileging public service over personal self-cultivation. To prepare for the examinations, however, many students sought instruction from scholars in secluded retreats who carried on a tradition of private education that was linked to personal self-cultivation. The origins of academies lie in this tradition of private education, transformed during the Five Dynasties-Northern Sung era, when academies developed as schools where students were trained for recruitment into the government bureaucracy. The role of academies in state education was eclipsed by government schools once the Northern Sung state began to support an official school system, beginning in the mid-eleventh century. When the relationship between the examination system and schools became a subject of controversy in the context of Northern Sung politics, the examination system itself was a target of some critics. By the late twelfth century many critics of the examination system—and by extension, government schools—were also involved with the revival of academies. Men who founded or restored academies in this period voiced objections to the kind of education provided by official schools, arguing that the content of the examinations determined what was taught in these schools, thus undermining the broader humanistic goal of cultivating human character. Chu Hsi and other True Way thinkers associated with the academy movement sharply criticized both the examination system and government schools for distorting learning in the interests of seeking "profit and salary." Chang Shih's stress on the "completion of human talents" rather than pedantic literary exercises designed to secure examination success exemplifies the attitude of many True Way thinkers that the goal of education ought to be the cultivation of human character. Not all commentary on contemporary education put the blame for what was wrong on the examination system, however. A wide spectrum of thinkers, including such diverse figures as Yeh Shih, Lu Yu, Chen Te-hsiu, and Lu Chiu-yuan, saw the examination system as simply a method of recruitment and selection, and therefore not the root of the problem.[2] The real problem lay in the education of the *shih* and their failure to take seriously their responsibility as a cultural elite.

The tension in Confucianism noted by Schwartz was reflected in a deep undercurrent of ambivalence that infused the academy movement in the thirteenth century and that was related to uncertainty over the proper role of the *shih*. Ambivalence was suggested, for example, by the use of White Deer Grotto Academy's regulations as a model at Illumined Way for the conduct of school sacrifices and rites at the shrine to Ch'eng Hao, while instructions concerning study, discipline, and testing mirrored those at the prefectural school.[3] Although the Southern Sung ideal of academy life may have originated in criticism of the examinations,[4] by the thirteenth century academies were absorbed into the examination culture of Southern Sung society. Even Marchmount Hill, after its revival in the late twelfth century, was clearly tied to the prefectural school, despite the academy's close association with Chang Shih. Both Marchmount Hill and White Deer Grotto, Chu Hsi's premier academy, were restored only with the approval and support of government authorities, and both provided training that prepared students to take the examinations. Other, less famed, academies, such as Purple Iris or White Egret Islet, were virtually indistinguishable from prefectural schools.

There was a contradiction between the legacy of private education and the benefits of state recognition and support, between the ideal of the personal teacher-student relationship fostered by the academy and the institutional character of a formal school supported by the government.[5] Although some academies retained the character of private schools, the granting of name plaques by the court and the allocation of land and other kinds of support were incentives that compromised the private nature of academies as the legacy of an earlier tradition. The politics of the academy movement reflected this contradiction and were evident already in the negotiations surrounding the restoration of White Deer Grotto by Chu Hsi.[6] The politicization of the academy movement as a whole, however, was a product of the thirteenth century and was intimately related to the reversal of the fortunes of True Way Learning during the reign of Li-tsung.

Like the shrine to Ch'eng Hao at Illumined Way, many shrines venerated members of the True Way pantheon—Chou Tun-i, the Ch'eng brothers, Chang Shih, Lü Tsu-ch'ien, Chu Hsi, and even Lu Chiu-yuan—along with local scholars who followed them or officials who had supported local education. The commemoration of local officials who had promoted schools or served the area in some other way, often through the pacification of bandits, was the motivation behind the founding of some academies. A prime example was Sleeping Dragon Academy in Fu-chien. A scattering of academy shrines were dedicated to other figures not directly associated with True Way Learning, such as Liu K'ai or Fan Chung-yen, but in these cases there was a local connection: a birthplace, the site of a study, or a place of office-holding. In some cases, a shrine that became the foundation for an academy was initially erected at the prefectural school—for example, the shrine to Hsieh Liang-tso was moved from the prefectural school to become the centerpiece of Shang-ts'ai Academy. The separation of shrines from prefectural schools and their transformation into academies provided a distinct space for the congregation of scholars, a place to associate with others like themselves and gain a new sense of identity as a scholarly community.

Rituals performed at academy shrines reinforced community identity by providing exemplars against which *shih* could measure their own accomplishments in self-cultivation. Academy students were exhorted to emulate the figures venerated at academy shrines and to live their lives in accord with ideals drawn from textual sources such as the *Four Books*. Ritual was a form of education, and the use of exemplary models was a pedagogical device of great antiquity. When shrines were combined with communal living in academy settings, and when students read the writings of scholars to whom sacrifices were dedicated, the power of these models was correspondingly enhanced. Liu Tsai, the chronicler of Su-chou's Tiger Hill Academy, founded in 1235 at a shrine to the Northern Sung scholar Yin Ch'un, commented: "Whoever walks on these grounds, recalls this person, and recites his writings, seeking their meaning."[7]

Figures venerated at academy shrines reminded *shih* of their obligations as a cultural elite, but these obligations could be interpreted in different ways, depending on the values represented by the individuals enshrined. Since academy shrines frequently revered local scholars or officials, the founding or restoration of an academy—and its recognition by the state through a name plaque or support—might be understood as a means of adapting the expression of local identity into a form sanctioned by the state and consonant with state interests. Men who suffered persecution, demotion, and even dismissal because of adherence to moral principles were as powerful models as those who successfully negotiated the vicissitudes of official careers. Shrines to such individuals at academies contributed to the reconstruction of historical memory and were a means to preserve an alternative historical record that commemorated political victims.

David Johnson has argued that the city-god cults of T'ang and Sung China reflect the outcome of a struggle between local religious beliefs and central ideological authority.[8] He suggests that this struggle resulted in the systematization and rationalization of local folk and "heretical" beliefs into a form consonant with the exercise of power through the appointed officials of the emperor. The authority of the local magistrate was enhanced by the merging of popular beliefs with ideas that supported the exercise of centralized bureaucratic power through him. More recently, James Watson and Valerie Hansen have made similar arguments concerning the interaction between local beliefs and state authority in the growth of the Ma-tsu cult in late imperial China and the transformation of popular deity cults in the Sung.[9] Watson stresses the ambiguity of symbols invoked in the evolution of the Ma-tsu cult, and Hansen points out the dual benefits to the state of recognizing popular deities—gaining both the deities' favor and popular support. Similarly, political victims enshrined at academies were ambiguous symbols that could be manipulated by both local elites and the court for different purposes.

Emphasis on the concept of "transformation through education" (*chiao-hua*) in numerous academy inscriptions suggests the extent to which anxiety about the proliferation of popular deity cults that drew on a variety of religious antecedents as well as the organization of lay congregational sects of Buddhism, documented from at least the early Northern Sung, may have inspired the building of academies by local prefects and magistrates who were known for quelling rebels, bandits, and heterodox cults. The dramatic expansion of the academy movement—particularly academies founded as shrines—in Southern Sung could be seen as a counterpart to the proliferation of deity cults, and the granting of titles by the court to deities that performed miracles was not unlike the awarding of name plaques to academies, signaling imperial approval and recognition.[10] By the late Southern Sung the appointment of headmasters by the court and the supervision of academy personnel by the Ministry of Personnel, like the *shih-fang* system of abbot selection for Buddhist monasteries, indicated the assumption of control by the state over the administration of academies, although it was far from a smoothly systematized practice.

As demonstrated by the affinities between academies and Buddhist monasteries, and by tensions expressed in competition for both material and human resources, there was a complex relationship between the academy movement and Buddhist monasticism. New institutions in the Sung, such as charitable estates and land endowments for schools, owed much to Buddhist precedents; and academies, too, can be seen as institutions that drew on Buddhist models of communal life. However, the dynamic of interaction between these two communities, Buddhist and Confucian, was often one of conflict, as each sought to strengthen their claims to "contested spaces." Such claims included both those to land and those to orthodoxy, at least seen through the rhetoric of commemorative inscriptions for academies. Inscription authors often praised academies as bastions of the Way in places that were overrun with Buddhist and Taoist temples as well as shrines to local deities. Like temples and shrines, academies as sites of ritual veneration of sages and scholars, especially the newly constructed True Way pantheon, became destinations on a True Way pilgrimage network, enabled by the relatively efficient transportation network and by the location of many academies at points where these routes intersected.

One of the original purposes of academies was the collection and storage of books, although there are no extant records of what books were included in academy libraries, apart from isolated references, such as Chu Hsi's donation to White Deer Grotto of a set of the *Han shu* and the bequest of the Nine Classics from the imperial government.[11] Technological changes associated with the commercial revolution of the Sung allowed some academies to print a scholar's works, such as the writings of Ch'eng Hao at Illumined Way or those of Lu Chiu-yuan at Elephant Mountain. Although records of what was printed at Sung academies are tantalizingly slim, clearly a wide range of works were printed, including such diverse items as Ssu-ma Kuang's *Comprehensive Mirror for Aid in Government*, T'ang commentaries on the *Han shu* and *Hou Han shu*, and even medical texts.[12] Since Fu-chien was a center of commercial printing in the Sung, records of medical texts printed at Fu-chien's Surrounding Peak Academy suggest that this school at least may have engaged in commercial printing for a market that extended well beyond the scholarly community associated with it. Modern scholars have linked the ability of Buddhist institutions to print the Buddhist canon to their wealth,[13] and it is reasonable to speculate that academy printing likewise indicates substantial economic resources available to invest in commercial printing.

We know as little about what texts were used at academies as we do about what texts were printed.[14] But we do know that many academies taught curricula that prepared students for the examinations.[15] Chu Hsi's own program of learning included standard historical texts such as the *Records of the Historian*, the *Tso Commentary*, and the *Comprehensive Mirror for Aid in Government*, although these works were secondary to the Confucian classics, especially the *Four Books*.[16] In a study of Chu Hsi's approach to learning, Daniel Gardner has claimed that there was a curricular shift to the *Four Books* contemporaneous with a literati retreat from central government politics documented by Robert Hartwell and Robert Hymes.[17] At the same time that many large academies such as Illumined Way and White Egret Islet prepared students for examination competition by training them in much the same way government schools did, there was a broad contextual shift to the *Four Books* perceptible in extant academy lectures.[18] The focus of opening convocation lectures at Illumined Way, for example, show this clearly, as lecturers based their remarks on texts drawn principally from the *Four Books*. The framework of study—the purpose of learning—shifted "from professional preparation for public service to a meaningful way of life in itself, a *vocation*."[19] According to Gardner, in Chu Hsi's view, "learning to be a sage" was a lifelong process, not merely a stage in one's career.[20]

Returning to themes evoked in the introduction to this book, we can see that the meaning and purpose of learning was transformed in the Southern Sung. Peter Bol has argued persuasively that the paradox of declining success and increasing participation in the examination system, particularly evident by the Southern Sung, was only apparent.[21] According to Bol, the function of the examination system had shifted from primarily a method of selection and recruitment for office to a means of confirming elite status as *shih*.[22] Viewed from this perspective, investment in education by local elites, either in family academies or in more "public" ones, was a means to gain recognition as legitimate members of a *shih* community, with or without taking examination degrees and holding office. Learning itself became a vocation. In sharp contrast to that formidable theorist of Chinese bureaucracy, Max Weber, who argued that the academic "calling" in the rationalized modern world was limited to objective knowledge and could not be extended to such things as character formation,[23] Chu Hsi saw his curriculum as providing learning that was specifically geared to the cultivation of human character, not training for bureaucratic office. This pedagogical agenda converged with social changes that made the competition for examination degrees fierce and the likelihood of failure great, so that *shih* were receptive to the ideas put forward by Chu Hsi and his True Way followers.

The "extraordinary achievement in cultural transformation"[24] described by Bol—participation in the examinations as a means for local elites to transform themselves into *shih*—worked two ways. At the same time that learning and participation in the examinations certified *shih* status, the institutional settings for these activities—both government schools and academies—provided a means for the integration of local elites into an empire-wide elite culture.[25] Men who had become dominant in their localities through wealth, charitable activities, affinal ties, and so on, were able to achieve recognition as *shih* outside their local communities through participation in educational institutions linked to the examination system. To a far greater extent than government schools, however, which were directly tied to the examinations, academies provided a *shih*-dominated alternative where men from different places congregated and associated on the basis of a common social and cultural identity. The increasing competition for, and the great difficulty of actually attaining, *chin-shih* degrees accounts for the popularity of an alternative that justified the lives of the *shih* as a scholarly elite in the absence of degree-taking or office-holding. The ideological basis of a new *shih* culture was articulated in the secondary discourse of True Way Learning, which sanctioned the role of the *shih* as local elites active in their communities, seeking education and self-cultivation, without necessarily having to achieve success as degree takers or officeholders.

In a recent essay on the examination system in late imperial China, Benjamin Elman focused on the dimensions of political, social, and cultural reproduction rather than social mobility.[26] Elman's line of argument is congruent with Bol's point that the examination system shifted in the Sung from a method of recruitment for government office to one of confirming elite status. Pushing this point further, as Bol suggests, participation in the examination culture alone—even without success—was also a way of confirming status as a member of the elite. Like the examination system, educational institutions were fundamentally means of social and cultural reproduction, but this did not mean they could not also be agents of cultural transformation. The Southern Sung academy movement was both the institutional expression of the cultural transformation of the *shih* and a means of constructing the new identity of the *shih*. This new identity was rooted in the idea of learning, not professional training for public service, as the vocation of the *shih*. Before the rise of the examination system, government office was not always a desirable way to achieve or maintain status. Charles Holcombe has argued that in the fourth century, for example, some of the most prominent aristocrats refused official appointments because the ideological value of reclusion gave their rejection of office meaning as social capital.[27] The validation of learning itself as a kind of cultural capital revitalized Southern Sung *shih* as a cultural elite with an identity apart from degrees and office. With the fall of the Southern Sung, reclusion gained new acceptance because of political conditions, but the justification for this alternative to service was deeply rooted not only in some of the earliest texts of the Confucian tradition,[28] but also in more recent institutional, social, and intellectual developments that converged in the Southern Sung academy movement.

Close to a century after Ch'en Fu-liang's assessment of the twelfth century academy movement as a response to the interdependence of government schools and the examination system, a very different picture emerges from late thirteenth century commentaries on the reasons for the flourishing of academies. Writing on Spring Mountain Academy in 1268, Liu K'o-chuang claimed that the writings of Chu Hsi were read throughout the empire, that his Way was honored in all the areas where he had been active, and that wherever men lectured on his doctrines and studied them, statues were erected and books were collected.[29] By this time, after the spread of the Chu Hsi cult in Fu-chien and the court's adoption of Chu Hsi's thought as imperial orthodoxy, the tension between True Way ideals of learning and examination education in government schools articulated by Ch'en Fu-liang and others was no longer a matter of controversy. But not only in Fu-chien was this the case: the association of Chu Hsi and his followers with academies was empire wide. According to Huang Chen, writing in 1273 on Lin-ju Academy (Fu, Chiang-hsi): "The *shih ta-fu* establish academies in order to chant and practice [Chu Hsi's] doctrine."[30]

By the end of the Southern Sung, learning had successfully been redefined according to True Way tenets as articulated by Chu Hsi and his followers. Writing in the early Yuan, Wu Ch'eng explained the academy movement of Southern Sung as a kind of educational revolution led by Chu Hsi, Chang Shih, and Lü Tsu-ch'ien. Homogenizing their ideas as a unified True Way, Wu Ch'eng stressed the difference between their educational philosophy and that of prefectural and county schools connected with the examination system.[31] How do we reconcile this difference with what we know of academy education in the thirteenth century, particularly the evidence of academies that were like prefectural schools and the relative similarity of formal education in both academies and government schools? Here I think we have to acknowledge the diversity of the academy movement and to reiterate the point that True Way Learning was not the only force behind the Southern Sung academy movement. A good example of this diversity can be seen in the variety of academies that coexisted in late Southern Sung Jun Prefecture on the southern banks of the Yangtze River where it intersected with the Grand Canal. Besides being the location of the prefectural school, the metropolitan county, Tan-t'u, was also the site of Huai-hai Academy, founded to serve refugee scholars, and Lien-hsi Academy, dedicated to the True Way patriarch Chou Tun-i and a destination for traveling *shih*.[32] Nearby Chin-t'an County was the home of Mount Mao Academy, on the Taoist mountain fortress, and Inculcating Duty Academy, the family school of the Chang.[33]

Founders of family academies, such as the Chang, were driven by a desire to improve, or at least sustain, the status of their lineages. To the extent that these schools provided opportunities for True Way scholars to teach and lecture, the True Way movement fused with a tradition of family schools that even predated the Northern Sung. The academy movement was shaped by social conditions such as increasing concern for the preservation of lineages and the coalescence of lineages into local elite communities. Family schools that were transformed into academies illustrate the links forged among local elites as individual lineages sought to enhance their status through support of local education. Academies were thus a prominent institutional manifestation of the growing importance of local identities. The apparent paradox of local or regional identities expressed in the veneration of local scholars at academies and emphasis on local landscapes, and the argument made here that academies shared a common institutional structure that transcended region, can be explained by seeing academies as places where *shih* congregated on the basis of social class affinities and where regional identities were expressed as part of an emerging *shih* culture. As *shih* traveled from their homes to study with famous scholars at academies, or to lecture at them, they participated in the building of both intellectual and social networks that contributed to the spread of True Way Learning and to the social integration of the *shih*.

The proliferation of academies in Southern Sung was as much the product of social conditions of the *shih* as academies were the institutional agency through which True Way Learning was propagated, and the relationship between the two was crucial. The construction of a new *shih* identity in Southern Sung was negotiated through the institutional form of the academy and expressed in the form of a secondary discourse in True Way Learning through which *shih* were encouraged to seek self-cultivation for its own sake and to disdain the rewards of office-holding. As articulated by academy administrators and scholars invited to lecture, the learning of the *shih* was defined as living according to the words and conduct of the sages presented in classical texts, especially the *Four Books*. The goal of learning was cultivation of innate, heaven-endowed human nature, not the attainment of degrees or office. This goal gained increasing credibility by the end of the Southern Sung, as the collapse of the dynasty intensified the conditions of moral choice: to reject office and seek refuge in the scholarly life of academies or to seek appointment under an alien regime.

Epilogue: The Transition from Sung to Yuan

In supporting the Yuan establishment of Ho-ching Academy at the grave of the Northern Sung scholar Yin Ch'un in K'uai-chi (Yueh), the Mongol governor pointed out that "[Yin Ch'un] died and was buried in Yueh. To enshrine him, but not to have a school—is this not inadequate?"[34] In his inscription on Ho-ching, the Chinese scholar Tai Piao-yuan (1244–1310) linked the establishment of schools to the need of the state to seek and recognize antecedents:

> The worthies of ancient times were . . . teachers in their communities. When they died, they were sacrificed to at the altars [*she*]. In the *Rites*, it says to please the ancestors. All begins with establishing schools, which is necessary to seek the

> foundations of the state. [People] sacrifice to the Former Sage and Former Worthies in the schools. If the state lacks its antecedents, it cannot distinguish itself from its neighbors. The worthiness of Suan-kung [Yin Ch'un] is in Yueh. I say that he ought to be sacrificed to at the altar, and that he ought to be regarded as a Confucian [*ju*] ancestor. How can we not establish schools and thus seek our antecedents?[35]

Reading this statement of a Chinese living under Mongol rule, one might interpret the seeking of antecedents as remembering Chinese scholars by erecting altars at academies to commemorate them. The Mongol governor's motives in supporting the establishment of Ho-ching Academy dedicated to Yin Ch'un, a symbol of the plight of scholar officials at the fall of the Northern Sung, are less clear. However, like his Chinese official counterparts in the waning years of the Southern Sung, who sought the support of local elites by founding and restoring academies, the Mongol governor's sanction of Ho-ching may be seen as a logical collaborative alliance with local elites, allowing them symbols of patriotism and moral rectitude embedded in a local institution that served the interests of state service as academies became part of the network of state schools under the Yuan.

Just as their Southern Sung predecessors erected academy shrines to Northern Sung True Way figures, Mongol officials similarly—and ironically—appropriated the symbols of Sung loyalist scholars. The founding of Kuang-hsin Academy, dedicated to the Southern Sung poet Hsin Ch'i-chi at his former residence in the final years of Southern Sung rule, recognized a loyalist poet whose official career was checkered at best, and might thus be seen as honoring the memory of someone who was persecuted by those in power.[36] With the end of the Southern Sung and the beginnings of Yuan rule, figures such as Yin Ch'un and Hsin Ch'i-chi were in turn appropriated by Mongol officials in an ambiguous use of these symbols. When Kuang-hsin was restored under the Mongols in 1298, it was renamed Chia-hsuan for Hsin Ch'i-chi's honorific. Mongol rulers could be at ease with commemorating a figure who personified the unhappy outcome of an idealistic scholar's political career and his consequent withdrawal from official life. Safely embalmed in an academy shrine, Hsin Ch'i-chi—loyalist poet and irridentist though he was—posed no real threat to the legitimacy of Yuan government.[37]

The transformation of shrines into academies meant the ossification of forces and symbols that might otherwise be used to challenge state authority. Enclosing a shrine in an academy enhanced its power, perhaps, by giving it a separate identity, but the very process of transforming a shrine into an academy also altered its meaning and potency. Shrines to figures such as Yin Ch'un, because of his ambivalent posture toward the court and his outspoken criticism of the emperor, or Hsin Ch'i-chi, a loyalist poet who was demoted and censured, might be used to focus resistance—to the Southern Sung court in its failure to prevent the Mongol onslaught, or to the new Mongol regime. The transformation of shrines into academies could be seen as a means to defuse such resistance and to appropriate potent symbols by placing them in structures that supported the authority of the state, whether by Southern Sung or by Yuan officials.

In an inscription on Pristine Wind Hall, the lecture hall at Angling Terrace Academy, Fang Hui related the name of the hall to Yen Kuang, whose exemplary influence linked him to the legendary Po-i, who starved in the wilderness rather than submit to an illegitimate sovereign: "Po-i preferred to die in order to complete his humanity. He was one who desired to clarify for myriad generations the proper relationship between ruler and minister. Tzu-ling [Yen Kuang] did not bend the Way in order to extend his life. He desired to clarify for myriad generations the proper relationship between friends."[38] The last sentence suggests the reason for Yen Kuang's objection to holding office: his intimate association with the emperor made it improper for him to be appointed. He resisted even the suggestion of using such personal ties in attaining office. The shrine and later the academy, especially Pristine Wind Hall, represented these ideals by linking contemporaries to past heroes such as Yen Kuang. The Southern Sung loyalist Hsieh Ao, who was buried at Angling Terrace, had deeply mourned Wen T'ien-hsiang's death at the hands of the Mongol conquerors, performing ritual mourning to "call back" Wen's soul from the north after his suicide.[39] He invoked Ch'ü Yuan, Yen Kuang, and Wen

T'ien-hsiang in a continuum of heroes in history.[40] These figures represent somewhat different ideals: Ch'ü Yuan, the loyal minister undeservedly dismissed by his ruler; Yen Kuang, upholding ideals of merit rather than personal ties as the criterion for office; and Wen T'ien-hsiang, a loyal martyr to the legitimate rule of his Chinese sovereign. But all of these ideals are related in a spectrum of values that define the principles of official service and justify the alternative of eremitism.

Ho Meng-kuei (1265 *chin-shih*), a late Southern Sung official who rejected service under the Yuan, wrote in an inscription on the renewal of the altar to Yen Kuang that with the rebuilding of the altar "we can raise up his *p'o* spirit."[41] The *p'o* spirit was the part of the soul (*hun-p'o*) that returned to earth upon death, and this statement imparts a distinctly religious element to the veneration of Yen Kuang specifically, and to the function of shrines in general. On the occasion of Angling Terrace's restoration in the Yuan (1341), Huang Chin wrote an inscription to commemorate it: "When gentlemen sequester themselves here and view the mountains and rivers . . . hear the 'wind' of the master, there will be none who are not inspired, and in the future the efforts of those former teachers who have contributed to its renewal and beautification will not be forgotten."[42] Clearly, the ideals associated with loyal service to a legitimate sovereign, a dimension of which is represented by Yen Kuang's refusal to presume on intimate ties with the emperor for personal privilege, were particularly attractive and important to men living under Mongol rule after the fall of the Southern Sung, and these ideals were symbolized in the academy. The restoration of Angling Terrace represents a subversion of this tradition, personified by Yen Kuang's refusal to serve, by the Mongol state, which incorporated the academy into its own educational framework by absorbing this local institution built around a shrine to a native culture hero into the Yuan imperial network of schools.

Just as the history of Angling Terrace illustrates the complex tradition associated with ideals of reclusion and service, Fang Hui's life and career exemplify the dilemma of *shih* living through the transition from Sung to Yuan. While prefect of Yen, Fang Hui wrote on Angling Terrace; when the Sung fell, he turned over the prefectural city to the

Mongol conquerors and was appointed in 1275 to the new post of prefect under the Yuan. Fang Hui's willingness to hold office under the Mongols contrasts sharply with the stance of his claimed relatives, the Fang brothers of Ch'un-an, who withdrew at the fall of the Sung to Stone Gorge Academy, for which Fang Hui composed a prose poem (see chapter 6). Fang Hui was condemned by his contemporaries for political opportunism, both under the Mongols and earlier under the notorious Chia Ssu-tao, whom he was said to have "flattered." Yet Fang Hui wrote eloquently of the righteous principles upheld by the legendary eremite, Po-i, in his inscription on Pristine Wind Hall at Angling Terrace. He also composed an inscription on the 1276 restoration of Purple Light Academy in his home county of She, Chu Hsi's native place, in which he compared the site of the academy with the state of Lu, Confucius' native place, claiming Chu Hsi as the heir of Confucius and Mencius. Finally, in his prose poem on Stone Gorge, Fang Hui referred to many aspects of the academy movement: Chu Hsi, White Deer Grotto, "ascending the hall" to hear lectures, the school rites, and venerating images of the former sage and worthies.[43] He also pointed out that, just as Confucius' disciples Yen and Tseng had no need to hold office, the gentleman could as well study at his family school or cultivate the fields.[44]

In contrast to the ambivalent posture of a figure such as Fang Hui, Wang Ying-sun, who was associated with Mount T'ao Tall Bamboo Academy in Yueh, was part of a circle of eremite literati centered on the Southern Sung capital of Hang-chou.[45] Wang Ying-sun was a poet and painter and part of a loyalist group that reburied the remains of the imperial family after the desecration of the imperial tombs at the fall of the Southern Sung. Hsieh Fang-te and Hsiung Ho, like Wang Ying-sun and the Fang brothers in Che-hsi, retreated to academies in Fu-chien when the Mongols established their rule over southern China. For these men, academies provided an alternative to government service under an alien regime.

The historical irony, however, came with the appropriation of many academies as part of the official educational hierarchy of the Yuan government. As Chu Hsi's commentaries on the Confucian canon were adopted by the Yuan as the official interpretations for the examinations, the academy movement identified with him and his followers was absorbed by the Yuan state. Academies became official institutions under the Yuan, standardized as government schools. Although Southern Sung academies were not by any definition "private" institutions, neither were they directly part of the system of government schools. Too little is known yet about academies in the Yuan, but considering the case of Fang Hui, it would not be injudicious to suggest that many *shih* who lived through the fall of the Southern Sung might well have found employment as educational officials under the new regime in academies restored after the conquest from Southern Sung antecedents.[46]

Appendix: Income and Expenditures for Illumined Way Academy

Income (*Chien-k'ang chih*, 29.4b–29.5a)

total land allocation: 4,908 *mou*, 3 *chueh*, 30 *pu*

Shang-yuan County

Tenant fields (*tien-t'ien*) of Intendant Hsu and two other households:

73 *mou* plus 38 *mou*

ti (uncultivated land) 21 *mou*, 1 *chueh*

Chiang-ning County

Tenant fields of Shao Jen and ten other households:

77 *mou*, 38 *pu*

Chu-jung County

Tenant fields of Tai Jih-te and forty other households:

386 *mou*, 2 *chueh*, 42 *pu*

ti 12 *mou*, 1 *chueh*, 25 *pu*

Miscellaneous property:

26 *mou*, 2 *chueh*, 20 *pu*

Li-shui County

Tenant fields of P'ing Teng-shih and thirteen other households:
3,542 *mou*, 47 *pu*

Li-yang County

Tenant fields and property of Yang Sheng-ssu and seventeen other households:
492 *mou*, 38 *pu*

ANNUAL GRAIN INCOME

Polished Rice (*mi*): 1,269 piculs
Unhulled Rice (*tao*): 3,662 catties (chin)
Beans and Wheat: 110 piculs
Tax money: 110 *kuan* (strings of cash), 700 *wen* (cash)

RENTAL PROPERTY INCOME

Annual rent on office in Ch'ang-chou, I-hsing county:
81 strings, 900 cash
Daily rental income from miscellaneous properties (after official reduction):
1 string, 10 cash; 1 string, 140 cash; 425 cash; 260 cash

PREFECTURAL GOVERNMENT MONTHLY ALLOCATION FOR SUPPORT OF SCHOLARS

5000 strings, 17 *chieh*; 40 bundles of firewood*

There was official supervision of the income and expenditures; if there were any discrepancies, a meeting would be held at the end of the year [to resolve them].

*In 1252, 2d mo., 2d da., the prefectural government announced that, annually, grain from the Chang estate would be converted into currency in the amount of 17 chieh, 100,000 strings to supplement student stipends; during Wang Yeh's tenure in office it was reduced to 5,000 strings.

EXPENDITURES (*Chien-k'ang chih*, 29.5a–29.5b)

MONTHLY SALARIES

Headmaster: 100 strings
Bursar (*ch'ien-liang kuan*): 20 strings
Dean (*t'ang-chang*): 100 strings; 2 piculs (hulled rice)
Registrar (*t'ang-lu*): 60 strings; 1 picul, 2 *tou* (hulled rice)
Lecturers (*chiang shu*): 50 strings; 1 picul, 5 *tou*
Hall guests (*t'ang-pin*): 26 strings; 1 picul, 2 *tou*
Rector (*chih-hsueh*): 24 strings; 1 picul, 2 *tou*
Guest lecturers (*chiang-pin*): 17 strings; 1 picul, 2 *tou*
Recorder (*ssu-chi*): 15 strings; 1 picul, 2 *tou*
Librarian (*chang-shu*): 15 strings; 1 picul, 2 *tou*
Shrine manager (*chang-ssu*): 14 strings; 1 picul, 2 *tou*
Dormitory manager (*chai-chang*): 10 strings; 1 picul
Students (*cheng-kung sheng-yuan*): 5 strings each
Medic: 7 *tou*

DAILY STIPENDS

Regular students (*shih-shih sheng-yuan*):
2 *sheng*, 5 *ho* polished rice; 300 cash for food preparation
Headmaster and hall master food subsidy: 700 cash
Registrar and lecturer food subsidy: 500 cash
Hall guest through dormitory supervisor food subsidy: 200 cash

Regular students who stayed in the dormitory would be given a nightly oil subsidy of 200 cash; hall master, registrar, and lecturer would each be given nightly 2 *liang* of oil. Coal allowance during the winter months for the headmaster on the days he entered the hall would be 5 catties; the hall master would be given 5 catties also; the registrar and the lecturer would each get 3 catties daily; each of the regular students would get 2 catties daily. This began from the first day of the tenth month and lasted until the end of the first month. All those who roomed and boarded fully would receive the full stipend; those who did not stay at the academy would receive half the stipend. All the payments used 18 *chieh* of official currency.

ALLOCATION FOR CH'ENG DESCENDANTS AND SUPPORT OF SHRINE (CHIEN-K'ANG CHIH, 29.16a–29.16b)

Grandmother Tseng: 500 strings, 17 *chieh* for robes

Shrine manager, Ch'eng Yu-hsueh: 500 strings, 17 *chieh* for clothing; 7 *tou*, 5 *sheng* of polished rice.

Natural father (*sheng-fu*) Ch'eng Tzu-ts'ai: 1000 strings; 4 rolls of local silk

Prefectural government monthly allotment to Ch'eng Chang-i for daily support of Grandmother Tseng: 300 strings, 17 *chieh* (for clothing expenses); 2.5 piculs of rice.

Monthly allotment to Illumined Way Academy for each person: 45 strings, 17 *chieh*.

Sacrificial food offerings and teachers' salaries: 50 strings, 17 *chieh*; 5 *tou* of polished rice

MEASURES

Land:

1 *chueh* = 60 *pu*
4 *chueh* = 1 *mou* (1/7 acre)

Capacity:

1 *ho* = .086 quarts
10 *ho* = 1 *sheng*
10 *sheng* = 1 *tou*
10 *tou* = 1 *tan* (picul, approx. 2.7 bushels)

Weight:

1 *chin* (catty) = 16 *liang* (1.3 lbs.)

Money:

1 *kuan* (string) = 1,000 *wen* (cash)
chieh = unit of paper currency

Notes

Abbreviations Used in the Notes

SJCC	Sung-jen chuan-chi tz'u-liao so-yin
SKCS	Ssu-k'u ch'üan-shu
SMTS	Ssu-ming ts'ung-shu
SPPY	Ssu-pu pei-yao
SPTK	Ssu-pu ts'ung k'an
SS	Sung shih
SYHA	Sung-Yuan hsueh-an
SYTFTS	Sung-Yuan ti-fang chih ts'ung-shu
TMTC	Ta-Ming I-t'ung-chih
TSCC	Ts'ung-shu chi-ch'eng

Introduction

1. Chou Ying-ho, comp., *Ching-ting Chien-k'ang chih*, 29.2b.
2. For Chou Ying-ho, see SJCC II.1495.
3. Chou Ying-ho, comp., *Ching-ting Chien-k'ang chih*, 29.30a–29.35b.
4. Ibid., 29.14b.
5. These were the "vegetarian offerings" (*shih-ts'ai or she-ts'ai*) to the Former Teacher, Confucius, and his disciples held at schools. See chapter 1.
6. Chou Ying-ho, comp., *Ching-ting Chien-k'ang chih*, 29.4b–29.5b.
7. Ibid., 29.5b.
8. Ibid., 29.5b–29.6a.
9. Lynn Thorndike, trans., *University Records and Life in the Middle Ages*, 91.
10. Ibid., 194.
11. See, for example, George Makdisi, *The Rise of Colleges in Islam and the West*.
12. See Gary Leiser, "The *Madrasa* and the Islamization of the Middle East: The Case of Egypt," 29–47.
13. Makdisi, *The Rise of Colleges*, 35 ff.
14. Ibid., 92–94.
15. The transformative social, economic, intellectual, and political changes of the Sung have been well documented. In addition to the important work by Robert Hartwell in economic history, studies on political and intellectual history by

James T. C. Liu, and the large body of work on social history by Patricia B. Ebrey, recent studies cited in the bibliography include Peter Bol, John W. Chaffee, Hugh R. Clark, Richard L. Davis, Valerie Hansen, Robert Hymes, Thomas H. C. Lee, Paul J. Smith, Hoyt Tillman, and Richard von Glahn.

16. See Thomas H. C. Lee, *Government Education and Examinations in Sung China*.
17. General histories of education, such as Ch'en Tung-yuan, *Chung-kuo chiao-yü shih*; Ch'en Ch'ing-chih, *Chung-kuo chiao-yü shih*; and Taga Akigorō, *Chūgoku kyōikushi* contain sections on academies. See also specifically on Sung education, Terada Gō, *Sōdai kyōikushi gaisetsu*; and Yuan Cheng, *Sung-tai chiao-yü: Chung-kuo ku-tai chiao-yü te li-shih-hsing chuan-che*. The classic general work on academies is Sheng Lang-hsi, *Chung-kuo shu-yuan chih-tu*. More recent studies include Chang Cheng-fan, *Chung-kuo shu-yuan chih-tu k'ao-lueh*; Ch'en Yuan-hui, *Chung-kuo ku-tai te shu-yuan chih-tu*; Pai Hsin-liang, *Chung-kuo ku-tai shu-yuan fa-chan shih*; Li Ts'ai-tung, *Chiang-hsi ku-tai shu-yuan chih-tu yen-chiu*. On Sung academies, see Sun Yen-min, *Sung-tai shu-yuan chih-tu chih yen-chiu*; Wu Wan-chu, *Sung-tai shu-yuan yü Sung-tai hsueh-shu chih kuan-hsi*; Ch'en Wen-i, "Yu kuan-hsueh tao shu-yuan: Ts'ung chih-tu yü li-nien te hu-tung kan Sung-tai chiao-yü te yen-pien."
18. See, for example, Wing-tsit Chan, "Chu Hsi and the Academies," 413.
19. Hoyt Cleveland Tillman, *Confucian Discourse and Chu Hsi's Ascendancy*, 3.
20. See Robert M. Hartwell, "Demographic, Political, and Social Transformations of China, 750–1550," 365–442; and Robert P. Hymes and Conrad Schirokauer, "Introduction," 1–58.
21. Although these two terms often appear to be used more or less interchangeably in Sung texts, it has become conventional in recent usage to understand *shih* as referring to the educated literati, apart from office-holding, while the term *shih ta-fu* is reserved for those who share in literary culture and are, have been, or are at least qualified to be officeholders.
22. I am using ideology here in the broad sense of both conscious and unconscious responses made by intellectuals to the world around them and to inherited traditions. For a brief and thoughtful critique of the many meanings of this term, see Thomas A. Wilson, *The Genealogy of the Way: The Construction and Uses of the Confucian Tradition in Late Imperial China*, 11–15.
23. See Louis Althusser, *Lenin and Philosophy and Other Essays*, 127–186.
24. This is, of course, counter to a strict Marxist view of ideology, which sees ideas as superstructural manifestations of economic relations and class interests. See Wilson, *Genealogy of the Way*, 12–13, for a critique of the Marxist concept of ideology.
25. See Hymes and Schirokauer, "Introduction," 51–54.
26. See Robert Hymes, "Lu Chiu-yuan, Academies, and the Problem of the Local Community," 442–444.
27. For this, see Robert P. Hymes, *Statesmen and Gentlemen: The Local Elite of Fu-chou, Kiangsi in Northern and Southern Sung*.
28. Of course, pedigree or descent was also an important component of status. See Peter K. Bol, *"This Culture of Ours": Intellectual Transitions in T'ang and Sung China*, 4 ff.
29. See Hymes, *Statesmen and Gentlemen*, 43–45, for details on the "family guarantee certificates" necessary to gain approval to enter the examination process.
30. Major differences in interpretation of the role of the examination system hinge on the degree to which there was a transformation in the nature of the elite

between Northern and Southern Sung. Some see a dramatic shift from an imperial elite, focused on examination success and government service, to local elites in Southern Sung who still participated in "examination culture," but whose primary arena of concern, activity, and source of status was the local community. Building on Hartwell's earlier work, Hymes' study of elite families in Fu-chou, Chiang-hsi, helped to define the differences between Northern and Southern Sung society and laid the groundwork for further studies documenting and refining the way we interpret these changes. See Hartwell, "Demographic, Political, and Social Transformations," and Hymes, *Statesmen and Gentlemen*. See also the extensive review of Hymes' study by Joseph McDermott, "Review of Statesmen and Gentlemen: The Elite of Fu-chou, Kiangsi in Northern and Southern Sung by Robert P. Hymes," 333–357. Recent work by Beverly Bossler has contributed to the modification and elaboration of views of the Sung elite. See Beverly J. Bossler, *Powerful Relations: Kinship, Status, and the State in Sung China, 960–1279*.

Whether elite continuity or change is stressed from Northern to Southern Sung, the role of the examination system remains critical. Did the examination system foster a relatively high degree of mobility or did it, in fact, operate through the use of the *yin* privilege and other means to perpetuate the advantages of an established elite and assure its continuity? In recognizing increased competition for a limited number of degrees and offices, did local elites in Southern Sung concentrate on local strategies, rather than imperial ones, for achieving, maintaining, or elevating status? Varied answers to these questions continue to define the parameters of debate on Sung social history. Patricia Ebrey has reviewed a series of works that deal with this issue, including books by Richard Davis, Thomas Lee, Robert Hymes, John Chaffee, and Umehara Kaoru. See Ebrey's review article, "The Dynamics of Elite Domination in Sung China," 493–519. A review article by Bol on John Chaffee's *The Thorny Gates of Learning in Sung China: A Social History of Examinations* specifically addresses the meaning of changes in the influence of the examination system by Southern Sung in relation to defining inclusion in the elite, the *shih*. See Bol, "The Examination System and the *Shih*," 149–171.

31. See the discussion in David L. Hall and Roger T. Ames, *Thinking through Confucius*, 43–46.
32. Ibid., 45.
33. On this, see Erik Zürcher, "Buddhism and Education in T'ang Times," 19–56.
34. See Bol, *"This Culture of Ours."*
35. In a classic article on the origins of academies in private retreats in the T'ang, Yen Keng-wang cited some two hundred instances of people preparing for government examinations in rustic mountain locales, often in Buddhist monasteries. See Yen Keng-wang, "T'ang-jen tu-shu shan-lin ssu-yuan chih feng-shang," 689–728. Many who studied in these settings later became famous in literary pursuits or government office. The places where they studied were identified by various terms, such as *shu-t'ang, hsueh-t'ang, ching-she,* and even *shu-yuan*. Terms for these institutions appear to have been used interchangeably. Only a handful were cases of scholars devoted to teaching students; most were groups of two to five scholars going into the mountains and making use of monasteries or temples to study for the examinations. On the development of private teaching and the ideal of the independent scholar in the T'ang, see David McMullen, *State and Scholars in T'ang China*, 47–51, 61–65.
36. Modern scholars have documented the first use of the term *shu-yuan* in T'ang

sources, referring to the building that housed the imperial book collection and to an institution with responsibility for the compilation and editing of historical documents. See, for example, Sheng Lang-hsi, *Chung-kuo shu-yuan chih-tu*, 1–7.

37. Chu Hsi, *Chu-tzu yü-lei*, 13.243.
38. Chaffee, *The Thorny Gates of Learning in Sung China*, 89. Data assembled for my study include nearly five hundred academies.
39. For this, see Chaffee, *The Thorny Gates of Learning in Sung China*, 35–41.
40. Bol, "The Examination System and the *Shih*," 152.
41. Ibid., 165 ff.
42. Hymes, *Statesmen and Gentlemen*, 132.
43. For a description of the physical layout and organization of a typical Ch'an monastery, see T. Griffith Foulk, "Myth, Ritual, and Monastic Practice in Sung Ch'an Buddhism," 167–191. Since Foulk argues persuasively that there was little to distinguish Ch'an monasteries from either Teaching or Vinaya monasteries, we can use this description as a model for Buddhist monasteries.
44. For a critical discussion of the origins and background of Ch'an regulations, see Foulk, "Myth, Ritual, and Monastic Practice in Sung Ch'an Buddhism," 156–159. For the more conventional view that prevailed before Foulk's pathbreaking work, see Yü Chün-fang, "Ch'an Education in the Sung: Ideals and Practices," 72–78. A summary of the content of the *Ch'an-yuan ch'ing-kuei* (1103), the earliest extant Sung code for Ch'an monasteries, is presented in Yü, "Ch'an Education in the Sung," note 44, 73–74. Compare the translation of Chu Hsi's rules for White Deer Grotto Academy, presented in W. Theodore de Bary, "Chu Hsi's Aims as an Educator," 202.
45. For this, see Daniel Gardner, "Modes of Thinking and Modes of Discourse in the Sung: Some Thoughts on the *yü-lu* ("Recorded Conversations") Texts," 574–603. At one point, Gardner explicitly makes a parallel between the use of the informal colloquial and the creation of an academy (589).
46. The most famous example is that of the Fan estate, documented by Denis Twitchett. See Twitchett, "The Fan Clan Charitable Estate, 1050–176"; for Buddhist precedents, see ibid., 102–103.
47. In a recent article on government schools, Richard Davis has pointed out the possible Buddhist influence on these schools' land endowments and administration. See Davis, "Custodians of Education and Endowment at the State Schools of Southern Sung," 99–100.
48. For example, Wilson, *Genealogy of the Way*, 112–143 argues that the genealogical model of lineage construction in Ch'an and T'ien-t'ai Buddhism paralleled developments in Confucianism during the Sung and later.
49. See Valerie Hansen, *Changing Gods in Medieval China, 1127–1276*; and Ellen Neskar, "The Cult of Worthies: A Study of Shrines Honoring Local Confucian Worthies in the Sung Dynasty (960–1279)."
50. See, for example, Daniel Overmyer, *Folk-Buddhist Religion: Dissenting Sects in Late Traditional China*, 87–88, citing Tsung-hsiao, *Ssu-ming chiao-hsing lu* (1202), on a large *nien-fo* society at a temple on Ssu-ming Mountain at the beginning of the thirteenth century (88).
51. Patricia B. Ebrey, *Family and Property in Sung China: Yuan Ts'ai's Precepts for Social Life (Yuan-shih shih-fan)*, 267.
52. It could be said, of course, that all elite public space was masculine, since elite women rarely ventured beyond the gates of their homes.
53. See Patricia B. Ebrey, *The Inner Quarters: Marriage and the Lives of Women in the Sung Period*, 41–42.

54. See Richard L. Davis, *Wind against the Mountain: The Crisis of Politics and Culture in Thirteenth-Century China*. Davis weaves discussion of concepts of masculinity and gender through his narrative of political and cultural crisis in the thirteenth century.

PART I: GEOGRAPHIES: INTELLECTUAL, ECONOMIC, AND SACRED

1. From Northern to Southern Sung: Academies and the True Way Movement

1. Lü Tsu-ch'ien, *Lü Tung-lai wen-chi*, 6.138–6.139. According to Lü Tsu-ch'ien's inscription on White Deer Grotto, the four outstanding academies of the empire were Sung-yang, Yueh-lu, Sui-yang (also known as Ying-t'ien), and White Deer Grotto. Wang Ying-lin (1223–1296), in his great thirteenth-century encyclopedia, *Yü hai*, adopted Lü Tsu-ch'ien's selection and discussed the same four in his section on academies (Taipei: Hua-wen ed., 167: 28b–32b). Hung Mai (1123–1202), in his *Jung-chai sui-pi wu-chi*, discussed only White Deer Grotto, Marchmount Hill, and Ying-t'ien (vol. 3, 46–47). Ma Tuan-lin's *Wen-hsien t'ung-k'ao* lists White Deer Grotto, Stone Drum, Ying-t'ien, and Marchmount Hill as the "four academies of the empire at the beginning of the Sung" (46.431). Ma Tuan-lin also mentioned both Sung-yang and Mao-shan Academies, noting, however, that neither of these were heard of in later times. Finally, the Ch'ing continuation of the *Wen-hsien t'ung-k'ao* gives White Deer Grotto, Stone Drum, Ying-t'ien, and Marchmount Hill, adopting Ma Tuan-lin's selection (*Ch'in-ting hsu wen-hsien t'ung-k'ao*, 50.3241]). This source also cites Wang Ch'i's Ming continuation of the *Wen-hsien t'ung-k'ao* as accepting Wang Ying-lin's designation of the "four great academies" that included Sung-yang and omitted Stone Drum.
2. For a good summary of the history of White Deer Grotto, see John W. Chaffee, "Chu Hsi and the Revival of the White Deer Grotto Academy, 1179–1181 A.D.," 40–62.
3. Chaffee, *The Thorny Gates of Learning in Sung China*, 42.
4. Li Han-chang, et al., eds., *Hu-nan t'ung-chih*, 68.1a. This account is supplemented by information in *Yü hai*, *Wen-hsien t'ung-k'ao*, and inscriptions by Wang Yü-ch'eng, *Hsiao-ch'u chi*; Chang Shih, *Nan-hsien wen-chi*, 10.1a–10.2b; and Ch'en Fu-liang, *Chih-chai wen-chi*, 39.7a–39.8b. General summary accounts may be found in Sun Yen-min, *Sung-tai shu-yuan chih-tu chih yen-chiu*, 51–52; and in Terada Gō, *Sōdai kyōikushi gaisetsu*, 7–8.
5. See Ou-yang Shou-tao, *Hsuan-chai wen-chi*, 7.14.
6. Wang Ying-lin, *Yü hai*, 167.30a.
7. Wang Yü-ch'eng, *Hsiao-ch'u chi*, 17.10b. For Wen Weng, see Pan Ku, *Han shu*, 89.3625–89.3626. For Wei Sa, see Fan Yeh, comp., *Hou Han shu*, 76.2458. Government traditionally included the notion of education, reflected in the term *cheng-chiao*, and thus was obligated to provide education and to preserve social order through proper governance.
8. See James T. C. Liu, *China Turning Inward: Intellectual-Political Changes in the Early Twelfth Century*, 37–38. Liu Po-chi, the author of a book on academies in Kuang-tung (*Kuang-tung shu-yuan chih-tu*), is also the author of a two-volume

work, *Sung-tai cheng-chiao shih*, written in commemoration of the founding of the Republic of China. One-third of this work is political and social history of the Sung, and the remainder consists of the history of Sung education and the examination system, including the educational philosophy of prominent thinkers and statesmen.

9. Wang Ying-lin, *Yü hai*, 167.30a. According to Liu Po-chi, this was the beginning of the formal use of the title of "headmaster" (*shan-chang*). See Liu Po-chi, *Kuang-tung shu-yuan chih-tu*, 831.
10. Wang Ying-lin, *Yü hai*, 167.30a.
11. For this, see Wang An-shih, *Wang Lin-ch'uan ch'üan-chi*, 38.213, whose poem on the T'an prefectural school makes this point.
12. For this description, see Sun Yen-min, "Sung-tai shu-yuan chih-tu," 8. Chiao Ping-nan estimates the range of size for academies of this period as from 10 or more rooms to 150, with book collections at large academies numbering several thousand *chuan*. See Chiao Ping-nan, "Sōdai no shoin seido ni tsuite," 74.
13. On this, see, for example, Sheng Lang-hsi, *Chung-kuo shu-yuan chih-tu*, 46, and Taga Akigorō, *Chūgoku kyōikushi*, 70. Both authors emphasize the relationship between the use of the term *shan-chang* for academy headmaster and Ch'an monastic influence.
14. For example, *tung-chang* was the term used for the administrative head of White Deer Grotto (*tung*) Academy. For a discussion of administrators' titles, see Chiao Ping-nan, "Sōdai no shoin seido ni tsuite," 8. Sun Yen-min, *Sung-tai shu-yuan chih-tu chih yen-chiu*, 100–114, provides a table of academies and administrative positions, including biographical information on many of the administrators and teachers.
15. Li Han-chang, et al., eds., *Hu-nan t'ung-chih*, 69.1a–69.2a; basic account in Sun Yen-min, *Sung-tai shu-yuan chih-tu chih yen-chiu*, 52–53. See also the inscription by Chu Hsi, *Hui-an hsien-sheng Chu Wen-kung wen-chi*, 79.22b–79.24a.
16. For Ch'i T'ung-wen, see SJCC III.2217. For a general summary of this academy's history, see Sun Yen-min, *Sung-tai shu-yuan chih-tu chih yen-chiu*, 68, and Terada Gō, *Sōdai kyōikushi gaisetsu*, 10.
17. Over fifteen hundred books were acquired, financial support allotted, and students formally began to study there. See Ch'i T'ung-wen's biography, SS 457/216: 13419; and Li T'ao, *Hsu tz'u-chih t'ung-chien ch'ang-pien*, 71.9a. The specific number of books is given in *Yü hai*, 117.30b, although Ma Tuan-lin gives a number of "several thousand" (*Wen-hsien t'ung-k'ao*, 46.31).
18. Wang Ying-lin, *Yü hai*, 117.30b. In 1006, Sung Prefecture, where the academy was located, was raised to a *fu* because it had been the former residence of T'ai-tsu; in 1014 it was established as Nan-ching, the "southern capital." It was under the latter name that Fan Chung-yen wrote about the academy. See Fan Chung-yen, *Fan Wen-cheng kung wen-chi*, 7.56a.
19. Wang Ying-lin, *Yü hai*, 117.30b.
20. Sun Yen-min, *Sung-tai shu-yuan chih-tu chih yen-chiu*, 68.
21. Wang Ying-lin, *Yü hai*, 117.32a. In 1010 the full name T'ai-shih Academy was granted along with more books.
22. At that time a headmaster (called *yuan-chang*) was appointed and one *ch'ing* of land was allotted for its support. See TMTC 29.12a.
23. Sun Yen-min, *Sung-tai shu-yuan chih-tu chih yen-chiu*, 64.
24. Chang Hsuan, comp., *Chih-cheng Chin-ling hsin-chih*, 9.13a.
25. W. Theodore de Bary, "A Reappraisal of Neo-Confucianism," 25.

26. For Sun Fu, see SJCC III.1898–III.1899; for Hu Yuan, see SJCC II.1570–II.1572; for Shih Chieh, see SJCC I.413–I.414.
27. Like Sun Fu's teaching at Mount T'ai Academy, Hu Yüan also taught students at what later became known as An-ting Academy at Yang-chou in Huai-tung. See TMTC 12.8a.
28. Shih Chieh, *Shih Tsu-lai wen-chi*, 6.11b–6.13a.
29. See Lee, *Government Education and Examinations in Sung China*, and Chaffee, *The Thorny Gates of Learning in Sung China*, for background on this.
30. Chaffee has estimated that, by the beginning of the Southern Sung, prefectural and county schools were allocated 1.5 million acres of land and supported about two hundred thousand students. See Chaffee, *The Thorny Gates of Learning in Sung China*, 78.
31. Chu Hsi, *Hui-an hsien-sheng Chu Wen-kung wen-chi*, 79.22b.
32. For this see Lee, *Government Education and Examinations in Sung China*, 115.
33. Ch'en Fu-liang, *Chih-chai wen-chi*, 39.7b. For background on the family certificates, see Chaffee, *The Thorny Gates of Learning in Sung China*, 60; Hymes, *Statesmen and Gentlemen*, 43–45.
34. Ch'en Fu-liang, *Chih-chai wen-chi*, 39.7b.
35. For one example of this, see Terada Gō, *Sōdai kyōikushi gaisetsu*, 266.
36. Lü Tsu-ch'ien, *Lü Tung-lai wen-chi*, 6.139.
37. Ibid.
38. For a discussion of this, see Conrad Schirokauer, "Neo-Confucians under Attack: The Condemnation of *Wei-hsüeh*," 163–198.
39. See James T. C. Liu, "How Did a Neo-Confucian School Become the State Orthodoxy?" 1–29.
40. See, for example, Linda Walton, "The Institutional Context of Neo-Confucianism: Scholars, Schools, and *Shu-yuan* in Sung-Yuan China," 492.
41. For a brief summary of this, see Chaffee, *The Thorny Gates of Learning in Sung China*, 89–90.
42. See, for example, Chaffee, "Chu Hsi and the Revival of the White Deer Grotto Academy, 1179–1181 A.D."
43. The term "intellectual geography" is used here to conceptualize intellectual history—particularly as reflected in academies—according to a geographical framework. This is not geographic determinism, nor is it the traditional geographic schools of thought approach. Rather, the concept of intellectual geography provides a meaningful way to organize a dense and complex array of persons and places.
44. For one example, see Wu K'ang, "Nan-Sung Hsiang-hsueh yü Che-hsueh," 39–59. The article was originally published in 1955, but the approach remains common in Chinese scholarship at least, as witnessed by its reprinting in 1981.
45. Tillman, *Confucian Discourse and Chu Hsi's Ascendancy*, 60–61.
46. For Hu An-kuo, see SJCC II.1591–II.1593 and Herbert Franke, ed., *Sung Biographies*, 434–436; for Hu Hung, see SJCC II.1558–II.1559 and Franke, *Sung Biographies*, 438–440. For a discussion of the Hu-Hsiang school at Marchmount Hill, see Yang Chih-ch'u, et al., *Yueh-lu shu-yuan shih-lueh*, 32–39. See also Tillman, *Confucian Discourse and Chu Hsi's Ascendancy*, 29–36.
47. For a thorough discussion of Chang Shih's ideas and of the intellectual relationship between Chang and Chu Hsi, see Tillman, *Confucian Discourse and Chu Hsi's Ascendancy*, 43–82. See also Conrad Schirokauer, "Chu Hsi and Hu Hung," 480–502.

48. For Ch'en Liang in the context of the True Way fellowship, see Tillman, *Confucian Discourse and Chu Hsi's Ascendancy*, 133–186.
49. See Yang Chih-ch'u, et al., *Yueh-lu shu-yuan shih lueh*, 25–27. Among Chang Shih's works is *Nan-hsien hsien-sheng Meng-tzu shuo*. For a brief description of this, see Etienne Balazs and Yves Hervouet, comps., *A Sung Bibliography*, 43.
50. Chang Shih, *Nan-hsuan wen-chi*, 10.1a–10.2b. Pacification commissioner for Hu-Kuang and prefect of T'an, Liu Kung (1122–1178), was responsible for the restoration. For Liu Kung, see SJCC V.3866. Four dormitories were added to the original foundations, and the number of students was set at twenty.
51. Chang Shih, *Nan-hsuan wen-chi*, 10.1b.
52. Wu I (1129–1177) was an eremite scholar from Fu-chien who came to Mt. Heng to study with Hu Hung. He rejected learning for the examinations and, after Hu Hung's death, studied with Chang Shih. See SJCC II.1107 and his "record of conduct" by Chu Hsi, *Chu-tzu wen-chi*, 16.552–16.553.
53. Chang Shih, *Nan-hsuan wen-chi*, 10.1b.
54. See Wu Ch'eng, *Wu Wen-cheng kung wen-chi*, 20.19a; see also Wing-tsit Chan, "Chu Hsi and the Academies," 406.
55. Ch'en Fu-liang, *Chih-chai wen-chi*, 39.7a–39.8b.
56. SYHA 71.1a.
57. Ch'en Fu-liang, *Chih-chai wen-chi*, 39.8a. For discussion of Chu-ko Liang in the Sung, see Hoyt Cleveland Tillman, "Ho Ch'ü-fei and Chu Hsi on Chu-ko Liang as a 'Scholar-General,'" 77–94.
58. For a brief description of this work, the *Li-tai ping-chih*, see Balazs and Hervouet, *A Sung Bibliography*, 184.
59. For his works, see the entries in Balazs and Hervouet, *A Sung Bibliography*, 184–185, 325–326, and 424–425. See also his biography in Franke, *Sung Biographies*, 103–107.
60. Since Chaffee has provided a solid and detailed study of the revival of White Deer Grotto under the direction of Chu Hsi, it is unnecessary to repeat here more than a general outline of events. See Chaffee, "Chu Hsi and the Revival of the White Deer Grotto Academy, 1179–1181 A.D."
61. See Lü Tsu-ch'ien, *Lü Tung-lai wen-chi*, 6.138–6.139.
62. For a discussion of the political complexities behind this, see John W. Chaffee, "Chu Hsi in Nan-k'ang: *Tao-hsüeh* and the Politics of Education," 414–431.
63. For a translation and discussion of these rules, see Chaffee, "Chu Hsi and the Revival of the White Deer Grotto Academy, 1179–1181 A.D.," 54–57; Wing-tsit Chan, "Chu Hsi and the Academies," 397–398; W. Theodore de Bary, *The Liberal Tradition in China*, 35–36; Daniel Gardner, trans., *Chu Hsi: Learning to be a Sage*, 29–30. For a comprehensive discussion of school rules in relation to academy rules, see Ch'en Wen-i, "Yu kuan-hsueh tao shu-yuan: ts'ung chih-tu yü li-nien te hu-tung k'an Sung-tai chiao-yü te yen-pien," 54–96.
64. See Chaffee, "Chu Hsi and the Revival of the White Deer Grotto Academy, 1179–1181 A.D.," 44, note 22, for details on this.
65. Lu Chiu-yuan, *Lu Hsiang-shan ch'üan-chi*, 23.174–23.175.
66. Ibid.
67. This restoration was carried out by Pan Chih, who was also responsible for the expansion of Marchmount Hill around the same time. See Chu Hsi, *Hui-an hsien-sheng Chu Wen-kung wen-chi*, 79.22b.
68. Ibid. See also the inscription on the land allotment by Liao Hsing-chih, *Sheng-chai chi*, 4.17a–4.18b.

69. Chu Hsi, *Hui-an hsien-sheng Chu Wen-kung-wen-chi*, 79.22b–79.24a.
70. Ibid., 79.23b
71. Chu Hsi, *Chu-tzu ta-ch'üan*, 100.13a–100.13b.
72. Ibid., 100.13b.
73. Li Han-chang, et al., eds., *Hu-nan t'ung-chih*, 68.1a.
74. Hymes has argued that this was due to his primary concern with managing his family affairs, rather than with a "middle-level" institution such as the academy. See Robert Hymes, "Lu Chiu-yuan, Academies, and the Problem of the Local Community."
75. See Lu Chiu-yuan's chronological biography (*nien-p'u*) in Lu Chiu-yuan, *Lu Hsiang-shan ch'üan-chi*, 36.330–36.331. For problems at the retreat and how students helped, see *Lu Hsiang-shan ch'üan-chi*, 14.121. For local background, see Jonathan O. Pease, "Lin-ch'uan and Fen-ning: Kiangsi Writers and Kiangsi Locales during the Sung," 63–64.
76. Pease, "Lin-ch'uan and Fen-ning," 63–64.
77. See Thomas H. C. Lee, "Chu Hsi, Academies and the Tradition of Private *Chiang-hsüeh*," 312.
78. Pease, "Lin-ch'uan and Fen-ning," 64.
79. Tillman, *Confucian Discourse and Chu Hsi's Ascendancy*, 92, 108.
80. Ibid., 114. See Lü Tsu-ch'ien, *Lü Tung-lai wen-chi*, 10.247. For discussion of Lü Tsu-ch'ien's rules, see Ch'en Wen-i, "Yu kuan-hsueh tao shu-yuan," 71.
81. See Ch'en Wen-i, "Yu kuan-hsueh tao shu-yuan," 71.
82. See, e.g., Z. D. Sung, ed. and trans., *The Text of Yi King*, 244.
83. Tillman, *Confucian Discourse and Chu Hsi's Ascendancy*, 84.
84. Lü Tsu-ch'ien, *Lü Tung-lai wen-chi*, 6.138–6.139; see also Tillman, *Confucian Discourse and Chu Hsi's Ascendancy*, 114.
85. SJCC I.569; Yang Yü-chien, et al., comps., *Chung-hsiu Nan-hsi shu-yuan chih*, 4.4a–4.4b.
86. SYHA 39.16a. For Chu Sung's father, Chu Shen, see SJCC I.579.
87. Ch'eng Tsu-lo, et al., eds., *Fu-chien t'ung-chih*, 65.21a, 65.23a. However, the anonymous Ch'ing work, *T'ien-hsia shu-yuan tsung-chih*, says that Chu Hsi, not his father, established Star Creek Academy (961). Chu Hsi likely built it at the site of his grandfather's grave, as he would later establish retreats at the sites of his mother's and father's graves, and therefore Star Creek had the character of an ancestral shrine. Chu Sung was also supposed to have established at the same time Cloud Kernel Academy in Cheng-ho. A similar discrepancy is found in the sources concerning this academy, one claiming that Cloud Kernel was founded by his father and one that it was founded by Chu Hsi (*Fu-chien t'ung-chih*, 65.23a; *T'ien-hsia shu-yuan tsung-chih*, 961).
88. Yang Yü-chien, et al., comps., *Chung-hsiu Nan-hsi shu-yuan chih*, 4.4b. This may have been the family of Cheng An-tao (1073 *chin-shih*) from Yu-ch'i (SJCC V.3688).
89. SJCC II.1577; V.3918, 3919, 3970.
90. Huang Kan, *Mien-chai chi*, 36.47a–36.47b. See Wing-tsit Chan, *Chu Hsi: New Studies*, 37.
91. For an account of Fu-chien academies established by Chu Hsi, see Wing-tsit Chan, "Chu Hsi and the Academies," 389–413. Prior to the Sung, there were private schools in Fu-chien that one author, at least, has associated with the later development of academies there. See Ch'en Ming-shih, "T'ang-Sung shih-ch'i Fu-chien te shu-yuan," 49–52. According to Ch'en Ming-shih, the first academy

in Fu-chien was Pine Islet, established in the beginning of the eighth century. Pine Islet was not just a place for private study and book storage, but was also used for lecturing (49). Ch'en Ming-shih also argues that the founding of Pine Islet Academy was earlier than the conventionally recognized first use of the term *shu-yuan* for one of the agencies of the T'ang central government (49).

92. Yü Chi, *Tao-yuan hsueh-ku lu*, 36.318; cited in Liu Ts'un-yan, "Chu Hsi's Influence in Yuan Times," 525–526.
93. TMTC 76.9a; Ch'eng Tsu-lo, et al., eds., *Fu-chien t'ung-chih*, 65.10a; Hsiung Ho, *Hsiung Wu-hsuan chi*, 4.19b–4.20b, 5.2b–5.4a.
94. For one example of a student who went there, see SYHA 69.35a.
95. Although the specific relationship between *ching-she* and academies is not clear, it is probably sufficient for our purposes here to accept a relatively simple distinction between the two: whatever Indian, Buddhist, Taoist, Confucian or other connotations the term may have had, during the Sung, *ching-she* were private scholarly retreats that sometimes became more public and more formalized as academies. It is significant, moreover, that although retreats could become academies, there is no case to my knowledge where an academy became a retreat, reverting from a more public to a more private function. See Wing-tsit Chan, "Chu Hsi and the Academies," 389–390. See also Thomas H. C. Lee, "Chu Hsi, Academies, and the Tradition of Private *Chiang-hsüeh*," 8–13, 21–27.
96. Ch'eng Tsu-lo, et al., eds., *Fu-chien t'ung-chih*, 65.14a–65.15a; TMTC 76.9a; Wing-tsit Chan, "Chu Hsi and the Academies," 340–343. For example, Pan Chih and his brother, Pan Ping, followed Chu Hsi at Wu-i. See SYHA 69.20a; SJCC V.3628, 3630. Yeh Wei-tao (1220 *chin-shih*) followed Chu Hsi at Wu-i after he was dismissed for supporting the thought of Ch'eng I at court. He eventually became an Imperial University professor (*t'ai-hsueh po-shih*) and lectured to Li-tsung, transmitting the teachings of Ch'eng I and Chu Hsi to the emperor (SS 438/197, 12986–12987). According to *T'ien-hsia shu-yuan tsung-chih*, Yeh Wei-tao established Creek Mountain Academy in Chien-yang County (934).
97. Ch'eng Tsu-lo, et al., eds., *Fu-chien t'ung-chih*, 65.10a–65.11b (inscriptions by Hsiung Ho and Yü Chi); TMTC 76.9a; *T'ien-hsia shu-yuan tsung-chih* also has the inscriptions by Hsiung Ho and Yü Chi (935–946). Hsiung Ho says that the retreat was built in 1194, but here I follow *Fu-chien t'ung-chih*, 65.10a, which agrees with Wang Mou-hung, *Chu-tzu nien-p'u*, 324. See also Wing-tsit Chan, "Chu Hsi and the Academies," 336.
98. Chu Hsi, *Chu-tzu ta-ch'üan*, 13.479–13.480. See Neskar, "The Cult of Worthies," 183–184, for a brief description of these rites.
99. Chu Hsi, *Chu-tzu yü-lei*, 107.2674.
100. Cheng Ts'ai (1188–1249), a native of Fu-an (Fu Prefecture) and a 1229 *chin-shih*, followed the disciples of Chu Hsi and was credited with the establishment of North Mountain Academy in his home county (SJCC V.3660; SYHA: supp. 64.20; Ch'eng Tsu-lo, et al., eds., *Fu-chien t'ung-chih*, 66.24b). The establishment of K'ao-t'ing Academy, also in Fu-an, and Stone Lake Academy in Fu-ting were both attributed to Chu Hsi (*Fu-chien t'ung-chih*, 66.25a, 66.21b).
101. These include Creek Mountain (Lu Tseng-yü, et al., comps., *Fu-chou fu chih*, 11.34b; *T'ien-hsia shu-yuan tsung-chih*, 918), Surrounding Creek (TMTC 74.9b; *Fu-chou fu chih*, 11.34b), and Indigo Field (*Fu-chou fu chih*, 11.34b; TMTC 74.9b).
102. Ch'eng Tsu-lo, et al., eds., *Fu-chien t'ung-chih*, 62; TMTC 74.9b. For Yü Ou, see SJCC II.1233 and Lu Tseng-yü, et al., comps., *Fu-chou fu chih*, 11.34b.
103. See Huang Chin-chung, "Chu Hsi yü Fu-chien shu-yuan k'ao-p'ing," 193. For discussion of the term *yu-chü* and similar ones, see chapter 4.

104. On increased competition for *chin-shih* degrees in Southern Sung, see Chaffee, *The Thorny Gates of Learning in Sung China*, 36–37.
105. Tillman, *Confucian Discourse and Chu Hsi's Ascendancy*, 255.
106. For this, see Neskar, "The Cult of Worthies." Ch'en Wen-i refers to this phenomenon as an "enshrinement culture." See Ch'en Wen-i, "Yu kuan-hsueh tao shu-yuan," 125–131. For possible parallels with the worship of popular deities, see Hansen, *Changing Gods in Medieval China*.
107. Hsiung Ho, *Hsiung Wu-hsuan chi*, 3.4b; Ch'eng Tsu-lo, et al., eds., *Fu-chien t'ung-chih*, 65.10b.
108. During the Yuan, Ts'ai Yüan-ting, Liu Yüeh, and Chen Te-hsiu were venerated at the academy, along with Huang Kan. See Hsiung Ho, *Hsiung Wu-hsien chi*, 3.3b.
109. Hsiung Ho, *Hsiung Wu-hsuan chi*, 3.2a. SJCC I.567. Chu I had been recommended for the post by Hsiung Ho's colleague, Hsieh Fang-te (SYHA: supp. 49.164b–49.165a).
110. Hsiung Ho, *Hsiung Wu-hsien chi*, 3.2a. According to Hsiung Ho, the academy had had a modest amount of land (ninety *mou*), but this was insufficient even for basic sacrifices. When the academy was renewed in the Yuan (1288 and 1305), more land was allocated to support the academy's activities (3.1b).
111. Ch'eng Tsu-lo, et al., eds., *Fu-chien t'ung chih*, 65.15a. For Tsai and Chien, see SJCC I.566, I.599; also SYHA 49.22b, 49.23a.
112. Ch'eng Tsu-lo, et al., eds., *Fu-chien t'ung-chih*, 65.15a. When the academy was expanded in 1268, Ch'eng Jo-yung (1268 *chin-shih*), a student of Jao Lu (1152–1221) and follower of Chu Hsi's thought, was made headmaster. See SJCC IV.3044, SYHA 83.4a. For Jao Lu, see SJCC V.4493. He studied with Huang Kan as a youth and built Stone Hollow Academy.
113. An inscription was written for this academy by Li Shao (1211 *chin-shih*) at the request of his younger cousin, the magistrate Li Hsiu. Both cousins studied together as youngsters at their family school, and Li Hsiu's father was a student of Huang Kan. See Yang Yü-chien, et al., comps., *Chung-hsiu Nan-hsi shu-yuan chih*, 4.4a–4.6b.
114. Yang Yü-chien, et al., comps., *Chung-hsiu Nan-hsi shu-yuan chih*, 4.5b.
115. For Huang Yen-sun, see SJCC IV.2923; SYHA: supp. 81.54a–81.54b.
116. SYHA: supp. 81.54b.
117. Ibid. For an extensive discussion of the "question and answer" method as it was presumably used here and in other academies, see Hayashi Tomoharu, "Chūgoku shoin ni okeru kyōikuhō no shūkyōteki teiryū." See especially 110 ff. for a textual analysis of *Chin-ssu lu* based on Hayashi's idea that the Socratic/Confucian method was the major pedagogical technique utilized by Chu Hsi and his followers.
118. During the Yuan, Chu Lin, a fourth-generation descendant of Chu Hsi, was appointed headmaster here, linking the academy to its original function as a shrine to Chu Hsi and his father. See SYHA: supp. 49.256b.
119. Ch'eng Tsu-lo, et al., eds., *Fu-chien t'ung-chih*, 63.20a. For Tsou Ying-lung, see SJCC IV.3293. Chu Hsi was supposed to have established two academies in Ch'üan-chou: Warm Mound and Small Mountain Clustered Bamboo. See Huai Yin-pu, ed., *Ch'üan-chou fu chih*, 13.85b–13.86a. In both cases, however, it seems likely that Chu Hsi might have visited these places, and perhaps lectured there, but the academies were actually founded at some later time.
120. Ch'eng Tsu-lo, et al., eds., *Fu-chien t'ung-chih*, 63.20a.
121. Ibid. There was a lecture hall, four dormitories, and a rites hall, which contained images of the two masters (Chu Hsi and his father). This academy was said to be structured like the prefectural and county schools. At the beginning of the

Pao-ch'ing era (1225–1227), Prefect Yu Chiu-kung allotted five *ch'ing* of abandoned temple land to support the academy (Ch'eng Tsu-lo, et al., eds., *Fu-chien t'ung-chih*, 63.20). For Yu Chiu-kung, see SJCC IV.2767. Since Yu Chiu-kung and his older brother, Yu Chiu-yen (1142–1206), were from Chien-yang, the home of Yu Tso (1053–1123; 1082 *chin-shih*), they likely were related to this Fu-chien disciple of the Ch'eng brothers. For Yu Chiu-yen, see SJCC IV.2768.

122. Observing Orchids Academy in Lung-ch'i County of Chang was established by a scholar named Ts'ai Ju early in the Sung. See Ch'eng Tsu-lo, et al., eds., *Fu-chien t'ung-chih*, 64.5a–64.5b.
123. TMTC 78.16a; Ch'eng Tsu-lo, et al., eds., *Fu-chien t'ung-chih*, 64.4b
124. SS, 415/174, 12452.
125. SJCC I.52; SYHA 55.8a.
126. Ch'eng Tsu-lo, et al., eds., *Fu-chien t'ung-chih*, 64.4b.
127. Ibid., 65.12a.
128. TMTC 76.9a.
129. Ch'eng Tsu-lo, et al., eds., *Fu-chien t'ung-chih*, 65.12a. There is reference in the latter source to another Hut Peak Academy in Ch'ung-an, also established by Ts'ai Ch'en during the same period, with the information that Li-tsung bequeathed a stone inscription bearing the two characters of the name in 1255 (Ch'eng Tsu-lo, et al., eds., *Fu-chien t'ung-chih*, 65.15b). The same source also states that Ts'ai Ch'en's grandson, Ts'ai Kung-liang, provided three hundred *mou* of land to support the academy (see also the entry for Ts'ai Kung-liang [1253 *chin-shih*] in SJCC V.3811). Since Chien-yang and Ch'ung-an Counties border on each other, it is conceivable that the academy lay on the boundary between them, and that these two references are to the same academy. It seems unlikely that Ts'ai Shen would have established two academies of the same name in such close proximity.
130. See SJCC V.3809; Franke, *Sung Biographies*, 1037–1039. Ts'ai Ch'en's son, Ts'ai Hang (1229 *chin-shih*), established Nine Peaks Academy, named after his father's honorific, in Ch'ung-an County at the first bend of the Nine Bends Stream (Ch'eng Tsu-lo, et al., eds., *Fu-chien t'ung- chih*, 65.15b).
131. Ch'eng Tsu-lo, et al., eds., *Fu-chien t'ung-chih*, 65.4a. For Wang Yeh, see SJCC I.167; see also chapters 2 and 5 of this book.
132. SS 420/179, 12577; SYHA 81.10a. Chen Te-hsiu established West Mountain Retreat in P'u-ch'eng County (Chien Prefecture) in 1221 (Ch'eng Tsu-lo, et al., eds., *Fu-chien t'ung-chih*, 65.18a).
133. SYHA 81.12b. There are other references indicating that by around 1260 an appointment as headmaster at an academy was concurrent with appointment as a prefectural professor. For these, see Terada Gō, *Sōdai kyōikushi gaisetsu*, 314.
134. SYHA: supp. 49.256b. Chu Pin's brother, Chu Lin, was headmaster at Southern Stream Academy. Another fourth-generation descendant of Chu Hsi, Chu Ch'un, became headmaster of K'ao-t'ing Academy, after the death of Chu I, a third-generation descendant of Chu Hsi (Ch'ün's father?) who had been recommended to the post of headmaster there by Hsieh Fang-te (SYHA: supp. 49.164b–49.165a).
135. SJCC V.3914.
136. SS 401/160, 12170.
137. Ibid., 12171.
138. Ibid.
139. See Ch'en Wen-i, "Yu kuan-hsueh tao shu-yuan," 163–164.
140. The Ch'en of P'u-t'ien had an illustrious ancestry, traced to the Latter Han. Dur-

ing the Five Dynasties they fled from the Huai-nan region to Fu-chien. Through the marriage of Ch'en Kao (d. ca. 1142–1143; 1111–1118 *chin-shih*) to a member of the Wang of Yin County in Ming Prefecture, one branch of the P'u-t'ien Ch'en came to be registered there. Although he relinquished any claim to property in P'u-t'ien, Ch'en Kao's son, Ch'en Chu-jen (1129–1197; 1151 *chin-shih*), did not entirely cut off his ties to family there. At the death of his uncle in P'u-t'ien, he helped to care for his orphaned cousins, establishing a charitable estate for them with two *ch'ing* (twenty-eight acres) of land. Ch'en Chu-jen was a nephew of Wang Ta-yu (1145 *chin- shih*), as was Lou Yueh (1137–1213), who composed a record of conduct for Chu-jen that details his ancestry and his relations with the Wang in Yin County. See Lou Yueh, *Kung-k'uei chi*, 89.1207, for background on ancestry and move to Yin; and 89.1220–89.1221 for relations with P'u-t'ien branch and charitable estate. For Ch'en Kao and Ch'en Chu-jen, see SJCC III.2500 and III.2533. Ch'en Mi must have belonged to the same P'u-t'ien Ch'en, and his grandfather, father, and brothers, as well as affinal ties, can be documented. For Ch'en Mi, see SJCC III.2441; for his father, Ch'en Hsun-ch'ing (1113–1186), his mother, and his paternal grandparents, see SJCC III.2601–III.2602. For his brothers Ch'en Ting (1150–1174) and Ch'en Shou (d. 1211), see SJCC III.2441, III.2434; for his cousin, Ch'en Yü, see SJCC III.2434. Ch'en Mi was married to the daughter of Liang K'o-chia (1128–1187) from Chin-chiang (Ch'üan-chou), first place *chin-shih* in 1160, prefect of Fu-chou, and compiler of the Ch'un-hsi era (1174–1189) gazetteer for Fu-chou, Liang K'o-chia, comp., *Ch'un-hsi San-shan chih* (see Balazs and Hervouet, *Sung Bibliography*, 149).

141. SYHA 69.13a.
142. Although it bears the same name as the prefecture, Yen-p'ing Academy was actually named for Li T'ung, Chu Hsi's teacher, who was a native of the area and whose honorific name was Yen-p'ing. See SYHA 69.12b–69.13a; TMTC, 77.6b; and the biographies of Ch'en Mi (SS 408/167, 12312) and Hsu Yuan-shu (SS 424/183, 12661).
143. *T'ien-hsia shu-yuan tsung-chih*, 962, says that this academy was built in 1375 and includes a Ming inscription, which is also recorded in *Fu-chien t'ung-chih* (Ch'eng Tsu-lo, et al., eds.), 64.24a–b. I think the weight of evidence, given the variety of corroborating sources, supports the Southern Sung dating in this case. There is another minor problem with the sources on this academy. According to SYHA 84.6a–84.6b, Ch'eng Chao-k'ai (1212–1280; 1268 *chin-shih*) built Southern Way Academy in Shang-jao County (Hsin, Chiang-hsi). This source, however, goes on to say that he built the academy for the purpose of uniting Chu Hsi's and Lu Chiu-yuan's two schools of thought, using a phrase from Mencius to name the academy that includes the words "tao-i"(the Way unified). So "Tao-nan," what I have translated as "Southern Way," has mistakenly been used in SYHA for Tao-i, which is the name of an academy in Hsin Prefecture founded by Ch'eng Chao-k'ai, who also held an administrative position at Elephant Mountain Academy in Hsin. For Ch'eng Chao-k'ai, see SJCC IV.3046.
144. Lin Hsueh-meng and his younger brother, Lin Hsueh-fu, were both students of Chu Hsi. See SJCC II.1404 and references in SYHA 69.30b and SYHA: supp. 69.120a–69.121a.
145. For Chao Fu, see SJCC IV.3327 and SYHA supp. 70.33a. His father, Chao Kang, and Kang's younger brother, Chao Wei, were known as the "Two Chao of Yu-ch'i" and transmitted their father, Chao Ch'i's, learning. See SJCC IV.3361, IV.3333. Chao Ch'i was a student of Shih Tun (1128–1182; 1145 *chin-shih*),

who was a colleague of Chu Hsi and who also served as prefect of Nan-k'ang. For Shih Tun, see SJCC I.417. Shi Tun's grandfather moved to T'ai's Lin-hai County from Yueh's Hsin-chang. The Shih of Hsin-ch'ang produced an extraordinary number of *chin-shih* during the Sung, beginning with Shih Shih-tan in 1019 (SJCC I.429). He built a charitable school (*i-shu*) and was revered by Fan Chung-yen, who appointed him headmaster of Chi-shan Academy. For more on the Shih, see chapter 5 of this book.

146. Mao Huaixin raises doubts about the tradition that Yang Shih, as a student of the Ch'eng brothers, brought their learning to the south when he returned to Fukien. See Mao, "The Establishment of the School of Chu Hsi and Its Propagation in Fukien," 504–505. In support of his argument, Mao cites Chu Hsi's criticisms of Yang Shih and other evidence to suggest that the tradition is a product of later times. However, in the thirteenth century, judging from the establishment of a number of academies dedicated to Yang Shih, the tradition that Yang Shih transmitted the thought of the Ch'eng brothers to the south, and was thus an intermediary between them and Chu Hsi and his followers, was very much alive. Other academies dedicated to Yang Shih include ones in Ch'ang and Hang in Che-tung and T'an in Hu-nan. See TMTC 10.9a, 38.13b, 63.14a.

147. An inscription by Liu Ch'en-weng (1231–1294) on this Turtle Mountain Academy contains an interesting, probably apocryphal, account of the origin of the shrine: "In 1127–1131 bandits destroyed Chiang-lo. Only when they got to the gate of Yang Shih did they stop and say that this was his home and could not be burned. From this time on his residence became a shrine" (*Hsu-ch'i chi*, 1.5b–1.6a.)

148. There is some discrepancy in the sources. Two Ch'ing sources and SYHA state that Turtle Mountain Academy was founded in 1267 by the prefect Feng Meng-te, a 1238 *chin-shih* and native of Chiang-lo. For Feng Meng-te, see SJCC IV.2760. Liu Ch'en-weng's inscription says that the academy was founded during the administration of Ch'en Mi, around 1225. Ch'eng Tsu- lo, et al., eds., *Fu-chien t'ung-chih*, 64.30a; *T'ien-hsia shu-yuan tsung-chih*, 971–972; TMTC 77.6b; and SYHA: supp. 25.112b all attribute the founding to Feng Meng-te ca. 1267. Despite the weight of evidence on the other side, I am inclined to accept the earliest account, which is that of Liu Ch'en-weng.

149. Huang Chi (1196–1266), a native of P'u-t'ien, and his elder brother, Huang Chen (1226 *chin-shih*), were followers of Ch'en Mi and Pan Ping, a former student of Chu Hsi at Wu-i Academy. For Huang Chi and his brother, see SJCC IV.2877, IV.2875. According to SYHA: supp. 47.53b, they were also followers of Liu K'o-chuang. Pan Ping and his elder brother, Pan Chih, heard Chu Hsi lecture at Wu-i and became his disciples (SYHA 69.20a). See SJCC V.3628, V.3630. After his death, there was a shrine to Pan Ping at Three Mountains Academy in Fu-chou. After the deaths of Ch'en Mi and Pan Ping, Huang Chi founded East Lake Academy to venerate the two scholars and requested official land to support sacrifices to them, and both Huang Chi and his brother lectured there. See SYHA 70.6b. See also the funerary inscription by Liu K'o-chuang for Huang Chi (*Hou-ts'un hsien-sheng ta ch'üan-chi*, 163.1452–163.1454). Huang Chi later became headmaster at Han River Academy, also in P'u-t'ien (TMTC 77, 276).

150. For Chao Hsi-ch'a, see SJCC IV.3487. According to Ho Chiao-yuan, comp., *Min shu*, Chao Hsi-ch'a was a maternal grandson of Chu Hsi (33.10b–33.13a). I am grateful to John Chaffee for this reference.

151. For Chao Shih-hsia, see SJCC IV.3554 and SYHA: supp.70.29b. He was an eighth-generation descendant of T'ai-tsu, and this particular branch of the impe-

rial clan was prominent in Ch'ü's Huang-yen County. Chao Shih-hsia and his three brothers all studied with Chu Hsi. See Sun Ying-shih, *Chu-hu chi*, 11.1a–11.5a. I am grateful to John Chaffee for this reference.

152. Liu K'o-chuang, *Hou-ts'un hsien-sheng ta ch'üan-chi*, 93.15b.
153. Ch'eng Tsu-lo, et al., eds., *Fu-chien t'ung-chih*, 12.4b.
154. Liu K'o-chuang, *Hou-ts'un hsien-sheng ta ch'üan chi*, 93.15b.
155. For more on the "community compact," see Monika Übelhör, "The Community Compact (*hsiang-yüeh*) of the Sung and Its Educational Significance."
156. SJCC V.3919, V.3970.
157. A second aspect of many of these figures who lived in the late Northern and early Southern Sung is their opposition in office to compromise with the Jurchen Chin. Nearly all were noted as confirmed opponents of peace with the Chin, and Chang Shih was the son of the general Chang Chün (1097–1164).
158. Liu K'o-chuang, *Hou-ts'un hsien-sheng ta ch'üan-chi*, 93.15a. Liu K'o-chuang has identified for us—at least from his perspective—the key areas of academy activity associated with Chu Hsi in the mid-thirteenth century, when Liu wrote this inscription at the founding of Spring Mountain Academy. Chien in Fu-chien was the location of more than twenty academies, most established in the Southern Sung and over half of which were directly associated with Chu Hsi. Nan-k'ang was the site of White Deer Grotto, and T'an-Heng in central Hu-nan was the site of four academies, including Stone Drum, where Chu Hsi had played a role in the academy's revival. Ching-T'an in northern Hu-nan was the site of eleven academies, including Marchmount Hill. The puzzling part of Liu K'o-chuang's statement deals with Hui (Chiang-tung), which was the site of perhaps four academies, three established in the Southern Sung. The most prominent of these was Purple Light, which was founded to venerate Chu Hsi. Even so, there is no indication from extant sources that it was a major academy in size or influence. Two considerations are prompted by Liu K'o-chuang's focus on Hui along with the other more obviously included areas. First, he has emphasized areas that were the site of model academies, such as White Deer Grotto or Marchmount Hill, irrespective of numbers of academies, although the region surrounding Marchmount Hill was dotted with academies. Second, the inclusion of Hui suggests either that Purple Light had an importance at the time not evident in extant sources or that there were other academies for which we have no documentation at all. It is possible that both are true. The possibility of lacunae in the sources suggested by this example serves as a reminder to exercise caution in numerical or geographical assessments.
159. At least twenty-five name plaques were awarded to academies by the court under Li-tsung. For a convenient list of these, see Wu Wan-chü, *Sung-tai shu-yuan yü Sung-tai hsueh-shu chih kuan-hsi*, 59–61.
160. Purple Light Academy in Chu Hsi's registered native place of Wu-yuan County (Hui, Chiang-tung) received a name plaque from the court in 1246. See TMTC 16.189.
161. Lou Yueh, *Kung-k'uei chi*, 54.756.

2. Shrines, Schools, and Shih*: The Thirteenth-Century Academy Movement*

1. For the concept of a national pantheon, see Neskar, "The Cult of Worthies," especially 216–270.

2. In earlier periods, men who were punished with cashiering or dismissal sometimes founded academies where they had been sent or retired. Eastern Isle Academy in Hu-pei's Lu-hsi County was established when Wang T'ing-kuei (1080–1172; 1118 *chin-shih*) was cashiered there by Ch'in Kuei and the local magistrate built the academy to accommodate the many *shih* who followed him. See Li Han-chang, et al., eds., *Hu-nan t'ung-chih*, 70.3b; SJCC I.326.
3. For these, see SJCC V.3875, V.3869, V.3995. For the academy, see Tseng Kuo-fan, et al., comps., *Chiang-hsi t'ung-chih*, 81.20a; Wang I-shan, *Chia-ts'un lei-kao*, 8.1a–8.4b. The academy was established by Ch'en Chang, younger brother of Ch'en Wei (see chapter 5), when he was prefect of Jui. See SJCC III.2529.
4. See Neskar, "The Cult of Worthies."
5. See, for example, Lee, *Government Education and Examinations in Sung China*, 29. See also Liu, "How Did a Neo-Confucian School Become the State Orthodoxy?" For a recent fuller account of both intellectual and political factors in the rise of True Way Learning, see Tillman, *Confucian Discourse and Chu Hsi's Ascendancy*.
6. For a brief discussion of this topic, see Foulk, "Myth, Ritual, and Monastic Practice in Sung Ch'an Buddhism," 163–164. Although T'ang monasteries that received name plaques from the court were granted certain privileges and benefits, by the Sung there were so many that the bestowal of a name plaque no longer had much significance. During the Sung a new designation of "public" monasteries, whose abbacies were overseen by the state, took the place of imperially sanctioned monasteries. State control of the appointment of abbots can be seen as similar to the appointment of headmasters at academies.
7. Neskar has named these "transmission shrines." See Neskar, "The Cult of Worthies," 216–270.
8. This academy was awarded a name near the end of Li-tsung's reign. See Li Han-chang, et al., eds., *Hu-nan t'ung-chih*, 69.25a. By far the most numerous academies dedicated by name to any True Way patriarch were those called Lien-hsi, after Chou Tun-i. They were widespread geographically: from northern Chiang-hsi, at the site of Chou Tun-i's study (Chiang); to his birthplace in Hu-nan (Tao); to places where he traveled or held office in Hu-nan and Kuang-tung; and even at the residence of his maternal relatives in Che-hsi (Jun). TMTC 52.21a (Chiang); 65.17b; Li Han-chang, et al., eds., *Hu-nan t'ung-chih*, 69.23a (Shao in Hu-nan); TMTC 79.11a, 81.10a (Kuang); TMTC 11.6a (Jun). Like academies dedicated to other members of the True Way pantheon, Chou Tun-i was also enshrined at academies named for a place, such as Dragon Creek in Wan-an County (Chi, Chiang-hsi). See Tseng Kuo-fan, et al., comps., *Chiang-hsi t'ung-chih*, 81.50b; TMTC 56.11a. Here local people established a shrine to Chou Tun-i to commemorate the fact that he held office in the area at a place called Dragon Creek near Fragrant Forest Temple, where he had visited.
9. Chu Hsi's son was said to have played a key role in the restoration of White Deer Grotto in 1217. See Huang Kan, *Mien-chai hsien-sheng Huang Wen-su kung wen-chi*, 18.5b. For the shrine at White Deer, see *Pai-lu shu-yuan chih*, 2.4a–2.4b.
10. For the date of its founding, see Fang Hui, *T'ung-chiang hsu-chi*, 131, where he says that 1276 was thirty-one years after the founding of the academy. For Li-tsung's bequest, see TMTC 16.189. For Han Pu, the prefect who established this academy, see SJCC V.4148. He and his younger brother, Han Hsiang (SJCC V.4139), took *chin-shih* degrees in 1223 and were students of Ch'eng-Chu learning. Li-tsung honored them with an inscription in his calligraphy also. See

SYHA: supp. 49.183b. Han Pu and his brother were from Yü-shan County in Shang-jao, which was also the residence of Han Yuan-chi in his old age, although he was originally from Kaifeng. Since Han Yuan-chi was prefect of Chien and wrote on Chu Hsi's Wu-i Academy, it is tempting to speculate that he belonged to the same Han family in Shang-jao, although I have found no direct evidence of this. Han Pu and his brother would have been about two generations after Han Yuan-chi, who died in 1187.

11. However, Chu Hsi never took the post. See Tseng Kuo-fan, et al., comps., *Chiang-hsi t'ung-chih*, 81.54a; see also Wu Ch'eng, *Wu Wen-cheng kung wen-chi*, 20.28a. For Feng Ch'u-chi, see SJCC IV.2752. According to the local history, this academy was said to imitate the Imperial University and therefore be different from other academies. However, not enough is known about this academy to clarify this point.
12. Yin Chi-shan, et al., eds., *Chiang-nan t'ung-chih*, 90.23b–90.24a.
13. TMTC 57.19b (3560); Tseng Kuo-fan, et al., comps., *Chiang-hsi t'ung-chih*, 81.24a.
14. Yuan Chueh, *Yen-yu Ssu-ming chih*, 14.38a. For Cheng Ch'ing-chih, see SJCC V.3704–V.3706; for Lou Fang, see SJCC V.3721–V.3722.
15. Tseng Kuo-fan, et al., comps., *Chiang-hsi t'ung-chih*, 81.3b–81.4a.
16. For example, Branch Mountain Academy in Ch'ü, Che-tung (Chi Hui-yun, et al., comps., *Che-chiang t'ung-chih*, 28.710). Mount Chi in Yueh (TMTC 45.10a), although dedicated to Chu Hsi and awarded a name plaque, left only a brief record.
17. Yin Chi-shan, et al., eds., *Chiang-nan t'ung-chih*, 90.5a. Founded in 1235, Tiger Hill was dedicated to Yin Ch'un (1071–1142). See chapter 5 of this book.
18. Yin Chi-shan, et al., eds., *Chiang-nan t'ung-chih*, 90.4b. According to the Yuan writer Yü Chi, a descendant of Wei Liao-weng told him that his great-grandfather was buried in Wu (the Su-chou region) because he had been unable to return to his home in Ssu-ch'uan before his death. See Yü Chi, *Tao-yuan hsueh-ku lu*, 7.2b–7.5a. According to standard sources, such as Wei Liao-weng's collected works and the dynastic history, Wei actually died in Fu-chou (Fu-chien), and the court granted his family a residence in Su-chou. See James T. C. Liu, "Wei Liao-weng's Thwarted Statecraft," 347.
19. For a concise summary of his life and sources, see SJCC V.4241–V.4244; see also Franke, *Sung Biographies*, 1180–1183, and Liu, "Wei Liao-weng's Thwarted Statecraft," 336–348.
20. Wei Liao-weng, *Ho-shan wen-ch'ao*, 11.10a–11.11a.
21. SYHA: supp. 80.37a5. For Wang Ta-fa, see SJCC I.713.
22. Wei Liao-weng, *Ho-shan wen-ch'ao*, 11.10b.
23. Ibid.
24. Ibid. Wei Liao-weng also described the extensive layout of the academy, with buildings for various purposes, including recreation and leisure.
25. Wei Liao-weng, *Ho-shan hsien-sheng ta ch'üan wen-chi*, 47: 1a–2b.
26. SS 437/196, 12968.
27. SJCC IV.3606. A refugee from the north at the fall of the Northern Sung, Fu Kuang retired to Ch'ung-te County (Hsiu, Che-hsi), where he established a study. See SJCC IV.3606; Hsu Shih, comp., *Chih-yuan Chia-ho chih*, 13.21a; 9b–12a. In 1269 the local magistrate established Ch'uan-i Academy at the site of his study, and enshrined both Fu Kuang and Chu Hsi there (*Chih-yuan Chia-ho chih*, 7.5a).

28. SJCC III.1850.
29. Lu Chiu-yuan, *Lu Hsiang-shan ch'üan-chi*, 36.345. See also Yuan Fu's inscription on Elephant Mountain Academy, dated 1233, in his *Meng-chai chi*, 13.186–13.188.
30. Yuan Chueh, *Yen-yu Ssu-ming chih*, 5.19a. See also Yuan Fu's lectures on the *Doctrine of the Mean* collected in *Meng-chai Chung-yung chiang-i*, in SMTS, collection 3.
31. Lu Chiu-yuan, *Lu Hsiang-shan ch'üan chi*, 35.347.
32. Ibid. For Ch'ien Shih, see SJCC V.4062–V.4063. Elephant Mountain had a long Buddhist history. Lu Chiu-yuan referred to this in a letter to Wang Chien-chung, recalling that the T'ang Chan master, Ma-tsu, had once resided on the mountain and that it became known as Chan Master Mountain. Lu Chiu-yuan said that he resided in the abbot's quarters of the ruins of the Ying-t'ien monastery (*Lu Hsiang-shan ch'üan-chi*, 9.76). This mountain was also known as Ying-t'ien Mountain, and thus the academy is referred to at times as Ying-t'ien shan Academy (not to be confused with the Northern Sung academy at Ying-t'ien *fu* in the north). See, e.g., SYHA 77.2b, 77.14a.
33. SJCC IV.2760; Yuan Fu, *Meng-chai chi*, 18.257.
34. Lu Chiu-yuan, *Lu Hsiang-shan ch'üan chi*, 35.346. The printing of Yuan Hsieh's work is cited in Huang Ch'ing-wen, *Chung-kuo ku-tai shu-yuan chih-tu chi ch'i k'o-shu t'an-yen* (Investigation into China's traditional academy system and printing), 100, and Liu Chih-sheng, "Chung-kuo shu-yuan k'o-shu chi-lueh," 411. Neither author has a reference for this, and I have been unable to track one down. Oddly, neither mention the printing of Lu Chiu-yuan's works, which is cited in the *nien-p'u* appended to his collected works.
35. Yuan Fu, *Mien-chai chi*, 13.187.
36. Lu Chiu-yuan, *Lu Hsiang-shan ch'üan-chi*, 36.347.
37. Yuan Fu, *Meng-chai chi*, 13.192. This was in 1235, according to an inscription by Ma T'ing- luan (1222–1289), written in 1289 (see Ma T'ing-luan, *Pi-wu wan-fang chi*, 17.10b).
38. Yuan Fu, *Meng-chai chi*, 13.192. For T'ang Chin, see SJCC IV.2771–IV.2772; for Chang Hsia, see SJCC III.2251 and SS 430/189, 12787.
39. See David Gedalecia, "Wu Ch'eng: A Yüan Dynasty Neo-Confucian Scholar," 304. T'ang Chin's elder brother, T'ang Ch'ien (1196 *chin-shih*), was a follower of Chu Hsi, as was his younger brother, T'ang Chung (1226 *chin-shih*). For T'ang Ch'ien and T'ang Chung, see SJCC IV.2772. See also SYHA 84.1b–84.2a.
40. This will be discussed further in chapter 5.
41. Yuan Fu, *Meng-chai chi*, 13.191.
42. Ibid., 14.202–14.203.
43. Ibid., 14.202.
44. Ibid.
45. For Wang Po, see SJCC I.143–I.144; for Ho Chi, see SJCC II.1257. In accordance with the practice by the 1260s, Ho Chi was concurrently professor at the Wu prefectural school and headmaster at Beautiful Pools Academy. See SS 45.884.
46. SS 45.884.
47. For a brief discussion of the connection to Huang Kan, see Tillman, *Confucian Discourse and Chu Hsi's Ascendancy*, 248. Ho Chi's father had held office in Lin-ch'uan County (Fu Prefecture, Chiang-hsi) when Huang Kan was county magistrate. See SS 438/197, 12979. So Ho Chi studied with Huang Kan, and Wang Po, in turn, studied with Ho, thus receiving Huang Kan's influence through his teacher. For Lü Tsu-ch'ien's influence, see Tillman, *Confucian Discourse and*

Chu Hsi's Ascendancy, 248–249, and John D. Langlois, Jr., "Political Thought in Chin-hua under Mongol Rule," 151.

48. Lin Shu-hsun, et al., eds., *Shao-chou fu-chih*, 18.1a.
49. For Yang Ta-i, see SJCC IV.3151. See also Lin Shu-hsun, et al., eds., *Shao-chou fu-chih*, 18.1a, which refers to his office as intendant of the Evernormal Granary. His official biography in the dynastic history, however, says that he was judicial intendant when he established this academy (SS 423/182, 12645).
50. The prefect was Chou Shun-yuan. For Chou Shun-yuan, see SJCC II.1491; for his building of the shrine, see SYHA: supp. 12.59b. According to Neskar, this was one of the earliest transmission shrines (Neskar, "The Cult of Worthies," 217–218). Neskar cites Chu Hsi's essay on its rebuilding, which dates the shrine to 1165; the *Shao-chou fu-chih* (Lin Shu-hsun, et al., eds.) dates it to 1170 (18.1a).
51. For Liao Te-ming, see SJCC IV.3305. For Chu Hsi's essay, see *Chu-tzu ta-ch'üan*, 79.9b–79.11a.
52. Lin Shu-hsun, et al., eds., *Shao-chou fu-chih*, 18.1b–18.2a; SS 423/182, 12645. Fang Ta-tsung (1183–1247; 1206 *chin-shih*) is quoted in this inscription as having expressed regret that his friend Yang Ta-i had to leave to take up his new post, but pleasure that it was an office formerly held by Chou Tun-i, and he urged that a shrine be erected to venerate Chou (18.1b). For Fang Ta-tsung, see SJCC I.68-69. Fang Ta-tsung belonged to the prominent Fang lineage of Fu-chien's P'u-t'ien County and held office as Nan-chien prefectural professor; he was also prefect of Lung-hsing and pacification commissioner of Kuang-nan. At the time he was quoted in this inscription, he was identified as *ching-shih*, "Classics Teacher," a court post for lecturing the emperor.
53. Lin Shu-hsun, et al., eds., *Shao-chou fu chih*, 18.2a. In addition to the five-bay shrine, Hsiang River Academy included a five-bay lecture hall (with two dormitories on either side, each of which was five bays), three gates, lands, and surrounding walls.
54. Lin Shu-hsun, et al., eds., *Shao-chou fu chih*, 18.1a.
55. For the first appointment of a headmaster at this academy, see SS 46.894. For the inscription, see Ou-yang Shou-tao, *Hsuan-chai wen-chi*, 14.1a–14.4b. For Yang Ch'ung-kung, see SJCC IV.3157.
56. For this academy, see Li Han-chang, et al., eds., *Hu-nan t'ung-chih*, 69.23a. Yang Ch'ung-kung earlier had been prefectural professor (*chiao-shou*), and then erudite of the National Academy (*kuo-tzu po-shih*). TMTC 65.17b; Ou-yang Shou-tao, *Hsuan-chai wen-chi*, 14.2b. Yang Ch'ung-kung also established an elementary school (*hsiao-hsüeh*) especially for the descendants of Chou Tun-i. For Yang Ch'ung-kung, see SJCC IV.3157. After Yang Ch'ung-kung served as supervisor of punishments for Kuang-tung, he was venerated by local people at a shrine there.
57. Ou-yang Shou-tao, *Hsuan-chai wen-chi*, 14.2b.
58. Liu Po-chi, *Kuang-tung shu-yuan chih-tu*, 21.
59. Ibid.
60. TMTC 83.10a. His cofounder was Chu Ssu-sun (1214–1280); for Chu Ssu-sun, see SJCC I.623. A native of Lang-chung in the Ssu-ch'uan basin, as a young man Chu Ssu-sun experienced the Mongol destruction of Ch'eng-tu in 1236 and barely escaped with his life. Chu Ssu-sun's experiences mirror one of the key elements in the Southern Sung academy movement during the mid-thirteenth century: the founding or support of academies by refugees who were displaced by warfare (see chapter 5). Paul Smith cites Chu Ssu-sun's experience as a young man during the destruction of Chengdu in 1236, recounted in the *San-mao lu*. See Paul J. Smith, "Family, *Landsmann*, and Status-Group Affinity in Refugee

Mobility Strategies: The Mongol Invasions and the Diaspora of Sichuanese Elites, 1230–1330," 671. Around the time Hsüan-ch'eng Academy was founded, Chu Ssu-sun was appointed pacification commissioner of Ching-hu, concurrently prefect of Chiang-ling.

61. Chi Ch'ing, et al., eds., *Kuang-hsi t'ung-chih*, 134.15b.
62. Wei Liao-weng, *Ho-shan hsien-sheng ta ch'üan chi*, 48.405–48.406. For Chao Pi-yuan, see SJCC IV.3418; for Chao Ju-yü, see Franke, *Sung Biographies*, 59–63.
63. Wei Liao-weng, *Ho-shan hsien-sheng ta ch'üan chi*, 48.3a. See also Ch'eng Pi, *Ming-shui chi*, 7.14a. For East Lake, see Tseng Kuo-fan, et al., comps., *Chiang-hsi t'ung-chih*, 81.3b–81.4a, and Yuan Hsieh, *Chieh-chai chi*, 10.148–10.149; for Lien-hsi, see Li Han-chang, et al., eds., *Hu-nan t'ung-chih*, 69.23a. This was the academy dedicated to Chou Tun-i in his native place and restored by Yang Ta-i's nephew, Yang Ch'ung-kung, who requested a name in 1262.
64. For Chang Ching, who composed Liu K'ai's record of conduct, see SJCC III.2290.
65. See Bol, "*This Culture of Ours*," for extensive discussion of the relationship between literary culture and ethical philosophy in Northern Sung.
66. See inscriptions by Lin Hsi-i (*Chu-ch'i chuan-chai shih-i k'ao hsu-chi*, 11.9b–11.11a) and Wu Ch'eng (*Wu Wen-cheng kung wen-chi*, 20.23b–20.25b). In these inscriptions, the shrine to Han Yü is called a *miao*, whereas normally the term for such a shrine is *tz'u*. The language used says that the people built a temple (*miao*) to enshrine (*tz'u*) Han Yü. See Wu Ch'eng, *Wu Wen-cheng kung wen-chi*, 20.24a. Lin Hsi-i also uses the term *miao*, e.g., Lin Hsi-i, *Chu-ch'i chuan-chai shih-i k'ao hsu-chi*, 11.9b.
67. For background on Han Yü, see Charles Hartman, *Han Yü and the T'ang Search for Unity*.
68. See Jao Tsung-i, "Sung-tai li Ch'ao kuan-shih yü Shu-hsueh chi Min-hsueh: Han-kung tsai Ch'ao-chou shou kao-tu ch'ung-ching chih yuan-yin," 167.
69. Ibid.
70. Ibid. For Ch'en Yao-tso, see SJCC III.2618.
71. For this, see Hartman, *Han Yü and the T'ang Search for Unity*, 93, 305–306. See also Jao Tsung-i, "Sung-tai li Ch'ao kuan-shih yü Shu-hsueh chi Min-hsueh," 167.
72. Lin Hsi-i, *Chu-ch'i chuan-chai shih-i k'ao hsu-chi*, 11.9b. For Cheng Liang-ch'en, see SJCC V.3689.
73. Lin Hsi-i, *Chu-ch'i chuan-chai shih-i k'ao hsu-chi*, 11.9b–11.11a. Lin Hsi-i also wrote an inscription in 1269 to commemorate the rebuilding of K'ai-yuan Temple in Ch'ao by his former student and friend, Lin Shih-chih (*Chu-ch'i chuan-chai shih-i k'ao hsu-chi*, 11.7b–11.9b). For Lin Shih-chih, see SJCC II.1381. Like the writers of other inscriptions, Lin Hsi-i undoubtedly was asked to do this for his friend and complied as a favor.
74. Lin Hsi-i, *Chu-ch'i chuan-chai shih-i k'ao hsu-chi*, 11.9b. Ch'en Kuei was prefect of Chang (Fu-chien) and later intendant of the Evernormal Granary for Kuang-tung. For Ch'en Kuei, see SJCC III.2435. Ch'en Kuei was also the son of Ch'en Mi, founder of three academies in Fu-chien. The amount of land allocated is unspecified.
75. Jao Tsung-i, "Sung-tai li Ch'ao kuan-shih yü Shu-hsueh chi Min-hsueh," 168.
76. As a Confucian scholar, Lin Hsi-i was deeply knowledgeable about Taoism, and he was the author of important Sung commentaries on Taoist works. See Balazs and Hervouet, *A Sung Bibliography*, 360–361, 363–364, 367–368.
77. SYHA: supp. 47.57.
78. SJCC III.2435.

79. In addition to being a direct disciple of Chu Hsi, Liao Te-ming was also known for destroying "licentious shrines" while magistrate of P'u-t'ien and for suppressing bandits in northern Shao Prefecture while judicial intendant for Kuang-tung. See his biography in SS 317/196, 12971.
80. Lin Hsi-i, *Chu-ch'i chuan-chai shih-i-k'ao hsu-chi*, 11.10a–11.10b. Wen Weng was an administrator of Shu during the Former Han who was known for carrying out *chiao-hua*; the establishment of schools there under Wu-ti was credited to him. Ch'ang Kun was a T'ang official who, like Han Yü, was cashiered to administer Ch'ao and later held office in Min, where he supported schools and was later venerated by local people for his work as an educator.
81. Lin Hsi-i, *Chu-ch'i chuan-chai shih-i k'ao hsu-chi*, 11.9b. For Chao Te, see *Chung-kuo jen-ming ta tz'u tien*, 1418. See also Hartman, *Han Yü and the T'ang Search for Unity*, 93. For Liao Te-ming, one of Chu Hsi's principal disciples from Fu-chien, see SJCC IV.3305. Double Peak Academy in Fu-chien's Nan-chien Prefecture was established at the end of the Southern Sung to honor him and Liao Kang. See Liu Ch'en-weng, *Hsu-ch'i chi*, 2.7b–2.9a, and Liu Chiang-sun, *Yang-wu chai chi*, 15.25a–15.28a, for inscriptions on this academy.
82. Another famous exile of the Northern Sung, Su Shih, penned an inscription on the earlier temple to Han Yü in which he claimed that Confucian learning in Ch'ao began with Han Yü's establishment of the school. See Hartman, *Han Yü and the T'ang Search for Unity*, 93, 305–306.
83. Yuan Chueh, *Yen-yu Ssu-ming chih*, 14.27b.
84. For Huang Chen, see SJCC IV.2780.
85. SJCC V.2439; SYHA 74.1414.
86. Yuan Chueh, *Yen-yu Ssu-ming chih*, 14.28a.
87. SJCC V.4239–4240.
88. I can identify Chao Yü-ho only by his titles at the end of his inscription and the geographic label of T'ien-t'ai as his native place.
89. Yuan Chueh, *Yen-yu Ssu-ming chih*, 14.26a–14.26b.
90. Ibid., 14.25b–14.27a. Chao Yü-ho's comments on the difference between Chu Hsi and Taoist eremitism echoes Han Yuan-chi's writing on Wu-i Academy in Fu-chien (see chapter 1).
91. Yuan Chueh, *Yen-yu Ssu-ming chih*, 14.26b.
92. Ibid., 14.27b–14.28a.
93. Yuan Chueh, *Yen-yu Ssu-ming chih*, 14.28a–14.29b.
94. Ibid., 14.30a. Although the date is not clear, an academy was founded to venerate Yang Chien in Lo-p'ing County (Jao, Chiang-hsi) sometime after his death because he had held office there. See Tseng Kuo-fan, et al., comps., *Chiang-hsi t'ung-chih*, 22.24b.
95. Yuan Chueh, *Yen-yu Ssu-ming chih*, 14.30a. For background on this, see Walton, "The Institutional Context of Neo-Confucianism," 473–474. For Liu Fu, see SJCC V.3908. Whether this represented usurpation of temple property is not made clear in the sources, although in the early Yuan, priests from this temple "usurped its land, destroyed its sacrificial images, and slandered all its students" (*Yen-yu Ssu-ming chih*, 14.30a), suggesting an ongoing struggle over land that alternately went either to the Confucian academy or the Buddhist temple. This temple was a "teaching" temple belonging to the Heavenly Platform sect (Huang Jun-yü, *Ning-po fu chien-yao chih*, 5.4b).
96. For Wen Chi-weng, see SJCC I.41. He also wrote an inscription on Ch'uan-i Academy in 1269 and was named education intendant at Illumined Way in Chien-k'ang (see below).

97. Yuan Chueh, *Yen-yu Ssu-ming chih*, 14.30b–14.32b. For Wen Chi-weng, see SJCC I.41.
98. Yuan Chueh, *Yen-yu Ssu-ming chih*, 14.30b–14.32b.
99. SJCC III.2586, III.2435.
100. The term *hsu-ling* is found in Chu Hsi's commentary on the opening line of the *Great Learning*, where it is part of the phrase *hsu-ling pu-mei*. Descriptive of the concept *ming-te* (inborn luminous virtue), Gardner translates this phrase as "unprejudiced, spiritual and completely unmuddled." See Daniel Gardner, *Chu Hsi and the Ta-hsüeh: Neo-Confucian Reflection on the Confucian Canon*, 89, 136 (Chinese text).
101. Extensive documentation on this academy is found in Chou Ying-ho, comp., *Ching-ting Chien-k'ang chih*, 29. This gazetteer was commissioner by the prefect Ma Kuang-tsu, and the compiler was Chou Ying-ho, headmaster at Illumined Way, thus accounting for the detailed coverage of the academy. Neskar, "The Cult of Worthies," 225, dates the founding of what she calls "Transmission" shrines to the 1170s. An inscription on the shrine was written in 1196 by Yu Chiu-yen (1142–1206), a native of Chien-yang (Fu-chien) and a follower of Chang Shih. Yu Chiu-yen laments the decline of the Way after Mencius, citing Hsun-tzu, Yang Hsiung, and Han Yü as exceptions whose writings followed the sages. Although various classicists arose from the Han on, they were not able to restore the flourishing of the rulers of antiquity. Reflecting the hagiography of transmission discussed by Neskar, Yu Chiu-yen treats Ch'eng Hao as the Sung link with the tradition of the Way, lost since Han Yü at least, and taught to Ch'eng Hao by Chou Tun-i. See *Ching-ting Chien-k'ang chih*, 29.6a–29.8a.
102. Chou Ying-ho, comp., *Ching-ting Chien-k'ang chih*, 29.10a.
103. Ibid.
104. Ibid., 29.1a.
105. Ibid., 29.2a.
106. Ibid.
107. Ibid. For Wu Yuan, see SJCC II.1105–II.1106.
108. Chou Ying-ho, comp., *Ching-ting Chien-k'ang chih*, 29.1b.
109. Ibid., 29.12b–29.13b. See chapter 1 for Wang Yeh's establishment of Chien-an Academy in Chien-ning (Fu-chien) while serving as prefect there. See SJCC I.167.
110. Chou Ying-ho, comp., *Ching-ting Chien-k'ang chih*, 29.11b. For Ma Kuang-tsu, see SJCC III.1836–III.1838. Like Wang Yeh, his predecessor as Chien-k'ang prefect, Ma Kuang-tsu was also a native of Chin-hua (Che-tung).
111. Chou Ying-ho, comp., *Ching-ting Chien-k'ang chih*, 29.14a.
112. Ibid., 29.14b.
113. For the functions of buildings at the prefectural school, see Chou Ying-ho, comp., *Ching-ting Chien-k'ang chih*, 28.11b. The Hall of Great Completion was a name given to central buildings in many academies, particularly during the Northern Sung, suggesting a close structural affinity between academies and schools.
114. Chou Ying-ho, comp., *Ching-ting Chien-k'ang chih*, 28.7a–28.11b.
115. Ibid., 29.15a; 28.14b–28.15a.
116. Ibid., 28.25a–28.28b. For a general discussion of the role of charitable estates in Southern Sung, see Linda Walton, "Charitable Estates as an Aspect of Statecraft in Southern Sung China."
117. Chou Ying-ho, comp., Ching-ting Chien-k'ang chih, 28.25a. For the category of shih-tzu, see Takahashi Yoshirō, "Sōdai shijin no mibun ni tsuite," 44 ff. Takahashi defines both *shih-tzu* and *shih-jen* as members of an intellectual class (*tu-*

shu jen) who were a legal category distinct from commoners and bureaucratic officeholders (*shih ta-fu*).

118. Ibid. A *tan* (or picul) equals 2.7 bushels.
119. Chou Ying-ho, comp., *Ching-ting Chien-k'ang chih*, 28.25b–28.26a.
120. Ibid., 28.25b–28.26b. The minimum requirement for an adult male in Sung times has been estimated to be about 2.5 *sheng* (one *sheng* equals .01 piculs, or .86 quarts). See Lee, *Government Education and Examinations in Sung China*, 135.
121. Chou Ying-ho, comp., *Ching-ting Chien-k'ang chih*, 28.26b.
122. A catty equals .01 piculs, or about 1.3 pounds.
123. The detailed economic information on Illumined Way is unique, but it does help in trying to assess levels of funding for academies in the Southern Sung. Lee has cited five to ten *ch'ing* (5,000 to 10,000 *mou*, or between 70 and 140 acres) as a fairly standard allotment for government schools in the twelfth century in moderately prosperous areas of the lower Yangtze region. See Lee, *Government Education and Examinations in Sung China*, 129 ff. Davis cites a 1071 mandate for prefectural schools to have a minimum of one thousand *mou*. See Davis, "Custodians of Education and Endowment at the State Schools of Southern Sung," 98. The local history of Ming Prefecture for the early thirteenth century (1227) records over four thousand *mou* of paddy lands spread over four of the five counties dedicated to school support. See Lo Chün, et al., comps., *Pao-ch'ing Ssu-ming chih*, 2.12a–2.13a. This amount does not include various other kinds of land, such as dry fields, lakelands, ponds, etc. These lands produced approximately 750 piculs of polished rice, 1,600 piculs of unhulled rice, and 2,215 piculs of grain. Other income in the form of cash came from taxes assessed on river marshes, mountains, etc. Looking at land prices and rents in Liang-che, McDermott cites statistics indicating that there was a great increase in the price of land in Liang-che from Northern to Southern Sung. See Joseph McDermott, "Land Tenure and Rural Control in the Liang-che Region during the Southern Sung," 275. The total amount of land—nearly five thousand *mou*—allotted to support the academy compares favorably with what we know of government school lands throughout the Sung. Davis' study of government school land endowments shows wide variations in levels of support, even in relatively similar economic conditions characteristic of prosperous areas of the coastal southeast.
124. Literally, the *mu-kuan*, or "behind the curtain" level of officials, such as assistant prefects, etc.
125. Chou Ying-ho, comp., *Ching-ting Chien-k'ang chih*, 29.14b. Wen Chi-weng's post is named as *chih-kan*, which seems to be a general term for a subordinate position in the prefectural government.
126. Chou Ying-ho, comp., *Ching-ting Chien-k'ang chih*, 29.20b. For Wu Chien, see SJCC II.1107–II.1108.
127. Chou Ying-ho, comp., *Ching-ting Chien-k'ang chih*, 29.20b.
128. Normally, academy headmaster was a concurrent appointment with the post of prefectural school professor. For example, Ho Chi was appointed Wu prefectural school professor, concurrently headmaster of Beautiful Pools Academy in 1264.
129. Ou-yang Shou-tao, *Hsuan-chai wen-chi*, 14.5a.
130. Chuang Chung-fang, comp., *Nan Sung wen-fan*, 46.12a–46.12b.
131. Chou Ying-ho, comp., *Ching-ting Chien-k'ang chih*, 29.15b.
132. Ibid., 29.15a.
133. Ibid., 29.15b. This was according to the *chao-mu* system, which stipulated the

order of lineal descendants as they were arranged at the ancestral shrines or grave.

134. Chou Ying-ho, comp., *Ching-ting Chien-k'ang chih*, 29.15b.
135. Ibid., 81.3b–81.4a; Yuan Hsieh, *Chieh-chai chi*, 10.148.
136. Yuan Hsieh, *Chieh-chai chi*, 10.148. East Lake Academy was located at a site associated with a tenth-century scholar, Li Yin, who was known along with his son, Li Hsu-chi (977 *chin-shih*), for attention to family as well as scholarship and service (SJCC II.864, II.1038). When East Lake was completed in 1211, it was altogether thirty-four bays in size, managed by a local scholar, and supported with two million cash and over one hundred piculs of polished rice (*Chieh-chai chi*, 10.149). Lu Chiu-yuan's son, Lu Chih-chih (1171–1225), later managed the academy (SYHA 58.2a; SJCC III.2668).
137. Lou Yueh, *Kung-k'uei chi*, 54.755–54.756. For Lou Yueh, see SJCC V.3728–V.3729.
138. Lou Yueh, *Kung-k'uei chi*, 54.755.
139. Ibid., 54.756.
140. Chou Pi-ta, *P'ing-yuan hsu-kao*, 19.7b–19.8b. There is some confusion about the name of this academy. Both Dragon Islet and White Egret (or simply Egret) Islet are used by various chroniclers of the academy at different times. Although never stated directly, it appears that Chou Pi-ta's Dragon Islet Academy is the same as the one Ou-yang Shou-tao, Hsieh Fang-te, and Liu Ch'en-weng wrote about as (White) Egret Islet. See Ou-yang Shou-tao, *Hsuan-chai wen-chi*, 14.5a–14.8b; Hsieh Fang-te, *Tieh-shan chi*, 9.2b–9.3b; Liu Ch'en-weng, *Hsu-ch'i chi*, 3.29a–3.31b.
141. Chou Pi-ta, *P'ing-yuan hsu-kao*, 19.8a.
142. Hsieh Fang-te, *Tieh-shan chi*, 9.2b–9.3a.
143. TMTC 57.6a; Chou Pi-ta, *P'ing-yuan hsu-kao*, 20.2a–20.3a. The name of the prefecture was changed from Yun to Jui in 1225. The commandery was Kao-an. For Wang Yen, see SJCC I.159.144. SJCC I.109; Franke, *Sung Biographies*, 1147–1153.
145. Chou Pi-ta, *P'ing-yuan hsu-kao*, 20.2b.
146. Ibid.
147. Ibid., 20.3a.
148. See Schirokauer, "Neo-Confucians under Attack," 190.
149. For Chiang Wan-li, see SJCC I.536–I.538.
150. For Ou-yang Shou-tao, see SJCC V.3761. Chiang Wan-li was also involved with Tsung-lien Academy in northeastern Chiang-hsi's Lung-hsing when he held office there. See Tseng Kuo-fan, et al., comps., *Chiang-hsi t'ung-chih*, 81.24a. This academy was founded at a shrine to Chou Tun-i, who held office there. Since this academy was dedicated to Chou Tun-i, it could be said that there was a link to True Way Learning, but it seems more appropriate to see Chiang Wan-li's connection with this academy as part of his duties as prefect.
151. Ou-yang Shou-tao, *Hsuan-chai wen-chi*, 14.5a.
152. For Huang Chia, see SJCC IV.2865.
153. Ou-yang Shou-tao, *Hsuan-chai wen-chi*, 14.5b.
154. Ibid., 14.6b.
155. Ibid., 7a.
156. Ibid., 14.7a.
157. Ibid., 14.7b.
158. Ibid., 14.7b–14.8b.
159. For Hsieh Fang-te, see SJCC V.4119.

160. Hsieh Fang-te, *Tieh-shan chi*, 9.2b.
161. Liu Ch'en-weng, *Hsu-ch'i chi*, 3.29a–3.31b. For Liu Ch'en-weng, see SJCC V.3947.
162. Liu Ch'en-weng, *Hsu-ch'i-chi*, 3.29a. Liu Ch'en-weng also composed inscriptions on two other academies in Chi: Orchid Jade, the family school of the Liu (perhaps his own?), and Double Creek. Liu Ch'en-weng served as headmaster at Dragon Creek in Chi's Wan-an County, an academy built at the site of a shrine to Chou Tun-i (*Hsu-ch'i chi*, 3.4a–3.6a; 1.6b–1.9b). He wrote inscriptions on Turtle Mountain and Double Peak Academies in Fu-chien's Nan-chien Prefecture as well (*Hsu-ch'i chi*, 1.5b–1.7a, 2.7b–2.9a). Another academy in the region associated with Chiang Wan-li—Origin of the Way Academy in Ta-yu County (Nan-an Prefecture)—was awarded a name plaque in 1269. Tao-yuan was founded in 1242 by Chiang Wan-li and the prefect. See Tseng Kuo-fan, et al., comps., *Chiang-hsi t'ung-chih*, 82.46b–82.47a.
163. See Neskar, "The Cult of Worthies."
164. Although Liu Ch'en-weng claimed that Chiang Wan-li was a disciple of Chu Hsi, there is no mention of this either in the SYHA references to him or in his SS biography. See Liu Ch'en-weng, *Hsu-ch'i chi*, 3.29a; SYHA 70.3b; SS 418/177, 12523–12525. However, given that Chiang Wan-li's native place was in Nan-k'ang commandery, there may be some assumed connection here.
165. McDermott quotes Sun Ti, writing in 1141 of *shih ta-fu* "parasites" who appropriated land in Liang-che as they fled their homes in the north. See McDermott, "Land Tenure and Rural Control in Liang-che during the Sung," 135. This phenomenon likely continued as the military situation worsened with the Mongols in the thirteenth century.
166. Fang Hui, *T'ung-chiang hsu-chi*, 130–134.
167. Ibid., 131.
168. This was at the request of Tseng Yuan-tzu (1250 *chin-shih*), vice director of the Ministry of Personnel. See Chuang Chung-fang, comp., *Nan-Sung wen-fan*, 46.12a. For Tseng Yuan-tzu, see SJCC IV.2830. See also Tseng Kuo-fan, et al., comps., *Chiang-hsi t'ung-chih*, 81.54a; TMTC 54.8a.
169. Chuang Chung-fang, comp., *Nan-Sung wen-fan*, 46.12a–46.12b.
170. Yuan Chueh, *Yen-yu Ssu-ming chih*, 14.33a–14.34b. See Wang Ying-lin's biographical sketch in Franke, *Sung Biographies*, 1167–1176.
171. Yuan Chueh, *Yen-yu Ssu-ming chih*, 14.35a. Huang Hsiang-lung, also a native of Ming Prefecture and the first headmaster appointed at Lin-ju Academy, wrote a commemorative inscription for a further restoration of Compassion Lake Academy later in the Yuan. See *Yen-yu Ssu-ming chih*, 14.35b–14.37b.
172. For Wang Yeh, see above under Illumined Way Academy.
173. For this academy, see Chi Hui-yun, et al., eds., *Che-chiang t'ung-chih*, 9.472. For Jen Shih-lin, see Umehara Kaoru and Kinugawa Tsuyoshi, comps., *Ryō-Kin-Gen jin denki sakuin*, 34.
174. Jen Shih-lin, *Sung-hsiang chi*, 1.6b.
175. For Yao Hsi-te, see SJCC II.1721–II.1722. For Hsieh Ch'ang-yuan, see SJCC V.4121; also Yuan Chueh, *Yen-yu Ssu-ming chih*, 5.29a. Hsieh Ch'ang-yuan went on to become minister of rites under the Yuan.
176. SYHA: supp. 76.23b.
177. Li Yen-p'ing was Chu Hsi's teacher, Li T'ung (1093–1163). See SJCC II.844.
178. Jen Shih-lin, *Sung-hsiang chi*, 1.6a–1.6b.
179. Yuan Chueh, *Yen-yu Ssu-ming chih*, 14.22a. In fact, in the 1280s Yuan Chueh was appointed to serve as headmaster at Beautiful Pools, although by that time

there may have been little left of Lü Tsu-ch'ien's intellectual influence. See SYHA 85.13b. In an essay entitled "The Learning of Eastern Che," the Ch'ing scholar Chang Hsueh-ch'eng (1738–1801) emphasized the Yuan lineage: "[T]he learning of Che-tung, although it was produced in Wu-yuan [Chu Hsi's birthplace], flowed out from the three Yuans [Yuan Hsieh, his son, Yuan Fu, and Yuan Chueh], who greatly revered Chiang-hsi Lu [Chiu-yuan]. But they also penetrated the Classics and served the ancient, not just with empty words about moral nature. Thus they did not go against the teachings of Master Chu" (Chang Hsueh-ch'eng, *Wen-shih t'ung-i*, 51).

180. See, for example, Chaffee, *The Thorny Gates of Learning in Sung China*, 45.
181. We can only assume this largely from the comments made by inscription writers, since, as pointed out earlier, we know very little about the actual content of teaching at academies. Ritual veneration, of course, continued to include other True Way patriarchs as well as local scholars.

3. *The Academy Movement: Economic and Sacred Geography*

1. Any statistical survey of Sung academies is problematic for at least two major reasons. The use of Ch'ing gazetteers is likely to inflate the numbers because the founding of an academy dedicated to a Sung person would be dated as Sung, although it may not have been established until later. A second, and in some ways more intractable, problem is how to define what is being counted. The term *shu-yuan* was used for a wide range of institutions, and in many cases these institutions are not distinct from others for which different names are used, such as *shu-t'ang*, *ching-she*, etc. Thus statistical surveys can be considered only approximations, suggesting general trends, and they must be used with caution. For a discussion of these problems, see Ch'en Wen-i, "Yu kuan-hsueh tao shu-yuan," 239–247. Ssu-ch'uan, in particular, presents a problem in assessing numbers of academies. One of the most prosperous regions, its geographical distance from the Southern Sung capital region and densely populated southeast, as well as its relatively early and destructive conquest by the Mongols, undoubtedly greatly affected the preservation of records. But Ssu-ch'uan was also not notably a center of True Way Learning, with the exception of Wei Liao-weng and his followers there. However, it is difficult to assess precisely what impact this may have had on the academy movement there.
2. On urbanization and the influence of commercialization on academies in the Ming and Ch'ing, see Ōkubo Eiko, *Min-Shin jidai shoin no kenkyū*, and Tilemann Grimm, "Academies and Urban Systems in Kwangtung."
3. Ou-yang Shou-tao, *Hsien-chai wen-chi*, 14.6b.
4. This was in Li Prefecture (Hu-pei). See Li Han-chang, et al., eds., *Hu-nan t'ung-chih*, 70.18a–70.18b.
5. Ibid., 79.18a.
6. Yuan Fu, *Meng-chai chi*, 14.202.
7. Chi Hui-yun, et al., comps., *Che-chiang t'ung-chih*, 28.1b.
8. Lu Chiu-yuan, *Lu Hsiang-shan ch'üan-chi*, 36.346.
9. See Shiba Yoshinobu, "Ningpo and Its Hinterland."
10. Tai Piao-yuan, *Yen-yuan Tai hsien-sheng wen-chi*, 10.6a.
11. Lou Yueh, *Kung-k'uei chi*, 54.755.
12. See Chang Ch'i-yun, et al., *Chung-kuo li-shih ti-t'u*, vol. II, 27, for a map showing these centers.
13. See, for example, the work of Hartwell on the iron and steel industry, cited in

Peter J. Golas, "The Mining Policies of the Sung Government," 411, note 1. Golas' bibliography (426–427) also contains references to works by Shiba Yoshinobu and other Japanese and Chinese scholars on the urban, commercial, and industrial transformations of the Sung.

14. I borrow this term from Daniels and Cosgrove, whose book of this title provides compelling theoretical perspectives drawn from the study of landscape largely in European and American contexts. See Stephen Daniels and Denis Cosgrove, eds., *The Iconography of Landscape: Essays on the Symbolic Representation, Design, and Use of Past Environments*, 1–10.
15. Alan R. H. Baker and Gideon Biger, eds., *Ideology and Landscape in Historical Perspective*, 4.
16. For a now-classic statement of this, see Clifford Geertz, *The Interpretation of Cultures*, 3–30.
17. In at least one case, a geomantic model has been applied in a cross-cultural study to the interpretation of Mesoamerican sites. See John B. Carlson, "A Geomantic Model for the Interpretation of Mesoamerican Sites: An Essay in Cross-Cultural Comparison."
18. Freedman termed the sense of organic connection between human history and the physical landscape reflected in geomancy "mystical ecology" (Maurice Freedman, *The Study of Chinese Society*, 313).
19. For an informative and perceptive discussion of Chinese geomancy in relation to urban sites, but with much broader implications, see Jeffrey Meyer, "*Feng-shui* of the Chinese City," 138–155. Meyer suggests that geomancy be understood not as "pseudo-science," but as a religious vocabulary describing the interplay of good and evil forces in the world (151–152); and that *feng-shui* beliefs may be comprehended as a "sacred text" (153) transmitted largely in practice.
20. Ebrey has discussed some aspects of geomancy in relation to burial practices in the Sung. She mentions attitudes toward geomancers that suggest some, at least, were of lower social classes. See Patricia B. Ebrey, "The Response of the State to Popular Funeral Practices," 215–220.
21. For brief descriptions of these, see Balazs and Hervouet, *A Sung Bibliography*, 130–131.
22. Translated by Chang Chun-shu and Joan Smythe as *South China in the Twelfth Century*. Richard Strassberg has recently compiled a collection of such works in *Travel Writing in Imperial China*.
23. See, for example, the poem by the Hang-chou poet Tung Ssu-kuo (fl. ca. 1260s) on Lien-hsi Academy at Mount Lu in Lu-shan chi, 5.7a; Hu Hung's poem on Jade Spring Academy in T'an (*Hu Hung chi, chüeh-chü*, 74); or Yeh Shih's poem on Wei Liao-weng's Crane Mountain Academy (*Shui-hsin wen-chi*, 7.77).
24. See the introduction to *Pilgrims and Sacred Sites in China*.
25. For China, see studies by Raoul Birnbaum: "Thoughts on T'ang Buddhist Mountain Traditions and Their Context," 5–24; "Secret Halls of the Mountain Lords: The Caves of Wu-t'ai Shan," 115–140.
26. The other four are Mount Heng in Shan-hsi, Mount Sung in Ho-nan, Mount Hua in Shen-hsi, and Mount Heng in Hu-nan.
27. See Ting Fu-pao, ed., *Fo-hsueh ta tz'u-tien*, 498.
28. Yü Chün-fang, "P'u-t'o Shan: Pilgrimage and the Creation of the Chinese Potalaka," 190.
29. Naquin and Yü, eds., *Pilgrims and Sacred Sites in China*, 17.
30. For a translation of this, see Burton Watson, trans., *Records of the Grand Historian of China*, vol. 2, 13–78.
31. Naquin and Yü, eds., *Pilgrims and Sacred Sites in China*, 11.

32. Ibid.
33. For a stimulating discussion of the links between poets and their locale, see Pease, "Lin-ch'uan and Fen-ning." Several papers presented at the conference on Mountains and the Cultures of Landscape in China, organized by William Powell and Peter Sturman and held at the Santa Barbara Museum of Art (January 14–16, 1993), treat topics in literary and visual representation of mountain landscapes.
34. For a discussion of this, see Andrew March, "Self and Landscape in Su Shih," 377–396.
35. Tung Kao, comp., *Ch'üan T'ang wen*, 888. This is cited in Chang Cheng-fan, *Chung-kuo shu-yuan chih-tu k'ao-lueh*, 84. The date of Hsü K'ai's inscription has been surmised by Terada Gō, *Sōdai kyōikushi gaisetsu*, 12.
36. See, for example, Yen Keng-wang, "T'ang-jen tu-shu shan-lin ssu-yuan chih feng-shang."
37. For this inscription, see Hsu Hsuan, *Ch'i-sheng chi*, 28, cited in Terada Gō, *Sōdai kyōikushi gaisetsu*, 13. For Hsu Hsuan, see SJCC III.2002, and Franke, *Sung Biographies*, 425–427. Hsu Hsuan and his brother (SJCC III.2013) were both known for their literary skills and were called "Big and Little Hsu." Hsu Hsuan was knowledgeable about and interested in Taoism, and he was one of the compilers of the early Sung Taoist canon. On this see Edward Schafer, *Mao-shan in T'ang Times*, 9. For the academy, see Hu Chung-yao's biography in SS 456/215, 13390.
38. Hsu Hsuan, *Ch'i-sheng chi*, 28, cited in Terada Gō, *Sōdai kyōikushi gaisetsu*, 13.
39. As a senior court scholar, Hsu Hsuan was the patron of Wang Yü-ch'eng (954–1001), one of three court scholars who composed poems to congratulate the Hu lineage in 994 for having maintained joint residence through four generations. These are cited in Terada Gō, *Sōdai kyōikushi gaisetsu*, 13–14. Ch'en Yao-sou (961–1017), one of the other presenters, took first-place *chin-shih* in 989.
40. This was also known as Thunder Dike Academy. See Yang I, *Wu-i hsin-chi*, 6.12b. See also Hung Wen-fu's biography in SS 456/215, 13392–13393.
41. Shih Chieh, *Shih Tsu-lai wen-chi*, 6.11b–6.13a.
42. Wang T'ung is the most problematic and controversial of this particular lineage of Confucianism. See Howard Wechsler, "The Confucian Teacher, Wang T'ung (584?–617): One Thousand Years of Controversy," 225–272.
43. Shih Chieh, *Shih Tsu-lai wen-chi*, 9.12b.
44. Li Han-chang, et al., eds., *Hu-nan t'ung-chih*, 69.1a–69.2a.
45. Ou-yang Shou-tao, *Hsuan-chai wen-chi*, 7.14.
46. Chu Hsi, *Chu-tzu ta-ch'üan*, 20.9a.
47. Ibid., 19.5a.
48. See Abe Chōichi, "Sōdai no Rozan: Zen to jūdō," 341, where he cites Wu Tsung-tz'u, *Lu-shan chih*, 9. These statistics represent the largest numbers for Buddhists and Taoists of all eras. I am unable to ascertain whether there was a shift from Northern to Southern Sung.
49. Abe Chōichi, "Sōdai no Rozan," 340.
50. Ibid., 341.
51. SJCC V.4431–5.4432; Abe Chōichi, "Sōdai no Rozan," 341.
52. For Chang Shang-ying, see SJCC 3.2404–3.2405; see also Abe Chōichi, "Sōdai no Rozan," 341. Chang Shang-ying is the subject of two recent studies. See Helwig Schmidt-Glintzer, "Zhang Shangying (1043–1122): An Embarrassing Policy Adviser under the Northern Song"; and Robert Gimello, "Chang Shang-ying on Wu-t'ai Shan."

53. On these, see Suzuki Chūsei, "Sōdai Bukkyō kessha no kenkyū," 303–333.
54. SJCC V.3875 (Liu Huan), III.2530–III.2533 (Ch'en Kuan). See also *Pai-lu shu-yuan chih*, 4.4a–4.4b.
55. Liu Huan's appellation, "West Brook Eremite"—gained while in retirement at Mount Lu—became the name of an academy founded to commemorate him in his native prefecture of Jui in Che-tung (see chapter 2).
56. Wang I-shan, *Chia-ts'un lei-kao*, 8.2a.
57. *Pai-lu shu-yuan chih*, 4.4b.
58. Ibid.
59. Abe Chōichi, "Sōdai no Rozan," 347.
60. During the Sung, the *shih-fang* system of abbot selection by the government became increasingly common. This meant that when a new abbot was needed, the local prefect ordered a Buddhist administrator to assemble the local clergy, select appropriate candidates with regard to age and qualifications, and report these names to him. The prefect would then name a new abbot from this group. For discussions of this system as it grew during the Sung, see Kanai Noriyuki, "Sōdai no Bukkyō ni tsuite—Sōdai shakai ni okeru ji-in to jūjisei no mondai," 52–58. See also Takao Giken, *Sōdai Bukkyōshi no kenkyū*, 60–63.
61. See, e.g., Hisayuki Miyakawa, "Local Cults around Mount Lu at the Time of Sun En's Rebellion."
62. See the work of Michel Strickmann, "The Mao Shan Revelations: Taoism and the Aristocracy," 1–64.
63. Yü Hsi-lu, comp., *Chih-hsun Chen-chiang chih*, 19.21b, 11.34a; see also Chang Hsuan, comp., *Chih-cheng Chin-ling hsin-chih*, 9.13a.
64. See chapter 1, note 1.
65. Lin Shu-hsun, et al., eds., *Shao-chou fu chih*, 18.2a.
66. Yuan Hsieh, *Chieh-chai chi*, 10.148–10.149.
67. Chang Hsuan, comp., *Chih-cheng Chin-ling hsin-chih*, 9.12b.
68. Lu Chiu-yuan, *Lu Hsiang-shan ch'üan-chi*, 9.7b.
69. Cited in Yuan Fu's "annunciatory prayer" for the opening school rites, Lu Chiu-yuan, *Lu Hsiang-shan ch'üan-chi*, 36.347.
70. This was in Yu-shan County (Hsin, Chiang-tung). See Chi Hui-yun, et al., comps., *Che-chiang t'ung-chih*, 82.23a.
71. Ch'eng Tsu-lo, et al., eds., *Fu-chien t'ung-chih*, 12.4b.
72. Yuan Chueh, *Yen-yu Ssu-ming chih*, 14.30a.
73. Ibid.
74. Yin Chi-shan, et al., eds., *Chiang-nan t'ung-chih*, 90.5a.
75. Ibid.
76. Cheng Yuan-yu, *Ch'iao-wu chi*, 9.356.
77. Yü Hsi-lu, comp., *Chih-hsun Chen-chiang chih*, 11.32b–11.33.
78. This was in Jun, Che-hsi. See Yü Hsi-lu, comp., *Chih-hsun Chen-chiang chih*, 11.27b–11.28a.
79. Cheng Yao and Fang Jen-jung, eds., *Ching-ting Yen-chou hsu-chih*, 3.3b.
80. Ibid.
81. Yuan Chueh, *Yen-yu Ssu-ming chih*, 14.38a.
82. Ibid., 14.38b.
83. This academy was in Shang-yu County (Nan-an, Chiang-hsi). See Tseng Kuo-fan, et al., comps., *Chiang-hsi t'ung-chih*, 82.48b.
84. Tseng Kuo-fan, et al., comps., *Chiang-hsi t'ung-chih*, 81.58b.
85. Ch'eng Tsu-lo, et al., eds., *Fu-chien t'ung-chih*, 63.20a.
86. This was in Jun, Che-hsi. See Wu Ch'eng, *Wu Wen-cheng kung wen-chi*, 20.25a.

87. Wu Ch'eng, *Wu Wen-cheng kung wen-chi*, 20.25a.
88. Yü Hsi-lu, comp., *Chih-hsun Chen-chiang chih*, 11.34a.
89. Ibid. See also SJCC I.167; SS 420/179, 12575–12577, for Wang Yeh.
90. See SJCC III.1914–3.1915 and SS 424/183, 12663–12665, for Sun Tzu-hsiu.
91. Huang Chin, *Chin-hua Huang hsien-sheng wen-chi*, 8.12a–8.13a.
92. Ibid., 8.12a–8.12b.
93. For this, see Linda Walton, "Southern Sung Academies as Sacred Places," 336.
94. See the discussion of this in Martin Collcutt, "The Early Ch'an Monastic Rule: *Ch'ing-kuei* and the Shaping of Ch'an Community Life."
95. This is mentioned by T. Griffith Foulk and Robert H. Sharf, "On the Ritual Use of Ch'an Portraiture in Medieval China," 179.
96. Chou Ying-ho, comp., *Ching-ting Chien-k'ang chih*, 29.14. Other examples of this term, suggesting it was commonplace, include Yuan Fu, *Meng-chai chi*, 13.193 (Elephant Mountain); Ma T'ing-luan, *Pi-wu wan-fang chi*, 17.11b (White Deer Grotto); and Ch'en I-chung, *Wu-tu wen-ts'ui hsu-chi*, 13.2b (Learning the Way). The term sheng-t'ang is also used for "ascend the hall" at academy shrines. See Li Han-chang, et al., eds., *Hu-nan t'ung-chih*, 70.14b (Create Anew Academy); Lü Tsu-ch'ien, *Lü Tung-lai wen-chi*, 6.140 (Angling Terrace); Chu Hsi, *Chu-tzu yü-lei*, 107.2674 (Ts'ang-chou).
97. Chou Ying-ho, comp., *Ching-ting Chien-k'ang chih*, 29.3a.
98. See Foulk, "Myth, Ritual, and Monastic Practice in Sung Ch'an Buddhism," 172–176, for a discussion of the function of patriarchs halls in Ch'an (and other) monasteries.
99. Liu K'o-chuang, *Hou-ts'un hsien-sheng ta ch'üan chi*, 93.15b.
100. Peter Jackson, *Maps of Meaning*, ix.
101. Daniels and Cosgrove, *The Iconography of Landscape*, 4.
102. Chu Hsi, *Hui-an hsien-sheng Chu Wen-kung wen-chi*, 79.22b.
103. Chang Shih, *Nan-hsuan wen-chi*, 10.1b.
104. Wu Ch'eng, *Wu Wen-cheng kung wen-chi*, 20.19a.
105. Chu Hsi, *Chu-tzu ta-ch'üan*, 78.12a.
106. Chu Hsi was the author of a series of poems about Wu-i and the retreat there that reveal his profound appreciation of the landscape. For these poems, see Chu Hsi, *Chu-tzu ta-ch'üan*, 9.2b–9.6a. See also Li Chi, "Chu Hsi the Poet," 110–112.
107. Deep appreciation of the landscape was not confined to Chu Hsi and his followers among True Way thinkers. Lu Chiu-yuan could also wax eloquent about the landscape of his Elephant Mountain Retreat. See Pease, "Lin-ch'uan and Fen-ning," 63–64.
108. Literally, *ch'ih*. In the Sung, a *ch'ih* equaled 30.72 cm., or about one foot.
109. Ch'eng Tsu-lo, et al., eds., *Fu-chien t'ung-chih*, 16.14a.
110. Han Yuan-chi, "Wu-i shu-yuan chi," in Tai Hsien, *Chu-tzu shih-chi*, 24b/696.
111. Ibid., 26a/699.
112. Locust Tree Hall was in Chin-hsi County (Fu, Chiang-hsi). See Tseng Kuo-fan, et al., comps., *Chiang-hsi t'ung-chih*, 81.58b.
113. Tseng Kuo-fan, et al., comps., *Chiang-hsi t'ung-chih*, 81.58b.
114. Li Han-chang, et al., eds., *Hu-nan t'ung-chih*, 70.18a.
115. This was in Jui-an County (Wen, Che-tung). See Ho Meng-kuei, *Ch'ien-chai wen-chi*, 9.19a–9.19b.
116. Chou Pi-ta, *P'ing-yuan hsu-kao*, 19.8a.
117. Ibid.
118. Ibid., 19.8b.

119. Chen Te-hsiu, *Hsi-shan hsien-sheng Chen Wen-chung kung wen-chi*, 26.446–26.447.
120. Stone Cavern Academy was located in Tung-yang County, Wu Prefecture (Che-tung).
121. Yeh Shih, *Shui hsin wen-chi*, 9.154–9.155. Wu-ling was the site associated with the poet T'ao Ch'ien's utopian vision of the Peach Blossom Spring.
122. See Bol, *"This Culture of Ours."*
123. Yang Yü-chien, et al., comps., *Chung-hsiu Nan-hsi shu-yuan chi*, 4.4a.
124. See Neskar, "The Cult of Worthies." See also Walton, "Southern Sung Academies as Sacred Places."
125. Scholarship on the rise of local elites and the apparent shift between Northern and Southern Sung is substantial. See especially Hymes, *Statesmen and Gentlemen*, and Bossler, *Powerful Relations*. This social historical perspective should be distinguished from the cultural or literary perspective represented by a study such as Pease, "Lin-ch'uan and Fen-ning." Pease sketches out through the writings of Northern Sung poets a sense of regional identity, and carries this forward into some Southern Sung figures, such as Lu Chiu-yuan. This is not to say that the social and cultural or literary are unrelated, but simply to suggest that one may observe different patterns and paces of historical change in each case.
126. Hsiung Ho, *Hsiung Wu-hsuan chi*, 4.17a–4.17b.
127. Cf. Chu Hsi's description of the landscape where he built Wu-i Retreat. Chu Hsi describes the fascinating beauty of the place, but does not attribute more to it than this. That is, he does not connect the landscape with transmission of the Way. That comes after him, with his apotheosis in the mid-thirteenth century.
128. Wu Ch'eng, *Wu Wen-cheng kung wen-chi*, 20.18b.
129. For this, see David Nemeth, *The Architecture of Ideology: Neo-Confucian Imprinting on Cheju Island, Korea*, 20.
130. Naquin and Yü, *Pilgrims and Sacred Sites in China*, 18.
131. Ibid.
132. At West Brook Academy, for example, scholars were allotted three days' worth of rice, but this could be extended for longer stays (Wang I-shan, *Chia-ts'un lei-kao*), 8.3b.
133. White Egret Islet, for example, was established at a site formerly used as a hostel. See chapter 2.
134. See, for example, Han-shan Academy in Ch'ao-chou (Kuang-tung), dedicated to Han Yü (Lin Hsi-i, *Chu-ch'i chuan-chai shih-i k'ao hsu-chi*, 11.9b–11.11a).
135. Huang Chin, *Huang Wen-hsien kung chi, 7 shang*, 265–266.
136. Lü Tsu-ch'ien, *Lü Tung-lai wen-chi*, 6.139. Hay has discussed the geomantic character of the site where this shrine was built. See Alan John Hay, "Huang Kung-wang's Dwelling in the Fu-ch'un Mountains: The Dimensions of a Landscape," 311. Hay also cites a poem by Huang T'ing-chien on Li Kung-lin's painting of Yen Kuang, called "Fishing the Shallows," along with a poem by Su Shih titled "Passing the Angling Terrace."
137. Lü Tsu-ch'ien, *Lü Tung-lai wen-chi*, 6.139.
138. Ibid., 6.139–6.140. After the shrine was renewed in 1180, disease struck neighboring prefectures, and the official responsible for the renewal requested that Lü Tsu-ch'ien write an inscription to commemorate the renewal. Although Lü Tsu-ch'ien is not explicit about this, it seems likely that the logical connection here is one of hoping to avoid disaster by placating the spirits of Yen Kuang and Fan Chung-yen, a practice not far removed from those associated with popular deity cults studied by Valerie Hansen and others. Lü Tsu-ch'ien, however, refused,

and his response to the official was to hold forth with a lengthy monologue scolding him for such petty concerns as the immediate welfare of his district rather than focusing on the long-term welfare of the empire.

139. For Lu Tzu-i, see SJCC III.2665.
140. Cheng Yao and Fang Jen-jung, eds., *Ching-ting Yen-chou hsu-chih*, 3.3a–3.3b.
141. Prior to his appointment as prefect of Yen, Lu Tzu-i had acquired a reputation for demon-quelling and the suppression of local religious beliefs and practices associated with shamanism. During his tenure as magistrate of Li-yang County in Chiang-ning (Chiang-tung), he "exorcised demons" and set up a school where rites were taught in order to transform local customs. See SJCC III.2665 for this summary and references.
142. Cheng Yao and Fang Jen-jung, eds., *Ching-ting Yen-chou hsu-chih*, 3.3b.
143. In Jui-an County, Wen Prefecture (Che-tung).
144. Wang Ying-sun was a minor official and painter from Yueh, thought to be a contributor to a collection of *tz'u* poetry compiled in the late thirteenth century by Sung loyalists. See SJCC I.323. See also Balazs and Hervouet, *A Sung Bibliography*, 475.
145. Lin Ching-hsi, *Chi-shan hsien-sheng chi*, 4.6a–4.7b.
146. See Franke, *Sung Biographies*, 261–268, for the biography of Chou Mi by Li Chu-tsing. See also Jennifer W. Jay, *A Change in Dynasties: Loyalism in Thirteenth-Century China*, 195–242.
147. Lin Ching-hsi, *Chi-shan hsien-sheng chi*, 4.7b.
148. Ibid.; SJCC 3.2649.
149. Nemeth, *The Architecture of Ideology*, 3.
150. For the concept of a "cognitive grid," see R. L. Gordon, "The Sacred Geography of a Mithraeum: The Example of Sette Sfere," 119–120.

PART 2: ACADEMIES IN THE SOCIETY AND CULTURE OF THE SOUTHERN SUNG *SHIH*

4. *Kin and Community: From Family School to Academy*

1. For an extended discussion of this and other conceptual issues in Sung political thought, see the introduction to Hymes and Schirokauer, eds., *Ordering the World*, especially 51–53.
2. See Walton, "Charitable Estates as an Aspect of Statecraft in Southern Sung China," 267, for the relationship between lineage and community charitable estates.
3. Patricia B. Ebrey, "Early Stages of Descent Group Organization."
4. For example, kinship networks might be used to combine wealth and power on a local level that could challenge the authority of local officials to collect taxes or maintain order. Kinship ties of court officials might undermine state policies by promoting the interests of kin members within the central government.
5. For background on the Ch'en family school, see Thomas H. C. Lee, "Politics, Examinations, and Chinese Society, 1000–1500: Reflections on the Rise of the Local Elite and Civil Society in Late Imperial China," 5–9; and Lee, "Sung Education and Schools Before Chu Hsi," 106. See also Yen Keng-wang, "T'ang-jen tu-shu shan-lin ssu-yuan chih feng-shang," 106, and Terada Gō, *Sōdai kyōikushi gaisetsu*, 12.

6. See Tung Kao, comp., *Ch'üan T'ang wen*, 883.3a–883.4a. There is a problem with the dating here. The passage from this source cited by Yen Keng-wang (706) concerning the Ch'en Family Academy states that the proclamation was issued in the *chung-hsing* era of the reign of the Southern T'ang emperor Li Sheng (937–943). There is no *chung-hsing* era during the reign of Li Sheng; the *chung-hsing* era is only one year, 958, during the reign of Li Ching. However, the *Nan T'ang shu* states that the school was founded in 939, which would place it in Li Sheng's reign. I think the evidence supports the earlier date.

   According to Hsu K'ai's inscription, there were a thousand people included in the Ch'en family's joint residence at the time he observed them and wrote about the school. The *Nan T'ang shu* says there were seven hundred people included in the Ch'en family at the time of the school's founding, which would have been about a generation earlier. As befitted the size of the lineage, the school itself was large: several tens of "frames" of buildings, including a library that held several thousand volumes, and twenty *ch'ing* of land for support (Tung Kao, comp., *Ch'üan T'ang wen*, 883.3a–883.4a).
7. Huang Ch'ing-wen, *Chung-kuo ku-tai shu-yuan chih-tu chi ch'i k'o-shu t'an-yen*, 140, has cited this academy as one known for holding an exceptionally high number of books.
8. In 1026, a member of the Ch'en lineage submitted a memorial to Jen-tsung (r. 1023–1063) detailing his family history, but exactly what happened to the Ch'en lineage after that is not clear. As the Yangtze basin began to develop, however, new immigrants provided a source of labor that made the unwieldy, and often troublesome, lineage communities increasingly obsolete, not to mention potentially threatening to the Sung state. At the same time, the government began to support local schools, obviating the need for schools like that of the Ch'en. For a brief discussion of the background of large-scale lineage communities that flourished in the Yangtze valley, especially concentrated in the P'o-yang Lake basin, see Richard von Glahn, *The Country of Streams and Grottoes: Expansion, Settlement, and the Civilizing of the Sichuan Frontier in Sung Times*, 164.
9. Floriate Forest Academy was a hundred "rooms" (*ch'ü*) in size, held five thousand volumes of books, and served "several tens" of students, according to an inscription by Hsu Hsuan, cited in Terada Go, *Sōdai kyōikushi gaisetsu*, 13.
10. SS 456/215, 13390.
11. Hu Chung-yao was appointed to a minor post as a temple administrator (*ssu-ch'eng*) by Li Yü (r. 961–975), the last ruler of the Southern T'ang. In 985 Sung T'ai-tsung honored the family with an imperial banner, and when Hu Chung-yao went to the capital to offer his gratitude, he was rewarded with two hundred catties of silver. Although the Sung dynastic history says that the banner was conferred in 985, Hsu Hsuan's inscription on Floriate Forest Academy says it was in 994. See SS 456/215, 13390.
12. In the 990s Hu Chung-yao was reported to have aided starving people from his own granary and to have contributed funds for the building of a bridge. T'ai-tsung commended Hu Chung-yao by appointing him prefectural assistant preceptor (*chu-chiao*), and in 994 his younger brother was awarded a post and rank at court. Hu Chung-yao himself eventually reached the post of registrar (*chu-pu*) of the imperial Directorate of Education (*kuo-tzu chien*). See SS 456/215, 13390.
13. See Hung Wen-fu's biography in SS 456/215, 13392–13393. In 995 T'ai-tsung honored the Hung for having had six generations residing together. Since the time of an ancestor who held office under the T'ang, the Hung were praised as having produced many descendants who resided together and who were known

for their filial piety and brotherly harmony. In his inscription on this academy, the Northern Sung literary scholar Yang I (974–1020) mentions as comparable institutions the Ch'en Family Academy (which he refers to as East Beauty Academy) and Floriate Forest Academy (Yang I, *Wu-i hsin-chi*, 6.12b). The biographies of both Hu Chung-yao, associated with Floriate Forest, and Hung Wen-fu (Thunder Lake Academy) are included in the "Filial and Righteous" biographical section of the Sung dynastic history, and the experiences of the two families who established these academies are remarkably parallel.

14. Around 995, after the school was built, T'ai-tsung bequeathed one hundred scrolls in imperial calligraphy, presumably for the school's library. Later, in recognition of the Hung family's joint residence and their promotion of education, T'ai-tsung bequeathed a banner in imperial calligraphy that read "righteous residence" (*i-chü*). See Yang I, *Wu-i hsin-chi*, 6.11b.
15. Hung Wen-fu's younger brother was named to the post of prefectural assistant preceptor, just as Hu Chung-yao had been, and there was a further proclamation in 997 honoring the Hung family joint residence (*men-lü*). Following this, the Hung sent their sons to take the examinations, and in 1000 Hung Wen-fu's eldest son took a *chin-shih* degree. See SS 415/256, 13393.
16. Tseng Kuo-fan, et al., comps., *Chiang-hsi t'ung-chih*, 81.6b–81.7a.
17. Pacification commissioner Wang Ming played a role in setting up the academy for Teng Yen to teach. For Wang Ming, see SJCC I.131–I.132. K'ung Wu-chung's inscription on Luxuriant Creek Academy is included in the local history. For K'ung Wu-chung, see SJCC I.393–I.394.
18. Li Han-chang, et al., eds., *Hu-nan t'ung-chih*, 68.20b–68.21a. The inscription on this academy by Wang Ting-min, magistrate of Hsiang-yin County during the 1086–1094 period, not only discusses the importance of schools in ordering the world and "transforming the people," but also describes the moving of shrines to accommodate the school, and the transformation of a shrine to the legendary sovereign Shun into a Confucian temple. For Wang Ting-min, see SJCC I.304.
19. One case of a family school documented for the late Northern Sung is that of Peach Spring Academy in Yin County (Ming, Che-tung). It was originally the family school of Wang Shuo (1010–1085), one of the local "Five Masters" of the Ch'ing-li era (1041–1048) and the first in his line to take a *chin-shih* degree (1041). The academy was established by imperial decree after the death of Wang Shuo and named with his honorific, Master Peach Spring. It was subsequently abandoned and later restored by Wang Shuo's descendants, probably sometime in the thirteenth century. See Walton, "The Institutional Context of Neo-Confucianism," 461–463, 477–478.
20. Bol, "The Examination System and the *Shih*," 167.
21. This was in Sung-yang County (Ch'u, Che-tung).
22. SYHA: supp. 69.192b. For Yeh Chen, see SJCC IV.3238. See also the inscription by the Yuan writer Wu Shih-tao, *Wu li-pu wen-chi*, 2.6a–2.7a.
23. Li Han-chang, et al., eds., *Hu-nan t'ung-chih*, 68.33a.
24. SYHA: supp./*pieh* 2.38b. Two hundred *mou* was allocated to support the academy.
25. Among activities Hymes identifies with membership in the Southern Sung elite is the founding and support of academies (Hymes, *Statesmen and Gentlemen*, 132). Hymes' work is of particular relevance for this study of academies because it suggests that academies are one kind of local institution reflecting the growing importance of local ties and local efforts in Southern Sung, in contrast to Northern Sung, when the state oversaw the important area of education through

the administration of state schools. In addition to his work on the Fu-chou elite, see also Hymes, "Lu Chiu-yuan, Academies, and the Problem of the Local Community." Here Hymes argues that the relative lack of importance given to academies by Lu Chiu-yuan reflected a particular vision of what the "community" should be. Nevertheless, Hymes' point in his study of the Fu-chou elite that academies were one kind of institution supported by the local elite as an indication of their local focus remains valid.

26. See the inscription for this academy by Hsieh Fang-te, *Tieh-shan chi*, 7.3b–7.36a.
27. On Chao Ju-yü's place in the intellectual debates of the time, including his relationship to Chu Hsi, see John W. Chaffee, "Chao Ju-yü, Spurious Learning, and Southern Sung Political Culture"; for mention of the academy, see 42.
28. Tseng Kuo-fan, et al., comps., *Chiang-hsi t'ung-chih*, 82; TMTC 50.7b. For Li Ch'un-nien, see SJCC II.1043; SYHA 51.21a–51.21b; Wei Liao-weng, *Ho-shan hsien-sheng ta-ch'üan wen-chi*, 75.4b. For Li Ta-yu, see SJCC II.940.
29. Wei Liao-weng, *Ho-shan hsien-sheng ta-ch'üan wen-chi*, 74.4b.
30. Ta-t'ung reached the post of minister of public works in the central government and has a biography in the dynastic history (SS 423/182, 12642–12643). Wei Liao-weng wrote a funerary inscription for Ta-yu, a follower of Lü Tsu-ch'ien (*Ho-shan hsien-sheng ta-ch'üan wen-chi*, 75.4b). We know the names of Ta-yu and Ta-t'ung's immediate ancestors (father, grandfather, and great-grandfather), that they both took *chin-shih* degrees, and that they both held office. We can speculate that these two brothers were the first of their line in Tung-yang to take *chin-shih* degrees, but that the Li must have had some local status prior to this.
31. There is a brief reference to another academy founded in Fu-liang County of Jao, called Ch'ang-hsiang. This academy was located in Ching-te chen and was established by someone surnamed Li. See TMTC 50.7b.
32. Another academy in Jao was also established by someone with the surname Li, but only the name of the academy and its founder are known. See Tseng Kuo-fan, et al., comps., *Chiang-hsi t'ung-chih*, 82.25a
33. Yeh Shih, *Shui-hsin wen-chi*, 9.155. For Kuo Ch'in-chih, see SJCC III.2340.
34. Yeh Shih, *Shui-hsin wen-chi*, 9.154-156.
35. Ibid., 9.155.
36. Ibid.
37. Ibid.
38. Ibid.
39. Ibid.
40. For Chang Chiu-ch'eng's thought, see Tillman, *Confucian Discourse and Chu Hsi's Ascendancy*, 24–29.
41. SYHA: supp. 73.35b; SYHA: supp. 69.156a.
42. For this academy, see SYHA 73.7a, 51.18b, 60.8a. Stone Brook Academy was also founded by Kuo Liang-ch'en, but we know nothing more about it. See SYHA 73.7a. Yeh Shih wrote funerary inscriptions for Kuo Liang-ch'en and his two sons. See Yeh Shih, *Shui-hsin wen-chi*, 13.245–13.247 (Kuo Liang-ch'en and Kuo Ch'eng); 23.460–23.461 (Kuo Chiang). Lü Tsu-ch'ien also wrote a separate funerary inscription for Kuo Ch'eng. See Lü Tsu-ch'ien, *Lü Tung-lai wen-chi*, 8.19.
43. Yeh Shih, *Shui-hsin wen-chi*, 13.246.
44. SYHA: supp. 40.41a; SYHA 51.21b. For Kuo P'u, see SJCC III.2121.
45. Yeh Shih, *Shui-hsin wen-chi*, 13.246.

46. SYHA: supp. 69.156b.
47. Ibid., supp. 40.41a. For T'ang Chung-yu, see SJCC III.1785; for Hsü Ch'iao, see SJCC III.2005–III.2006; for Tu Yü, see SJCC II.807.
48. Tillman, *Confucian Discourse and Chu Hsi's Ascendancy*, 134. On T'ang Chung-yu's relationship with Chu Hsi, see ibid., 134–136.
49. See SYHA 60.8a (biography of Wu K'uei); for Hsueh Shu-ssu, see SJCC V.4194.
50. SS 422/181, 12614.
51. SYHA 1.24b. The five brothers were known for their outstanding scholarly abilities as the "Chin-hua Five Kao," for the second character in their *t'zu*.
52. SHYA 73.4b.
53. See SJCC III.2115.
54. Ch'en Liang, *Ch'en Liang chi*, 26.393. See also Bossler, *Powerful Relations*, 136.
55. Aoyama Sadao, *Sōjin denki sakuin*, 137, lists the father, grandfather, and great-grandfather.
56. Yeh Shih, *Shui-hsin wen-chi*, 13.246. See also Bossler, *Powerful Relations*, 146.
57. See Chikusa Masaaki, "Sōdai kanryō no kikyō ni tsuite," 28–57.
58. Yeh Shih, *Shui-hsin wen-chi*, 13.247–13.248. In his funerary inscription for Kuo Liang-hsien, Yeh Shih notes that Liang-hsien's wife's surname was Yeh, and that two of his daughters married men with the surname Yeh. Conceivably, these individuals were related to Yeh Shih, thus accounting for his efforts in writing these inscriptions.
59. Yeh Shih, *Shui-hsin wen-chi*, 13.247.
60. Ibid.
61. Chi Hui-yun, et al., comps., *Che-chiang t'ung-chih*, 28, 705. The continuing prominence of the Kuo is suggested by the fact that the county magistrate in 1290 was named Kuo Ying-jen. It is not clear if he was a descendant of the Kuo, but it is reasonably likely.
62. I have not traced the marriage ties of the Kuo, accepting Yeh Shih's statement at face value.
63. Yeh Shih, *Shui-hsin wen-chi*, 7.332–7.334.
64. Ibid., 6.311–6.312.
65. SYHA 60.8a5.
66. Ibid., supp. 60.34b. For Wu Wen-ping, see SJCC II.1138 and Yeh Shih's funerary inscription for his son (*Shui-hsin wen-chi*, 25.498).
67. According to Wu K'uei's biography, over one hundred people came there from elsewhere (SYHA 60.8a).
68. When there was a famine in the area during the Ch'un-hsi era (1174–1190), Wu K'uei "nourished the living and mourned the dead" (Yeh Shih, *Shui-hsin wen-chi*, 25.498).
69. Yeh Shih, *Shui-hsin wen-chi*, 25.498.
70. Ibid. For Hsu Chi, see SJCC III.2002.
71. SYHA 60.6b states that Fu Yin was T'ang Chung-yu's *chung-piao* (son of T'ang's maternal aunt or uncle or paternal aunt). SYHA 60.8a calls Fu Yin T'ang Chung-yu's *wai-ti* (maternal cousin). Both T'ang Chung-yu and Lü Tsu-chien (d. 1196), Lü Tsu-ch'ien's younger brother, praised his learning, and he was eventually invited to Lü Tsu-ch'ien's Beautiful Pools Academy (60.6b).
72. Yeh Shih, *Shui-hsin wen-chi*, 25.498; SYHA 60.8a.
73. Wu K'uei did not take a degree, but he did hold a minor local office. There is a brief notice in SYHA of another academy in Tung-yang founded at the beginning of the Southern Sung by Chiang Ch'ang-tao to teach his agnatic relatives. A student of Lü Tsu-ch'ien and native of Tung-yang, Ch'iao Hsing-chien (1156–1241;

1193 *chin-shih*), was invited to teach there. For this, see SYHA: supp. 73.38a2; SJCC IV.2972; SYHA 73.2a.

74. Ebrey, *Family and Property in Sung China*, 229–230.
75. Soft Stream Academy in Huang-yen County (T'ai, Che-tung) was established at the family school (*shu*) of the Huang, although there is no date for this. See SYHA: supp. 82.155b, 82.212b.
76. Tseng Kuo-fan, et al., comps., *Chiang-hsi t'ung-chih*, 82.10b.
77. Wang Ying-ch'en, *Wen-ting chi*, 9.17a.
78. Ibid.
79. Ibid., 9.17b. For Kao K'o-yang, see SJCC III.1753.
80. Wang Ying-ch'en, *Wen-ting chi*, 9.18b.
81. See the inscription for this academy by Tseng Feng, *Yuan-tu chi*, 4.32a–4.33a. Tseng Feng was from Lo-an County (Fu, Chiang-hsi), so we may assume that the academy was also located there, although there is no positive evidence of this. It is, of course, possible that the marriage relative, whom I cannot identify further, resided elsewhere. Tseng Feng linked the name of the academy, which was built on a hillock planted with apricot trees, to the Apricot Altar associated with Confucius; and he distinguished it from the apricot groves on Mount Lu connected with Taoists, and the apricot city in the northwest, identified with Buddhists. See *Yuan-tu chi*, 4.32b.
82. Tseng Feng, *Yuan-tu chi*, 4.32a.
83. Ibid., 4.33a.
84. Yang Wan-li, *Ch'eng-chai chi*, 75.3b–75.5a.
85. For Liao Yen-hsiu, see SJCC IV.3304.
86. Yang Wan-li, *Ch'eng-chai chi*, 75.3b–75.4a. Huang Ch'ing-wen, *Chung-kuo ku-tai shu-yuan chih-tu chi ch'i k'o-shu t'an-yen*, 140, lists this as one of the most important Sung academies for the storage of books.
87. Yang Wan-li also wrote an inscription on another family academy elsewhere in T'an (*Ch'eng-chai chi*, 76.8b–76.10a)—the school of the Chou family, although neither father nor sons can be identified. In addition to Yang Wan-li's commemorative inscriptions for both this school, called Luxuriant Creek Academy, and the Liao family's Dragon Pool Academy, there is another common link: Hsieh E (1121–1194; 1157 *chin-shih*), a student of the Ch'eng brothers' thought, was invited to teach at both places. For Hsieh E, see SJCC V.4108. Yang Wan-li also composed a funerary inscription for him (*Ch'eng-chai chi*, 121.11).
88. Chen Te-hsiu, *Chen Hsi-shan wen-chi*, 26.446–26.447.
89. Ibid., 26.446.
90. For Huang Ts'ung-lung, the only member of this descent group I can identify, see SJCC IV.2912. See also Chen Te-hsiu, *Chen Hsi-shan wen-chi*, 26.446–26.447. According to SYHA: supp. add 2.57a, Huang Ts'ung-lung was a local scholar who lived at the end of the Sung and beginning of the Yuan.
91. Chen Te-hsiu, *Chen Hsi-shan wen-chi*, 26.447.
92. Lu Hsien, et al., comps., *Chia-ting Chen-chiang chih*, 10.7a.
93. See James Legge, trans., *The Chinese Classics*, vol. 1, 131.
94. Liu Tsai, *Man-t'ang wen-chi*, 21.34b.
95. For Chang Kang, see SJCC III.2308. Under the heading for this academy, TMTC 11.6a (like *Chia-ting Chen-chiang chih*) states that it was established as a *chia-shu* by Chang Kao, Chang Kang's grandson and thus the generation following Chang Tsung-ti, Chang Kang's nephew, whom the SYHA credits with establishing the academy (SYHA: supp. 3.199b–3.200a); for Chang Tsung-ti, see SJCC III.2385.

96. Liu Tsai, *Man-t'ang wen-chi*, 21.32a–21.35b.
97. Ibid., 21.33a.
98. For this, and a discussion of Liu Tsai's philanthropic activities in general, see James T. C. Liu, "Liu Tsai (1165–1238): His Philanthropy and Neo-Confucian Limitations," 1–29.
99. Tseng Kuo-fan, et al., comps., *Chiang-hsi t'ung-chih*, 81.6b.
100. Ibid.
101. Ch'eng Pi, *Ming-shui chi*, 7.18a–7.20a.
102. Ibid., 7.18b–7.19a. For Wu Ying-ch'ou, see SJCC II.1171, although this is the only reference to him.
103. Ch'eng Pi, *Ming-shui chi*, 7.19a. Ch'eng Pi tells of lightning that struck a teak tree without burning it; the wood was then used to make statues of Confucius and Mencius.
104. Ch'eng Pi, *Ming-shui chi*, 7.18b.
105. Ibid., 7.19b.
106. Ibid.
107. Ibid. Ch'eng Pi also mentions here being asked to write an inscription for Sun Valley Academy, although he was unable to do so. I can find no other reference to this academy, suggesting the likelihood that there were other similar family academies not recorded. Records of academies were in many instances dependent on the willingness of a colleague, relative, or acquaintance to write an inscription.
108. Recall that Ch'eng Pi also wrote an inscription for Clear Hsiang Academy in Ch'üan Prefecture (Hu-nan).
109. Ho Meng-kuei, *Ch'ien-chai wen-chi*, 9.18b–9.21a. For Ch'en Tou-lung, see SJCC III.2547; for his father, see SJCC III.2550. Ch'en T'ien-tse was a student of Yeh Ts'ai, who wrote the major commentary on the *Reflections on Things at Hand*.
110. SYHA: supp. 49.218a; TMTC 48.8a. This suggests one of the functions of academies in Southern Sung and thus one of the reasons behind the Southern Sung academy movement: providing occupation for men out of office, in mourning or for other reasons. See chapter 5.
111. SYHA: supp. 47a. According to this source, the fifth-generation ancestor of Ch'en T'ien-tse fled the north at the time of the fall of the Northern Sung and took up residence in Hang-chou. Ch'en T'ien-tse then retired to Jui-an, which is given as his son's (Ch'en Tou-lung) native place. Wen Chi-weng wrote a funerary piece for Ch'en T'ien-tse, which was placed at his grave. A shrine to the "Three Gentlemen" was erected at the academy.
112. Tseng Kuo-fan, et al., comps., *Chiang-hsi t'ung-chih*, 81.19a.
113. Ibid., 81.19a–81.20a.
114. Ibid.
115. For Chung Ju-yü, see SYHA 71.10b; for his son, Chung Chen, see SYHA: supp. 69.173b; for the inscription on the academy, see Ch'eng Chu-fu, *Hsueh-lou chi*, 12.8a–12.9b.
116. South Marchmount Academy was established in the early thirteenth century (1205–1207) at the side of South Marchmount Temple, in close proximity to Marchmount Hill Academy.
117. Chung Ju-yü's third-generation descendant, Chung Meng-li, restored the academy in 1294 after it had been taken over by "powerful families" in the chaos caused by the Mongol invasions. He allotted his own land to increase the academy's support to a total of one thousand *mou*. The academy clearly was regarded as a family institution, and although it is not explicit in the sources, the allo-

cation of land likely was seen as a means to prevent the dismemberment of family property by partible inheritance.

118. For Liu Yen, see SJCC V.3861; also Aoyama Sadao, *Sōjin denki sakuin*, 216. See also the inscription on this academy by Liu Ch'en-weng, *Hsu-ch'i chi*, 3.4a–3.5b. Since Liu Ch'en-weng was also from Chi—Liu Yen's native place and the site of the academy—there is a reasonable likelihood that they belonged to a common descent group. There is, however, no positive evidence of this assertion.
119. There is no date given for this academy, but it almost certainly was the late twelfth or thirteenth century, considering the date of Liu Yen's death and the dates of the inscription's writer. The name of this academy is a reference to a classical phrase associated with the famous Hsieh surname of the era of Northern and Southern Dynasties. Sons of the Hsieh were considered particularly virtuous, and the descendants of Liu Yen were favorably compared with them, as rare in the extent of their virtue as "fragrant orchids and jade trees." See Liu I-ch'ing, *Shih-shuo hsin-yü*, 35, and Richard Mather's translation of this, *A New Account of Tales of the World*, 72.
120. There are more extant inscriptions for academies attributed to Liu Ch'en-weng than to any other Sung writer. In addition to inscriptions for Orchid Jade above and Double Peak below, Liu Ch'en-weng wrote on both Double Creek and White Egret Islet in his home prefecture of Chi and Turtle Mountain in Fu-chien's Nan-chien Prefecture. He was recommended by Chiang Wan-li, for whom White Egret Islet was established. For Double Creek, White Egret Islet, and Turtle Mountain, see his collected works, *Hsu-ch'i chi*, 1.6b–1.9b, 3.29a–3.31b, 1.5b–1.7a. A 1262 *chin-shih* from Chi (Chiang-hsi), Liu Ch'en-weng was headmaster of Lien-hsi Academy, held high office in the central government, and retired home at the fall of the Southern Sung. For Liu Ch'en-weng, see SJCC V.3947.
121. See the inscriptions on this academy by Liu Ch'en-weng, *Hsu-ch'i chi* (2.6b–2.7b), and his son, Liu Chiang-sun (b. 1257), *Yang-wu chai chi* (15.25a–15.28a). The relationship between Liao Kang and Liao Te-ming is not clear. For general biographical references, see SJCC IV.3299, IV.3305.
122. Liu Chiang-sun, *Yang-wu chai chi*, 15.25a.
123. Liu Ch'en-weng, *Hsu-ch'i chi*, 2.6b–2.7a.
124. Ibid., 2.7b.
125. SS 374/133, 11590. For Liao Ch'ih, see SJCC IV.3301. For the brothers, see SJCC IV.3300, IV.3301, IV.3302.
126. SS 374/133, 11590.
127. SS 317/196, 12971.
128. Liu Chiang-sun, *Yang-wu chai chi*, 2.6b.
129. Liu Ch'en-weng, *Hsu-ch'i chi*, 2.7b.
130. See Walton, "The Institutional Context of Neo-Confucianism," 477, 478–479.
131. For Ying Su and Ying Hsu, see SJCC V.4092, V.4093.
132. The family connection continued with the restoration of Weng Islet Academy at the end of the thirteenth century by a descendant of Ying Hsü, Ying Hsiang-sun. In 1295–1296 Ying Hsiang-sun led his relatives to allot property to the academy for the support of teaching and was appointed headmaster at the academy, which then acquired official status. See Walton, "The Institutional Context of Neo-Confucianism," 484–485.
133. Feng Fu-ching, comp., *Ta-te Ch'ang-kuo chou t'u-chih*, 2.10b–2.11a.
134. See, for example, Wang Yuan-kung, *Chih-cheng Ssu-ming hsu-chih*, 8.6a.
135. See Walton, "The Institutional Context of Neo-Confucianism," 468, 478.

136. Wang Ying-lin, *Ssu-ming wen-hsien chi*, 1.16b–1.18b. Wang Ying-lin calls this school a *shu-shu*, and apparently the term *shu-yuan* was only used in the Yuan.
137. Wang Ying-lin, *Ssu-ming wen-hsien chi*, 1.16b.
138. Ibid., 1.17a.
139. Ibid., 1.17b.
140. Ibid.
141. Ibid. For Ch'i T'ung-wen, see SJCC III.2217; for Tseng Kung, see SJCC IV.2810–IV.2812; for Liu Ch'ing-chih, see SJCC V.3975–V.3976, especially SS 437/196, 12956–12957.
142. Wang Ying-lin, *Ssu-ming wen-hsien chi*, 1.18a.
143. Tseng Kuo-fan, et al., comps., *Chiang-hsi t'ung-chih*, 81.58a.
144. Kawakami Kyōji, "Sōdai no toshi to kyōiku—shūkengaku o chūshin ni," 377.
145. For this point, see Takahashi Yoshirō, "Sōdai shijin no mibun ni tsuite," 68–69.
146. Kawakami Kyōji, "Sōdai no toshi to kyōiku," 376.
147. Ibid., 377.
148. Robert Hymes, "Marriage, Descent Groups, and the Localist Strategy in Sung and Yuan Fu-chou," 96.

5. *Social Integration and Cultural Legitimacy: Academies and the Community of* Shih

1. Chikusa has made a significant contribution to the social history of the Sung in his work on *hsien-kuan*—"leisured officials"—a term used to refer to *shih* with official positions but no administrative responsibilities. He documents this term as a category of *chi-chü*, "sojourners," or officials who resided where they had held office rather than in their native areas. This phenomenon began to be noted in the late Northern Sung and was prevalent by the Southern Sung. *Shih* with official status but no administrative posts created problems for local government, and this led to official regulations on them and their activities. At the same time, as Chikusa suggests, they made important contributions to local culture. See Chikusa Masaaki, "Sōdai kanryō no kikyō ni tsuite." Chikusa cites examples from the Sung dynastic history alone that document cases of over ten years as "leisured residents" (31). Undoubtedly many more cases could be culled from a survey of other biographical sources. Chikusa also cites the "extreme" case of Chu Hsi, who spent only nine years of the fifty years after he took a *chin-shih* degree in official posts and only forty days at court (31).
2. Chikusa, "Sōdai kanryō no kikyō ni tsuite," 29.
3. SJCC V.3761, V.3756.
4. Ou-yang Shou-tao's first appointment at an academy was as lecturer at Chiang Wan-li's White Egret Islet Academy, established in 1241, the same year Ou-yang took his *chin-shih* degree.
5. SS 411/170, 12364–12365; SYHA, 88.1a, 88.2a.
6. Tseng Kuo-fan, et al., comps., *Chiang-hsi t'ung-chih*, 81.3b.
7. Chu Hsi, *Chu-tzu ta-ch'üan*, 100.13b. This amount was one *sheng*, four *tou* of rice, plus sixty cash. One *sheng* is slightly less than a liter, and four *tou* is less than four deciliters. According to Chu Hsi, this followed the regulations of the prefectural school.
8. Wang I-shan, *Chia-ts'un lei-kao*, 8.3b.
9. This and the following statements are based on ideas proposed by Hymes.
10. For Yü Ch'ou, see SJCC IV.3199–IV.4000.

11. Takahashi has identified a new social category of *shih-jen* or *shih-tzu* (scholars), distinct from *shih ta-fu*. See Takahashi Yoshirō, "Sōdai shijin no mibun ni tsuite." In making this distinction, Takahashi argues that office-holding was the defining characteristic of the *shih ta-fu*, while *shih-jen* shared scholarly standing as intellectuals and formed the core of examination candidates not yet eligible for office. In the introduction to her translation of Yuan Ts'ai's *Yuan-shih shih-fan*, Ebrey refers to the category of *shih* or *shih-jen* as essentially identical with *shih ta-fu*. See Ebrey, *Family and Property in Sung China*, 3–7. See especially 5, note 3. Yü Ch'ou's memorial similarly uses the term *shih-tzu*, clearly referring to individuals who have scholarly qualifications (or at least pretensions) and yet reject the official educational institutional structure and hierarchy.
12. *Ch'in-ting hsu wen-hsien t'ung-k'ao*, 50.3241. The date of the memorial is uncertain, but it is probably around 1200.
13. Takahashi further describes a social hierarchy beginning with local officials (*hsiang-kuan*), followed by sojourners (*chi-chü*), then *shih-jen*, and finally, commoners. In this formulation, the upper two categories would be broadly considered *shih ta-fu*, members of an office-holding elite. As Takahashi points out, *shih-jen* were conscious of their scholarly status and played a role of leadership in local affairs consistent with it. At the same time, they could also use their position to further their own self-interest. In this sense, the activities and behavior of *shih-jen* were similar to Chikusa's description of the problems created locally by "leisured officials" without administrative appointments but with official status. *Shih-jen* were also eager, however, to validate their status through participation in the scholarly community associated with academies. They could participate in a variety of ways: as founders, supporters, teachers, temporary lecturers, or even as students of a famed teacher invited to lecture.
14. For discussion of this, see Lee, *Government Education and Examinations in Sung China*, 116.
15. Ibid., 118–119.
16. Ch'en Ch'i-ch'ing (ca. 1180–1236), comp., *Chia-ting Ch'ih-ch'eng chih*, 34.20b.
17. Ibid. See also SJCC II.1224. Not all who moved to T'ai were as illustrious as Lü I-hao. In sharp contrast to Lü I-hao, in around 1175 a little-known scholar from Ch'u named Ying Shu, who was praised by Chu Hsi, lodged in Huang-yen County (*Chia-ting Ch'ih-ch'eng chih*, 34.23a). By the reign of Hsiao-tsung (1163–1189), the academy movement was well underway with the revival of Northern Sung academies such as White Deer Grotto, Stone Drum, and Marchmount Hill. One of the earliest recorded academies in T'ai, Creek Mountain Number One Academy (Chi Hui-yun, et al., comps., *Che-chiang t'ung-chih*, 27.30b), located in Lin-hai County, was distinguished by a plaque written by Chu Hsi. Since this academy was probably established in 1175, Chu Hsi likely wrote the plaque during his stay there when he became acquainted with Ying Shu.
18. SJCC V.4116; Franke, *Sung Biographies*, 413–415.
19. Hsieh Liang-tso was imprisoned, stripped of official status, and reduced to the status of an ordinary citizen for expressing a frank opinion at court about a change in reign name. See Franke, *Sung Biographies*, 414.
20. SJCC V.4117.
21. SJCC V.4117. The *tz'u* of both are the same. TMTC 47.10b says that Hsieh Liang-tso's sons and grandsons traveled to T'ai, where the prefect received them and asked to conduct rites to Hsieh in the prefectural school. If this was during the Chia-ting period (1208–1224), as the account states, it would have had to be Hsieh Liang-tso's grandsons or great-grandsons.

22. There were a number of Hsieh in Lin-hai, several of whom took *chin-shih* degrees in the late twelfth and early thirteenth century, including the family of Li-tsung's Empress Hsieh. She was the granddaughter of Hsieh Shen-fu (1166 *chin-shih*). For Hsieh Shen-fu, see SJCC V.4125; for Empress Hsieh, see SJCC V.4124. In her father's generation, two brothers took *chin-shih* degrees in 1202. See SJCC V.4121, V.4128. Two other Hsieh from Lin-hai also took degrees in 1172 and 1177, although their relationship to each other and to other Hsieh is not clear. See SJCC V.4129.
23. Yeh Shih, *Shui-hsin wen-chi*, 10.165–10.166.
24. Ibid., 10.165.
25. SYHA 82.16b; Chi Hui-yun, et al., comps., *Che-chiang t'ung-chih*, 27.34b. The prefect who established Shang-ts'ai Academy is identified in several sources as Wang Hua-p'u, sometimes Wang Shih-weng, and there is an entry in SYHA (82.16b) for him, but I cannot locate any other information about him.
26. A second Shang-ts'ai Academy was founded in T'ai's Hsien-chü County in the late Southern Sung by Chao Pi-sheng, a native of T'ai who served as magistrate of I-wu County in Wu (Chi Hui-yun, et al., comps., *Che-chiang t'ung-chih*, 26; SJCC IV.3416). At the end of his career, he returned home and requested permission from the court to found the academy, imitating the example of Shang-ts'ai Academy in Lin-hai.
27. SS 421/180, 12586.
28. See Smith, "Family, *Landsmann*, and Status-Group Affinity in Refugee Mobility Strategies," 680. Both Yang Tung's father, Yang Ju-ming, and his grandfather had taken *chin-shih* degrees (1172 and 1193). See SJCC IV.3160, IV.3150. Yang Ju-ming established Five Peaks Academy in Lu-chou along the southern frontier of the Ssu-ch'uan basin (Ch'ang Ming, ed., *Ssu-ch'uan t'ung-chih*, 79.406).
29. Ch'eng Tsu-lo, et al., eds., *Fu-chien t'ung-chih*, 63.1b; SS 421/180, 12586.
30. This is according to SYHA 82.16b, under the biographical sketch of Wang Pen, who subsequently became headmaster after Wang Po. There is an extant lecture by Wang Po at Shang-ts'ai that deals with Hsieh Liang-tso's concept of "always being alert" (SYHA: supp. 82.23b–82.24a); see also Wing-tsit Chan, trans. and ed., *Neo-Confucian Terms Explained (The Pei-hsi tz'u-i by Ch'en Ch'un, 1159–1223)*, 102. According to his biography in the dynastic history, Chao Ching-wei (1241 *chin-shih*) was first asked, but he declined because of illness. Chao Ching-wei was subsequently appointed prefect of T'ai. See SS 425/184, 2673; SJCC IV.3582. According to Wang Po's biography in the dynastic history, he was appointed teacher at both Wu's Beautiful Pools and T'ai's Shang-ts'ai Academies under the respective tenures of Ts'ai Hang and Yang Tung in Wu and Chao Ching-wei in T'ai. See SS 438/197, 12981.

    Wang Po was descended from a distinguished scholarly lineage in Wu. His father, Wang Han (d. 1211), was a student of both Chu Hsi and Lü Tsu-ch'ien (SJCC I.232; SYHA 73.3). Wang Po's grandfather, Wang Shih-yü (1122–1190; 1148 *chin-shih*), studied with Yang Shih and Lü Pen-chung (SJCC I.335; SYHA 25.21). If not foremost in their careers, military concerns were a persistent undercurrent in the lives of many of these Southern Sung scholars and officials. Wang Han was noted for his drawings of eighty-nine "items" of military heroes from King Wu to K'ou Chun of the Northern Sung (SJCC I.232). As a young man, Wang Po greatly admired Chu-ko Liang, even to the point of taking a sobriquet identified with him (SS 438/197, 12980).
31. SYHA 82.16b; see also SJCC I.192.
32. SJCC I.123. Wang Pi held office in Fu-chien and in 1254 established Three Mountain Academy in Fu Prefecture. For Three Mountain Academy, see TMTC

74.9b and Lu Tseng-yü, et al., comps., *Fu-chou fu chih*, 11.29a. Like other officials involved with academies, Wang Pi was perhaps inspired to establish Three Mountain Academy in Fu-chou following his experience with Angling Terrace Academy in Yen. As prefect of Yen in 1251, Wang Pi had been responsible for appointing new offices at Angling Terrace there (Cheng Yao and Fang Jen-jung, eds., *Ching-ting Yen-chou hsu-chih*, 3.2b). He also wrote a great deal on both Chen Te-hsiu and Chu Hsi (SYHA 82.16a). Wang Pi is of further interest because of his family background. He was from Chin-hua, the grandson of Wang Huai (1126–1189; 1145 *chin-shih*), a prominent official under Hsiao-tsung who disliked Chu Hsi, attacked True Way Learning, and was instrumental in the False Learning prohibition of 1195 (SJCC 1.159). However, Wang Pi also studied with Chu Hsi's disciple, Jao Lu, and when he held office in Fu-chien he was said to have "opened up" Chen Te-hsiu's doctrine of "right *ch'i*." He was also supposed to have written a lengthy commentary on Chu Hsi, although the editors of the *Ssu-k'u ch'üan-shu* expressed doubts about this attribution. See SYHA: supp. 82.146b. In the mid-1250s, Wang Pi established Willow Lake Academy at the lecturing place of Ch'eng Tuan-meng, one of Chu Hsi's disciples, in Jao's Tehsing County (Tseng Kuo-fan, et al., eds., *Chiang-hsi t'ung-chih*, 82.24a). In any case, it is clear that Wang Pi did not maintain the negative view of Chu Hsi and his followers expressed by his grandfather. This may suggest the degree to which Chu Hsi's views had come to be accepted as orthodoxy by the mid-thirteenth century, rather than any personal idiosyncrasy. Serving in office in Fu-chien, where Chu Hsi's followers were very active, may also have had an influence on Wang Pi. Yang Tung, who became the first headmaster of Shang-ts'ai Academy, was prefect of Hsing-hua during the Ch'un-yu (1241–1252) era, close to the time Wang Pi held office as vice fiscal commissioner (*chuan-yün fu-shih*) of Fu-chien.

33. SS 418/177, 12527.
34. See SJCC I.429 (father Shih Shih-tan, 1019 *chin-shih*), I.427 (son Shih Ya-chih [b. 1026]; 1034–1038 *chin-shih*), I.424 (son Shih Hsiu-chih [1017–1093]; 1038 *chin-shih*), I.434 (son Shih Lin-chih, 1049 *chin-shih*), I.427 (nephew Shih Mu-chih [1015–1093]; 1045 chin-shih). Shih Ya-chih's cousin, Shih Mu-chih, was magistrate of T'ien-t'ai (T'ai) and was known along with Wang An-shih, magistrate of Yin County (Ming) and Ch'en Hsien, magistrate of Hsien-chu County (T'ai), as the "Three Worthy Administrators" (SJCC I.427).
35. SYHA: supp. 14.19a; SJCC 1.427 says Shih Ya-chih took his degree in the 1034–1038 period, but the local history says he took a degree in 1042. A further discrepancy in the sources concerns the academy itself. Although Shih Ya-chih took a degree at age seventeen, he rejected holding office and was eventually appointed erudite of the Court of Imperial Sacrifices (*t'ai-ch'ang po-shih*). It seems likely that the Drum Mountain where he built a lodging place and study would have been located in his home county of Hsin-ch'ang, but the gazetteer places Stone Drum in Lin-hai, where his descendants later moved.
36. SJCC I.417. Shih Yen held office as prefect of Nan-k'ang and was admired by Chu Hsi, who wrote an epitaph for him (*Chu Wen-kung wen-chi*, 92.1622–92.1623). He was also the teacher of the Tu brothers, Chih-jen and Yü, of Huang-yen County, who lectured at a place in Huang-yen that later became a shrine to Chu Hsi (who also had lectured there) and then Fan River Academy, established sometime after 1200. For the Tu brothers, see SJCC II.811, II.807–II.808; for the academy, see Yü Ch'ang-lin, et al., comps., *T'ai-chou fu chih*, 27.31b. The Tu brothers were sons of Tu Ch'un, for whom Yeh Shih wrote an epitaph, and whose grandfather was Tu I (fl. 1052), known for his filial piety

(SJCC II.801, 802). The Tu brothers were also great-uncles of Tu Fan (1182–1245; 1208 *chin-shih*), who studied with Chu Hsi as well as with Tu Fan's great-uncles, and whose residence at the burial place of his ancestors became Fan River Academy. For Tu Fan, see SJCC II.803–804; Franke, *Sung Biographies*, 1077–1079.

37. For Yang Tung's Han River Academy, see TMTC 77. 27b; for Wang Pi's Three Mountains Academy, see note 32.
38. SYHA 82.17a; Smith, "Family, *Landsmann*, and Status-Group Afinity in Refugee Mobility Strategies," 678. Smith points out that affinal connections were important in the ability of Chang Hsu's father to move his family out of Ssu-ch'uan into the relative safety of the southeast.
39. Smith, "Family, *Landsmann*, and Status-Group Affinity in Refugee Mobility Strategies," 690.
40. SJCC I.94–I.97.
41. This is according to Ts'ao Pin's biography in the dynastic history, appended to that of his kinsman, Ts'ao Shu-yuan (SS 416/175.12482). Liu Tsai's inscription on the academy attributes the founding of a shrine to Ch'en Fei, who was prefect in the 1208–1224 (ca. 1213) era (*Man-t'ang wen-chi*, 23.30a). However, according to his dynastic history biography, Li Fei (d. 1276) established the academy when he was fiscal intendant for Che-hsi (SS 450/209.13254). I cannot resolve this inconsistency. For Ch'en Fei, see SJCC III.2459; for Li Fei, see SJCC II.852.
42. SJCC I.733.; see also Irving Yucheng Lo, *Hsin Ch'i-chi*.
43. Yü Chi, *Tao-yuan hsueh-ku lu*, 10.6a. The year T'ang Chen made Hsin Ch'i-chi's residence into official land is given as *hsin-chi*, but this would be either 1221 or 1281, either too early or too late. T'ang Chen (SJCC III.1780) took a *chin-shih* in 1253 and was prefect of Jao around 1270, so I have taken the date *hsin-wei* (1271) to have been mistakenly recorded as *hsin-chi*. Both T'ang Chen and his elder brother died in the capture of Jao by Mongol troops, so neither could have been active in 1281. According to both *Chiang-hsi t'ung-chih* (Tseng Kuo-fan, et al., comps.), 82.14a, and TMTC 51.6b, this academy was first named Gourd Spring.
44. SYHA: supp. 84.31a.
45. Yü Hsi-lu, comp., *Chih-hsun Chen-chiang chih*, 11.27b; SJCC V.4505.
46. Yü Hsi-lu, comp., *Chih-hsun Chen-chiang chih*, 11.27b; SJCC III.2078, III.2075 (Chang Yen's father).
47. Yü Hsi-lu, comp., *Chih-hsun Chen-chiang chih*, 11.27b.
48. Ibid.
49. The name plaque was granted in 1249. See Yin Chi-shan, et al., eds., *Chiang-nan t'ung-chih*, 90.23b.
50. Yü Hsi-lu, comp., *Chih-hsun Chen-chiang chih*, 11.32b. For Hsu Li, see SJCC III.2001. This academy was located at the site of Chou Tun-i's maternal kin's home.
51. Yü Hsi-lu, comp., *Chih-hsun Chen-chiang chih*, 11.32b.
52. SJCC II.1300–II.1301; Franke, *Sung Biographies*, 779–786.
53. SJCC III.2107–III.2108 for K'ou Chun. For the academy, see Li Tseng-po, *K'o-chai tsa-kao*, 5.1a–5.2b.
54. Kao Ssu-te, *Ch'ih-t'ang ts'un-kao*, 4.5a–4.7a; Ch'eng Chu-fu, *Ch'eng Hsueh-lou chi*, 2.16b–2.17b.
55. Kao Ssu-te, *Ch'ih-t'ang ts'un-kao*, 4.5b. There is discrepancy in the sources with regard both to the dates of founding and to the location of Nan-yang Academy. Kao Ssu-te locates Nan-yang at Wu-ch'ang County in E, but the gazetteer places

it in Chiang-ling (*Hu-pei t'ung-chih*, 59.42a–59.42b). Ch'eng Chu-fu's inscription also places it in E (*Ch'eng Hsueh-lou chi*, 2.17a). I am inclined to accept the testimony of the inscriptions over the Ch'ing gazetteer. Sun Yen-min, *Sung-tai shu-yuan chih-tu chih yen-chiu*, 69, dates both academies in the Chia-hsi period (1237–1240), citing as evidence Meng Kung as prefect of Chiang-ling at that time. Li Tseng-po's inscription on Kung-an Academy states that it was begun in 1242 and received a name place in 1243 (Li Tseng-po, *K'o-chai tsa-kao*, 5.1a). Ch'eng Chu-fu also states that Nan-yang Academy was begun in the Ch'un-hsi era (1241–1252). Again, I am inclined to follow the inscriptions over the gazetteer.

56. Kao Ssu-te, *Ch'ih-t'ang ts'un-kao*, 4.5b.
57. Ibid.
58. Li Tseng-po, *K'o-chai tsa-kao*, 5.2b.
59. Ibid., 5.1b. Headmaster Lei I-chung (1247 *chin-shih*) was said not to have gotten along with Chia Ssu-tao, and yet he expanded the academy. For Lei I-chung, see SJCC IV.3092.
60. Li Tseng-po, *K'o-chai tsa-kao*, 5.1b.
61. In a meticulous study comparable to that of Chikusa on sojourners, Huang K'uan-ch'ung has examined the phenomenon of *kuei-cheng jen*, literally, "men who returned to the upright," or those who moved south fleeing from either the Jurchen or the Mongols in the Southern Sung. Citing various terms by which they were referred to in the sources, such as *kuei-ming, kuei-ch'ao, kuei-fu*, and *chung-i*, Huang K'uan-ch'ung discusses the complex and shifting views of these men implemented in government policies toward them, as well as changing attitudes on their part toward the Southern Sung court. See Huang K'uan-ch'ung, "Lueh-lun Nan-Sung shih-tai te kuei-cheng jen" (Concerning political refugees in the Southern Sung period).
62. Huang K'uan-ch'ung, "Lueh-lun Nan-Sung shih-tai te kuei-cheng jen," 209–216.
63. SS 424/183, 12661. Ch'eng Tsu-lo, et al., eds., *Fu-chien t'ung-chih*, 63.4b. Hsu Yuan-shu studied with Ch'en Wen-wei (1154–1239), a disciple of Chu Hsi's who was also from Shang-jao (SJCC III.2545). For Ch'en Wen-wei's connections with academies, see chapter 6.
64. Lin Hsi-i, *Chu-ch'i chuan-chai shih-i k'ao hsu-chi*, 11.2.
65. SS 420/179, 12575.
66. SJCC 3.1914–3.1915; SS 424/183, 12664 (his restoration of Mount Mao Academy).
67. SJCC 1.188.
68. SS 424/183, 12663.
69. Ibid.
70. Ibid. Although it was not connected with Mount Mao Academy, when Sun Tzu-hsiu subsequently took charge of problems with salt piracy in Ch'ü, he was assisted by someone described as *yu-shih* (lodging scholar), another term used to refer to members of a scholarly elite not resident in their native areas and not in office where they resided.
71. For this academy, see Cheng Yao and Fang Jen-jung, eds., *Ching-ting Yen-chou hsu-chih*, 3.2a–3.4a.
72. SJCC III.2665.
73. For a discussion of this philosophical background, see the introduction to Chan, trans. and ed., *Neo-Confucian Terms Explained*, 22–32.
74. SJCC III.2529.
75. For the inscription on this academy, see Ch'en Yuan-chin, *Yü-shu lei-kao*, 5.4b–5.7a.
76. For other examples of the practice of erecting *sheng-tz'u*, see Chu I, *I-chueh liao*

tsa-chi, 2.20b–2.21a; Chu Pien, *Ch'ü-wei chiu-wen*, 3.20; and Kung Ming-chih, *Chung-wu chi-wen*, 2.5a–2.5b, 4.9b–4.10a. I am grateful to Judith Boltz for these references.

77. Chen Te-hsiu, *Hsi-shan hsien-sheng Chen Wen-chung kung wen-chi*, 25.392 *shang*–25.393.
78. This term is commonly used by Buddhists, although it probably does not have a specific Buddhist meaning here. However, it is still significant that this term is used, because it has an ambivalent connotation, particularly given the context here.
79. Chen Te-hsiu, *Hsi-shan hsien-sheng Chen Wen-chung kung wen-chi*, 25.392.
80. Ti Jen-chieh was also venerated at Southern Lake Academy in Fu-chou, Hu-pei. See TMTC 66.3b. His biography in Liu Hsu, *Chiu T'ang shu*, 89.2895, records a *sheng-tz'u* established in honor of him.
81. According to his biography in Liu Hsu, *Chiu T'ang shu* (89.28945), Ti Jen-chieh was also noted for having destroyed 1,700 "licentious shrines" (*yin-tz'u*) in an effort to stamp out popular deity cults. Ch'en Ch'un cited this in his *Pei-hsi tz'u-i* as part of his diatribe against popular religious practices. See Chan, trans., *Neo-Confucian Terms Explained*, 160, and Hansen, *Changing Gods in Medieval China*, 99. Although Chen Te-hsiu's account of the shrine to Ch'en Wei stresses popular support, it seems unlikely that Ti Jen-chieh would have been regarded as a hero among the people for his service at court and even more unlikely that his vehement suppression of popular deity cults would have made him a hero to the common people.
82. Chen Te-hsiu, *Hsi-shan hsien-sheng Chen Wen-chung kung wen-chi*, 25.393 *shang*.
83. Wen T'ien-hsiang, *Wen Wen-shan ch'üan-chi*, 9.18b–9.19a.
84. That is, those who are sunburnt from labor in the fields.
85. Wen T'ien-hsiang, *Wen Wen-shan ch'üan-chi*, 9.19a.
86. Ibid., 9.19b.
87. Hsieh Fang-te, *Tieh-shan chi*, 9.2b.
88. Liu Ch'en-weng, *Hsu-ch'i chi*, 3.31b.
89. Liu Tsai, *Man-t'ang wen-chi*, 23.29a–23.29b
90. Ibid., 23.30b.
91. Ibid., 23.30a.
92. Ibid., 23.30b.
93. Huang K'uan-ch'ung points out that, in addition to the contributions refugees made to the development of the Chiang-nan region during the Southern Sung, they also created social and economic problems. See Huang K'uan-ch'ung, "Lueh-lun Sung-tai shih-tai te kuei-cheng jen."

6. *Academies and the Learning of the* Shih, *ca. 1225–1275*

1. Chou Ying-ho, comp., *Ching-ting Chien-k'ang chih*, 29.17a–29.20a. Although anonymous and undated, this lecture was probably presented sometime between the founding of the academy in 1241 and the first dated lecture in 1252.
2. Chou Ying-ho, comp., *Ching-ting Chien-k'ang chih*, 29.17a.
3. Ibid., 29.17b. For a gloss on *ch'ing*, rendered here as "circumstances," see Kidder Smith, Jr., et al., *Sung Dynasty Uses of the I Ching*, 255.
4. Chou Ying-ho, comp., *Ching-ting Chien-k'ang chih*, 29.18a. Ch'eng Hao held office in Shang-yuan County early in his career. See, inter alia, Franke, *Sung Biographies*, 169.

5. Chou Ying-ho, comp., *Ching-ting Chien-k'ang chih*, 29.18b.
6. Ibid., 29.19a–29.19b.
7. Ibid., 29.20a.
8. Ibid., 29.20b–29.22a. For Wu Chien, see SJCC II.1107–II.1108.
9. I can find no information on Hu Ch'ung.
10. Chou Ying-ho, comp., *Ching-ting Chien-k'ang chih*, 29.25a.
11. Ibid., 29.25b–29.27a. For Chu P'i-sun, see SJCC I.624.
12. Chou Ying-ho, comp., *Ching-ting Chien-k'ang chih*, 29.25b. According to glosses on this term as used in the *Rites of Chou*, which he quotes in the beginning of this passage, the *pin-hsing* was the method of selecting officials carried out by local officials (*ch'ing ta-fu*) of the Chou, who announced those who were talented in the "local libation ceremonies" (*hsiang yin-chiu li*) and then recommended those named to the ruler for appointment to office.
13. Chou Ying-ho, comp., *Ching-ting Chien-k'ang chih*, 29.25b.
14. Ibid., 29.26b.
15. Ibid., 29.27a.
16. Ibid., 29.27a–29.28a. I can find no information on Chao Ju-chou.
17. Chou Ying-ho, comp., *Ching-ting Chien-k'ang chih*, 29.28a–29.30a.
18. See Smith, Jr., *Sung Dynasty Uses of the I Ching*, 15.
19. Chou Ying-ho, comp., *Ching-ting Chien-k'ang chih*, 29.28b.
20. Ibid.
21. Ibid., 29.29a.
22. Ibid., 29.29b.
23. Ibid., 29.30a–29.35b.
24. Ibid., 29.30a.
25. Ibid., 29.30b. For the translation of *ch'i* as "psychophysical stuff," see Gardner, trans., *Chu Hsi: Learning to be a Sage*, 50–51 *passim*. Since *chih* is translated by Chan as "natural substance, simple stuff" (*Reflections on Things at Hand*, 115, note 133), I have rendered *ch'i-chih* as "psychophysical stuff."
26. Chou Ying-ho, comp., *Ching-ting Chien-k'ang chih*, 29.31a. For the translation of this passage, see Legge, trans., *The Chinese Classics*, vol. I, 137.
27. Chou Ying-ho, comp., *Ching-ting Chien-k'ang chih*, 29.31b.
28. Ibid., 29.32a–29.32b.
29. Ibid., 29.32b.
30. Ibid., 29.33b.
31. Ibid., 29.33a.
32. Ibid.
33. Ibid., 29.33b–29.34a.
34. Ibid., 29.35a–29.35b.
35. Ibid., 29.35b.
36. Ibid., 29.36a. For Chang Hsien, see SJCC III.2339. Chang Hsien was recommended for appointment to the History Bureau by Ma Kuang-tsu, who was prominently involved with Illumined Way Academy when he held office here.
37. Chou Ying-ho, comp., *Ching-ting Chien-k'ang chih*, 29.36a–29.38a.
38. Ibid., 29.36a–29.37b. For this passage, see Legge, trans., *The Chinese Classics*, vol. I, 413.
39. Chou Ying-ho, comp., *Ching-ting Chien-k'ang chih*, 29.38a.
40. Ibid., 29.37b.
41. Ibid., 29.38a. I cannot find other information on Hu Li-pen.
42. Chou Ying-ho, comp., *Ching-ting Chien-k'ang chih*, 29.38a–29.38b.
43. Ibid., 29.38b.
44. Ibid., 29.40a–29.42a. For Weng Yung, see SJCC III.1975.

45. Chou Ying-ho, comp., *Ching-ting Chien-k'ang chih*, 29.40b.
46. Four of them (Hu Ch'ung, Hu Li-pen, Chao Ju-chou, and Pan Chi) cannot be identified beyond the offices listed for them accompanying their lectures. Three of the remaining five, however, took *chin-shih* degrees in the same year (1244), and two of them, Chang Hsien and Chou Ying-ho, were supported by Ma Kuang-tsu.
47. SJCC III.2545.
48. Chen Te-hsiu, *Chen Hsi-shan wen-chi*, 26.446–26.447.
49. Ch'en Wen-wei, *K'o-chai chi*, 8.8a–8.9b.
50. Ibid., 8.8b–8.9a.
51. Ibid.
52. Ibid., 8.9a.
53. Ibid., 8.12a–8.14a. For the academy, see TMTC 57.19b.
54. Ch'en Wen-wei, *K'o-chai chi*, 8.9b–8.12a.
55. Ibid., 8.9b–8.10a.
56. His own father, Ch'en Pang-hsien (1133–1226), was an eremite scholar, known as Master Bamboo Grove (see SJCC III.2545, where he is appended to his son's biographical entry).
57. Ch'en Wen-wei, *K'o-chai chi*, 3.15b
58. Ibid., 3.16a. Legge, trans., *The Chinese Classics*, vol. I, 407.
59. Ch'en Wen-wei, *K'o-chai chi*, 3.16b. Legge, trans., *The Chinese Classics*, vol. I, 407–408.
60. Ch'en Wen-wei, *K'o-chai chi*, 8.14a.
61. Ibid., 8.17b–8.22b.
62. Ibid., 8.18a–8.19a. Legge, trans., *The Chinese Classics*, vol. I, 428–430, 411.
63. Ch'en Wen-wei, *K'o-chai chi*, 8.20a.
64. Ibid., 8.20a–8.20b. Legge, trans., *The Chinese Classics*, vol. I, 175–176, 179–180.
65. Ch'en Wen-wei, *K'o-chai chi*, 8.21b. Legge, *The Chinese Classics*, vol. I, 331.
66. Ch'en Wen-wei, *K'o-chai chi*, 8.22a.
67. For an eloquent treatment of Wen T'ien-hsiang's personal and professional life, see Davis, *Wind Against the Mountain*, 4 ff. See also Jay, *A Change in Dynasties*, 93–136.
68. For Wen T'ien-hsiang, see SJCC I.37–I.40; Franke, *Sung Biographies*, 1187–1201. For this lecture, see Wen T'ien-hsiang, *Wen Wen-shan ch'üan-chi*, 11.369–11.372.
69. Wen T'ien-hsiang, *Wen Wen-shan ch'üan-chi*, 11.369.
70. Ibid.
71. Ibid., 11.372.
72. Both Liu Huan and Liu Shu were recognized by Chu Hsi in a shrine he erected at Nan-k'ang while in office there. See Wang Mou-hung, *Chu-tzu nien-p'u*, 2.78.
73. An inscription written in 1285 for the restoration of the academy by Wang I-shan cites the establishment of a shrine to the three Liu in the Shao-hsing period (1131–1165), nearly a century before the founding of the academy in 1236. See Wang I-shan, *Chia-ts'un lei-kao*, 8.1a–8.4b. Wang I-shan noted that Chiang Wan-li established White Egret Islet Academy in Lu-ling to venerate Ch'eng Hsiang and his two sons, and likened the honoring of these two generations to the three generations represented at West Brook Academy (8.2b–8.3a). Other sources on White Egret Islet, however, make no mention of this; possibly by the time of Wang I-shan's writing, however, such a shrine had been erected at White Egret Islet. Wen T'ien-hsiang was a native of Lu-ling and studied under Ou-yang

Shou-tao at White Egret Islet as a youth. See Franke, *Sung Biographies*, 1187–1188; see also Davis, *Wind against the Mountain*, 138.

74. SJCC IV.3044.
75. SYHA 83.4a.
76. Peck Peak Academy was named for the honorific of Li Po-yü (1235 *chin-shih*), who was said to have established it. For Li Po-yü, see SJCC II.982. For the academy, see Tseng Kuo-fan, et al., comps., *Chiang-hsi t'ung-chih*, 22.26b. For Ch'eng Jo-yung's lecture there, see SYHA 83.4a–83.6b. The academy likely was founded after Li Po-yü's death, or at least late in his career, by someone else, perhaps at his residence or study, since he was also from Yu-kan County. Thus the academy was probably founded sometime in the latter half of the thirteenth century.
77. SYHA 83.4a.
78. Ibid., 83.5a.
79. Ibid., 83.6a. Translated by Liu Ts'un-yan in his "Chu Hsi's Influence in Yuan Times," 525.
80. SYHA 83.6b.
81. For Fang Feng-ch'en, see SJCC I.81–I.83. For the lecture, see SYHA 82.14a–82.14b.
82. See the inscription by Fang I-k'uei (fl. ca. 1265) in Fang Feng-ch'en's collected works, *Chiao-feng wai-chi*, 3.32ba–3.34b.
83. SYHA 82.14a–82.14b.
84. Fang Feng-ch'en, *Chiao-feng wai-chi*, 3.33a. Fang I-k'uei was a contemporary of Ho Meng-kuei (1265 *chin-shih*). For Fang I-k'uei, see SJCC I.67; SYHA: supp. 82.143b; for Ho Meng-kuei, see SJCC II.1283.
85. For Fang Feng-chen, see SJCC I.83.
86. Fang Hui, *T'ung-chiang hsu-chi*, 1.13–1.17.
87. For Fang Feng-chia, see SJCC I.83.
88. SYHA 64.9b; SYHA: supp. 64.47b. For Hsiung Ho, see SJCC IV.3620; for Hsieh Fang-te, see SJCC V.4119.

Conclusion

1. Benjamin Schwartz, "Some Polarities in Confucian Thought," 5.
2. See the discussion in Ch'en Wen-i, "Yu kuan-hsueh tao shu-yuan," 184–190. For examples, see Yeh Shih, *Shui-hsin wen-chi*, 3.673, 13.798–13.802.
3. Chou Ying-ho, comp., *Ching-ting Chien-k'ang chih*, 29.5b–29.6a.
4. "Yu kuan-hsueh tao shu-yuan," 178.
5. Ibid., 136 passim.
6. See Chaffee, "Chu Hsi and the Revival of the White Deer Grotto Academy, 1179–1181 A.D."; see also Chaffee, "Chu Hsi in Nan-k'ang: *Tao-hsüeh* and the Politics of Education."
7. Liu Tsai, *Man-t'ang wen-chi*, 23.30a.
8. David Johnson, "The City-God Cults of T'ang and Sung China," 363–457.
9. See James Watson, "Standardizing the Gods: The Promotion of T'ien Hou ('Empress of Heaven') along the South China Coast, 960–1960"; Hansen, *Changing Gods in Medieval China*, 162.
10. See Hansen, *Changing Gods in Medieval China*, 79–104.
11. Chu Hsi, *Chu-tzu wen-chi*, 81.24a; cited in Chan, "Chu Hsi and the Academies," 401.

12. Huang Ch'ing-wen, *Chung-kuo ku-tai shu-yuan chih-tu chi ch'i k'o-shu t'an-yen*, 102. See also Liu Chih-sheng, "Chung-kuo shu-yuan k'o-shu chi-lueh," 410–412; Yeh Te-hui (1864–1927), *Shu-lin ch'ing-hua*, 74–75; P'an Mei-yüeh, "Liang-Sung Shu-k'o te t'e-se," 45–55; Ku Jui-lan, "Chung-kuo shu-yuan k'an-k'o t'u-shu k'ao," 27–44.
13. Huang Min-chih, "Sung-tai Fu-chien te ssu-yuan yü she-hui," 316; Chikusa Masaaki, "Fukken no ji-in to shakai," 186.
14. Chan pointed out that, even at the premier academy of the Southern Sung, White Deer Grotto, we have no record of what was taught or what texts were used. See Wing-tsit Chan, "Chu Hsi and the Academies," 399.
15. For that matter, we know little about the curricula at government schools, other than that teaching was based on Confucian canonical texts that would be tested in the examinations. See Lee, *Government Education and Examinations in Sung China*, 110.
16. Gardner, trans., *Chu Hsi: Learning to be a Sage*, 41.
17. Ibid., 79.
18. Hilde de Weerdt, a graduate student at Harvard University working on Southern Sung examination essays, has found that there is a steady increase in True Way thought and style in these expositions traceable over the course of Li-tsung's reign, suggesting that by the mid-thirteenth century True Way Learning had a substantial impact on the content of the examinations. Personal communication, August 15, 1996.
19. Gardner, trans., *Chu Hsi: Learning to be a Sage*, 79.
20. Ibid., 80.
21. Bol, "The Examination System and the Shih," 169.
22. Ibid., 155, 169.
23. See his famous address at Munich in 1918, in H. H. Gerth and C. Wright Mills, trans. and ed., From *Max Weber: Essays in Sociology*, 129–156. Michael Shwehn, in *Exiles from Eden*, points out that Gerth and Mills' translation of *Wissenschaft* as "science" is better reflected by the term "academics" (6).
24. Bol, "The Examination System and the *Shih*," 167.
25. Ibid., 166, citing Chaffee, *The Thorny Gates of Learning in Sung China*, 142.
26. Benjamin A. Elman, "Political, Social, and Cultural Reproduction via Civil Service Examinations in Late Imperial China," 7–28.
27. Charles Holcombe, "The Exemplar State: Ideology, Self-Cultivation, and Power in Fourth-Century China," 93–139. See also Charles Holcombe, *In the Shadow of the Han: Literati Thought and Society at the beginning of the Southern Dynasties*.
28. On eremitism in early China, see Aat Vervoorn, *Men of the Cliffs and Caves: The Chinese Eremitic Tradition to the End of the Han Dynasty*.
29. Liu K'o-chuang, *Hou-ts'un hsien-sheng ta ch'üan chi*, 93.15a.
30. Chuang Chung-fang, comp., *Nan-Sung wen-fan*, 46.12b.
31. Wu Ch'eng, *Wu Wen-cheng kung wen-chi*, 23.30b.
32. For these, see Yü Hsi-lu, comp., *Chih-hsun Chen-chiang chih*, 11.27b–11.34a.
33. For Mount Mao Academy, see Yü Hsi-lu, comp., *Chih-hsun Chen-chiang chih*, 11.34a–11.35b; for Inculcating Duty Academy, see Lu Hsien, et al., comps., *Chia-ting Chen-chiang chih*, 10.7a.
34. Tai Piao-yuan, *Yen-yuan Tai hsien-sheng wen-chi*, 10.3b.
35. Ibid., 10.4a.
36. In his political career, Hsin Ch'i-chi suffered several demotions and two major censures, and after 1182 he withdrew to spend the remaining twenty years of his

life as a recluse. He composed the vast majority of his poems during this period of retirement. See Lo, *Hsin Ch'i-chi*, 30.

37. Similarly, the restoration in 1285 of West Brook Academy, dedicated to the "Three Liu" as persecuted worthies under the Sung, exemplifies the appropriation of symbols of *ju* ideals under the Yuan. See the inscription by Wang I-shan, Chia-ts'un lei-kao, 8.1a–8.4b.
38. Fang Hui, *T'ung-hsiang hsu-chi*, 5.5a.
39. SJCC V.4111.
40. For discussion of the poetic and artistic tradition surrounding Angling Terrace and Yen Kuang Academies, including this reference to Hsieh Ao, see Hay, "Huang Kung-wang's Dwelling in the Fu-ch'un Mountains," 311 ff.
41. Ho Meng-kuei, *Ch'ien-chai wen-chi*, 8.9b.
42. Huang Chin, *Chin-hua Huang hsien-sheng wen-chi, 7 shang*, 266.
43. Fang Hui, *T'ung-hsiang hsu-chi*, 1.15–1.16.
44. Ibid., 1.16–1.17.
45. SJCC I.323.
46. Fang Feng-ch'en's three sons, for example, and one son of his brother, Fang Feng-chen, became education officials under the Yuan, as did the two sons of Ho Meng-kuei, a colleague of the Fang brothers who also wrote on Angling Terrace Academy. See Jay, *A Change in Dynasties*, 167.

Glossary

Characters for academies, terms, phrases, and people cited in the text are provided below; those mentioned only in the notes are not included. Characters for authors and works cited are given in the bibliography. Geographical names, era names, rulers, and official titles easily found in standard reference sources are not glossed here.

An-hu (Peace Lake) 安湖
An-t'ien (Peaceful Fields) 安田
Cha-hsi (Wooden Slip Creek) 札溪
chai-chang 齋長
Ch'an 禪
Ch'an-yuan ch'ing-kuei 禪苑清規
Chang Chiu-ch'eng 張九成
Chang Chiu-ling 張九齡
Chang Hsia 張洽
Chang Hsien 張顯
Chang Hsu 張盨
Chang Kang 張綱
Chang Kao 張鎬
Chang Shang-ying 張商英
Chang Shih 張式
chang-shu 掌書
chang-ssu 掌司
Chang Tsai 張載
Chang Tsung-shih 張宗湜
Chang Yen 章琰
Ch'ang-tsung Chao-chueh 常總照覺
Chao Fu 趙阜
Chao Hsi-ch'a 趙希忭
Chao Ju-ching 趙汝靚
Chao Ju-ch'ou 趙汝詶
Chao Ju-yü 趙汝愚
Chao Pi-yuan 趙珌愿
Chao Shih-hsia 趙師夏
Chao Yü-ho 趙與沶
Ch'en Ch'un 陳淳
Ch'en I-chung 陳宜中
Ch'en K'ai 陳塏
Ch'en Kuan 陳瓘
Ch'en Kuei 陳圭
Ch'en Mi 陳宓
Ch'en-shih 陳氏

Ch'en T'ien-tse 陳天澤
Ch'en Tou-lung 陳斗龍
Ch'en Ts'un 陳存
Ch'en Wei 陳韡
Ch'en Yao-tso 陳堯佐
Ch'en Yung-pin 陳用賓
Cheng Ch'ing-chih 鄭清之
cheng-hsin 正心
cheng-kung sheng-yuan 正供生員
Cheng Liang-ch'en 鄭良臣
ch'eng 誠
Ch'eng Chang-i 程掌義
Ch'eng-Chu 程朱
Ch'eng Hao 程顥
Ch'eng I 程頤
ch'eng-i 誠義
Ch'eng Jo-yung 程若庸
Ch'eng-nan shu-chuang 城南書莊
Ch'eng Tzu-ts'ai 程子材
Ch'eng Yu-hsueh 程幼學
Ch'eng Yen-sun 程偃孫
Chi chieh hsin 輯解尋
chi-chü 寄居
ch'i 氣
ch'i-chih 氣質
Ch'i T'ung-wen 戚同文
chia 家
chia-chuan 家傳
chia-chuang 家狀
chia-fa 家法
chia-shu 家塾
Chia Ssu-tao 賈似道
chiang-pin 講賓
chiang-she 講舍
chiang-shu 講書
Chiang Wan-li 江萬里
chiao 教
chiao-hua 教化
chiao-shou 教授
ch'iao-chü 僑居
ch'iao-yü 僑寓
chieh 界
chieh-she 結社
chien 間
Chien-an (academy) 建安
ch'ien 乾
Ch'ien-kang (Seal Ridge) 鈐岡
ch'ien-liang kuan 錢糧官
Ch'ien Shih 錢時
Ch'ien-yang (Seal Light) 鈐陽
chih (know) 知
chih (moral substance) 質
chih (wisdom) 智
chih-hsueh 直學
chih-shih sheng-yuan 職事生員
chin 斤

chin-shih 進士
Ch'in Kuei 秦檜
ching-hsueh 經學
ching-she 精舍
ching-shen 精神
ch'ing (circumstances) 情
ch'ing (land measure) 頃
Ch'ing-hsiang (Clear Hsiang) 清湘
ch'iung-li 窮理
Chou Mi 周密
Chou Tun-i 周敦頤
Chu Chien 朱鑑
Chu-i (academy) 主一
Chu-ko Liang 諸葛亮
Chu-lin (Bamboo Grove) 竹林
Chu P'i-sun 朱貔孫
Chu Sung (Wei-chai) 朱松 (畏齋)
Chu Tsai 朱在
chü-ching 居敬
Ch'ü Yuan 屈源
Ch'üan-shan (Spring Mountain) 泉山
chueh 角
chün-tzu 君子
chung (centrality) 中
chung (loyalty) 忠
Chung Chen 鍾震
chung-ho 衆合
Chung Ju-yü 鍾如惠
fa-t'ang 法堂
Fan Chung-yen 范仲淹
Fang Feng-chen 方逢振
Fang Feng-chia 方逢嘉
Fang I-k'uei 方一夔
Fang Lai 方來
Fang-yü sheng-lan 方輿勝覽
feng 風
feng-ch'i 風氣
Feng Ch'ü-chi 馮去疾
Feng Hsing-tsung 馮興宗
feng-shan 封禪
feng-shui 風水
fu (hexagram 24) 復
fu (prose poem) 賦
Fu Kuang 輔廣
fu-ti 福地
Fu Yin 傅寅
Han-ch'üan (Cold Spring) 寒泉
Han-shan 韓山
Han T'o-chou 韓侂冑
Han Yuan-chi 韓元吉
Han Yü 韓愈
ho 合
Ho Chi 何基
Ho-ching 和靖
Ho-shan (Crane Mountain) 鶴山

Hou Chung-liang 侯仲良

Hsi-chien (West Brook) 西澗

Hsi-yuan (West Garden) 西園

hsiang (form) 象

hsiang (school) 庠

Hsiang-chiang (Hsiang River) 湘江

hsiang-chü 鄉舉

Hsiang-hsi (Fragrant Creek) 香溪

Hsiang-shan (Elephant Mountain) 象山

hsiang-shih 鄉士

hsiang-tang 鄉黨

hsiang yin-chiu li 鄉飲酒禮

hsiao (imitate) 效

hsiao (school) 校

Hsieh Ch'ang-yuan 謝昌元

Hsieh Chieh 謝傑

Hsieh K'o-chia 謝克家

Hsieh K'o-nien 謝克念

Hsieh Liang-tso 謝良佐

Hsien-ch'eng 軒成

hsin 信

Hsin Ch'i-chi (Yu-an, Chia-hsuan) 辛棄疾 (幼安，稼軒)

hsin-hsueh 心學

Hsin Nan-jung 辛南容

Hsin-t'ien (New Field) 新田

Hsin Yuan-lung 辛元龍

hsing (actions) 行

hsing (essence, nature) 性

Hsing-wu (Apricot Embankment) 杏塢

Hsiu-hsi (Luxuriant Creek) 秀溪

hsiu-shen 修身

Hsu Chi 徐幾

Hsu Chi 徐畸

Hsu Ch'iao 徐僑

Hsu K'ai 徐鍇

Hsu Li 徐桌

hsu-ling 虛靈

hsu-ling pu-mei 虛靈不昧

Hsu Yuan-chieh 徐元杰

Hsua-hsien (Former Worthies) 先賢

hsueh erh shih hsi 學而時習

hsueh 學

hsueh-lu 學錄

Hsueh Shu-ssu 薛叔似

Hu An-kuo 胡安國

Hu-ch'iu (Tiger Hill) 虎丘

Hu Chung-yao 胡仲堯

Hu Ch'ung 胡崇

Hu-feng (Peck Peak) 斛峰

Hu-hsi (Tiger Creek) 虎溪

Hu Hsien 胡憲

Hu Hung 胡宏

Hu Li-pen 胡立本

Hu Yin 胡寅

Hu Yuan 胡瑗
Hua-lin (Floriate Forest) 華林
Huai-hai 淮海
Huai-t'ang (Locust Tree Hall) 槐堂
Huai-yü (Embracing Jade) 懷玉
Huan-feng (Surrounding Peak) 環峰
Huang Chen 黃震
Huang Chia 黃嘉
Huang Hsing-chih 黃性直
Huang Ts'ung-lung 黃從龍
Hui-yuan 慧遠
hun-p'o 魂魄
Hung Wen-fu 洪文撫
Hung-yuan (Vast Spring) 洪源
i (propriety) 義
i-chuang 義莊
i-chü ssu-fang-chih shih 以居四方之士
i kuan yu-hsueh-chih shih 以館遊學之士
i-shu 義塾
i-yü 醫諭
Jao Lu 饒魯
jen 仁
ju 儒
ju-hsueh 儒學
ju-shu 儒術
Ju Shu chi 入蜀記
k'ai-shan 開山
k'ai-t'ang 開堂
Kao K'o-yang 高可仰
Kao K'uan-jen 高寬仁
K'ao-t'ing 考亭
ko-wu chih-chih 格物致知
K'ou Chun 寇準
kuan (official) 官
kuan (string of cash) 貫
kuan-hui 官會
Kuang-hsin 廣信
Kuang-p'ing 廣平
Kuei-feng (Turtle Peak) 龜峰
Kuei-shan (Turtle Mountain) 龜山
Kuei-yen (Cassia Cliff) 桂巖
k'un 坤
Kung-an chu-lin (Kung-an Bamboo Grove) 公安竹林
Kung Chi-hsien 龔基先
kung-shih 貢士
K'ung Wu-chung 孔武仲
Kuo Ch'eng 郭澄
Kuo Chiang 郭江
Kuo Chin 郭津
Kuo Ch'in-chih 郭欽止
Kuo Hao 郭浩
kuo-hsueh 國學
Kuo Liang-ch'en 郭良臣

Kuo Liang-hsien 郭良顯
Kuo P'u 郭溥
Lan-t'ien (Indigo Field) 藍田
Lan-yü (Orchid Jade) 蘭玉
Le-shan 樂善
Lei-hu (Thunder Lake) 雷湖
Lei-t'ang (Thunder Dike) 雷塘
li (principle) 理
li (ritual) 禮
Li Ch'un-nien 李椿年
Li Hsiao 李瀟
Li Hsiu 李脩
li-hsueh 理學
Li K'an 李侃
Li Kung-lin 李公麟
Li Po 李渤
Li Ta-t'ung 李大同
Li Ta-yu 李大有
Li Te-chün 李德俊
Li-tse (Beautiful Pools) 麗澤
Li T'ung 李侗
Li-yang 澧陽
Li Yang-lei 李陽雷
liang 兩
liang-hsin 良心
Liao Ch'ih 廖遲
Liao Jung 廖融
Liao Pang-chieh 廖邦傑
Liao Te-ming 廖德明
Liao T'ien-ching (Wen-po) 廖天經 (文伯)
Liao Yang-chih (Chung-kao) 廖仰之 (仲高)
Liao Yen-hsiu 廖彥脩
Lien-hsi 濂溪
Lin Cheng-chung 林正仲
Lin-ch'i 臨濟
Lin Chieh 林岊
Lin Hsueh-meng 林學蒙
Lin-ju 臨汝
Lin Shih-chih 林式之
ling (order) 令
ling (spirit) 靈
Liu Chi-chang 劉季章
Liu Ch'ing-chih 劉清之
Liu Fu 劉黻
Liu Hsi-chung 劉羲仲
Liu Huan 劉渙
Liu Mien-chih 劉勉之
liu-shih 流士
Liu Shu 劉恕
liu-su 流俗
Liu Tzu-hui 劉子翬
Liu Tzu-i 劉子怡
Liu Tzu-yü 劉子羽
Liu Yen 劉弇

Liu Yueh 劉鑰
Lo-feng (Conch Peak) 螺峰
Lo Ts'ung-yen 羅從彥
Lou Fang 樓昉
Lu (mountain) 盧
Lu-chou (Egret Islet) 鷺洲
Lu-feng (Hut Peak) 盧峰
Lu Tien 陸佃
Lu Tzu-yü 陸子遹
Lü I-hao 呂頤浩
Lü Ta-chün 呂大鈞
Lü Ta-lin 呂大臨
Lü-shih hsiang-yueh 呂氏鄉約
lü-shu 閭塾
Lung-chiang (Dragon River) 龍江
Lung-chin (Dragon Ford) 龍津
Lung-chou (Dragon Islet) 龍州
Lung-shan (Dragon Mountain) 龍山
Lung-t'an (Dragon Pool) 龍潭
Ma Kuang-tsu 馬光祖
Mao (mountain and academy) 茅
Meng Kung 孟珙
mi 米
miao-hsueh 廟學
ming (fate, decree) 命
Ming-cheng (Clear Orthodoxy) 明正
Ming-ching (Clarified Classics) 明經
ming-lun t'ang 明論堂
ming ming-te 明明德
Ming-shan (Illumined Good) 明善
Ming-tao (Illumined Way) 明道
mo-kuan-chih t'ien 沒官之田
Nan-hsi (Southern Stream) 南溪
Nan-hsua 南軒
Nan-hu (South Lake) 南湖
Nan-k'ang 南康
Nan-shan (South Mountain) 南山
Nan-tao (Southern Way) 南道
Nan-yang 南陽
Nan-yueh (South Marchmount) 南嶽
nien-fo 念佛
Ou-yang Hsin (Chung-ch'i) 歐陽新(仲齊)
Ou-yang Hsiu 歐陽秀
Pai-chang hsi (Hundred *Chang* Creek) 百丈溪
Pai-lu chou (White Egret Islet) 白鷺洲
Pai-lu tung (White Deer Grotto) 白鹿洞
P'an Chi 潘驥
pao-chia 保甲
Pao-feng chieh-mao 寶峰結茅
Pao-feng k'o-wen 寶峰克文
pen-hsin 本心
pin-hsing 賓興
pin-hsing shih-shuai 賓興師帥

P'ing-shan (Level Mountain) 平山
Po I 伯夷
p'o 魄
pu (divine) 卜
pu (land measure) 步
P'u-chi 菩濟
san-she fa 三舍法
shan 善
shan-chang 山長
Shan-hai ching 山海經
shan-lin 山林
shan-men 山門
Shang-ch'ing 上清
shang-t'ang 上堂
Shang-ts'ai 上蔡
Shao Yung 邵雍
she-ts'ai 舍菜
Shen-i (Inculcating Duty) 申義
sheng 升
Sheng-chu (Bamboo Flute) 笙竹
sheng-fu 生父
sheng-ling 生靈
sheng-tz'u 生祠
shih (events) 事
shih (scholar) 士
Shih 施
Shih chi 史記
Shih Chieh 石介
Shih-ching (Stone Well) 石井
shih chün-tzu 士君子
shih-fang 十方
Shih-hsia (Stone Gorge) 石峽
shih-jen 士人
Shih-ku (Stone Drum) 石鼓
Shih Mi-chung 史彌忠
Shih Mi-yuan 史彌遠
shih ta-fu 士大夫
shih-ts'ai 釋菜
Shih Tun 石塾
Shih-tung (Stone Cavern) 石洞
shih-tzu 士子
Shih Ya-chih 石亞之
shu 術
Shu Ch'i 叔齊
shu-fang 書房
Shu Lin 舒霖
Shu Mi 舒泌
shu-she 書舍
shu-t'ang 書堂
shu-yuan 書院
Shuang-feng (Double Peak) 雙峰
shui-hsien t'ai-pao 水仙太保
Shun 舜
ssu (private, selfish) 私
ssu-chi 司計
Ssu-ma Ch'ien 司馬遷

Ssu-ma Kuang 司馬光

ssu-ta ming-shan 四大名山

Su Shih 蘇軾

Sui-yang 睢陽

Sun Fu 孫復

Sun Tzu-hsiu 孫子秀

Sung-yang 嵩陽

ta-ch'eng tien 大成殿

Tai (mountain and academy) 岱

T'ai (mountain and academy) 泰

T'ai (mountain and academy) 臺

t'ai-chi 太極

T'ai-fu 太傅

T'ai-shih (mountain and academy) 太室

tan 石

Tan-yang (Cinnabar Sun) 丹陽

tang 黨

t'ang-chang 堂長

T'ang Chen 唐震

T'ang Chin 湯巾

T'ang Chung-yu 唐仲友

t'ang-lu 堂錄

t'ang-pin 堂賓

tao (unhulled rice) 稻

tao-hsin 道心

tao-hsueh 道學

T'ao Hung-ching 陶弘景

T'ao-shan hsiu-chu (Mount T'ao Tall Bamboo) 陶山脩竹

te 德

teng-t'ang 登堂

Teng Wu 鄧武

Teng Yen 鄧晏

Ti Liang-kung (Jen-chieh) 狄梁公 (仁傑)

Tiao-t'ai (Angling Terrace) 釣台

tien-chiao 典教

tien-t'ien 佃田

t'ien-li 天理

T'ien-men (Heaven Gate) 天門

t'ien-ming 天命

T'ien-t'ai 天台

tou 斗

Ts'ai Ching 蔡京

Ts'ai Shen 蔡沈

Ts'ai Yuan 蔡淵

Ts'ai Yuan-ting 蔡元定

Ts'ang-chou 滄州

Ts'ao Pin 曹豳

Tseng Kung 曾鞏

Tsou Ying-lung 鄒應龍

tsu 祖

tsu tzu-ti 祖子弟

tsung-hsueh 宗學

Tsung-hui (Honoring Chu Hsi) 宗晦

tsung-p'u 宗譜

tsung-tsu 宗祖

tsung-yin tzu-ti 宗姻子弟

Tu Yü 杜旗

t'u-chu pu-chi yu-hsueh-chih jen 土著不及遊學之人

tuan 端

tui 兑

Tung-hu (East Lake) 東湖

Tung-shan (East Mountain) 東山

tung-t'ien 洞天

T'ung-wen (Harmony Culture) 同文

T'ung Yao 童幼

T'ung-yuan (Teak Spring) 桐源

Tzu-chih (Purple Iris) 紫芝

Tzu-chih t'ung-chien kang-mu 資治通鑑綱目

tzu-jan er jan 自然而然

Tzu-yang (Purple Light) 紫陽

Tz'u-hu (Compassion Lake) 慈湖

Wang An-shih 王安石

Wang Pi 王賁

Wang Pi 王佖

Wang Po 王柏

Wang Shao 王韶

Wang Sui 王遂

Wang Ta-fa 王大發

Wang Tan 王旦

Wang T'ung 王通

Wang Yeh 王埜

Wang Yen 王淹

Wang Ying-ch'en 汪應辰

Wang Ying-sun 王英孫

Wang Yueh 王鑰

Wei Chi 危積

wei-chi 為己

Wei Chü 魏榘

wei-hsueh 偽學

wei Huai-shih liu-yü-che i-ye-chih suo 為淮士流寓者肄業之所

Wei Sa 衛颯

wei-wo 為我

wen (culture, cash) 文

Wen Chi-weng 文及翁

Wen-ching 文敬

Wen-kung 文公

Wen Weng 文翁

Weng-chou (Weng Islet) 翁洲

Weng Yung 翁泳

Wo-lung (Sleeping Dragon) 臥龍

wu 物

Wu Chien 吳堅

Wu-i (mountain range and academy) 武夷

Wu K'uei 吳葵

Wu Shun-shen 吳舜申

Wu Sui 吳燧

Wu Tzu-liang 吳子良

Wu Wen-ping 吳文炳

Wu Ying-yu 吳應酉
Wu Yuan 吳淵
wu-yü 物欲
Yang Chien 楊簡
Yang Hsiung 楊雄
Yang Shih 楊時
Yang Ta-i 楊大異
Yang Tung 楊楝
Yang Ying-kuei 楊應桂
Yang Yun-kung 楊允恭
yao 妖
Yao 堯
Yao Hsi-te 姚希得
yeh 業
Yeh Chen 葉震
yen-chü t'ang 燕居堂
Yen Kuang (Tzu-ling) 嚴光 (子陵)
Yen-p'ing (academy) 延平
Yin Ch'un (Su-kung) 尹淳 (肅公)
Yin I 尹沂
yin-yang 陰陽
Yin Yen-te 尹彥德
Ying Su 應傃
ying-t'ang 影堂
Ying-t'ien 應天
Ying Yu 應繇
yu-chi 遊記
Yu Chiu-yen 游九言
Yu Tso 游酢
yü 寓
Yü Ch'ou 虞儔
yü-chü 寓居
yü-lu 語錄
Yü Ou 余偶
Yü-ti chi-sheng 輿地紀勝
Yuan Ts'ai 袁采
Yueh Fei 岳飛
Yueh-lu (Marchmount Hill) 嶽麓
yun 慍
Yun-chuang (Cloud Manor) 雲莊
Yung-chia 永嘉
Yung-tung (East Yung) 甬東

BIBLIOGRAPHY

PRE-1900 CHINESE SOURCES

The following abbreviations are used for standard editions:

SKCS	Ssu-k'u ch'üan-shu 四庫全書
SMTS	Ssu-ming ts'ung-shu 四明叢書
SPPY	Ssu-pu pei-yao 四部備要
SPTK	Ssu-pu ts'ung-k'an 四部備刊
SYTFTS	Sung-Yuan ti-fang chih ts'ung-shu 宋元地方之叢書
TSCC	Ts'ung-shu chi-ch'eng 叢書集成

Chang Chung-hsin 張仲炘, eds. and comps. *Hu-pei t'ung-chih* 湖北通志 (Hu-pei gazetteer). 1921 ed.

Chang Hsuan 張鉉, comp. *Chih-cheng Chin-ling hsin-chih* 至正金陵新志 (Chin-ling new gazetteer for the 1341–1368 era). 1344. SYTFTS ed.

Chang Hsueh-ch'eng 章學誠 (1738–1801). *Wen-shih t'ung-i* 文史通義 (Comprehensive meaning of literature and history). Hong Kong: T'ai-p'ing ed.

Chang Shih 張栻 (1133–1180). *Nan-hsua wen-chi* 南軒文集 (Collected works of Chang Shih). SPTK ed.

Ch'ang Ming 常明 ed. *Ssu-ch'uan t'ung-chih* 四川通志 (Ssu-ch'uan gazetteer). 1816 ed.

Chen Te-hsiu 真德秀 (1178–1235). *Chen Hsi-shan wen-chi* 真西山西文集 (Collected works of Chen Te-hsiu). TSCC ed.

———. *Hsi-shan hsien-sheng Chen Wen-chung kung wen-chi* 西山先生真文忠公文集 (Collected works of Chen Te-hsiu). SPTK ed.

Ch'en Ch'i-ch'ing 陳耆卿, comp. *Chia-ting Ch'ih-ch'eng chih* 嘉定赤城志 (T'ai-chou gazetteer for the 1208–1224 era). 1223. SYTFTS ed.

Ch'en Fu-liang 陳傅良 (1137–1203). *Chih-chai wen-chi* 止齋文集 (Collected works of Ch'en Fu-liang). SPTK ed.

Ch'en Liang 陳亮 (1143–1194). *Ch'en Liang chi* 陳亮集 (Collected works of Ch'en Liang). Peking: Chung-hua ed.

Ch'en Shun-yü 陳舜俞 (d. 1074). *Lu-shan chi* 廬山記 (Record of Mount Lu). TSCC ed.

Ch'en Wen-wei 陳文蔚 (1235 *chin-shih*). *K'o-chai chi* 克齋集 (Collected works of Ch'en Wen-wei). SKCS ed.

Ch'en Yuan-chin 陳元晉 (1211 *chin-shih*). *Yü-shu lei-kao* 魚墅類稿 (Collected works of Ch'en Yuan-chin). SKCS ed.

Cheng Ch'iao 鄭樵 (1104–1162). *T'ung chih lueh* 通治略 (Digest of government institutions). SPPY ed.

Cheng Yao 鄭瑤 and Fang Jen-jung 方仁榮, comps. *Ching-ting Yen-chou hsu-chih* 景定嚴州續志 (Yen-chou continued gazetteer for the 1260–1264 era). 1262. SYTFTS ed.

Cheng Yuan-yu 鄭元祐 (1292–1364). *Ch'iao-wu chi* 僑吳集 (Collected works of Cheng Yuan-yu). Yuan-tai chen-pen wen-chi ed.

Ch'eng Chu-fu 程鉅夫 (1249–1318). *Hsueh-lou chi* 雪樓集 (Collected works of Ch'eng Chu-fu). Yuan-tai chen-pen wen-chi ed.

Ch'eng Pi 程珌 (1164–1242). *Ming-shui chi* 洺水集 (Collected works of Ch'eng Pi). SKCS ed.

Ch'eng Tsu-lo 程祖洛, et al., eds. *Fu-chien t'ung-chih* 福建通志 (Fu-chien gazetteer). 1835 ed.

Ch'eng Tuan-hsueh 程端學 (1278–1334). *Chi-chai chi* 積齋集 (Collected works of Ch'eng Tuan-hsueh). SMTS ed.

Ch'eng Tuan-li 程端禮 (1271–1345). *Wei-chai chi* 畏齋集 (Collected works of Ch'eng Tuan-li). SMTS ed.

Chi Ch'ing 吉慶, et al., eds. *Kuang-hsi t'ung-chih* 廣西通志 (Kuang-hsi gazetteer). 1801 ed.

Chi Hui-yun 稽會筠, et al., eds. *Che-chiang t'ung-chih* 浙江通志 (Che-chiang gazetteer). 1736 ed.

Ch'ien Ku 錢穀 (1508–ca. 1578), comp. *Wu-tu wen-ts'ui hsu-chi* 吳都文粹續集 (Literary gems of the Wu capital, continued collection). SKCS ed.

Ch'in Hui-t'ien 秦蕙田 (1702–1764), comp. *Wu-li t'ung k'ao* 五禮通考 (Comprehensive investigation of the five rites). Taipei: Kuang-wen ed.

Ch'in-ting hsu wen-hsien t'ung-k'ao (Imperially ordered continued comprehensive investigation of literary materials). Compiled beginning in 1747. Taipei: Hsin-hsing ed.

Chou Pi-ta 周必大 (1126–1204) *P'ing-yuan hsu-kao* 平園續稿 (Continued draft from Level Garden). In *Chou I-kuo wen-chung kung chi* 周益國文忠公集 (Collected works of Chou Pi-ta). 1851 ed.

Chou Ying–ho 周應合, comp. *Ching-ting Chien-k'ang chih* 景定建康志 (Chien-k'ang gazetteer for the 1260–1264 era). 1261. SYTFTS ed.

Chu Hsi 朱熹 (1130-1200). *Chu-tzu ta-ch'üan* 朱子大全 (Great collection of Master Chu). SPPY ed.

———. *Chu-tzu wen-chi* 朱子文集 (Collected works of Master Chu). TSCC ed.

———. *Chu-tzu yü-lei* 朱子語類 (Sayings of Master Chu). Peking: Chung-hua ed.

———. *Hui-an hsien-sheng Chu Wen-kung wen-chi* 晦庵先生朱文公集 (Collected works of Chu Hsi). SPTK ed.

———. *Pai-lu-tung shu-yuan chiao-kuei* 白鹿洞書院教規 (Rules for White Deer Grotto Academy). TSCC ed.

Chu I 朱翌 (1097–1167). *I-chueh liao tsa-chi* 猗覺寮雜記 (Miscellany of Chu I). Pi-chi hsiao-shuo ta-kuan ed.

Chu Pien 朱弁 (d. 1144). *Ch'ü-wei chiu-wen* 曲洧舊聞 (Miscellany of Chu Pien). TSCC ed.

Chuang Chung-fang 莊仲方 (1780–1857), comp. *Nan-Sung wen-fan* 南宋文範 (Literary documents of the Southern Sung). 1888 ed.

Ch'üan Tsu-wang 全祖望 (1705–1755). *Chieh-ch'i t'ing chi* 鮚埼亭集 (Collected works of Ch'üan Tsu-wang). SPTK ed.

Fan Chung-yen 范仲淹 (989–1052). *Fan Wen-cheng kung wen-chi* 范文正公文集 (Collected works of Fan Chung-yen). SPTK ed.

Fan Yeh 范曄 (398–446), comp. *Hou Han shu* 後漢書 (History of the Latter Han). Taipei: Ting-wen ed.

Fang Feng-ch'en 方逢辰 (1221–1291). *Chiao-feng wai-chi* 蛟峰外集 (Collected works of Fang Feng-ch'en). SKCS ed.

Fang Hui. 方回 (1227–1306). *T'ung-chiang hsu-chi* 桐江續集 (Collected works of Fang Hui). SKCS ed.

Feng Fu-ching 馮福京, comp. *Ta-te Ch'ang-kuo chou t'u-chih* 大德昌國州圖志 (Ch'ang-kuo gazetteer for the 1297–1307 era). 1298. SYTFTS ed.

Fu-chien t'ung-chi 福建通紀 (Complete records of Fu-chien). Taipei: Ta-t'ung, 1968 reprint of 1922 ed.

Ho Ch'iao-yuan 何喬遠 (1558–1632), comp. *Min shu* 閩書 (Treatise on Fu-chien). 1630 ed.

Ho Meng-kuei 何夢桂 (1265 *chin-shih*). *Ch'ien-chai wen-chi* 潛齋文集 (Collected works of Ho Meng-kuei). SKCS ed.

Hsieh Fang-te 謝枋德 (1226–1289). *Tieh-shan chi* 疊山集 (Collected works of Hsieh Fang-te). SPTK ed.

Hsiung Ho 熊禾 (1253–1312). *Hsiung Wu-hsua chi* 熊勿軒集 (Collected works of Hsiung Ho). Cheng-i t'ang ch'üan-shu ed.

Hsu Hsuan 徐鉉 (916–991). *Ch'i-sheng chi* 騎省集 (Collected works of Hsu Hsuan). SKCS ed.

Hsu Shih 徐碩, comp. *Chih-yuan Chia-ho chih* 至元嘉禾志 (Chia-ho gazetteer for the 1271–1294 era). 1288. SYTFTS ed.

Hu Hung 胡宏 (1105–1155). *Hu Hung chi* 胡宏集 (Collected works of Hu Hung). Peking: Chung-hua ed.

Huai Yin-pu 懷陰布, et al., comps. *Ch'üan-chou fu-chih* 泉州府志 (Ch'üan-chou gazetteer). 1763 ed.

Huang Chin 黃溍 (1277–1357). *Chin-hua Huang hsien-sheng wen-chi* 金華黃先生文集 (Collected works of Huang Chin). SPTK ed.

———. *Huang Wen-hsien kung chi* 黃文獻公集 (Collected works of Huang Chin). SKCS ed.

Huang Jun-yü 黃潤玉 (1389–1477). *Ning-po fu chien-yao chih* 寧波府簡要志 (Essential records of Ning-po prefecture). SMTS ed.

Huang Kan 黃幹 (1152–1221). *Mien-chai chi* 勉齋集 (Collected Works of Huang Kan). SKCS ed.

———. *Mien-chai hsien-sheng Huang Wen-su kung wen-chi* 勉齋先生黃文肅公文集. Pei-ching t'u-shu-kuan chen-pen ts'ung-k'an ed.

Huang Tsung-hsi 黃宗羲 (1610–1695), Ch'üan Tsu-wang 全祖望, et al., eds. *Sung-Yuan hsueh-an* 宋元學案 (Records of Sung-Yuan Confucian scholars). SPPY ed.

Hung Mai 洪邁 (1123–1202). *Jung-chai sui-pi wu-chi* 容齋隨筆五集 (Five collections of notes from my studio). Taipei: Taiwan Commercial Press ed.

Hung Tzu-k'uei 洪咨夔 (1179–after 1239). *P'ing-chai wen-chi* 平齋文集 (Collected works of Hung Tzu-k'uei). SPTK ed.

Jen Shih-lin 任士林 (1253–1309). *Sung-hsiang chi* 松鄉集 (Collected works of Jen Shih-lin). SKCS ed.

Juan Yuan 阮元, ed. *Kuang-tung t'ung-chih* 廣東通志 (Kuang-tung gazetteer). 1822 ed.

Kao Ssu-te 高斯得 (1229 *chin-shih*). *Ch'ih-t'ang ts'un-kao* 恥堂存稿 (Collected works of Kao Ssu-te). Wu-ying tien palace ed.

Kung Ming-chih 龔明之 (1091–1182). *Chung-wu chi-wen* 中吳紀聞 (Miscellany of Kung Ming-chih). Pi-chi hsiao-shuo ta-kuan ed.

Li Han-chang 李瀚章 et al., eds. *Hu-nan t'ung-chih* 湖南通志 (Hu-nan gazetteer). 1885 ed.

Li T'ao 李燾 (1115–1184). *Hsu tzu-chih t'ung-chien ch'ang-pien* 續資治通鑑長編 (*Continued comprehensive mirror for aid in government, long draft*). Taipei: Shih-chieh ed.

Li Tseng-po 李曾伯 (?–after 1265). *K'o-chai hsu kao ch'ien* 可齋續稿前 (Continued draft of Li Tseng-po's writings, first part). SKCS ed.

Liang K'o-chia 梁克家 (1128–1187), comp. *Ch'un-hsi San-shan chih* 淳熙三山志 (Fu-chou gazetteer for the 1174–1189 era). SYTFTS ed.

Liao Hsing-chih 廖行之 (1137–1189). *Sheng-chai chi* 省齋集 (Collected works of Liao Hsing-chih). SKCS ed.

Liao Kang 廖剛 (1070–1143). *Kao-feng wen-chi* 高峰文集 (Collected works of Liao Kang). SKCS ed.

Lin Ching-hsi 林景熙 (fl. ca. 1275). *Chi-shan hsien-sheng chi* 霽山先生集 (Collected works of Lin Ching-hsi). Chih pu-tsu chai ts'ung-shu ed.

Lin Hsi-i 林希逸 (ca. 1210–ca. 1273). *Chu-ch'i chuan-chai shih-i k'ao hsu-chi* 竹溪鬳齋十一槀續集 (Collected works of Lin Hsi-i). SKCS ed.

Lin Shu-hsun 林述訓, et al., eds. *Shao-chou fu-chih* 韶州府志 (Shao-chou gazetteer). 1874 ed.

Liu Ch'en-weng 劉辰翁 (1231–1294). *Hsu-ch'i chi* 須溪集 (Collected works of Liu Ch'en-weng). SKCS ed.

Liu Chiang-sun 劉將孫 (1257–?) *Yang-wu chai chi* 養吾齋集 (Collected works of Liu Chiang-sun). SKCS ed.

Liu Hsu 劉昫 (fl. ca. 940). *Chiu T'ang shu* 舊唐書 (Old history of the T'ang dynasty). Peking: Chung-hua ed.

Liu I-ch'ing 劉義慶 (403–444). *Shih-shuo hsin-yü* 世記新語 (New account of tales of the world). Taipei: Hua-lien, 1973.

Liu K'o-chuang 劉克莊 (1187–1269). *Hou-ts'un hsien-sheng ta-ch'üan chi* (Collected works of Liu K'o-chuang). SPTK ed.

Liu Tsai 劉宰 (1166–1239). *Man-t'ang wen-chi* 漫塘文集 (Collected works of Liu Tsai). SPTK ed.

Lo Chün 羅濬, et al., comps. *Pao-ch'ing Ssu-ming chih* 寶慶四明志 (Ming-chou gazetteer for the 1225–1227 era). 1227. SYTFTS ed.

Lou Yueh 樓鑰 (1137–1213). *Kung-k'uei chi* (Collected works of Lou Yueh). TSCC ed.

Lu Chiu-yuan 陸九淵 (1139–1192). *Lu Hsiang-shan ch'üan-chi* 陸象山全集 (Collected works of Lu Chiu-yuan). Taipei: Shih-chieh ed.

Lu Hsien 魯憲, et al., comps. *Chia-ting Chen-chiang chih* 嘉定鎮江志 (Chen-chiang gazetteer for the 1208–1224 era). 1213. SYTFTS ed.

Lu Tseng-yü 魯曾煜, et al., comps. *Fu-chou fu chih* 福州府志 (Fu-chou gazetteer). 1751 ed.

Lü Tsu-ch'ien 呂祖謙 (1137–1181). *Lü Tung-lai wen-chi* 呂東萊文集 (Collected Works of Lü Tsu-ch'ien). TSCC ed.

———. *Tung-lai Lü T'ai-shih wen-chi* 東萊陸太史文集 (Collected works of Grand Historian Lü Tsu-ch'ien). TSCC ed.

Lu Yu 陸游 (1125–1210). *Wei-nan wen-chi* 畏南文集 (Collected Works of Lu Yu). SPTK ed.

———. *Lu Fang-weng ch'üan-chi* (Complete Works of Lu Yu). Hong Kong: Kwong-ch'i ed.

Ma T'ing-luan 馬廷鸞 (1222–1289). *Pi-wu wan-fang chi* 碧梧玩芳集 (Collected works of Ma T'ing-luan). Yü-chang ts'ung-shu ed.

Ma Tuan-lin 馬端臨 (1254–1325). *Wen-hsien t'ung-k'ao* 文獻通考 (Collected literary documents). Taipei: Hsin-hsing ed.

Ou-yang Shou-tao 歐陽守道 (1209–after 1267). *Hsuan-chai wen-chi* 選齋文集. (Collected works of Ou-yang Shou-tao). SKCS ed.

Pai-lu shu-yuan chih 白鹿書院志 (Record of White Deer Academy). First preface dated 1687. 1883 ed.

Pan Ku 班固 (32–92). *Han shu* 漢書 (Han history). Peking: Chung-hua ed.

Shen Ting-yun 沈定均 et al., comps. *Chang-chou fu-chih* 章州府志 (Chang-chou gazetteer). 1878 ed.

Shih Chieh 石介 (1005–1045). *Shih Tsu-lai wen-chi* 石徂徠文集 (Collected works of Shih Chieh). SKCS ed

Shih-ku shu-yuan chih 石鼓書院志 (Record of Stone Drum Academy). First preface dated 1533. Ming Wan-li woodblock ed., Peking University Library.

Sun Ying-shih 孫應時 (1154–1202). *Chu-hu chi* 燭湖集 (Collected works of Sung Ying-shih). SKCS ed.

Sung-chi san-ch'ao cheng-yao 宋季三朝政要 (Important government events of the last three reigns of the Sung). After 1280. TSCC ed.

Ta Ming i-t'ung-chih 大明一通志 (Gazetteer of the Ming empire). 1461. Photographic reprint of manuscript in National Central Library, Taipei.

Tai Hsien 戴銑 (1496 *chin-shih*). *Chu-tzu shih-chi* 朱子實紀 (True records of Master Chu). Taipei: Kuang-wen ed.

Tai Piao-yuan 戴表元 (1244–1310). *Yen-yuan Tai hsien-sheng wen-chi* 剡源戴先生文集 (Collected works of Tai Piao-yuan). SPTK ed.

T'ien-hsia shu-yuan tsung-chih 天下書院總志 (Complete gazetteer of academies in the empire). First preface dated 1702. Taipei: Kuang-wen ed.

T'o T'o 脱脱, et al., comps. *Sung shih* 宋史 (Sung history). Peking: Chung-hua ed.

Tseng Feng 曾丰 (1142–?). *Yuan-tu chi* 緣督集 (Collected works of Tseng Feng). 1851 ed.

Tseng Kuo-fan 曾國藩, et al., eds. *Chiang-hsi t'ung-chih* 江西通志 (Chiang-hsi gazetteer). 1881 ed.

Tung Kao 董誥 (1740–1818), comp. *Ch'üan T'ang wen* 全唐文 (Complete T'ang prose). Peking: Chung-hua ed.

Tung Ssu-kuo 董嗣果 (fl. ca. 1280). *Lu-shan chi* 廬山集 (Mount Lu collection). SKCS ed.

Wang An-shih 王安石 (1021–1086). *Wang Lin-ch'uan ch'üan-chi* 王臨川全集 (Collected works of Wang An-shih). Taipei: Shih-chieh ed.

Wang I-shan 王義山 (1214–1287). *Chia-ts'un lei-kao* 稼村類稿 (Collected works of Wang I-shan). SKCS ed.

Wang Mou-hung 王懋竑 (1668–1741). *Chu-tzu nien-p'u* 朱子年譜 (Chronological biography of Chu Hsi). Taipei: Shih-chieh ed.

Wang T'ing-kuei 王庭珪 (1080–1172). *Lu-hsi wen-chi* 盧溪文集 (Collected works of Wang T'ing-kuei). SKCS ed.

Wang Tz'u-ts'ai 王梓材, Feng Yun-hao 馮雲濠, comps. *Sung-Yuan hsueh-an pu-i* 宋元學案補遺 (Supplement to the records of Sung-Yuan Confucian scholars). 1838. Taipei: Shih-chieh ed.

Wang Ying-ch'en 汪應辰 (1118–1176). *Wen-ting chi* 文定集 (Collected works of Wang Ying-ch'en). SKCS ed.

Wang Ying-lin 王應麟 (1223–1296). *Ssu-ming wen-hsien chi* 四明文獻集 (Collection of literary documents from Ming-chou). SMTS ed.

———. *Yü hai* 玉海 (Sea of jade encyclopedia). Taipei: Hua-wen ed.

Wang Yü-ch'eng 王禹偁 (954–1001). *Hsiao-ch'u chi* 小畜集 (Collected works of Wang Yü-ch'eng). Wu-ying tien palace ed.

Wang Yuan-kung 王元恭. Comp. *Chih-cheng Ssu-ming hsu-chih* 至正四明續志 (Ming-chou continued gazetteer for the 1341–1368 era). 1342. SYTFTS ed.

Wei Liao-weng 魏了翁 (1178–1237). *Ho-shan hsien-sheng ta-ch'üan wen-chi* 鶴山先生大全文集 (Collected works of Wei Liao-weng). SPTK ed.

———. *Ho-shan wen-ch'ao* 鶴山文鈔 (Literary documents of Wei Liao-weng). 1874 ed.

Wen T'ien-hsiang 文天祥 (1236–1283). *Wen Wen-shan ch'üan-chi* 文文山全集 (Complete works of Wen T'ien-hsiang). Taipei: Shih-chieh ed.

Wu Ch'eng 吳澄 (1247–1331). *Wu Wen-cheng kung wen-chi* 吳文正公集 (Collected works of Wu Ch'eng). SKCS ed.

Wu Shih-tao 吳師道 (1283–1344). *Wu li-pu wen-chi* 吳禮部文集 (Collected works of Wu Shih-tao). Hsü Chin-hua ts'ung-shu ed.

Yang I 楊億 (974–1020). *Wu-i hsin-chi* 武夷新集 (Collected works of Yang I). SKCS ed.

Yang Wan-li 楊萬里 (1127–1206). *Ch'eng-chai chi* 誠齋集 (Collected works of Yang Wan-li). SKCS ed.

Yang Yü-chien 楊毓健, et al., comps. *Chung-hsiu Nan-hsi shu-yuan chih* 重修南溪書院志 (Revised record of Southern Stream Academy). 1870 ed.

Yeh Meng-te 葉夢得 (1077–1148). *Shih-lin chü-shih Chien-k'ang chi* 石林居士建康集 (Collected works of Yeh Meng-te). SKCS ed.

Yeh Shih 葉適 (1150–1223). *Shui-hsin wen-chi* 水心文集 (Collected works of Yeh Shih). In *Yeh Shih chi* 葉適集 (Collection of Yeh Shih's writings). Taipei: Ho-lo t'u, 1974.

Yin Chi-shan 尹繼善, et al., eds. *Chiang-nan t'ung-chih* 江南通志 (Chiang-nan gazetteer). 1736 ed.

Yü Ch'ang-lin 喻長霖, et al., comps. *T'ai-chou fu chih* 台州府志 (T'ai-chou gazetteer). 1936 ed.

Yü Chi 虞集. *Tao-yuan hsueh-ku lu* 道園學古錄 (Collected works of Yü Chi). SPTK ed.

Yü Hsi-lu 俞熙魯, comp. *Chih-hsun Chen-chiang chih* 至順鎮江志 (Chen-chiang gazetteer for the 1330–1331 era). 1332. SYTFTS ed.

Yuan Chueh 袁桷 (1266–1327). *Ch'ing-jung chü-shih chi* 清容居士集 (Collected works of Yuan Chueh). SPPY ed.

———. *Yen-yu Ssu-ming chih* 延祐四明志 (Ming-chou gazetteer for the 1314–1320 era). SYTFTS ed.

Yuan Fu 袁甫 (1214 *chin-shih*). *Meng-chai chi* 蒙齋集 (Collected works of Yuan Fu). TSCC ed.

———. *Meng-chai Chung-yung chiang-i* 蒙齋中庸講義 (Lectures on the *Mean* by Yuan Fu). SMTC ed.

Yuan Hsieh 袁燮 (1144–1224). *Chieh-chai chi* 絜齋集 (Collected works of Yuan Hsieh). TSCC ed.

Modern Asian Language Sources

Abe Chōichi 阿部肇一. "Sōdai no Rozan: Zen to judō 宋代の廬山 : 禪と儒道 (Mount Lu in the Sung period: Ch'an and Confucianism)." *Shūkyōgaku ronshū* (Komazawa daigaku) 宗教學論集(駒澤大學) 13 (1987): 339–349.

Aoyama Sadao 青山定雄, et al., comps. *Sōjin denki sakuin* (Sung biographical index). Tokyo: Tōyō bunko, 1968.

Chang Cheng-fan 張正藩. *Chung-kuo shu-yuan chih-tu k'ao-lueh* 中國書院制度考略 (Investigation of the Chinese academy system). Taipei: Chung-hua shu-chu, 1982.

Chang Ch'i-yun 張其均, et al. *Chung-kuo li-shih ti-t'u* 中國歷史地圖 (Historical atlas of China). Taipei: Chung-kuo wen-hua ta-hsueh, 1980.

Ch'ang Pi-te 昌彼德, Wang Te-i 王德毅, et al. *Sung-jen chuan-chi tzu-liao so-yin* 宋人傳記資料索因 (Index to Sung biographical materials). 6 vols. Taipei: Ting-wen, 1974–1976.

Ch'en Ch'ing-chih 陳清之. *Chung-kuo chiao-yü shih* 中國教育史 (History of Chinese education). Taipei: Commercial Press, 1971.

Ch'en Ming-shih 陳名實. "T'ang-Sung shih-ch'i Fu-chien te shu-yuan" 唐宋時期福建的書院 (Fu-chien academies during the T'ang and Sung). *Wen-hsien ch'ing-pao hsueh-k'an* 文獻情報學刊 (Fu-chien sheng kao-hsiao t'u-shu ch'ing-pao wei-yuan hui) 2 (1990): 49–52.

Ch'en Shun-ying 陳舜英. "Fo-chiao tui Chung-kuo chiao-yü ho shu-yuan chih-tu te ying-shang" 佛教對中國教育和書院制度的影响 (Influence of Buddhism on Chinese education and the academy system). In Hunan ta-hsueh Yueh-lu shu-yuan wen-hua yen-chiu suo, eds., *Yueh-lu shu-yuan i-ch'ien-nien ling i-shih chou nien chi-nien wen-chi* 岳麓書院一千年零一十周年紀念文集 (Collection in commemoration of Marchmount Hill Academy's 1,010th anniversary), vol. 1. Ch'ang-sha: Hu-nan jen-min ch'u-pan she, 1986.

Ch'en Tung-yuan 陳東原. "Ch'an-lin te hsueh-hsiao chih-tu" 禪林的學校制度 (School system in Ch'an monasteries). *Min-tuo tsa-chih* 民鐸雜誌 6(3) (1936): 1–10.

———. *Chung-kuo chiao-yü shih* 中國教育史 (History of Chinese education). Taipei: Commercial Press, 1970 (1937).

———. "Lu-shan Pai-lu-tung shu-yuan yen-ko k'ao" 盧山白鹿洞書院沿革考 (Investigation of the history of Mount Lu's White Deer Grotto Academy). *Min-tuo tsa-chih* 民鐸雜誌 7(1) (1937): 1–32; 2: 1–25.

Ch'en Wen-i 陳雯怡. "Yu kuan-hsueh tao shu-yuan: Ts'ung chih-tu yü li-nien te hu-tung kan Sung-tai chiao-yü te yen-pien" 由官學到書院:從制度與理念的互動看宋代教育的演變 (From official education to academies: Transformations in Sung education from the perspective of the interaction between institutions and ideals). M.A. thesis, National Taiwan University, 1996.

Ch'en Yuan-hui 陳元暉. *Chung-kuo ku-tai te shu-yuan chih-tu* 中國古代的書院制度 (China's traditional academy system). Shanghai: Chiao-yü ch'u-pan she, 1981.

Ch'iao Ping-nan 喬炳南. "Sōdai no shoin seido ni tsuite" 宋代の書院制度について (Concerning the Sung academy system). *Tezukayama daigaku ronshū* 帝塚山大學論集 14 (April 1977): 64–89.

Chikusa Masaaki 竺沙雅章. "Fukken no ji-in to shakai" 福建の寺院と社會 (Temples and society in Fu-chien). Reprinted in Chikusa Masaaki, *Chūgoku Bukkyō shakaishi kenkyū* 中國佛教社會史研究 (Studies in the social history of Chinese Buddhism). Kyoto: Dōbōsha, 1982.

———. "Sōdai kanryō no kikyō ni tsuite 宋代官僚の寄居について (Concerning the temporary residence of Sung bureaucrats)." *Tōyōshi kenkyū* 東洋史研究 41: 1 (1982): 28–57.

Ch'iu Chao-wei 邱兆偉. "Sung-tai shu-yuan chiao-yü chih ch'eng-yin" 宋代書院教育之原因 (Completion of Sung academy education). *Taiwan chiao-yü fu-tao yueh-k'an* 台灣教育輔導月刊 17(2) (February 1967): 12–16.

Chu Jui-hsi 朱瑞熙. "Nan-Sung Fu-chien Yen Meng-piao ch'i-i" 南宋福建晏夢彪起義 (Uprising of Yen Meng-piao in Southern Sung Fu-chien). In *Sung-shih lun-chi* 宋史論集 (Collected essays in Sung history). Honan: Hsin-hua, 1983.

Fei Hai-chi 飛海幾. "Sung-tai shu-yuan hsin-k'ao" 宋代書院新考 (A New Investigation of Sung Academies). *Hsien-tai hsueh-yuan* 現代學園 1(11) (February 1965): 21–24.

———. "Sung-tai shu-yuan te hsin yen-chiu" 宋代書院的新研究 (New studies of Sung academies). *Hsueh-yuan* 學園 8(3) (Juanuary 1973): 13–14; 8(4) (February 1973): 7–8.

Hayashi Tomoharu 林友春. "Chūgoku ni okeru shoin no sui-i" 中國における書院の推移 (Transition of academies in China). In Hayashi Tomoharu, ed., *Kinsei higashi Ajia kyōikushi kenkyū* 近世東アジア教育史研究 (Studies in the educational history of modern East Asia). Tokyo: Gakujutsu shuppankai, 1970.

———. "Chūgoku shoin ni okeru kyōikuhō no shūkyōteki teiryū" 中國書院における教育法の宗教的底流 (Religious undercurrents of the educational method in Chinese academies). In Taga Akigoro 多賀秋五郎, ed., *Chūsei Ajia kyōikushi kenkyū* 中世アジア教育史研究 (Studies in the educational history of middle period Asia). Tokyo: Kokushokan, 1980.

———. "Tō-Sō shoin no hassō to sono kyōiku" 唐宋書院の發生とその教育 (Development of T'ang-Sung academies and their education). *Gakushūin daigaku bungakubu kenkyū nempō* 學習院大學文學部研究年報 2 (1954): 133–156.

Ho Yu-sen 何佑森. "Liang Sung hsueh-feng te ti-li fen-pu" 兩宋學風的地理分佈 (Geographical distribution of Sung traditions of learning). *Hsin Ya hsueh-pao* 1(1) (August 1955): 331–379.

Huang Chin-chung 黃金鍾. "Chu Hsi yü Fu-chien shu-yuan k'ao-p'ing" 朱喜與福建書院考評 (Investigation of Chu Hsi and Fu-chien academies). In Wu-i Chu Hsi Research Center, ed., *Chu Hsi yü Chung-kuo wen-hua* 朱喜與中國文化 (Chu Hsi and Chinese culture). Shanghai: Hsueh-lin, 1989.

Huang Ch'ing-wen 黃晴文. *Chung-kuo ku-tai shu-yuan chih-tu chi ch'i k'o-shu t'an-yen* 中國古代書院制度及其刻書探研 (Investigation into China's traditional academy system and printing). Taipei: 1984.

Huang K'uan-ch'ung 黃寬重. "Lueh-lun Nan-Sung shih-tai te kuei-cheng jen" 略論南宋時代的歸正人 (Concerning political refugees in the Southern Sung period). In Huang K'uan-ch'ung, *Nan-Sung shih yen-chiu chi* 南宋史研究集 (Collected studies on Southern Sung history). Taipei: Hsin wen-feng ch'u-pan kung-ssu, 1985.

Huang Min-chih 黃敏枝. "Sung-tai Fu-chien te ssu-yuan yü she-hui" 宋代福建的寺院與社會 (Temples and society in Sung period Fu-chien). *Ssu yü yen* 思與言 16(4) (November 1978): 311–340.

———. "Sung-tai Liang-che lu te ssu-yuan yü she-hui" 宋代兩浙路的寺院與社會 (Temples and society in Sung period Liang-che circuit). *Ch'eng-ta li-shih hsueh-pao* 成大歷史學報 5 (July 1978): 319–349.

Jao Tsung-i 饒宗頤. "Sung-tai li Ch'ao kuan-shih yü Shu-hsueh chi Min-hsueh: Han-kung tsai Ch'ao-chou shou kao-tu ch'ung-ching chih yuan-yin" 宋代蒞潮官師與蜀學及閩學:韓公在潮州受高度崇敬之原因 (Sung period officials stationed at Ch'ao-chou and the Shu school and the Min school: The reasons for the high reverence shown to Han Yu at Ch'ao-chou). In Kinugawa Tsuyoshi, ed., *Liu Tzu-chien hakushi shosu kinen Soshi kenkyū ronshū* 劉子健博士頌壽紀念宋史研究論集 (Collected studies in Sung history to commemorate the seventieth birthday of Professor James T. C. Liu). Kyoto: Dōbōsha, 1989.

Kanai Noriyuki 金井德幸. "Sōdai no Bukkyō ni tsuite—Sōdai shakai ni okeru ji-in to jūjisei no mondai" 宋代の佛教について — 宋代社會における寺院と住持制の問題 (Concerning Sung Buddhism—temples in Sung society and the problem of the abbacy system). *Rekishigaku kyōiku* 歷史學教育 10(8) (August 1962): 52–58.

Kawakami Kyōji 川上恭司. "Sōdai no toshi to kyōiku—shūkengaku o chūshin ni" 宋代の都市と教育:州縣學お中心に (Sung cities and education—with special attention to prefectural and county schools). In *Chūgoku kinsei no toshi to bunka* 中國近世の都市と文化 (Cities and culture in China's modern period). Kyoto: Kyōto daigaku jimbunkagaku kenkyūjō, 1984.

Kinugawa Tsuyoshi 衣川強. *Sō-Gen gakuan; Sō-Gen gakuan hō-i: Jinmei jikō betsumei sakuin* 宋元學案;宋元學案補遺:人名字號別名索引 (Index of names in the *Sung-Yuan hsueh-an* and its supplement). Kyoto: Kyoto daigaku jimbunkagaku kenkyūjō, 1974.

Ku Jui-lan 辜瑞蘭. "Chung-kuo shu-yuan k'an-k'o t'u-shu k'ao" 中國書院刊刻圖書

考 (Investigation into the woodblock print libraries of Chinese academies). *Kuo-li chung-yang t'u-shu-kuan kuan-k'an* (new series) 9(2) (1976): 27–44.

Li Ts'ai-tung 李才棟. *Chiang-hsi ku-tai shu-yuan chih-tu yen-chiu* 江西古代書院制度 (Traditional academy system of Chiang-hsi). Nan-ch'ang: Chiang-hsi chiao-yü ch'u-pan she, 1993.

———. *Pai-lu-tung shu-yuan shih-lueh* 白鹿東書院史略 (Brief history of White Deer Grotto Academy). Peking: Chiao-yü k'o-hsueh, 1989.

Liang Keng-yao 梁庚堯. *Nan Sung te nung-ts'un ching-chi* 南宋的農村經濟 (Rural economy of the Southern Sung). Taipei: Lien-ching, 1984.

———. *Sung-tai she-hui ching-chi shih lun-chi* 宋代社會精濟史論集 (Collected writings on the social and economic history of the Sung). Taipei: Yun-ch'en wen-hua, 1997.

Liu Chih-sheng 劉志盛. "Chung-kuo shu-yuan k'o-shu chi-lueh" 中國書院刻書紀略 (Summary of Chinese academy printing). In Hu-nan ta-hsueh Yueh-lu shu-yuan wen-hua yen-chiu suo, eds., *Yueh-lu shu-yuan i-ch'ien-nien i-shih chou nien chi-nien wen-chi,* vol. 1 (1986). Changsha: Hu-nan jen-min ch'u-pan she, 1986.

Liu Po-chi 劉伯驥. *Kuang-tung shu-yuan chih-tu* 廣東書院制度 (Academy system of Kuang-tung). Taipei: Kuo-li pien-shih kuan Chung-hua ts'ung-shu pien-pan wei-yuan-hui, 1978 (1958).

———. *Sung-tai cheng-chiao shih* 宋代政教史 (History of politics and education in the Sung Period). Taipei: Chung-hua shu-chu, 1971.

Mai Chung-kuei 麥仲貴. *Sung-Yuan li-hsueh-chia chu-shu nien-piao* 宋元理學家著書年表 (Chronological table of bibliographical and biographical data for Sung and Yuan Neo-Confucian philosophers). Hong Kong: Hsin Ya yen-chiu she, 1968.

Makino Tatsumi 牧野修二. "Gendai byōgaku shoin no kibō ni tsuite" 元代廟學書院の規模について (Concerning the structure of temple schools in the Yuan). *Ehime daigaku hōbungakubu ronshū (bungakubu)* 12 (December 1979): 29–55.

Ōkubo Eiko 大久保英子. *Min-Shin jidai shoin no kenkyū* 明清時代書院の研究 (Studies on Ming and Ch'ing academies). Tokyo: Kokushōkan, 1976.

Pai Hsin-liang 白新良. *Chung-kuo ku-tai shu-yuan fa-chan shih* 中國古代書院發展史 (History of the development of China's traditional academies). Tientsin: T'ien-chin ta-hsueh ch'u-pan she, 1995.

P'an Mei-yueh 潘美月. "Liang-Sung Shu-k'o te t'e-se" 兩宋蜀刻的特色 (Special characteristics of printing in Ssu-ch'uan during the Sung). *Kuo-li chung-yang t'u-shu-kuan kuan k'an (hsin)* 國立中央圖書館館刊(新) 9(2) (1976): 45–55.

Sheng Lang-hsi 盛郎西. *Chung-kuo shu-yuan chih-tu* 中國書院制度 (The Chinese academy system). Taipei: Commercial Press, 1978 (1936).

Sun Yen-min 孫彥民. "Sung-tai shu-yuan chih-tu" 宋代書院制度 (The academy system of the Sung period). *Nü-shih shu hsueh-pao* 女師書學報 2 (August 1978): 1–12.

———. *Sung-tai shu-yuan chih-tu chih yen-chiu* 宋代書院制度之研究 (Studies on the Sung academy system). Taipei: Cheng-chih ta-hsueh, 1963.

Suzuki Chūsei 鈴木中正. "Sōdai Bukkyō kessha no kenkyū" 宋代佛教結社の研究 (Studies on Buddhist associations in the Sung period). *Shigaku zasshi* 史學雜志 52 (1941): 65–98, 205–241, 303–333.

Taga Akigorō 多賀秋五郎. *Chūgoku kyōikushi* 中國教育史 (History of Chinese education). Tokyo: Iwasaki shōten, 1955.

Takahashi Yoshirō 高橋芳郎. "Sōdai shijin no mibun ni tsuite" 宋代士人の身分について (Concerning the status of *shih-jen* in the Sung period). *Shirin* 史林 69(3) (May 1986): 39–70.

Takao Giken 高雅義堅. *Sōdai Bukkyōshi no kenkyū* 宋代佛教の研究 (Studies on Sung-period Buddhism). Kyoto: Hyakkaen, 1975.

T'an Ch'i-hsiang 譚其驤, et al. *Chung-kuo li-shih ti-t'u chi* 中國歷史地圖集 (Historical maps of China). Peking: Ti-t'u, 1982–1987.

Terada Gō 寺田剛. *Sōdai kyōikushi gaisetsu* 宋代教育史概説 (Overview of Sung education). Tokyo: Hakubunsha, 1965.

Ting Fu-pao 丁福保, ed. *Fo-hsueh ta tz'u-tien* 佛學大辭典 (Encyclopedic dictionary of Buddhism). Fu-chien P'u-t'ien Kuang-hua ssu ed., 1990.

Umehara Kaoru 梅原郁, Kinugawa Tsuyoshi 衣川強, comps. *Ryō-Kin-Gen jin denki sakuin* 遼金元人傳記索引 (Index to biographical data for Liao, Chin, and Yuan people). Kyoto: Kyoto University Research Institute for Humanistic Studies, 1972.

Wu K'ang 吳康. "Nan-Sung Hsiang-hsueh yü Che-hsueh" 南宋湘學與浙學 (The Hsiang School and the Che School in the Southern Sung). In *Sung-shih yen-chiu chi* 宋史研究集 (Collected Studies in Sung History) 13 (1981): 39–59.

Wu Tsung-tz'u 吳宗慈. *Lu-shan chih* 廬山志 (Record of Mount Lu). Shanghai: Wen-hai, 1933.

Wu Wan-chü 吳萬居. *Sung-tai shu-yuan yü Sung-tai hsueh-shu chih kuan-hsi* 宋代書院與宋代學術之關奚 (Relationship between Sung academies and Sung thought). Taipei: Wen-shih che ch'u-pan she, 1991.

Yang Chih-ch'u, et al. *Yueh-lu shu-yuan shih-lueh* 岳麓書院史略 (Brief history of Marchmount Hill Academy). Ch'ang-sha: Yueh-lu shu-she, 1986.

Yang Chin-hsin 楊金鑫. *Chu Hsi yü Yueh-lu shu-yuan* 朱熹與岳麓書院 (Chu Hsi and Marchmount Hill Academy). Shanghai: Hua-tung shih-fan ta-hsueh ch'u-pan she, 1986.

———. "Hu-nan Sung-tai shu-yuan kai-k'uang" 湖南宋代書院概況 (Outline of Sung academies in Hu-nan). *Yüeh-lu shu-yuan t'ung-hsun* 岳麓書院通訊 1 (1983): 49–56.

Yeh Hung-sa 葉鴻灑. "Lun Sung-tai shu-yuan chih-tu chih fa-sheng chi ch'i ying-hsiang" 論宋代書院制度之發生及其影響 (Concerning the development of the Sung academy system and its influence). In Sung-shih tso-t'an hui, eds. and comps., *Sung-shih yen-chiu chi,* vol. 9 (1977): 417–473.

———. "Sung-tai shu-yuan chiao-yü t'e-se chi ch'i tsu-chih" 宋代書院教育特色及

其組織 (Special characteristics of Sung academy education and its structure). *T'an-chiang hsueh-pao* 淡江學報 15 (1977): 57–79.

Yeh Te-hui 葉德輝. *Shu-lin ch'ing-hua* 書林清話 (Clear conversations from the forest of books). Peking: Ku-chi ch'u-pan she, 1957.

Yen Keng-wang 嚴耕望. "T'ang-jen tu-shu shan-lin ssu-yuan chih feng-shang" 唐人讀書山林寺院之風尚 (The trend of T'ang people studying in secluded temples). *Chung-yang yen-chiu-yuan li-shih yü-yen hsueh-yuan yen-chiu ch'i-k'an* 中央研究院歷史語言學院研究期刊 30(2) (1960): 689–728.

Yü Ying-shih 余英時. *Chung-kuo chin-shih tsung-chiao lun-li yü shang-jen ching-shen* 中國近世宗教倫理與商人精神 (The religious ethic and mercantile spirit in modern China). Taipei: Lien-ching, 1987.

Yuan Cheng 袁征. *Sung-tai chiao-yü: Chung-kuo ku-tai chiao-yü te li-shih-hsing chuan-che* 宋代教育:中國教育的歷史性轉折 (Sung education: A pivotal turn in traditional Chinese education). Canton: Kuang-tung kao-teng chiao-yü ch'u-pan she, 1991.

Western Language Sources

Althusser, Louis. *Lenin and Philosophy and Other Essays* (New York and London: Monthly Review Press, 1971).

Baker, Alan R. H., and Gideon Biger, eds. *Ideology and Landscape in Historical Perspective* (Cambridge: Cambridge University Press, 1992).

Balazs, Etienne, and Yves Hervouet, comps. *A Sung Bibliography* (Hong Kong: Chinese University of Hong Kong Press, 1978).

Birnbaum, Raoul. "Secret Halls of the Mountain Lords: The Caves of Wu-t'ai Shan." *Cahiers d'Extreme-Asie* 5 (1989–1990): 115–140.

———. "Thoughts on T'ang Buddhist Mountain Traditions and Their Context." *Tang Studies* 2 (1984): 5–24.

Bol, Peter K. *"This Culture of Ours": Intellectual Transitions in T'ang and Sung China* (Stanford: Stanford University Press, 1992).

———. "The Examination System and the *Shih*." *Asia Major* (3d series) 3(2) (1990): 149–171.

Bossler, Beverly J. *Powerful Relations: Kinship, Status, and the State in Sung China, 960–1279* (Cambridge, Mass.:Harvard University Press, 1998).

Carlson, John B. "A Geomantic Model for the Interpretation of Mesoamerican Sites: An Essay in Cross-Cultural Comparison." In *Mesoamerican Sites and World-Views*, ed. Elizabeth P. Benson (Washington, D.C.: Dumbarton Oaks, 1981).

Chaffee, John W. *The Thorny Gates of Learning in Sung China: A Social History of Examinations* (Cambridge: Cambridge University Press, 1986).

———. "Chao Ju-yü, Spurious Learning, and Southern Sung Political Culture." *Journal of Sung-Yuan Studies* 22 (1990–1992): 22–61.

———. "Chu Hsi in Nan-k'ang: *Tao-hsüeh* and the Politics of Education." In *Neo-Confucian Education: The Formative Stage*, ed. W. Theodore de Bary and John W. Chaffee (Berkeley and Los Angeles: University of California Press, 1989), 414–431.

———. "'To Spread One's Wings': Examinations and the Social Order in Southeastern China during the Southern Sung." *Historical Reflections/Reflexions Historiques* 9 (1982): 305–322.

———. "Chu Hsi and the Revival of the White Deer Grotto Academy, 1179–1181 A.D." *T'oung pao* 71 (1985): 40–62.

Chan, Wing-tsit. *Chu Hsi: New Studies* (Honolulu: University of Hawai'i Press, 1989).

———. "Chu Hsi and the Academies." In *Neo-Confucian Education: The Formative Stage*, ed. W. Theodore de Bary and John W. Chaffee (Berkeley and Los Angeles: University of California Press, 1989).

———. trans. and ed. *Neo-Confucian Terms Explained (The Pei-hsi tz'u-i by Ch'en Ch'un)* (New York: Columbia University Press, 1986).

———, trans. *Reflections on Things at Hand: The Neo-Confucian Anthology Compiled by Chu Hsi and Lü Tsu-ch'ien* (New York: Columbia University Press, 1967).

Chang Chun-shu and Joan Smythe, trans. *South China in the Twelfth Century* (Hong Kong: Chinese University of Hong Kong Press, 1981).

Clark, Hugh R. *Community, Trade, and Networks: Southern Fujian Province, from the Third to the Thirteenth Century* (Cambridge: Cambridge University Press, 1991).

Collcutt, Martin. "The Early Ch'an Monastic Rule: *Ch'ing-kuei* and the Shaping of Ch'an Community Life." In *Early Ch'an in China and Tibet*, ed. Whalen Lai and Lewis R. Lancaster. Berkeley Buddhist Studies Series (Berkeley: University of California Press, 1983).

Daniels, Stephen, and Denis Cosgrove, eds. *The Iconography of Landscape: Essays on the Symbolic Representation, Design, and Use of Past Environments* (Cambridge: Cambridge University Press, 1988).

Davis, Richard L. *Court and Family in Sung China, 960–1279: Bureaucratic Success and Kinship Fortunes for the Shihs of Ming-chou* (Durham, N.C.: Duke University Press, 1986).

———. "Custodians of Education and Endowment at the State Schools of Southern Sung." *Journal of Sung-Yuan Studies* 25 (1995): 95–119.

———. *Wind against the Mountain: The Crisis of Politics and Culture in Thirteenth-Century China* (Cambridge, Mass.: Harvard University Press, 1996).

de Bary, W. Theodore. *The Liberal Tradition in China* (New York: Columbia University Press, 1983).

———. "A Reappraisal of Neo-Confucianism." In *Studies in Chinese Thought*, ed. Arthur F. Wright (Chicago: University of Chicago Press, 1967 [1953]).

Ebrey, Patricia B. *The Inner Quarters: Marriage and the Lives of Women in the Sung Period* (Berkeley and Los Angeles: University of California Press, 1993).

———. *Family and Property in Sung China: Yuan Ts'ai's Precepts for Social Life (Yuan-shih shih-fan)* (Princeton, N.J.: Princeton University Press, 1984).

———. "The Response of the State to Popular Funeral Practices." In *Religion and Society in T'ang and Sung China*, ed. Patricia B. Ebrey and Peter N. Gregory (Honolulu: University of Hawai'i Press, 1993).

———. "The Dynamics of Elite Domination in Sung China." *Harvard Journal of Asiatic Studies* 48 (1989): 493–519.

———. "Early Stages of Descent Group Organization." In *Kinship Organization in Late Imperial China, 1000–1940*, ed. Patricia B. Ebrey and James L. Watson (Berkeley and Los Angeles: University of California Press, 1986).

Elman, Benjamin A. "Political, Social, and Cultural Reproduction via Civil Service Examinations in Late Imperial China." *Journal of Asian Studies* 50(1) (1991): 7–28.

Foulk, T. Griffith. "Myth, Ritual, and Monastic Practice in Sung Ch'an Buddhism." In *Religion and Society in T'ang and Sung China*, ed. Patricia B. Ebrey and Peter N. Gregory (Honolulu: University of Hawai'i Press, 1993).

Foulk, T. Griffith, and Robert H. Sharf. "On the Ritual Use of Ch'an Portraiture in Medieval China." *Cahiers d'Extreme-Asie* 7 (1993–1994): 155–219.

Franke, Herbert, ed. *Sung Biographies* (Wiesbaden: Franz Steiner verlag, 1976).

Freedman, Maurice. *The Study of Chinese Society* (Stanford: Stanford University Press, 1979).

Gardner, Daniel K. "Modes of Thinking and Modes of Discourse in the Sung: Some Thoughts on the *yü-lu* ("Recorded Conversations") Texts." *Journal of Asian Studies* 50(3) (August 1991): 574–603.

———, trans. *Chu Hsi and the Ta-hsüeh: Neo-Confucian Reflection on the Confucian Canon* (Cambridge: Harvard University Press, Council on East Asian Studies, 1986).

———, trans. *Chu Hsi: Learning to be a Sage* (Berkeley and Los Angeles: University of California Press, 1990).

Gedalecia, David. "Wu Ch'eng: A Yüan Dynasty Neo-Confucian Scholar." *Journal of Chinese Philosophy* 20 (1993): 293–311.

Geertz, Clifford. *The Interpretation of Cultures* (New York: Basic Books, 1973).

Gerth, H. H., and C. Wright Mills, trans. and ed. *From Max Weber: Essays in Sociology* (New York: Oxford University Press, 1974 [1946]).

Gimello, Robert. "Chang Shang-ying on Wu-t'ai Shan." In *Pilgrimage and Sacred Sites in China*, ed. Susan Naquin and Yü Chün-fang (Berkeley and Los Angeles: University of California Press, 1992).

Golas, Peter J. "The Mining Policies of the Sung Government." In *Collected Studies on Sung History Dedicated to Professor James T. C. Liu in Celebration of His Seventieth Birthday*, ed. Kinugawa Tsuyoshi (Kyoto: Dohōsha, 1989), 411–427.

Gordon, R. L. "The Sacred Geography of a Mithraeum: The Example of Sette Sfere." *Journal of Mithraic Studies* 1(2) (1976): 119–165.

Grimm, Tilemann. "Academies and Urban Systems in Kwangtung." In *The City in Late Imperial China*, ed. G. William Skinner (Stanford: Stanford University Press, 1977).

———. "The Inauguration of *T'i-chü hsüeh-shih ssu* (Education Intendants) during the Northern Sung Dynasty." *Études Song*, vol. 1 (1976): 259–274.

Hall, David L., and Roger T. Ames. *Thinking Through Confucius* (Albany: State University of New York Press, 1987).

Hansen, Valerie. *Changing Gods in Medieval China, 1127–1276* (Princeton, N.J: Princeton University Press, 1990).

Hartman, Charles. *Han Yü and the T'ang Search for Unity* (Princeton, N.J.: Princeton University Press, 1986).

Hartwell, Robert M. "Demographic, Political, and Social Transformations of China, 750–1550." *Harvard Journal of Asiatic Studies* 42(2) (December 1982): 365–442.

Hay, Alan John. "Huang Kung-wang's Dwelling in the Fu-ch'un Mountains: The Dimensions of a Landscape." Ph.D. dissertation, Princeton University, 1978.

Holcombe, Charles. *In the Shadow of the Han: Literati Thought and Society at the Beginning of the Southern Dynasties* (Honolulu: University of Hawai'i Press, 1994).

——— "The Exemplar State: Ideology, Self-Cultivation, and Power in Fourth-Century China." *Harvard Journal of Asiatic Studies* 49(1) (June 1989): 93–139.

Hucker, Charles O. *A Dictonary of Official Titles in Imperial China* (Stanford: Stanford University Press, 1985).

Hymes, Robert P. *Statesmen and Gentlemen: The Local Elite of Fu-chou, Kiangsi in Northern and Southern Sung* (Cambridge: Cambridge University Press, 1986).

———. "Marriage, Descent Groups, and the Localist Strategy in Sung and Yuan Fuchou." In *Kinship Organization in Late Imperial China*, ed. Patricia B. Ebrey and James L. Watson (Berkeley and Los Angeles: University of California Press, 1986).

———. "Lu Chiu-yuan, Academies, and the Problem of the Local Community." In *Neo-Confucian Education: The Formative Stage*, ed. W. Theodore de Bary and John W. Chaffee (Berkeley and Los Angeles: University of California Press, 1989).

Hymes, Robert P., and Conrad Schirokauer. "Introduction." In *Ordering the World: Approaches to State and Society in Sung Dynasty China*, ed. Robert P. Hymes and Conrad Schirokauer (Berkeley: University of California Press, 1993).

Jackson, Peter. *Maps of Meaning* (London: Unwin Hyman, 1989).

Jay, Jennifer W. *A Change in Dynasties: Loyalism in Thirteenth-Century China* (Bellingham, Wash.: Western Washington University Press, 1991).

Johnson, David. "The City-God Cults of T'ang and Sung China." *Harvard Journal of Asiatic Studies* 45(2) (December 1985): 363–457.

Langlois, John D., Jr. "Political Thought in Chin-hua under Mongol Rule." In *China under Mongol Rule*, ed. John D. Langlois, Jr. (Princeton, N. J.: Princeton University Press, 1981), 137–185.

Lee, Thomas Hung-chi. *Government Education and Examinations in Sung China* (Hong Kong: Chinese University Press of Hong Kong, 1985).

———. "Politics, Examinations and the Chinese Society, 1000–1500: Reflections on the Rise of the Local Elite and the Civil Society in Late Imperial China." Paper presented to the conference on Family Process and Political Process in Modern Chinese History, Institute of Modern History, Academia Sinica. Taipei, June 1992.

———. "Chu Hsi, Academies, and the Tradition of Private *Chiang-hsüeh*." *Chinese Studies* 2(1) (June 1984): 301–329.

Legge, James, trans. *The Chinese Classics*, 4 vols. (Taipei: Wen-shih che, 1974).

Leiser, Gary. "The *Madrasa* and the Islamization of the Middle East: The Case of Egypt." *Journal of the American Research Center in Egypt* 22 (1985): 29–47.

Li Chi. "Chu Hsi the Poet." *T'oung pao* 58 (1972): 55–119.

Liu, James T. C. *China Turning Inward: Intellectual-Political Changes in the Early Twelfth Century*. (Cambridge, Mass.: Harvard University Press, 1988).

———. "Wei Liao-weng's Thwarted Statecraft." In *Ordering the World: Approaches to State and Society in Sung Dynasty China*, ed. Robert P. Hymes and Conrad Schirokauer (Berkeley and Los Angeles: University of California Press, 1993).

———. "Liu Tsai (1165–1238): His Philanthropy and Neo-Confucian Limitations." *Oriens Extremus* 25(1) (1978): 1–29.

———. "How Did a Neo-Confucian School Become the State Orthodoxy?" *Philosophy East and West* 23(4) (1973): 483–505.

Liu Ts'un-yan. "Chu Hsi's Influence in Yuan Times." In *Chu Hsi and Neo-Confucianism*, ed. Wing-tsit Chan (Honolulu: University of Hawai'i Press, 1986).

Liu Xinru. "Buddhist Institutions in the Lower Yangtze Valley during the Sung Dynasty." *Bulletin of Sung-Yuan Studies* 21 (1989): 31–51.

Lo, Irving Yucheng. *Hsin Ch'i-chi* (New York: Twayne Publishers, Inc., 1971).

Makdisi, George. *The Rise of Colleges in Islam and the West* (Edinburgh: Edinburgh University Press, 1981).

Mao Huaixin. "The Establishment of the School of Chu Hsi and Its Propagation in Fukien." In *Chu Hsi and Neo-Confucianism*, ed. Wing-tsit Chan (Honolulu: University of Hawai'i Press, 1986).

March, Andrew. "Self and Landscape in Su Shih." *Journal of the American Oriental Society* 86(4) (1986): 377–396.

Mather, Richard, trans. *A New Account of Tales of the World* (Minneapolis: University of Minnesota Press, 1976).

McDermott, Joseph. "Land Tenure and Rural Control in the Liang-che Region during the Southern Sung." Ph.D. dissertation, Cambridge University, 1979.

———. "Review of *Statesman and Gentlemen: The Elite of Fu-chou, Kiangsi in Northern and Southern Sung* by Robert P. Hymes." *Harvard Journal of Asiatic Studies* 51 (1993): 333–357.

McMullen, David. *State and Scholars in T'ang China* (Cambridge: Cambridge University Press, 1988).

Meyer, Jeffrey. "*Feng-shui* of the Chinese City." *History of Religions* 18 (1978): 138–155.

Miyakawa, Hisayuki. "Local Cults around Mount Lu at the Time of Sun En's Rebellion." In *Facets of Taoism*, ed. Holmes Welch and Anna Seidel (New Haven, Conn.: Yale University Press, 1979).

Naquin, Susan, and Yü Chün-fang. "Introduction." In *Pilgrims and Sacred Sites in China*, ed. Susan Naquin and Yü Chün-fang (Berkeley and Los Angeles: University of California Press, 1992).

Nemeth, David. *The Architecture of Ideology: Neo-Confucian Imprinting on Cheju Island, Korea* (Berkeley: University of California Publications in Geography, 1987), vol. 26.

Neskar, Ellen. "The Cult of Worthies: A Study of Shrines Honoring Local Confucian Worthies in the Sung Dynasty (960–1279)." Ph.D. dissertation, Columbia University, 1993.

Overmyer, Daniel P. *Folk-Buddhist Religion: Dissenting Sects in Late Traditional China* (Cambridge, Mass.: Harvard University Press, Council on East Asian Studies, 1976).

Pease, Jonathan O. "Lin-ch'uan and Fen-ning: Kiangsi Writers and Kiangsi Locales during the Sung." *Asia Major*, (3d series) 4(1) (1991): 39–85.

Schafer, Edward. *Mao-shan in T'ang Times*. Monograph no. 1 (Boulder, Colo.: Society for the Study of Chinese Religions, 1980).

Schirokauer, Conrad. "Chu Hsi and Hu Hung." In *Chu Hsi and Neo-Confucianism*, ed. Wing-tsit Chan (Honolulu: University of Hawai'i Press, 1986).

———. "Neo-Confucians Under Attack: The Condemnation of *Wei-hsüeh*." In *Crisis and Prosperity in Sung China*, ed. John W. Haeger (Tucson: University of Arizona Press, 1975).

Schmidt-Glintzer, Helwig. "Zhang Shangying (1043–1122): An Embarrassing Policy Adviser under the Northern Song." In *Collected Studies on Sung History Dedicated to Professor James T. C. Liu in Celebration of His Seventieth Birthday*, ed. Kinugawa Tsuyoshi (Kyoto: Dohōsha, 1989).

Schwartz, Benjamin. "Some Polarities in Confucian Thought." In *Confucianism and Chinese Civilization*, ed. Arthur F. Wright (Stanford: Stanford University Press, 1964).

Shwehn, Michael. *Exiles from Eden* (New York: Oxford University Press, 1993).

Smith, Kidder, Jr., et al. *Sung Dynasty Uses of the I Ching* (Princeton, N. J.: Princeton University Press, 1990).

Smith, Paul J. *Taxing Heaven's Storehouse: Horses, Bureaucrats, and the Destruction of the Sichuan Tea Industry, 1074–1224* (Cambridge, Mass.: Harvard University Press, Council on East Asian Studies, 1991).

———. "Family, *Landsmann*, and Status-Group Affinity in Refugee Mobility Strategies: The Mongol Invasions and the Diaspora of Sichuanese Elites, 1230–1330." *Harvard Journal of Asiatic Studies* 52(2) (December 1992): 665–708.

Steele, John, trans. *I-li, or Book of Ceremonial and Etiquette* (Taipei: Ch'eng-wen, 1968 [1917]).

Strassberg, Richard. *Travel Writing in Imperial China* (Berkeley and Los Angeles: University of California Press, 1994).

Strickmann, Michel. "The Mao-shan Revelations: Taoism and the Aristocracy." *T'oung pao* 63(1) (1977): 1–64.

Sung, Z. D., ed. and trans. *The Text of Yi King* (Taipei: Wen-hua t'u-shu, 1983).

Thorndike, Lynn, trans. and introd. *University Records and Life in the Middle Ages* (New York: W. W. Norton, 1975 [1944]).

Tillman, Hoyt Cleveland. "Ho Ch'ü-fei and Chu Hsi on Chu-ko Liang as a 'Scholar General.'" *Journal of Sung-Yuan Studies* 25 (1995): 77–94.

———. "A New Direction in Confucian Scholarship: Approaches to Examining Differences between Neo-Confucianism and *Tao-hsüeh*." *Philosophy East and West* 42(3) (July 1992): 455–474.

Twitchett, Denis. "The Fan Charitable Estate, 1050–1760." In *Confucianism in Action*, ed. David S. Nivison and Arthur F. Wright (Stanford: Stanford University Press, 1959).

Übelhör, Monika. "The Community Compact (*hsiang-yüeh*) of the Sung and Its Educational Significance." In *Neo-Confucian Education: The Formative Stage*, ed. W. Theodore de Bary and John W. Chaffee (Berkeley and Los Angeles: University of California Press, 1989).

Vervoorn, Aat. *Men of the Cliffs and Caves: The Development of the Chinese Eremitic Tradition to the End of the Han Dynasty* (Hong Kong: Chinese University of Hong Kong Press, 1990).

von Glahn, Richard. *The Country of Streams and Grottoes: Expansion, Settlement, and the Civilizing of the Sichuan Frontier in Song Times* (Cambridge, Mass.: Harvard University Press, Council on East Asian Studies, 1987).

Walton, Linda. "Charitable Estates as an Aspect of Statecraft in Southern Sung China." In *Ordering the World: State and Society in Sung Dynasty China*, ed. Robert P. Hymes and Conrad Schirokauer (Berkeley and Los Angeles: University of California Press, 1993).

———. "Southern Sung Academies as Sacred Places." In *Religion and Society in T'ang and Sung China*, ed. Patricia B. Ebrey and Peter N. Gregory (Honolulu: University of Hawai'i Press, 1993).

———. "The Institutional Context of Neo-Confucianism: Scholars, Schools, and Shu-yuan in Sung-Yuan China." In *Neo-Confucian Education: The Formative Stage*, ed. W. Theodore de Bary and John W. Chaffee (Berkeley and Los Angeles: University of California Press, 1989).

Watson, Burton, trans. *Records of the Grand Historian of China*. 2 vols. (New York: Columbia University Press, 1961).

Watson, James. "Standardizing the Gods: The Promotion of T'ien Hou ('Empress of Heaven') along the South China Coast, 960–1960." In *Popular Culture in Late Imperial China*, ed. David Johnson, Andrew Nathan, and Evelyn Rawski (Berkeley and Los Angeles: University of California Press, 1985).

Wechsler, Howard. "The Confucian Teacher Wang T'ung (584?–617): One Thousand Years of Controversy." *T'oung pao* 63(4–5) (1977): 225–272.

Wilson, Thomas A. *The Genealogy of the Way: The Construction and Uses of the Confucian Tradition in Late Imperial China* (Stanford: Stanford University Press, 1995).

Yü, Chün-fang. "P'u-t'o Shan: Pilgrimage and the Creation of the Chinese Potalaka." In *Pilgrimage and Sacred Sites in China*, ed. Susan Naquin and Yü Chün-fang (Berkeley and Los Angeles: University of California Press, 1992).

———. "Ch'an Education in the Sung: Ideals and Practices." In *Neo-Confucian Education: The Formative Stage*, ed. W. Theodore de Bary and John W. Chaffee (Berkeley and Los Angeles: University of California Press, 1989).

Zürcher, Erik. "Buddhism and Education in T'ang Times." In *Neo-Confucian Education: The Formative Stage*, ed. W. Theodore de Bary and John W. Chaffee (Berkeley and Los Angeles: University of California Press, 1989), 19–56.

INDEX